Psychotherapy and Personality Change

AUTHORS

JOHN M. BUTLER

DESMOND S. CARTWRIGHT

ROSALIND F. DYMOND

THOMAS GORDON

DONALD L. GRUMMON

GERARD V. HAIGH

EVE S. JOHN

CARL R. ROGERS

ESSELYN RUDIKOFF

JULIUS SEEMAN

ROLLAND R. TOUGAS

MANUEL J. VARGAS

All of the authors are members or former members of the Staff of the Counseling Center, University of Chicago

Psychotherapy and Personality Change

CO-ORDINATED RESEARCH STUDIES
IN THE CLIENT-CENTERED APPROACH

Edited by

CARL R. ROGERS

and

ROSALIND F. DYMOND

THE UNIVERSITY OF CHICAGO PRESS

CHICAGO & LONDON

Standard Book Number: 226–72374-7
Library of Congress Catalog Card Number: 54-11211

THE UNIVERSITY OF CHICAGO PRESS, CHICAGO 60637

The University of Chicago Press, Ltd., London

Printed in the United States of America

Preface

The complex and ramified research program whose initial findings are presented in this volume could not have come into being or have been carried through to its present degree of completion without the assistance of many individuals and groups who have, directly and indirectly, made this project possible. The authors wish in this preface to indicate their indebtedness to some of these persons and organizations.

We are grateful to the University of Chicago for establishing and maintaining the Counseling Center, in the face of some opposition and considerable skepticism. This action has enabled a group to develop a program in which counseling service, training of therapists, research, and formulation of theory have proceeded hand in hand. Dr. Ralph W. Tyler, former Dean of the Division of the Social Sciences, Robert M. Strozier, Dean of Students, and Lawrence A. Kimpton, former Dean of Students and now Chancellor of the University, deserve special mention in this respect for the backing they have given to the Center.

Our thanks also go to the Department of Psychology and its chairman, Dr. James G. Miller. The departmental policy of permitting and encouraging a very large proportion of faculty time for research has enabled faculty members to devote much of their energy to this project. The department and its chairman have also facilitated the work through assistance in providing funds, through many administrative aids, and by a friendly interest in the whole program.

We feel a very special debt to the Rockefeller Foundation, which took a trail-blazing step in deciding to support this research through its Medical Sciences Division. Without the two generous grants which the foundation made to cover a five-year period, the program could not have been undertaken. Dr. Alan Gregg and Dr. Robert S. Morison have helped the program by their willingness for the research to follow its own developing leads without any restrictive influences.

The conceptualization of the program and its implementation would not have been possible without the previous scholarly work of a whole host of workers in the fields of psychology and psychotherapy. Particular mention should be made of the many research workers who had in previous years completed significant objective studies in client-centered therapy, providing a basis upon which this program could be built; of William Stephenson, whose development of the Q-technique supplied us at a most appropriate time with an instrument of great subtlety, stimulating our investigation of areas heretofore beyond our reach; of the many other psychologists whose study and research have provided the other tests and instruments which we have used; and of the many colleagues in psychology, psychiatry, and related fields whose suggestions and criticisms have been given in most friendly and helpful fashion.

In the planning of the research program we invited the participation of three consultants: Dr. O. Hobart Mowrer, research professor of psychology, University of Illinois; Dr. David Shakow, chief psychologist, Illinois Neuropsychiatric Institute, and professor of psychology, University of Illinois; and Dr. James G. Miller, professor of psychology and chairman of the Department of Psychology, University of Chicago. Their faithful attendance at the meetings of the Research Group and their penetrating criticisms and insightful suggestions helped significantly in creating an improved design for the total program, in avoiding certain pitfalls, and in enriching our thinking about implementation. Though they should not be held accountable for the conduct of the research or of the analysis of the material, we are grateful to them for the important contributions they made in the initial stages.

The research would not have been possible without *work*—much of it, as in any research program, being routine in nature, yet exacting in its demands. While we the authors have, we hope, done our share, we owe a tremendous debt to the loyal and unremitting efforts of a small army of counselors, research assistants, psychometrists, transcribers, and others. Some of these carried heavy responsibilities over a considerable period of time, counseling clients or developing a subproject; others helped primarily in the planning of the studies; others carried on the analysis of the data for one or more projects; still others worked faithfully at the particularly frustrating though fascinating task of transcribing the recorded interviews. Without attempting to assess the varying degrees to which the research is indebted to them, we wish to list the names of the people who have made the research a reality. Those who served as therapists in the research (and often in several other capacities as well) are: Robert P. Anderson, Russell Becker, Daniel V. Bergman, Frank Brogno, John M. Butler, Thomas Gordon, Donald L. Grummon, Gerard V. Haigh, Bill L. Kell, Elias H. Porter, Jr., Nathaniel J. Raskin, Carl R. Rogers, Esselyn Rudikoff, Julius Seeman, Eugene Streich, and William Watson. Those who served as co-ordinators of the research efforts for varying periods of time are: John M. Butler, Rosalind Dymond, Donald L. Grummon, and Julius Seeman. Those who served primarily as psychometrists, research assistants, or associates are: Desmond Cartwright, Sarah Counts, Rosalind Dymond, Richard Farson, Melvin Feffer, Rosslyn Gaines, Gerald Gratch, Margaret Hartley, Leonard Hersher, Richard Jenney, Eve S. John, Frank Kirk, Kanwal Mehra, Donald Nachand, Jack Saporta, and Samuel Sutton. Those who completed special studies based upon data in the research are: Paul Bowman, Jacques Boyer, Elaine Dorfman, Margaret Fox, B. Clark Lutes, Donald Nachand, Richard Reed, Frank Tate, Rolland Tougas, and Manuel Vargas. Those who served primarily as transcribers, research secretaries, or in other capacities are: Dorothy Becker, Katherine Biddle, Jean Brody, Madeleine Chevalier, Lois Delattre, Charlotte Ellinwood, Victor Fujiu, Virginia Goulding, Virginia Hallman, Jeanne Harper, Rosalie Jones, Florence Kennedy, Laura Kruh, Margaret Long, Elizabeth MacGregor, Elaine McMaster, Mary Frances Morris, Elizabeth Morse, Marjorie Page, Carol Parsch, Judith Roothaan, Hellene Sarett, Mary Shumway, Ruth Struik, Yvonne Vines, Jeanne Weil, Curtis Williams, Helen Wills, and Isabelle Wright.

Two of us, Rosalind Dymond and Carl Rogers, undertook the editorial duty of co-ordinating these discrete studies into book form. Those who aided in this preparation are: Charlotte Ellinwood, Virginia Garvey, Virginia Hallman, Jeanne Harper, Elaine McMaster, Marjorie Page, Mary Shumway, Isabelle Wright, and Alexander Zelchenko.

Our appreciation also goes to the *Psychological Service Center Journal* and its editor, Russell G. Leiter, for permission to use material from its pages. Chapters 2, 3, and 15 of this volume were first published, in modified form, in that journal.

Finally, we wish to acknowledge the generous aid given by our clients. Without their willingness, in the midst of their personal difficulties, to devote long hours over a period of one to three years to the taking of tests, the sorting of innumerable Q-sort cards, and the other tasks of the research, the project would have died in its infancy. It is our sincere hope that the knowledge and insight gained from this study will mean that later clients, both in our Center and in therapists' offices throughout the land, will be dealt with more perceptively, with deeper understanding, and with greater likelihood of personal benefit.

THE AUTHORS

CHICAGO, ILLINOIS

Table of Contents

I. INTRODUCTION

1. Introduction 3
   Carl R. Rogers

2. Developing a Program of Research in Psychotherapy . . . 12
   Thomas Gordon, Donald L. Grummon, Carl R. Rogers, and Julius Seeman

3. Design, Procedures, and Subjects for the First Block . . . 35
   Donald L. Grummon

II. FINDINGS

4. Changes in the Relation between Self-concepts and Ideal Concepts Consequent upon Client-centered Counseling . . . 55
   John M. Butler and Gerard V. Haigh

5. Adjustment Changes over Therapy from Self-sorts 76
   Rosalind F. Dymond

6. A Comparative Study of the Changes in the Concepts of the Self, the Ordinary Person, and the Ideal in Eight Cases . . 85
   Esselyn C. Rudikoff

7. Counselor Judgments of Therapeutic Process and Outcome . 99
   Julius Seeman

8. Adjustment Changes over Therapy from Thematic Apperception Test Ratings 109
   Rosalind F. Dymond

9. Changes over Client-centered Therapy Evaluated on Psychoanalytically Based Thematic Apperception Test Scales . . 121
   Donald L. Grummon and Eve S. John

10. Changes in Self-awareness during Client-centered Therapy . 145
    Manuel J. Vargas

11. The Effect of Psychotherapy upon Certain Attitudes toward Others 167
    Thomas Gordon and Desmond S. Cartwright

12. Ethnocentrism as a Limiting Factor in Verbal Therapy . . 196
    Rolland R. Tougas

13. Changes in the Maturity of Behavior as Related to Therapy . 215
Carl R. Rogers

14. Personality Changes as a Function of Time in Persons Motivated for Therapy 238
Donald L. Grummon

III. CASE STUDIES

15. The Case of Mrs. Oak: A Research Analysis 259
Carl R. Rogers

16. The Case of Mr. Bebb: The Analysis of a Failure Case . . 349
Carl R. Rogers

IV. CONCLUSION

17. An Overview of the Research and Some Questions for the Future 413
Carl R. Rogers

INDEX

Index 437

PART I

Introduction

CHAPTER 1

Introduction

CARL R. ROGERS

I. THE PROGRAM AND ITS ORIGIN

This volume describes a large-scale research program in psychotherapy which has been under way for more than four years at the Counseling Center of the University of Chicago. It is a continuing program, and the present report is a statement of findings to date rather than a closing of the door upon something completed and finished.

The program is, first of all, a research in the outcomes or concomitants of psychotherapy. This is particularly true of the studies contained in this book. It is also, however, an investigation of the processes which operate in psychotherapy, as will be evident in some of the following chapters and in studies still to be completed. It is a study of the outcomes and process of one approach to therapy—the approach usually known as client-centered or nondirective. In these various respects the program grows naturally out of the views and interests of the group which is responsible for it.

The Counseling Center of the University of Chicago is, as its name indicates, a resource for individuals who desire personal counseling or psychotherapy. It has become a focal center for the objective investigation of many aspects of psychotherapy, for the continuing formulation of a developing theory of personality and therapy, and for the training of counselors and therapists.

The staff of the Center, in endeavoring to be of the most effective help to disturbed or maladjusted individuals, has come to utilize certain hypotheses in regard to the capacities of the client, the function of the therapist, and the process of therapy. The formulation of these hypotheses as a group of tentative principles constitutes the client-centered approach to psychotherapy. This point of view has been set forth in a number of books and many articles. It is the continuous testing of these hypotheses which has been the motivation for the previous research conducted by the staff and for this present research program as well.

II. THE HYPOTHESES OF CLIENT-CENTERED THERAPY

Without attempting to describe in any complete sense the client-centered approach, it may be helpful to remind the reader of a few of its central hypotheses. These are the working principles of the staff—hypotheses which appear to be supported by our clinical experience and which we wish increasingly to test by our research.

1. The first hypothesis is that the individual has within himself the capacity, latent if not evident, to understand those aspects of himself and of his life which are causing him dissatisfaction, anxiety, or pain and the capacity and the tendency to reorganize himself and his relationship to life in the direction of self-actualization and maturity in such a way as to bring a greater degree of internal comfort.

2. This capacity will be released, and therapy or personal growth will be most facilitated, when the therapist can create a psychological climate characterized by (*a*) a genuine acceptance of the client as a person of unconditional worth; (*b*) a continuing, sensitive attempt to understand the existing feelings and communications of the client, as they seem to the client, without any effort to diagnose or alter those feelings; and (*c*) a continuing attempt to convey something of this empathic understanding to the client.

3. It is hypothesized that, in such an acceptant, understanding, and nonthreatening psychological atmosphere, the client will reorganize himself at both the conscious and the deeper levels of his personality in such a manner as to cope with life more constructively, more intelligently, and in a more socialized as well as a more satisfying way. More specifically it is hypothesized that the client will change in his perception of self, will become more understanding of self and others, more accepting of self and others, more creative, more adaptive, more self-directing and autonomous, more mature in his behavior, less defensive, and more tolerant of frustrations.

4. It is hypothesized that the therapeutic relationship is only one

instance of interpersonal relationships and that the same lawfulness governs all such relationships. Thus, if the parent creates such a climate for his child, the child will become more self-directing, socialized, and mature; if the teacher creates such a climate for his class, the student will become a self-initiated learner, more original, more self-disciplined; if the administrator or executive creates such a climate for his organization, the staff will become more self-responsible, more creative, better able to adapt to new problems, more basically co-operative.

These four hypotheses are a distillation of the experience of the staff. It should be clear that they all imply, or build upon, a confidence in the essentially constructive nature of the human organism. The reader who wishes to understand the way in which such hypotheses become operative in the counseling relationship, or who wishes to understand the personality theory which is developing out of experience with them, will do well to consult other sources.[1] This statement of hypotheses may, however, suggest at least the trend of experience and thinking out of which this ramified program grows.

III. THE CONTENTS OF THIS VOLUME

In endeavoring to introduce the reader to the total investigation to be reported, there keeps coming to mind the oft-repeated statement of Robert Hutchins about the university of which he was chancellor: "It isn't a good university; it's just the best that there is." One can perceive in this epigram nothing but pride and confidence; on the other hand, one can perceive in it a deep disappointment in falling so far short of the aim. In very much the same ambivalent spirit I am tempted to say of what follows in this book, "It isn't a good research in psychotherapy; it's just the best that there is." Perhaps I can indicate a few of the reasons why, on the one hand, we take a certain pride in presenting this investigation

1. The most complete and up-to-date volume is Carl R. Rogers, *Client-centered Therapy* (Boston: Houghton Mifflin Co., 1951). which contains material on the practice and theory of client-centered therapy and summarizes much of the earlier research. Chapters by Nicholas Hobbs, Thomas Gordon, and Elaine Dorfman present material on this approach in the fields of group therapy, group leadership, and play therapy, respectively. The extensive Bibliography gives references to most of the other books and articles presenting this point of view.

to the public and why, on the other hand, we feel that it falls far short of what we would like it to be.

"*We Point with Pride*"

This is essentially a pioneering venture. Though a number of studies of psychotherapy have previously been made, some by the same investigators, this is the first thoroughly objective study of outcomes of psychotherapy in which adequate controls have been utilized. Not only are there two different types of control groups but other control features have been developed, to the end that we will not deceive ourselves in regard to our findings. We can, with a reasonable degree of assurance, sort out those changes which occur as concomitants of psychotherapy from those which occur as a result of other factors.

In other respects, too, it is a pathfinding study. It uses, on a large scale, the newly developed Q-technique as a means of assessing many subtle changes. It makes an exploratory effort in the direction of testing certain hypotheses in regard to personality change through the objective investigation of the single case. While it is a preliminary testing, to be sure, it may, as a method, open up a number of deep problems of personality dynamics to scientific study. It makes extensive use of "blind" ratings of clinical material in order to avoid any possible bias in making judgments. Thus it has, in a number of ways, pioneered in using and developing new methods of scientific investigation in this difficult field.

Another basis for pride in the program is that it has resolutely taken account of, and paid attention to, those clients who have not accepted therapy—the "drop-out" or "attrition" group—and those for whom the experience has been a failure. It is our conviction that the field of psychotherapy cannot come of age until it understands its failures as well as it understands its successes, and, though we have not achieved this goal in our research, we have at least moved in this direction.

Another aspect of the program concerning which we feel satisfaction is that it is one of the very few large-scale attempts to test a coherent set of hypotheses growing out of a consistent body of personality theory. We have endeavored to avoid the testing of atomistic hypotheses whose proof or disproof has little relationship to any larger body of theory. We have, on the contrary, attempted to make sure that each hypothesis which we have tested has a significant place in the developing theory of personality in client-centered therapy or in the burgeoning theoretical system of the field of perception. Thus the empirical support of a hypothesis tends to confirm a whole body of theory; the disproof of such a hypothesis tends to cast doubt upon the related theoretical system. It is in this way, we believe, that we avoid piling up a meaningless body of isolated facts and promote instead the genuine advance of science.

"*We View with Disappointment*"

Many of our disappointments with the total research could be summed up in one sentence. It is a study of fallible individuals made by fallible individuals. We have learned to our sorrow the extreme difficulty of keeping in touch with a group of clients and a group of controls over periods of one to four years, when some of the clients are dissatisfied with their experience and do not wish to be contacted, other clients and controls move to distant cities or even out of the country, still others go into military service, and the like. At times the life of the psychologist who deals with animals, whose subjects are safely locked in cages, has seemed like a very simple one by contrast.

We have learned—or relearned—that the most competent therapists are likely to be highly individual and that it is not easy, over a period of years, to keep them confined within a research design which endeavors to obtain from them comparable data on each and every research client. We have also had to face the fact that, when the welfare of the client conflicts in any way with the requirements of the research, it is the latter which must give way. We all approve of this policy, yet its effect on the research is sometimes a matter for regret.

All this adds up to a certain lack of "neatness" in the research. There are gaps in the data. There are unfortunate failures to obtain follow-up data on some clients. There is, occasionally, a lack of strict comparability in the material obtained. These deficiencies we greatly regret.

In another way, too, the study seems to lack neatness. This

grows out of our puzzlement as to when to close the books on our first block of clients. Should we wait until every client has completed therapy and a follow-up period, running the risk that our research staff might disperse or lose its motivation for carrying through the initial projects—the risk that the data would be unused? Or should we permit the data to be analyzed when the client group is sufficiently large to test satisfactorily the particular hypotheses under investigation? We chose the second policy, and the reader will discover that the numbers in the therapy group in the various chapters differ somewhat, depending on the date on which the analysis of the material began. Indeed, even as this is written, there is one client in our first block of therapy cases who is still in therapy, with more than a hundred and seventy interviews. The results of therapy for this client are included in none of the present studies.

Another respect in which we are disappointed is that these studies involve only one approach to psychotherapy. We have, from the first, had hopes that other therapeutic viewpoints might be included. When a well-qualified, medically trained psychiatrist and psychoanalyst requested the opportunity to participate in the research and asked to have the same measures applied in the same way to his patients in psychoanalysis, we were greatly pleased. This would permit, we believed, at least a small and preliminary investigation of the differences between therapies in terms of outcomes. This project was under way, with the research tests given to the co-operating patients and with all interviews being recorded, when the analyst was taken into military service. This represented a real loss to the program.

These are a few of the deficiencies which we see and regret. We are keenly aware of the fact that this is an investigation which is in some ways imperfect and in some ways incomplete.

The Order of Presentation

Since a volume of research is not likely to be read straight through from beginning to end like a novel, a few comments about the order in which the material is presented may be helpful as a guide to the reader.

Chapter 2 gives the fabric of thinking in which the research was planned and the major policies which developed. It also describes briefly a number of projects not yet completed and not reported in this volume, in order to provide a picture of the total context of the program.

Chapter 3 gives the basic design for the projects based on the first block (Block I) of cases. All the studies in this book gathered their data from this block of clients, and an understanding of this over-all design is essential for the most complete understanding of the material which follows.

Once the reader has completed chapter 3, any of the remaining chapters may be read as a separate unit. Each has been written in such a fashion as to be complete in itself, provided the reader understands the general design of which it is a part.

In chapter 4 we begin by looking at the hypothesis that changes occur in the perceived self of the client during therapy and in the relation of that perceived self to the desired or ideal self. Q-technique is the instrument, and data are presented from control individuals as well as from clients in therapy.

In chapter 5 the attempt is made to relate these inner and phenomenological alterations in self-perception to an external criterion of adjustment, formulated by clinicians. Data are given both for clients and for controls.

Chapter 6 is a much more exhaustive analysis of the material gained through the Q-sorts. In eight cases in which we had the data during a waiting period prior to therapy, during therapy, and over a follow-up period, the changes in perception of the self, of the ideal, and of the ordinary person are analyzed.

In chapter 7 we leave the purely phenomenological data and consider the changes in the client as judged from the vantage point of the counselor. The relationship of counselor judgments to other variables is also presented.

Chapter 8 moves on to an even more external basis of judgment. It presents the data from a blind analysis of the Thematic Apperception Test on both therapy and control individuals, investigating the degree of personality change in each group.

Chapter 9 analyzes the same basic data, the protocols from the

Thematic Apperception Test, approaching the task with a scale based upon classical psychoanalytic formulations, and again studying both clients and controls as to changes in their mental health status as viewed from a different theoretical framework.

Chapter 10 investigates the hypothesis that the emergence of new elements of self-awareness is a significant aspect of the process of therapy. The criteria for this investigation of process are drawn from four of the preceding chapters (chaps. 5, 7, 8, and 9).

Chapter 11 considers the hypothesis that therapy brings about a change in attitudes toward others, using as its instrument a complex paper-and-pencil scale of attitudes and comparing clients and controls.

Chapter 12 takes one portion of the data from the preceding chapter and investigates the hypothesis that ethnocentric attitudes may militate against the success of client-centered or other forms of psychotherapy. It is one of the few studies which have been made regarding the limitations of therapy.

Chapter 13 studies the hypothesis that therapy results in an increase in the maturity of behavior of the client. The Willoughby Emotional-Maturity Scale is the instrument for both the experimental and the control individuals.

In chapter 14 a detailed investigation is made to determine whether clients who are motivated for therapy change in the absence of therapy. Is it, in other words, the motivation which induces change, or the therapy?

Part III of the book is devoted to the objective analysis of single cases. Each of these is best thought of as a vertical slice which cuts down through each of the horizontal studies in terms of one individual client. Chapter 15 presents the case of Mrs. Oak, giving many excerpts from the recorded interviews to give the clinical flavor of the therapy but focusing primarily on the objective findings from each of the major studies mentioned above, illuminating their meaning in terms of an individual. In addition, this chapter formulates and tests certain hypotheses in this single case. While Mrs. Oak is a client in whom psychotherapy seems to have occurred, chapter 16 makes an equally thorough analysis of the material on Mr. Bebb, a client whose therapy was a failure.

Part IV gives in chapter 17 a brief, nontechnical résumé of the whole program, weaving the many findings into an integrated pattern of results and pointing up some of the major issues which call for further investigation.

It is hoped that these brief comments may serve to some extent as an aid to the reader in selecting those portions of the book which for him hold primary interest. We turn now to the way in which the whole program developed.

CHAPTER 2

Developing a Program of Research in Psychotherapy

THOMAS GORDON, DONALD L. GRUMMON,
CARL R. ROGERS, AND JULIUS SEEMAN

The purpose of this chapter is to describe something of the development of the program and the thinking and planning which preceded the specific research enterprises themselves. It is felt that an analysis of this preliminary phase will perhaps be of help to others faced with similar problems in attacking a broad and complex field of study. It will also provide a meaningful context for the understanding not only of the later chapters in this book but of the further research reports which will be published subsequently.

I. THE BACKGROUND

The Place of Research in Psychotherapy

For more than fifty years the practice and the study of psychotherapy have made a profound contribution to the behavioral sciences. This contribution has not been limited to the personal help which has been gained by persons in emotional distress but consists even more importantly of significant insights into personality and behavior. Much of what we tentatively know about the dynamics of human behavior has come either directly or indirectly from the field of psychotherapy. Insights derived from the practice of psychotherapy have gained such a degree of public interest and acceptance that it is difficult to name an area of endeavor involving human relationships which has not been affected. There is no doubt that modern man deals differently with the problems of education, child-rearing, criminality, illness, personnel selection, and international relationships—to mention a few—because of the understanding of human behavior which has come from psychotherapy. The outstanding influence here is the theoretical framework which Freud grounded upon observations made during therapeutic hours. Contributions have also come from the practice and thinking of Jung, Adler, Rank, Horney, Sullivan, and Fromm and from the work of Rogers and the group interested in client-centered therapy. It is safe to say that every branch of social science and many of society's functions have been affected by the thinking of workers in the field of psychotherapy.

Viewing this significant influence, one might suppose that a considerable body of carefully planned and executed research would have evolved in this field, developing and refining the truths which had been glimpsed in clinical practice. Such, however, is not the case. The reasons seem to be twofold. In the first place, psychotherapy is an extremely complex matter, involving emotional and cognitive functions, the process of learning, physiological determinants of behavior, social attitudes, ethical values—in fact, most of the areas of study which are important to the behavioral sciences. To plan or carry on well-controlled objective research in such an area seems to some a well-nigh impossible task, and the formidable obstacles are without question one of the reasons why there has not been more research.

A second reason is perhaps even more important. Psychotherapy is, among other things, one of the most subtle arts known to man. It is a rich and delicate relationship in which the nuances may have more significance than the obvious elements. Because of this, many competent therapists have felt that this is an area in which research, in the usual sense of objectively controlled studies, could never enter. Some of these workers not only have felt skeptical but have been definitely opposed to any attempt to measure or test the intangible and intuitive elements which loom so large in the actual practice of psychotherapy.

The group which has developed the present research program recognizes the large element of truth in both of these contentions. It is hard to imagine a field in which research is more difficult. It is also recognized that the essential elements of therapy are almost certainly subtle, are frequently intuitive, and often lie below the surface of the obvious situation. Yet this group has the conviction that Thorndike's dictum is essentially correct—that "anything that exists, exists in some quantity that can be measured." It also has the belief, as it reviews the history of science, that important advances in science frequently follow when common observations are rigorously measured, under carefully controlled conditions, and when commonly held theories are put to objective empirical test. It is on such a basis that research in therapy is predicated.

A Foundation of Research in Client-centered Therapy

Such a view as to the possibility of research in psychotherapy has been implemented by a decade of research in client-centered therapy, in which several of the present group have participated. It is within the context of this earlier research that the present program acquires its fullest meaning. It would not be appropriate here to undertake a systematic review of this research, since a survey and analysis of it is already available in published form (32). In Table 1, however, the reader will find a synopsis which indicates the major areas in which work has been done and an illustrative and partial list of the studies which have been completed in each area.

A study of this table reveals in broad outline the areas which have thus far been tapped by research in client-centered therapy. In regard to the process itself, some attention has been given to the counselor's behavior in interviews, and a beginning has been made in considering the client-therapist interaction. With regard to the client, some initial measurements have been made of the changes which take place in the self-concept, in insight, in attitudes toward others, in defensiveness, in reported behavior, and the like, during the series of interviews. As to outcomes, while the scope of the studies is small in relation to all the questions which might be asked, yet a diversity of effort is seen in the studies which tap behavior on personality tests, physiological changes in stress situations, and behavior in social situations. A start has been made, in a variety of ways, in investigating the complex phenomenon which is therapy, and the results have been sufficiently promising to encourage further development.

The Aims of the Present Research Program

It is out of the beginnings briefly described in the preceding section that research in psychotherapy has reached a point in its development where the tentative, groping quality of the earlier investigations can give way to more comprehensive planning and

TABLE 1

SUMMARY OF RESEARCH AREAS IN CLIENT-CENTERED THERAPY

STUDIES IN THE THERAPEUTIC PROCESS

Counseling Method:

The development and evaluation of a measure of counseling interview procedures: Porter (25).

An investigation of counselor behavior in nondirective psychotherapy: Snyder (34), Seeman (30).

Process in the Client:

A. Studies in the self.

Self-reference in counseling interviews: Raimy (26), Snyder (34), Seeman (30).

The relationship between attitudes toward self and attitudes toward others: Sheerer (33), Stock (35).

B. Study of other concepts related to process.

Insight: Curran (9).

Defensive behavior in client-centered therapy: Hogan (18), Haigh (13).

The locus of evaluation in therapy: Raskin (27).

The use of grammatical and psychogrammatical categories of language in therapy: Grummon (12).

Reported behavior changes in therapy: Hoffman (17).

Interaction of Client and Counselor:

Relationship between counseling method and client response: Bergman (3).

Therapeutic relationships as created by experts and non-experts: Fiedler (10).

STUDIES IN OUTCOMES OF THERAPY

Personality-Test Assessment:

Personality changes in individuals undergoing client-centered therapy: Muench (23), Carr (8), Haimowitz (14).

A study of changes in perception in relation to psychotherapy: Jonietz (19).

A study of measures currently used in evaluating personality change in therapy: Mosak (22).

Situational Behavior:

Measurement of physiological response to frustration before and after therapy: Thetford (36).

Study of Psychosocial Adjustment:

Data on the personal adjustment of veterans after counseling: Bartlett (2).

Effect of therapy on the reading function in children: Bills (4, 5).

orderly development. In planning the present research in the autumn of 1949, it became evident to the Research Group of the staff of the Counseling Center that we had achieved a clearer idea of the questions we wanted to ask and the research directions which seemed promising. We recognized that we had reached the point where our research might be of the sort which has been called "program design." Marquis defines program design as "the planning of an integrated series of research activities focussed on a central problem and involving a number of scientists for several years" (21, p. 432). As we met to plan our comprehensive activities in this field, this achievement of a program design became our primary aim. We wished to develop a flexible, ongoing design in which many workers of varying shades of opinion regarding therapy might find a congenial conceptual framework in which they could attack related problems in a related fashion. This aim has been in the background of all our specific planning. Its fulfilment has been recognized as being a matter of attitude as well as of research design and staff organization.

The more immediate objectives of the program as it developed in our thinking were threefold: (*a*) the investigation of the internal dimension of therapy—the discovery of those lawful relationships inherent in the process of therapy which are involved in the reorganization of personality in therapy; (*b*) the investigation of the external dimension of therapy—the discovery of the correlates of the therapeutic process in the larger psychological, physiological, and sociological field of the individual; and (*c*) the relation of these findings to personality theory and to present knowledge about personality.

II. THE RESEARCH PLANNING

Before proceeding to a description of the specific projects by which we endeavored to implement these aims, it will be helpful to describe the way in which the planning was done, for the process has many implications which have affected the decisions and the thinking of the group.

The Research Group

The planning and the conduct of the program have at all times been in the hands of the Research Group. The size of this group has varied from time to time, inasmuch as there is a continuous flow of researchers coming into the group, participating for a period, and then leaving upon the completion of their project or their special mission. The total group has been as large as twenty-five or thirty and as small as fifteen or twenty. The number of persons having more or less continuous functions in the group is approximately ten. These are the people who have permanent or semipermanent positions on the staff of the Counseling Center. At any one time six to eight of these also have had faculty appointments in the University of Chicago. In addition to the group that functions fairly continuously in the program, there is a large group of advanced graduate students who are carrying out specific studies or who are performing certain specialized tasks in the program, such as statistical work, testing, conducting pilot studies, etc. As of this writing, for example, nine doctoral dissertations and four Master's theses based on data collected in the research program have been completed, and at least an equal number are in process.

The Research Group also included three regular consultants who worked very closely with those actually carrying on the research during the early planning stages. Frequently, faculty members of the Department of Psychology also have been asked to participate in the group in the capacity of consultants.

Several times it has been necessary to include a large proportion of the total staff of the Counseling Center in some of the research meetings. This has been necessary when the group concerns itself with problems that involve the many counselors on the staff who are doing the actual counseling of the research cases. In short, the Research Group has consisted of varying members of faculty, other Center staff members, and students and consultants, each of whom carries out certain functions in the group of a permanent or relatively impermanent nature.

The Functioning of the Research Group

One of the distinctive features of the research program has been the way the participants have functioned as a group. As might be expected, the group has learned that it is most comfortable operating in a way that is consistent with the social philosophy which has gradually developed alongside of client-centered therapy. In short, the conduct of the research program has been "group-centered." Like most groups that fit such a description, the research group had to grow into this manner of functioning. Thus it seemed expedient at first to select a director and to think in terms of such questions as who should have authority over whom or what should be the chain of command and the channels of communication. In some of the earlier formal proposals, as a matter of fact, certain members were listed as "director" or "principal investigator." Yet, in fact, the research has never had a director. It has operated in such a way that all the participants have felt free to assume functional leadership whenever the quality of their contribution warranted this. No staff member has been required to participate in the program by being assigned to the research group, though persons with specialized psychometric or research skills have been employed to exercise those skills in connection with the program. The research has been carried on primarily by those who have wished to participate, each person doing those tasks which had the most meaning for him within the context of the group's own goals. To a great extent each person defines for himself the area of responsibility he wishes to assume, and the group in turn has structured itself on the basis of the various functions which are voluntarily taken over by its members. Form thus follows function, not the reverse of this. This has meant that the form and the organizational structure of this group, unlike most other groups in our society, have not been elevated to a position of importance over and above the purpose and desires of the individuals who comprise the group. It has meant that structure has not had the quality of permanence that it has in most groups. On the contrary, the organizational structure of the research group has been in constant change.

It would be a mistake to assume that such a fluid process has always functioned smoothly. At times it has seemed inefficient and confusing to some, and at times others have felt that a slightly more traditional organizational form would better suit our needs. Proposals for changes in our way of working are frequent, and many of these have been adopted. As one studies the decisions made by the group, however, a pattern is clearly discernible. The group as a whole, despite temporary swings by the whole group and persistent skepticism on the part of some individuals, has maintained an "organic" and flexible type of functioning in which direction by one person is absent and in which the thinking and criticism of every member of the group are equally available in regard to any specific plan or decision. Whether this fluid mode of functioning has "paid off" in terms of quality and significance of the actual accomplishments of the group is something which only time and the judgment of the whole profession can decide. It is clear that the Research Group, by and large, has believed that it will.

How do outside consultants fit into such a fluid mode of functioning? One of the perplexing problems in all program research has been how to make effective use of consultants. The potential contribution of "outside" consultants is usually taken for granted, yet it is also recognized that it is often difficult for consultants to acquire sufficient familiarity with a program to enable them to make appropriate contributions. An attempt was made to alleviate this difficulty by bringing in the consultants during the earliest stages of hypothesis construction and project planning. Thus the consultants and staff developed a common background. Like all other members of the group, the consultants had to work through the puzzling problems that inevitably plague researchers during this early planning stage. They shared in the initial gropings of the group and likewise in the gradual process of formulating solutions to such complex problems as research design, controls, criteria, and the like. This has meant that, instead of a research staff *and* consultants, there has been simply a group working together on research. It was hoped that the consultants, like any of the other group members, would feel free to participate in any way they wished, to attend certain meetings or not to attend, to consult only with individuals or with the total group. Although their participation necessarily had to be limited by the demands of their regular positions and their geographical locations, nevertheless they made frequent and significant contributions to the group and have themselves acquired significant learnings from their membership in the group. As the research took form and the major task became the carrying-through of the agreed-upon plans, their functions diminished, and their participation for the most part ceased. Their aid was greatest during the planning period.

A Basic Decision regarding Theory

In the earliest stages of our thinking many "good ideas" as to specific projects were proposed. It was soon evident that it would be quite possible to undertake a variety of "good" studies which would be nothing but a hodgepodge. At this point an important decision was made. It was agreed that the greatest research advance would be made if the hypotheses tested were derived from, and related to, a body of theory sufficiently coherent to allow progressive integration of knowledge as new research facts became available. This decision has increasingly justified itself. Each of the separate studies which have been undertaken has derived its major hypothesis from existing psychological theory. Up to the present time three bodies of theory have primarily been utilized. The first is the personality theory which has been evolving in client-centered therapy, exemplified in Rogers' recent volume (28); the second is the field of learning theory; and the third is the body of psychological theory which has grown up around the process of perception. Other bodies of theory will undoubtedly be utilized in the future.

Viewed from this perspective, research and theory development are reciprocal processes, the theory providing significant hypotheses for investigation by research, and the research contributing to the evaluation and the enrichment of psychological theory. In this context, therapy is seen not only as an applied clinical technique for helping the individual but also as a most valuable window opening upon the dynamic processes of personality organization and change. Findings based upon this type of broad orientation will, it is believed, have a generality and significance which will extend far beyond the field of psychotherapy itself.

Operating in terms of this fundamental thinking, it was decided that each project to be considered by the Research Group would involve (*a*) the formulation of a hypothesis grounded in some explicit body of pertinent psychological theory; (*b*) the further elaboration of the hypothesis in operational terms so that both the testability of the hypothesis and the appropriate method of testing it would be made clear; (*c*) the selection of instruments to carry out the necessary operations; and (*d*) consideration of samples and controls. It is emphasized that in this order of hypothesis development the tests and other instruments used to measure outcomes are chosen for their specific utility in providing evidence for particular theory-based hypotheses rather than for their general clinical usefulness or popularity.

The Issue of Controls

An issue upon which the group spent many hours of discussion was the problem of controls. Some felt that controls, though theoretically desirable, were actually almost impossible to achieve because of the complexity of the variables involved. For example, it was questioned whether certain personality variables and the elusive but important phenomenon of "therapeutic readiness" or motivation could be controlled in any really adequate sense. Yet it was also recognized that one could have only limited objective confirmation of the effects of therapy without the use of controls. Out of the discussion came a clearer recognition that the important concept regarding controls is not so much the concept of *control groups* as the concept of *control phenomena*—that is, the importance of controls lies in the adequate accounting for variables presumed to be relevant to therapy. Such controls can be instituted in many ways. Sometimes it means using separate control groups. At other times the best controls may come from different measures of the same person, that is, the "own-control" method. In still other instances controls lie in data rather than in people. For example, if one wishes to describe those points in therapy which counselors characterize as "deep," an essential part of such a description comes out of a comparison of such points with randomly selected passages. Finally, effective control methods lie in statistical controls as a supplement to experimental controls. For example, if one wishes to institute controls where continuous measurement is involved (e.g., recognition time in a perception experiment), a method of choice may be analysis of covariance, where the effect of initial differences between experimental and control groups is partialed out and the groups equated by statistical means. The general policy of the Research Group is to utilize the principle of control phenomena and in any given design to use that method or combination of control methods which will make it most possible to isolate and study the effect of the experimental variable of therapy upon the personality and behavior of clients.

III. THE STUDIES APPROVED

Working this way, and thinking in these terms, the Research Group has considered and approved a wide range of related projects. A number of the major projects have been completed and are reported in this volume, as are also some of the smaller special studies. Other investigations have been completed and published in journals. A number of others are available as unpublished doctoral dissertations. Still others are in the stages of data collection or analysis, while others are only approved proposals, with the investigators wrestling with problems of methodology and instrumentation. Like any organic development, all phases of growth—the bud, the full-blown flower, and the museum specimen gathering dust in a glass case—are exemplified in our projects.

Among the studies under way or planned are many which will rely upon data collected from therapy with individuals, but there are others which will collect their data from play therapy. There are studies concerned with process and with outcomes. There are researches in which the object of study will be the client's visual perception, his physiological reactions during the interviews, his verbal productions, his social attitudes, his concepts of himself, his values, his social behavior. Looked at from another point of view, there are represented in the program studies of the client alone, of the therapist alone, and of the relationship between client and therapist. If this gives some picture of the range of projects, it will perhaps be less confusing if we consider a number of these projects in a very brief and general way, thinking of them particularly as (*a*) studies in the process of therapy and as (*b*) studies in the correlates or outcomes of therapy. As the studies to be reported in this book will be dealt with in detail in the next chapter, we will here touch only on some of the other projects approved under this program to give the reader some notion of the variety of the work. These studies are either completed or now in progress and are available as indicated in the references at the end of this chapter.

Studies of Process

With regard to study of the internal dimension of therapy, we are endeavoring, by our projects, to raise particular questions which will add to our understanding of the nature of therapy and the nature of personality organization. A full investigation of this area involves many facets, the first and most obvious being the study of the therapeutic process itself—that is, observations of the order which is inherent in therapy at successive stages of the interviews.

Bowman (6) has completed a study, based upon an analysis of the recorded interviews, in which he studies, throughout the process of therapy, the changing relationship between the current concept of self, the wished-for self, and the "proper" or socially demanded self. Fox (11) has studied the changing interrelationships between a number of categories of the client's verbal productions as therapy proceeds. Categorizing the client's statements about self, others, social institutions, and the like, she has studied the underlying order which exists in these data. Hartley (15) has completed a study in which the changes in the client's concept of self throughout therapy are analyzed and related to concepts of the ideal self and counselor concepts. This study was a forerunner of much of the work with Q-technique which is reported in this book. Rogers is embarked upon a study of the manner in which the individual becomes more open to his experience—less defensive—during therapy. Commencing with elements which are present in the diagnostic picture but not in the client's awareness, he is attempting to trace, through a variety of means, the emergence of this material into awareness. Anderson (1) is analyzing the data obtained in an investigation which seeks to compare certain continuing physiological measurements (heart rate and the like) of the client during the therapeutic hours with his verbal productions during these same hours. These brief descriptions may give some picture of the range of the several studies which are attempting to investigate the process of therapy within the client and some of its ramifications.

Approaching the internal dimension from another angle, Seeman (31) is asking about those points in therapy which therapists regard as "deep." The intention is not only to arrive at an operational definition of depth but also to compare the characteristics of the therapeutic process at these presumably significant points with those at other points.

A further line of inquiry about process consists of comparing clients who complete therapy with those who do not. Rudikoff (29) has embarked upon such a study, which seems to offer a direct avenue to clues about the relationship of personality and motivation to therapy. It also provides the possibility of understanding better the nature of failure in therapy. Another attack on this last issue is being made by making very complete analyses of all the research data on cases in which therapy and change clearly took place and equally complete studies of cases in which therapy and change did not occur. It is hoped that hypotheses in regard to failure in therapy may emerge, as well as further hypotheses in regard to therapy when it does occur.

A facet of the therapeutic process to which increasing emphasis has been given is that which concerns itself with the therapeutic relationship or the psychological climate of therapy. Several studies give attention to this question. Bown (7) is completing a study in which the client and the counselor independently picture the way in which each perceives the relationship at progressive stages of therapy. Available for comparison also is the way each pictures the ideal therapeutic relationship both before and after therapy. Kell (20) has investigated a factor which may have a bearing on the counselor's capacity for empathy. He has measured the ability of three different groups to predict the self-concept of a client from hearing a therapeutic interview. The groups were experienced counselors, counselors in training, and a group of chemists.

These, then, are some of the researches in the process of therapy which the Research Group has approved. As the program proceeds, we shall expect not only that the foregoing lines of investigation will be further developed but that new questions will be asked, new methods devised, new hypotheses considered. All these developments will converge upon the central point of understanding more deeply what it is that constitutes the process of therapy, what elements are crucial or significant for this process, and what factors may block it, impede it, or prevent it from occurring.

Studies of Outcomes

The study of those correlates of the therapeutic process which are thought of as outcomes has thus far occupied the major portion of our time, though not necessarily of our thinking. A number of the studies approved in this field are completed and being reported in later chapters. Here we will mention some of the other studies still in process.

Several of these studies attempt to measure aspects of personality change. Various hypotheses are being investigated in a study involving several of the staff, using as instruments the Thematic Apperception Test (TAT), the Stein Sentence Completion Test, and the Rorschach given tachistoscopically. It should perhaps be stressed again that the question of how the client changes on the TAT or on the Rorschach is to us a matter of secondary interest, because by themselves such findings would constitute only isolated facts. It is only as a particular aspect of a theory of therapy or a theory of personality may be tested by these or other instruments that our interest becomes primary.

Since the theory of therapy hypothesizes change in attitudes toward others as one outcome, investigations have been made in this field. One study by Gordon and others in which the data are now being analyzed uses a role-playing situation to assess the changes in attitudes toward others.

In its consideration of outcome studies the Research Group discerns a certain trend. In the studies mentioned thus far we believe that there hangs about them a faint aroma of proving that therapy is "good." The hypotheses upon which we now are working are concerned, we believe, with even more basic correlates and have less of any value flavor about them. For example, a study being conducted by Seeman deals with the relationship between therapy and perception. Does therapy, in any measurable way, affect perception as it may be tested in the laboratory? Does perception become more flexible or more rigid? More open to stimuli or less? Another study contemplates an investigation of the relationship between therapy and learning. Does therapy affect the basic learning process of the individual? The major postulate in these plans is that personal reorganization occurs in therapy and modifies the ways in which individuals use their personal resources in the tasks of learning and perceiving. It is believed that such investigations will open up avenues of even more fundamental knowledge of personality and its dynamic processes.

We may summarize some of these research plans for measuring outcomes by observing that the chief characteristic is a multidirectional approach to the assessment of personality and behavioral concomitants of the therapeutic process. In the long run we may be able to make a number of valid statements about the concomitants of therapy which will permit an adequate social judgment as to its usefulness.

The Magnitude of the Problem of Data Collection

Since this is a relatively new field of research, it may be appropriate to close this section regarding the specific aspects of our research by commenting on a problem which is not well understood. The task of making intensive studies of clients is far from a simple one. Not only are the ethical and professional problems perplexing ones, each needing careful consideration if we are to protect the interests of both the client and science, but the purely physical problem of data collection tends to be staggering. As an example, in the first of our research "blocks" (Block I) there are approximately twenty-five therapy cases and twenty-five controls. A battery of five research instruments is administered three times to half of the clients and controls, four times to the other half. In addition, one of the instruments is given at other times during therapy and at matched times to the controls. All the interviews are recorded, and it is hoped that they can all be transcribed. Here is an estimate of the time involved for gathering the raw data from one forty-interview case and one matched control case:

		Hours
Counselor	Interviewing	40
	Checking and editing transcription	80
Psychometrist	Three test batteries to client	18
	Three test batteries to control	18
Client	Time given to research tasks	18
Control subject	Time given to research tasks	18
Transcribers	Transcription of tests and recorded interviews, preliminary checking of same, duplication and assembling of interviews	480

These are actually minimum time allotments, provided everything moves smoothly. It should also be borne in mind that this work cannot be done all at once on any one client but that the tasks are spaced out over a period of at least a year and often two or three years. Thus nearly seven hundred man-hours is invested in gathering the data on this one case, without any account of the time needed for analyzing the material thus gathered. Perhaps this will convey some notion of the magnitude of effort which is involved in collecting the data for studies such as we have been describing. The data are already proving their worth, but they also make it obvious that, at present, research in psychotherapy will move forward slowly.

IV. THE APPROACH TO THE CRITERION PROBLEM

What is the criterion for research in psychotherapy? This is a most perplexing issue. Psychotherapy is a complex process involving multiform changes in a complex organism, and the question as to the criterion with which measurements are to be compared constitutes a stumbling block in this field. Much of the viewpoint of the Research Group regarding this problem is already implicit in the preceding sections, but it is a sufficiently important question that it seems worth while to discuss the evolving thinking of the group as it has become clarified.

"Success" as a Criterion

There is no doubt that in the initial stages of our planning we were strongly, even though often unconsciously, influenced by the criterion of "success." Our thinking often took the form of discussing what measures would demonstrate the "success" or "failure" of therapy. Certainly this is the criterion which occurs to most people when they think of studying psychotherapy. From this point of view, psychotherapy is conceived as something which makes people "better," or "adjusted," and hence the therapy is successful or unsuccessful in achieving this aim. Or it is conceived as a "cure" for a "mental illness," and research then becomes involved in ambiguity piled upon ambiguity, in which the question is whether a mythical entity has or has not been removed. The consequence of this use of criteria based upon value judgments has been that each investigator endeavors to prove that therapy does produce certain changes which have value to him, a rather unsatisfactory basis for science. The fact that there are various more or less competitive therapeutic orientations still further complicates this manner of using selected definitions of success.

The basic difficulty here is that, to be in any way satisfactory, such a criterion as "success" in therapy must have a solid, known meaning which is acceptable to all. But psychology does not know enough as yet to provide any such definition. The bald fact is that our science lacks an incontestable body of knowledge about personality and that there is no general agreement about the precise nature of adjustment and maladjustment. Murray has stated, "If the psychologist of personality had to limit his discourse to theories that were securely proved, he would have nothing to recount. In this realm there are no certainties" (24, p. xii). For example, the removal of symptoms might be one definition of success, but this definition will be unacceptable to many, because a symptom may disappear but leave unchanged the deeper psychological disturbance out of which the symptom arose. But if deep personality change is made the definition of success, not only is the definition of the direction of that change a matter of dispute, but it may also be claimed that therapy may be successful without involving personality change. The client may simply increase in his ability to cope with pressing environmental problems. Again, success might be defined as a point at which the client feels satisfied and content within himself, but this immediately arouses the objection that such evaluations are untrustworthy and subject to the "hello-goodbye" effect described by Hathaway (16). Others object that such statements may be simply a "flight into health," while still others point out that the client may be satisfied with behaviors which are asocial or even antisocial. If the attempt is made to define success in terms of social behavior and adjustment, the difficulties are equally great. A divorce or a change in a job may be "good" or "bad," depending upon one's interpretation of the interaction between client and environment, and such interpretations differ from clinician to clinician. Increased productivity on the job may mean improvement or may mean a surrender to the demands of the status quo. Better grades can mean increased rigidity as well as better adjustment. In short, it is quite impossible at the present time to define "success" or "adjustment" in such a way that the definition is both operationally clear and acceptable to all. And even to the degree that there is concurrence of judgment in such a definition, it is simply a pooling of value judgments, which is a most unsatisfactory basis for a research program.

The Conclusion regarding Criteria

As a consequence of this type of consideration we have come to the conclusion that "success," no matter how it is phrased or defined, is not a usable or useful criterion for research in psychotherapy. In some ways our practice does not fully live up to this conclusion, since the decision has been a gradual one, and we have not been able entirely to rid ourselves of this older method of thought. We may still use the terms "success" and "failure," but they should be understood as being in quotes. We will also obtain judgments from both counselor and client as to whether they regarded the experience of therapy as "successful," since such material may be valuable data for comparison with other measures. But in every meaningful way we have given up the concept of "success" as the criterion against which our research measurements will be compared. When, in this book, we use such a phrase as "These are the successful cases, according to counselor judgment," it should be understood that we are using the counselor's rating as one datum for our study but are in no way implying that such cases meet some generally acceptable operational definition of success.

Perhaps we may most briefly explain the criteria which we have substituted by saying that we have ceased asking, "What tests and other instruments will demonstrate success or failure of therapy?" and are asking the question, "What are the concomitants of therapy?" Let us look at this more specifically. Therapy is a series of events. What are the characteristics of those events as predicted by theory? Do these characteristics, operationally defined, occur or fail to occur in the experience of clients in therapy? This decision means abandoning entirely the idea of one general criterion for our studies and substituting many clearly defined personality variables, specific to the individual hypotheses being investigated. It also means the abandonment of any value judgment in the criteria and the provision instead of an objectively verified description of a variable about which social value judgments can be separately made. For example, the theory of client-centered therapy predicts that the individual will change in the direction of increasingly viewing others as persons of worth. It also predicts that after therapy the individual is able to be aware of a greater proportion of his total organismic reponse to any situation. Each of these predictions can be operationally defined and verified or disproved. Whether they are regarded as "good," whether a person is "better" because he has moved in these directions, whether he is "cured," whether therapy is to be regarded as a "success" because these and other changes have occurred—these are issues of social value judgment which can be made by any person or any group in terms of the cultural standards they hold. But such value judgments are different from the questions of fact—the questions as to whether such predicted changes did, as a matter of measurement, occur.

Perhaps an example may be given to clarify this line of thought. A study which we have discussed, but which has not as yet been initiated, is as follows. According to the theory developed by Hogan (18) regarding defensiveness, therapy should result in a larger proportion of sensory stimuli being available to awareness. The more data a person has available to awareness, the more effective he should be in formulating possible solutions to problem situations. Hence a hypothesis might be constructed from theory that "following therapy an individual will be more effective in problem-solving." All that is needed to turn this into a research project is to give operational definitions to each term in the hypothesis. Once the research is undertaken, it should either support or disprove the hypothesis. If supported, then it would permit the statement that psychotherapy—defined in such-and-such operational terms—tends to increase the effectiveness of individuals in problem-solving situations to such-and-such a degree. Is this "success" in therapy? It is when we ask the question in such a context that "success" is seen for what it is—purely a value judgment. Perhaps this hypothetical illustration will make clear what we mean when we say that we plan to substitute many specific variables, each operationally described, for the global criterion of "success."

Put in another way, our thinking about criteria for research in psychotherapy means that eventually we should be able to make a series of statements of this order: "Client-centered therapy, operationally defined in this way, tends to produce changes *a*, *b*, *d*, and *f* in clients. No change is found in characteristics *c* and *e*." When such a series of statements is available, the profession and the lay public will be in a position to make a sound value judgment as to whether they will regard as a "success" a process which produces these changes.

Perhaps one of the most important consequences of this line of thinking about criteria is that it not only will produce new learnings about psychotherapy itself but will contribute much toward advancing an ongoing process of discovering new knowledge about personality and toward the development and evaluation of personality theory. We see our research as contributing as much to the field of personality as to the field of psychotherapy. In psychotherapy we hope to make a contribution by investigating the degree of change in a considerable number of specific variables, clearly defined and objectively measured. In the area of personality knowledge and theory it is our hope that we may contribute not only by studies of the detailed characteristics of individuals but even more importantly by adding the dimension of change, by making it possible to know not only something of the degree to which personality characteristics alter but also the effective dynamics of such change.

REFERENCES

1. ANDERSON, ROBERT, P. "An Exploratory Investigation of the Relationship between Verbal Behavior and Physiological Behavior during Client-centered Therapy." Ph.D. dissertation (in progress), University of Chicago.
2. BARTLETT, MARION R. "A Six Month Follow-up of the Effects of Personal Adjustment Counseling of Veterans," *Journal of Consulting Psychology*, XIV (1950), 393–94.
3. BERGMAN, DANIEL V. "Counseling Method and Client Responses," *Journal of Consulting Psychology*, XV (1951), 216–24.
4. BILLS, ROBERT E. "Nondirective Play Therapy with Retarded Readers," *Journal of Consulting Psychology*, XIV (1950), 140–49.
5. ———. "Play Therapy with Well-adjusted Retarded Readers," *ibid.*, pp. 246–49.
6. BOWMAN, PAUL. "A Study of the Consistency of Current, Wish, and Proper Self-concepts as a Measure of the Therapeutic Process." Ph.D. dissertation, University of Chicago, 1951.
7. BOWN, OLIVER. "An Investigation of the Therapeutic Relationship in Client-centered Psychotherapy." Ph.D. dissertation, University of Chicago, 1954.
8. CARR, ARTHUR C. "An Evaluation of Nine Nondirective Psychotherapy Cases by Means of the Rorschach," *Journal of Consulting Psychology*, XIII (1949), 196–205.
9. CURRAN, CHARLES A. *Personality Factors in Counseling*. New York: Grune & Stratton, 1945.
10. FIEDLER, FRED E. "A Comparison of Therapeutic Relationships in Psychoanalytic, Nondirective and Adlerian Therapy," *Journal of Consulting Psychology*, XIV (1950), 436–45.
11. FOX, MARGARET. "A Quantitative Study of Changes in Verbal Behavior Occurring in Counseling." Ph.D. dissertation, University of Chicago, 1951.
12. GRUMMON, DONALD L. "The Use of Language Categories for the Study of Personality and Psychotherapy." Ph.D. dissertation, University of Chicago, 1950.
13. HAIGH, GERARD V. "Defensive Behavior in Client-centered Therapy," *Journal of Consulting Psychology*, XIII (1949), 181–89.
14. HAIMOWITZ, NATALIE READER and MORRIS L. "Personality Changes in Client-centered Therapy," in W. WOLFF (ed.), *Success in Psychotherapy*, chap. 3. New York: Grune & Stratton, 1952.
15. HARTLEY, MARGARET. "Changes in the Self-concept during Psychotherapy." Ph.D. dissertation, University of Chicago, 1951.
16. HATHAWAY, S. R. "Some Considerations Relative to Nondirective Counseling as Therapy," *Journal of Clinical Psychology*, IV (1948), 226–31.
17. HOFFMAN, A. EDWARD. "A Study of Reported Behavior Changes in Counseling," *Journal of Consulting Psychology*, XIII (1949), 190–95.

18. HOGAN, RICHARD A. "The Development of a Measure of Client Defensiveness in the Counseling Relationship." Ph.D. dissertation, University of Chicago, 1948. (Summary published in *Journal of Consulting Psychology*, XVI, [1952], 417–24.)
19. JONEITZ, ALICE K. "A Study of the Phenomenological Changes in Perception after Psychotherapy as Exhibited in the Content of Rorschach Percepts." Ph.D. dissertation, University of Chicago, 1950.
20. KELL, BILL L. "An Experimental Study of the Ability To Predict the Self-concept of an Individual from His Therapeutic Interview Behavior." Ph.D. dissertation, University of Chicago, 1950.
21. MARQUIS, DONALD G. "Research Planning at the Frontiers of Science," *American Psychologist*, III (1948), 430–38.
22. MOSAK, HAROLD. "Evaluations in Psychotherapy: A Study of Some Current Measures." Ph.D. dissertation, University of Chicago, 1950.
23. MUENCH, GEORGE A. "An Evaluation of Nondirective Psychotherapy by Means of the Rorschach and Other Tests," *Applied Psychological Monographs*, XIII (1947), 1–163.
24. MURRAY, HENRY A., *et al. Explorations in Personality*. New York: Oxford University Press, 1938.
25. PORTER, E. H., JR. "The Development and Evaluation of a Measure of Counseling Interview Procedures," *Educational and Psychological Measurement*, III (1943), 105–26, 215–38.
26. RAIMY, VICTOR C. "Self-reference in Counseling Interviews," *Journal of Consulting Psychology*, XII (1948), 153–63.
27. RASKIN, NATHANIEL J. "An Objective Study of the Locus-of-Evaluation Factor in Psychotherapy," in W. WOLFF (ed.), *Success in Psychotherapy*, chap. 6. New York: Grune & Stratton, 1952.
28. ROGERS, CARL R. *Client-centered Therapy*. Boston: Houghton Mifflin Co., 1951.
29. RUDIKOFF, ESSELYN. "A Study of the Self-concept, the Concept of the Ordinary Person, and the Self-ideal in Relationship to Client-centered Psychotherapy." Ph.D. dissertation (in progress), University of Chicago.
30. SEEMAN, JULIUS. "A Study of the Process of Nondirective Therapy," *Journal of Consulting Psychology*, XIII (1949), 157–68.
31. ———. "A Proposal for the Study of Depth in Psychotherapy." Counseling Center, University of Chicago, 1951. (Mimeographed.)
32. SEEMAN, JULIUS, and RASKIN, NATHANIEL J. "Research Perspectives in Client-centered Therapy," in O. H. MOWRER (ed.), *Psychotherapy: Theory and Research*, chap. 9. New York: Ronald Press Co., 1953.
33. SHEERER, ELIZABETH T. "An Analysis of the Relationship between Acceptance of and Respect for Self and Acceptance of and Respect for Others in Ten Counseling Cases," *Journal of Consulting Psychology*, XIII (1949), 169–75.

34. Snyder, William U. "An Investigation of the Nature of Nondirective Psychotherapy," *Journal of General Psychology*, XXXIII (1945), 192–223.
35. Stock, Dorothy. "An Investigation into the Interrelations between the Self-concept and Feelings Directed toward Other Persons and Groups," *Journal of Consulting Psychology*, XIII (1949), 176–80.
36. Thetford, William N. "An Objective Measure of Frustration Tolerance in Evaluating Psychotherapy," in W. Wolff (ed.), *Success in Psychotherapy*, chap. 2. New York: Grune & Stratton, 1952.

CHAPTER 3

Design, Procedures, and Subjects for the First Block

DONALD L. GRUMMON

A basic element in the planning of the research program was, as indicated in the preceding chapter, the use of one group or "block" of clients as a unit on which a number of separate hypotheses might be tested. In this chapter we describe the basic design, the data-gathering procedures, and the subjects involved in the first such block (Block I). All the later chapters are based on this first block and give some of the findings which have grown out of the projects here briefly described.

I. THE GENERAL AIM FOR THE FIRST BLOCK

The broad objective in this first block was to study the outcomes of client-centered therapy and at the same time to provide data out of which studies of the process of psychotherapy might also be made. By "outcomes," we refer to those behavioral and psychological changes which may occur in the client undergoing psychotherapy; by "process," we refer to those experiences of the client and other events of the therapeutic hours which are related to outcomes. More simply, what changes occur in the client, if any? Why does he change? And how are these two sets of events interrelated?

A subsidiary objective is to set forth procedures whereby other kinds of psychotherapy can be studied in a comparable manner, thus eventually making it possible to obtain meaningful cross-comparisons between different therapies.

The general plan of the research calls for measures of several selected psychological and behavioral characteristics to be made before, during, and following the psychotherapy of persons undergoing client-centered counseling at the University of Chicago's Counseling Center. All the counseling interviews are electrically recorded on permanent disks and will be studied in a variety of ways to add understanding about the process of therapy.

II. THE HYPOTHESES AND THE PSYCHOLOGICAL TESTS EMPLOYED TO INVESTIGATE THEM

A detailed statement of the hypotheses and their basis in theoretical thinking about personality and psychotherapy will be left to the reports of specific projects to follow. However, to orient the reader, we will here present a general statement about the problems studied in these projects and list the tests used to obtain appropriate measurements.

Project No. 1

The first project had to do primarily with changes in self-perception. A universe of self-referent statements (which we have termed the "SIO Q-Sort") was developed by Butler and Haigh for this project following the methods of Stephenson (3). These statements are printed on cards which the client sorts to describe (*a*) himself (the self-sort), (*b*) how he would like to be (the ideal-sort), and (*c*) what the ordinary person is like (the ordinary sort). The subject is instructed to place each card in one of nine piles arranged along a continuum from "least like" to "most like." A specified number of cards must be placed in each of the nine piles so as to achieve a quasi-normal distribution and the ready assignment of scale values. These data are then analyzed by correlational methods and factor analysis.

The project examines a number of specific hypotheses about changes in perceptions of self and others during therapy such as: the correlation between the self-sort and the ideal-sort will increase during the later stages of therapy. Chapters 4, 5, and 6 report results from this project.

Project No. 2

The second project was designed to study changes in the total personality make-up of the client as well as to examine more specific hypotheses relating to personal adjustment. The Thematic Apperception Test (TAT) was chosen as the instrument. Included in this project are such hypotheses as: (*a*) personality change occurs in a direction definable as improved adjustment; (*b*) clients after therapy will perceive and describe social relationships in a more mature way; and (*c*) following therapy there will be a greater congruence between the client's perception of self and the clinical diagnosis revealed by the TAT. Chapters 8 and 9 are two studies addressed to hypothesis *a*. Chapters 15 and 16 include results of these hypotheses in two case studies.

Project No. 3

This project measures possible changes in the client's attitudes toward others. Two measuring devices are used: (*a*) The Self-Other Attitude Scale (S-O Scale) designed to measure the following attitudes; antidemocratic trends, ethnocentrism, political-economic conservatism, dependence upon experts, acceptance of differences of opinions, belief in democratic means, acceptance of the worth of others, and desire to change others. (*b*) A role-playing situational test developed by Gordon for this research and designed to measure the response of individuals to others in certain critical interpersonal situations. The results of the S-O Scale are found in chapters 11 and 12. The role-playing material is still in process of analysis.

Project No. 4

This project studies changes in the emotional maturity of behavior as indicated by the Villoughby Emotional-Maturity Scale (E-M Scale), which was standardized for a similar purpose. The client describes his own behavior on the E-M Scale and, in addition, provides the names of two friends who are asked to submit to the test examiner independent ratings of the client's behavior. These friends also rate the behavior of still another friend, a procedure which supplies control data, since changes in the ratings of these friends can be compared with any changes in the ratings of the client under study. The report of this study will be found in chapter 13.

Process Studies

Another whole group of projects is utilizing the recorded interviews and other information to investigate the internal dimensions of the psychotherapeutic hours.

This chapter will make no further mention of these process studies, because they tend to have unique designs which are best reported separately. However, it would be wrong for the reader to gain the impression that the process studies have been awarded a secondary place in the minds of our research group. In fact, we believe that the greatest reward will probably come from such process studies. It is here that we are most likely to learn about the crucial question in the area of psychotherapy—namely, how improved personal adjustment is achieved by the client. Chapter 10 is one such study.

III. THE OVER-ALL DESIGN FOR THE FIRST BLOCK

The general framework for this first co-ordinated series of projects may be seen from the diagram in Figure 1. It will be dis-

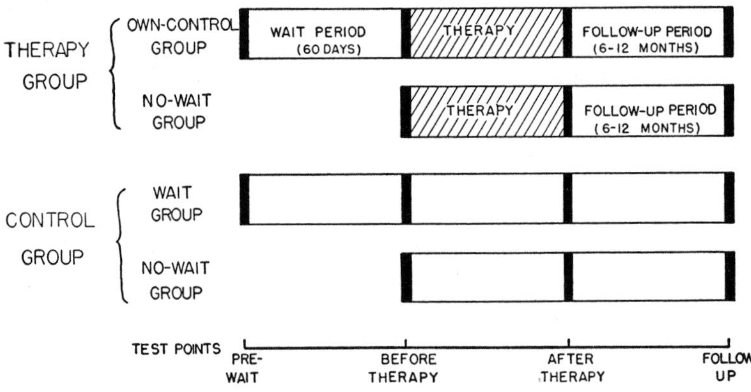

FIG. 1.—General design for first block

cerned that there is a therapy, or experimental, group and a control group. A portion of the therapy group is set apart as the own-control group in which there is a sixty-day wait period, preceded and followed by the administration of the research tests, before therapy starts. This group is also matched in the so-called "wait group" of the controls.

The rationale of the design is that, through the own-control group, we can control for personality factors and motivation for therapy. This is accomplished by comparing changes made during the wait and the therapy periods. The no-therapy control group provides a more precise control for the passage of time and the effects of repeated administration of the tests. If change occurs in the therapy and follow-up period which is greater than the change in the waiting period of the own-control group, or in the equivalent period for the control group, then we would have strong evidence that therapy produces change which is not accounted for on other grounds.

So much for the over-all rationale of the design. Let us now examine the composition of each of these groups.

IV. THE THERAPY GROUP

The experimental group (see Table 1) consists of twenty-nine clients ranging in age between twenty-one and forty years, with an average of twenty-seven years. There were eighteen men and eleven women; sixteen were students at the University of Chicago, and thirteen were persons from the surrounding community.

Space does not permit an adequate description of the presenting problems or the personality characteristics of each of these clients. However, a cursory description of a hypothetical average client will be presented. (Case studies of individual clients also appear in chaps. 15 and 16.)

A sketch of a typical client would be one who belongs to the middle class and is above average in intelligence and education. He is defensively organized and attempts to intellectualize and minimize his problems. He is hesitant about seeking professional help and doubtful—yet hopeful—about therapy.

The client is making a reasonably successful adjustment to his life-situation as this would be judged by the untrained observer in close contact but not intimately acquainted with the client. Some idiosyncrasies and atypical emotional reactions would be noted but not considered as too serious or important. Inwardly, however, the client feels considerable disturbance. He experiences frequent anxiety, a sense of failure, and guilt. He feels that he is socially inadequate, that he lacks positive goals for his life, and that he has difficulty making decisions. In addition, he is concerned about one or more specific problems such as an unhappy marital life, impending failure on the job or in school, homosexual urges (usually not being acted upon), or aggressive impulses.

The diagnostically oriented clinician would observe many neu-

TABLE 1

CLIENTS IN THE EXPERIMENTAL GROUP

Client	Sex	Age	Student (S) or Non-student (NS)	No. of Interviews	Weeks in Therapy
	Closed Cases				
Oak	F	40	NS	40*	23
Babi	F	29	NS	6	13
Bacc	F	21	S	9	4
Bajo	M	27	S	11	6
Bame	M	28	S	38	46
Bana	M	24	NS	33	24
Bann	M	31	NS	16	14
Barr	M	28	S	41*	20
Bayu	M	24	S	15	9
Bebb	M	24	S	9	6
Beda	F	37	NS	46	55
Beel	F	21	S	11	7
Beke	M	30	S	56	32
Bela	M	21	S	31	38
Bene	F	22	S	10	9
Benz	M	28	NS	23	33
Beri	M	26	S	56	31
Beso	F	36	S	12	11
Bett	F	23	S	64	72
Bico	F	26	NS	33	36
Bifu	M	24	NS	8	6
Bime	F	28	NS	13	18
Bina	M	27	NS	48†	52
Bink	F	33	NS	37	78
Bira	M	30	S	64	91
Bisk	M	26	S	108†	137
Bixy	M	22	NS	16	12
Blen	M	27	NS	32	39
	Still Active Cases				
Bipi	M	24	S	168‡	....
Total	29	....	....	....	....
Subtotal	18M, 11F	....	16S, 13NS	....	....
Mean	....	27	....	31§	33§
Range	....	21–40	....	6–108§	4–137§

* There were eight additional interviews after the follow-up testing.

† Some of these are double interviews, lasting one and a half to two hours. Double interviews are counted as two interviews.

‡ To date.

§ Does not include the still active case.

rotic characteristics in the client serious enough to merit immediate attention; he would not, however, classify the client as a severe neurotic.

The above paragraphs would describe in a general way roughly the middle range of the clients in the therapy group. A sizable number of the clients were more seriously disturbed even to the point of being borderline psychotics. Another small group of clients evidenced more healthy personalities and came to counseling because of uncertainties and emotional tensions associated largely with some immediate environmental problem.

V. PROCEDURES FOR SELECTING THE EXPERIMENTAL GROUP

The researcher investigating psychotherapy faces many difficult questions when he attempts to set forth a rationale for selecting his experimental group. He might wish to sample randomly all maladjusted persons who could conceivably benefit from psychotherapy, but the characteristics of this parent-population are unknown. Should the experimental group be limited to persons who actively seek psychotherapy for themselves? Should only persons with similar problems and personality characteristics be included? Should particular kinds of maladjustment be eliminated—for example, narcotic addiction, intellectual deficit, psychosis, or minor maladjustment which appears to be associated primarily with some temporary environmental stress?

We find no fully satisfactory answers to such questions. We doubt, also, their relevance because of the infancy of research in this area.

Our solution to the problem was to select clients for study by randomly sampling the adult clientele of the Counseling Center.[1] The only factors used to stratify this sample were the sex and student or nonstudent status in the proportions found among the clients at the Center during the six months prior to the beginning of this research. Our procedure was this: When it was

1. The Counseling Center serves both the students of the University and the general public. Most clients are self-referred, although we get referrals from physicians, psychiatrists, clergymen, and various community organizations. We avoid accepting a client who might possibly require institutional treatment, and we let it be clearly known that we cannot be responsible for medical problems. See Grummon and Gordon (1) for a more complete description of the Counseling Center's operation.

determined that testing time and a therapist were both available, the next person requesting counseling (provided he fitted the sex and student-nonstudent vacancies) was referred to a preliminary interviewer, who asked the client to participate in the research.[2] When a client refused to participate (as did approximately 50 per cent of those asked),[3] the receptionist was notified and the procedure repeated for the next prospective client appearing at the Center. In a few instances extraneous factors influenced the selection of the experimental group. For example, one client is included because he had been waiting several months to see a particular counselor who still had no opening other than for a research case. While exceptions of this kind cannot be justified from the standpoint of good research design, more service-oriented values sometimes dictate them. It is difficult to be completely hardheaded about research in an organization whose staff is genuinely concerned about the welfare of the client. An exception to our design was made only after considerable thought indicated it was necessary to protect the interests of a particular client.

These procedures provided an experimental group that is reasonably typical of the clients customarily seen at the Counseling Center.[4] The procedures also avoided biasing the sample by prejudgments about such things as the client's readiness for counseling or the therapist's desire to work with particular types of personalities or particular problems.

2. In the earlier stages of the research the receptionist presented the prospective client with a card which explained the research and asked for the client's participation. We dropped this procedure because too many clients failed to get an adequate understanding of what was expected of them, and the number of refusals to participate was consequently high.

3. Clients gave a variety of reasons for not wanting to participate in the research. About one-fifth of this group had tentative plans to leave the city in the near future. About one-third claimed they could not afford the time required for the testing. (The testing did require quite a large time commitment and was especially demanding on persons who worked and lived some distance from the Counseling Center.) Almost half of the group refusing to participate expressed concern about having to wait sixty days before beginning counseling. Some clients expressed concern about the recording of their interviews. Others were not sure that they really wanted counseling. Some persons agreed to participate and then made arrangements for therapy elsewhere.

4. Although we have no concrete evidence on this point, our subjective impression is that the clients in the research do not as a group differ materially from the usual clientele of the Counseling Center.

One further consideration was involved in selecting the experimental group. In this research we wished to study how and why a client changes during the course of psychotherapy, and therefore it was desirable to select cases in which there was a presumption that some change had taken place. Studying unsuccessful cases can hardly provide the investigator with information about how therapeutic changes do occur, although, of course, it may well provide information as to how therapeutic changes fail to occur. On the other hand, if we select for study only those cases that, for example, the therapist rates as successful, we obviously have a biased sample which limits the scope of the investigation.

We arrived at a compromise solution to the problem. Our experimental group consists of all cases started in the research who completed six or more therapeutic interviews.[5] We assumed, rather arbitrarily, that in six or more interviews there is at least an opportunity for change to occur.

This procedure is bound to include cases where both the therapist and the client agree that little or no benefit was derived from the therapeutic interviews. Consequently, subgroups are also studied. One group includes only those clients who terminated therapy after six or more interviews, stating that they felt no need for further therapeutic help. Comparisons are also made between cases rated as most and least "successful" by the therapists.

VI. THE ATTRITION GROUP

Those cases that failed to complete six or more therapeutic interviews, labeled the "attrition group," are studied separately. In most instances these clients were not given post-therapy tests. One question studied here is: "Do the clients of the attrition group differ in significant ways from other clients who apparently make more extensive use of their therapy?" Table 2 summarizes the information about the termination status of these twenty-five clients. Most of them failed to get really started in therapy.

5. Nine cases were dropped from the experimental group because it was impossible to get the necessary post-therapy tests. In a few of these cases the client either refused to take the post-therapy tests or repeatedly failed to keep the appointments; in other instances, situational factors over which the client had no control prevented the post-therapy testing. According to ratings made by the counselors, these nine cases considered collectively were less successful than the average case in the experimental group. Only one of the nine was considered to be a marked success by the counselor.

VII. THE CONTROL GROUPS

In planning this research, considerable attention was given to the question of control cases. Ideally, control cases should be instituted for at least the following variables: (1) passage of time; (2) important environmental influences; (3) personality characteristics, including kind and degree of disturbance; (4) motivation for therapy; (5) the client's expectations of therapy (e.g., does he see therapy as involving ways of meeting specific environmental pressures, or does he see therapy as a means of deeper personality change?); and (6) biosocial characteristics: (*a*) age, (*b*) sex, and (*c*) social class status.

TABLE 2

SUMMARY OF THE TERMINATION STATUS OF THE CASES IN THE ATTRITION GROUP

No. of Clients	No. of Interviews per Client	Reason for Termination of Therapy
3	0	Took pre-wait tests but failed to show for first therapy interview
1	0	Referred to a psychiatrist because he showed signs of psychosis at time of testing
1	1	Removed from research because he was leaving the city soon
4	1	Came in more to inquire about therapy than to actually begin therapy
9	1 or 2	Dissatisfied with the therapy and quit
1	5	Decided he needed psychoanalysis
6	3–5	Left therapy, with both client and counselor feeling that a moderate amount of help had been received; in most instances the client mastered a stressful situation rather than deeply exploring self

It is not practical to control all these variables. Matching individuals on more than five characteristics is a formidable undertaking under most circumstances. Many of these variables are difficult to specify in any precise and measurable way, and to institute controls for some variables raises ethical and professional considerations. For example, to match groups in their motivation for psychotherapy while also controlling time would have required keeping some people waiting more than a year for therapy even though they were desperately in need of immediate help. Furthermore, the importance of these variables to the therapeutic process can only be surmised.

With the foregoing considerations in mind, we set up two types of control groups. (In addition, other control features are implemented in the design of some specific projects.)

1. To form the *own-control group*, half[6] of the clients agreeing to participate in the research were asked to defer their therapy for sixty days. The test battery was administered before and after this sixty-day waiting period. It is thus possible to compare any personality changes in the waiting period with changes that may take place during the therapy period.

2. The subjects in the *equivalent-control group* were selected from those persons who volunteered to serve as subjects for a "research on personality." The control group was matched with the therapy group for sex, for student-nonstudent status, for age (within two or three years), and for an approximation of socio-economic status. Table 3 lists the equivalent-control subjects and their matching data. The intervals between testing for the control subjects correspond to the intervals for the matched experimental subjects. Approximately half of them, being matched with the own-control therapy group, were tested at four points in the research. The others were matched with the "no-wait" therapy group and were tested at three points in the research as indicated in Figure 1.

The own-control plan controls motivation for therapy and, indeed, for most of the factors listed above except passage of time and environmental influences. The equivalent-control plan controls the time factor to fill out the control design. Environmental influences are not controlled, but it is assumed that environmental influences other than therapy are randomly distributed between the therapy and the control groups. In both groups it is expected that individuals may be attacked by disease, may form new friendships or break old ones, will experience success or failure, and the like.

One possible limitation in the selection of the own-control sub-

6. One-half the clients started in the research were own-control cases. However, a somewhat higher attrition rate was experienced with these clients, so that less than half of the experimental group are own-control cases.

jects should be noted. During the first testing session the examiner, after having consulted the preliminary interviewer's recommendation, decided whether the client should be placed in the own-control group or go immediately into therapy. A client was placed in the own-control group only if it seemed that waiting was not likely to cause him serious discomfort or harm. Otherwise the assignment was random except that a balance was kept between

TABLE 3

SUBJECTS IN THE CONTROL GROUP

Subject	Sex	Age	Student (S) or Non-student (NS)	Socio-economic Status*
Adis	F	44	NS	UL
Akim	F	29	NS	LM
Abor	F	19	S	LM
Abco	M	30	NS	LM
Agaz	M	24	S	LM
Aban	M	29	S	UM
Abif	M	25	S	LM
Abet	M	23	S	UM
Agiv	F	31	NS	LM
Acme	F	24	NS	LM
Abok	F	27	NS	UL
Afit	M	30	S	LM
Akor	M	21	S	LM
Abbe	M	22	S	LM
Ajil	M	30	S	LM
Abex	M	23	S	UM
Abul	F	35	NS	LM
Adir	F	30	NS	LM
Acro	F	25	S	LM
Afim	F	27	NS	UL
Abed	F	26	NS	LM
Ajac	M	28	S	UL
Abri	M	26	NS	LM

* LM = Lower Middle; UL = Upper Lower; UM = Upper Middle.

the wait and no-wait groups with respect to sex and student and nonstudent status. An assignment to the wait group was occasionally changed to the no-wait group, if, for example, the client developed anxiety during the waiting period or, as happened in one case, the student's college adviser requested such a move. Thus we sometimes violated the best sampling procedures when those procedures would act against the needs of a client. Actually, as Hartley and Rudikoff (2) pointed out in an early progress report, "absolute random assignment of persons [to the wait and no-wait groups] was not essential. . . . We did not intend to compare the [wait and no-wait] groups in any way, i.e., one was not the control group for the other. Each of these groups had similar control groups of persons not in therapy who were tested over the same time span."

A comment is also in order in regard to the selection of the equivalent-control group. Initially we selected control subjects by matching them individually with experimental subjects, and most of our controls were obtained in this manner. Later, however, we were forced to change this procedure. We lost numerous control subjects because these individuals left the city or for other reasons could not be reached for all the testing. Therefore we shifted our goal to that of selecting a control group which, on the various matching variables, would be matched in mean and standard deviation with the therapy group. Table 4 gives the composition of

TABLE 4

TOTAL GROUP CHARACTERISTICS FOR ALL EXPERIMENTAL AND CONTROL SUBJECTS

Group	Age		Sex		Occupation		Socioeconomic Status*			
	Range	Mean	M	F	S	NS	LL	UL	LM	UM
Experimental ($N=29$)	21–40	27.25	17	11	18	10	1	6	19	2
Control ($N=23$)	19–44	27.30	12	11	12	11	0	4	16	3

* LL = Lower Lower; UL = Upper Lower; LM = Lower Middle; UM = Upper Middle.

the control and therapy groups. It is clear that the matching is satisfactory on the age factor, though only moderately satisfactory on the other three variables. As many others have discovered before, we found that matching on four variables is a difficult problem, especially where contact with each control subject must be maintained for from one to three years.

VIII. THE SELECTION OF RESEARCH COUNSELORS

In this research we wished to study client-centered counseling as it occurs on the usual "journeyman" level. This meant that the counselors could not be selected from only the most expert client-centered therapists, or from the clearly unqualified therapists, or those in the early stages of their training.

All members of the Counseling Center staff (which includes many trainees) were invited to participate as research counselors provided they met the following more or less arbitrary criteria defined in terms of experience as a counselor:

1. The counselor should have been intensively engaged in doing counseling for a period of at least one year (but not necessarily full time).
2. His experience as a client-centered counselor should cover not less than 341 therapeutic interviews. (This figure of 341 was selected because it was the median number of interviews handled by staff members at that time.)
3. He should have had enough experience with recording his interviews to be comfortable in the recording situation.

All but a few staff members meeting these requirements participated as research counselors. This group represents a wide range of experience. Of the twelve counselors having cases in the experimental group, five were relatively inexperienced and near the minimum requirements outlined above. One counselor had been engaged in this work for twenty-two years, while the remaining six counselors had between four and six years of experience (some of it part time).

The assignment of research counselors was set up so that a number of different therapists would be utilized and so that, in so far as possible, all therapists would handle an approximately equal number of cases. Eight therapists each saw between three and five clients in the experimental group. The remaining four therapists saw either one or two cases.

Many of our clients come to the Counseling Center requesting a specific counselor. Some assignment of counselors was made on this basis, but no more than half of any counselor's research cases were assigned in this manner.

Although the therapists on the Counseling Center staff follow the client-centered orientation in a general way, there are real differences among us in our approach to clients. We decided to side-step the difficult question of determining just who is and who is not a client-centered counselor by leaving this up to the individual counselor. The counselor participated if he felt he was following essentially the client-centered orientation. A more careful study of the client-centeredness of the counseling was left to the later study of the recorded and transcribed therapeutic protocols.

IX. CHRONOLOGY OF THE DATA-GATHERING PROCEDURES

1. *Preliminary interviews.*—This interview was usually quite short, lasting no longer than ten to twenty minutes. The client was asked to participate in a research investigating personality. The interviewer, himself a counselor, covered the following points about the research:

a) Participation in the research would be of no personal value to the client, but in the long run it might be of great benefit to others.

b) The client's participation would require that he take a battery of psychological tests on several occasions, each occasion requiring two sessions of three hours or less. He was not told that these research tasks would come at particular phases of his therapy.

c) The therapeutic interviews would be recorded.

d) Everything, including both tests and the client's therapy, would be kept confidential. The precautions to insure this, such as the use of code names and the editing of records, were explained.

e) We were not experimenting with types of therapy; the client's therapy would be the same whether he participated in the research or not. Furthermore, his therapist would not know about the results of his tests.

f) Getting therapy at the Center was not dependent upon participation in the research.

g) The client might have to wait sixty days before beginning his therapy, but, if he participated in the research, his wait would certainly not be longer than this, and it might be much less.

h) The client was not told that personality changes over therapy were being investigated, although several clients assumed this to be the case.

Some, but not all, of the preliminary interviews were recorded. The interviewer filled out a brief form which provided information about the client's reaction to the research, the reason he came to the Counseling Center, and some of his expectations about therapy.

2. *Pre-wait tests.*—Figure 1 diagrams the way in which the research instruments were administered. The first testing session took place as soon after the preliminary interview as possible. In addition to the test battery (TAT, E-M Scale, SIO Q-Sort, S-O Scale, and the role-playing situational test), a short personal history form was filled out which was used primarily to make socioeconomic identifications. The client also provided the names of

two friends who knew him well and whom he was willing to have us contact for the purpose of rating him on the E-M Scale.

This session is, of course, equivalent to the pre-therapy testing for persons not in the own-control group.

3. *Pre-therapy tests.*—The same battery of tests was administered a second time to the client. (This would be the first testing session for clients in the no-wait group.)

4. *Begins counseling.*—Counseling was begun within a few days after the pre-therapy testing. All interviews were electrically recorded on the Gray Audograph and the disks stored for later transcription.

5. *In-therapy tests.*—The SIO Q-Sort was the only instrument administered during the course of the therapy. The cards were sorted to depict the self, the self-ideal, and the ordinary person after the seventh, twentieth, and each succeeding twenty interviews until the termination of therapy. At the end of the seventh interview the counselor also sorted the SIO Q-Sort cards as he predicted the client would sort them.

6. *Post-testing.*—At the conclusion of therapy the entire test battery was readministered, and the counselor again sorted the SIO Q-Sort cards as he predicted the client would sort them.

7. *Counselor rating.*—The counselor filled out a rating scale which had several items under each of the general categories of (*a*) the outcomes of therapy, (*b*) the nature of the relationship between the client and the counselor, and (*c*) the nature of the therapeutic process.

8. *Follow-up tests.*—The test battery was given again between six months and one year following the termination of therapy. In several instances the client had left the city, and it was necessary to have psychologists at other universities administer the follow-up tests as well as the follow-up interview mentioned below.

9. *Follow-up interviews.*—Two follow-up interviews were conducted soon after the follow-up tests were given. Both were recorded. One of these interviews was conducted by the test administrator who knew nothing about how the client had responded to the therapy. This was an open-ended interview in which the following questions were asked:

a) I am interested in your reaction to your counseling experience and whether or not it meant anything to you then or during these last months.

b) Has it in any way changed your feelings about yourself?

c) Has it in any way changed your behavior?

d) Has it influenced your relations with your family? Employer? Instructors?

e) What was it in the counseling that made it (effective) (ineffective)?

A follow-up interview by the counselor proceeded along much the same pattern except that more pointed questions about the therapy were sometimes raised. In most instances the counselor's follow-up interview was omitted if the client had left the city.

10. *Follow-up questionnaire.*—The client filled out a questionnaire aimed at getting information about (*a*) the client's evaluation of his therapy, (*b*) an account of significant life-experiences that had occurred since the termination of therapy, and (*c*) whether the client had sought out or was thinking of seeking out additional help.

X. THE TESTING SITUATION

Two examiners did nearly all the testing in this research. The tests were administered in a set order, and usually they were completed in two three-hour sessions which were separated by a maximum of five days and usually less. The tests were administered individually, and the examiner remained in the room with the subject even for those tests on which the subject worked alone. The TAT and the role-taking tests were electrically recorded. The examiner routinely kept notes on the subject's test behavior and particular reactions to the specific test instruments.

The examination was conducted in accordance with the usual clinical procedures except that approval for specific test responses was avoided. We felt that approval might, in some instances, tend to bring forth the same client response on later examinations. The examiner avoided revealing the design of the research and the purposes for which the tests were being given.

Both examiners were persons who easily developed warm relationships with their subjects. A leisurely psychological atmosphere was maintained which encouraged casual talk, and not infrequently the subjects felt that they had struck up a real acquaintanceship with the examiner.

XI. SUMMARY

This chapter has described the design, the procedures, and the subjects employed in our first major research block. This block is the basis for a co-ordinated series of researches investigating change in the client's self-perceptions, in his personality, in his attitudes toward others, and in his behavior. The detailed statement of the hypotheses and findings of each of these researches is contained in the following section of this book.

The over-all design in this block is to make psychological and behavioral measures before, during, and following the therapy (including long-term follow-up) and to record all interviews which serve as the basic data for studies examining the process of client-centered psychotherapy. The *therapy* or *experimental group* consists of twenty-nine unselected clients who had undergone six or more therapeutic interviews. Twenty-five clients who started in the project but dropped therapy before six interviews form the *attrition group*. An *own-control group* is employed in which about one-half of the therapy group received the test battery, waited sixty days, retook the test battery, and then began therapy. An *equivalent-control group*, which is matched with the experimental group for age, sex, student-nonstudent status, and an approximation of socio-economic status, was selected from among persons volunteering to participate in a research on personality. The research counselors were selected to represent fairly "journeyman" client-centered counselors.

The testing situation and the chronology of the data-gathering procedures were described.

REFERENCES

1. GRUMMON, DONALD L., and GORDON, THOMAS. "The Counseling Center at the University of Chicago," *American Psychologist*, III (1948), 166–71.
2. HARTLEY, MARGARET, and RUDIKOFF, ESSELYN. "Selection of Cases and Standard Operating Procedures." Progress report. Counseling Center, University of Chicago, 1950. (Mimeographed.)
3. STEPHENSON, WILLIAM. *The Study of Behavior: Q-Technique and Its Methodology*. Chicago: University of Chicago Press, 1953.

PART II

Findings

CHAPTER 4

Changes in the Relation between Self-concepts and Ideal Concepts Consequent upon Client-centered Counseling

JOHN M. BUTLER AND GERARD V. HAIGH

I. INTRODUCTION

This chapter reports a study which grows out of the theoretical interest which has been focused upon the self-concept as a useful construct in understanding the dynamics of personality and of behavior. The self-concept, or self-structure, is defined by Rogers (4) as an organized, fluid but consistent, conceptual pattern of the characteristics of the "I" or the "me" which are admissible into awareness, together with the values attached to those concepts. Since this self-concept is seen as the criterion determining the "repression" or awareness of experiences and as exerting a regulatory effect upon behavior (4, chap. 11), its relevance to any study of counseling or psychotherapy is clear. How such a seemingly intangible notion is to be used in an objective fashion is less clear.

Theoretical Assumptions of This Study

Let us first consider the basic logic involved in arriving at some operational use of this construct. We start with the notion of Rogers that the self-concept consists of an organized conceptual pattern of the "I" or "me" together with the values attached to those concepts. This implies that many single self-perceptions, standing in relation each to the other, exist for the same individual. It is quite possible for the individual to order these self-percepts along a subjective or psychophysical continuum from "unlike me" to "like me." Thus, if a given characteristic such as "intelligence" is held by the individual to apply to himself, this characteristic may be perceived by the individual to be more or less like himself than another characteristic, such as "introversion." Thus, if asked, the individual may say, "It is more characteristic of me that I am intelligent than it is that I am introverted. However, I am both intelligent and introverted." To put this in terms of the logic of science, we may say that the fundamental relation involved is the transitive asymmetrical relation, in which if *A* is greater than *B*, and *B* greater than *C*, then *A* is greater than *C*. Thus one assumption is that the individual is able to make this type of judgment about his self-perceptions and to order them along a continuum.

This subjective scale does not, however, yield any clues as to the values attached to the self-concepts. For instance, an individual might say, "I am intelligent and glad of it" (or "I am not stupid and glad of it"). He might say, "I am introverted and am unhappy about it" (or "I am not extroverted and am unhappy about it"). In order to take care of this crisscross of metrics, we introduce the notion of the ideal self-concept. This is here defined as the organized conceptual pattern of characteristics and emotional states which the individual consciously holds as desirable (and undesirable) for himself. The assumption is that the individual is able to order his self-perceptions along a continuum of value from "what I would most like to be" to "what I would least like to be" or, more briefly, from "like my ideal" to "unlike my ideal." This subjective scale could then yield a distribution of the same characteristics or self-perceptions which were ordered along the scale of "like me" to "unlike me."

The discrepancy between the placements of a given characteristic on the self scale and the ideal scale would yield an indication of self-esteem. It would indicate operationally not only the way in which the individual perceived himself as possessing this given characteristic but the degree to which he values this state. The discrepancies between self and ideal on all these characteristics would yield an index of self-esteem or self-value.

The Instrument

These assumptions about the ordering of characteristics were implemented by means of a list of self-referent statements. A set of one hundred such statements was taken at random from available therapeutic protocols (actually the statements were selected on an accidental sampling rather than a strictly random basis), reworded for clarity, and given to both control and client subjects. The subjects were required to sort the items on the metrics "like-me" to "unlike-me" and "like-ideal" to "unlike-ideal." The sort was a forced normal sort with nine piles.[1] The subjects were given the following instructions:

1. *Self-sort.* Sort these cards to describe yourself as you see yourself today, from those that are least like you to those that are most like you.
2. *Ideal sort.* Now sort these cards to describe your ideal person—the person you would most like within yourself to be.

The nature of the items to be sorted on these two scales may be suggested by these illustrations: "I am a submissive person"; "I am a hard worker"; "I really am disturbed"; "I am afraid of a full-fledged disagreement with a person"; "I am likable."

It should be noted that the forced sorting of these items into an approximately normal distribution is not a fundamental requirement. Transitive asymmetrical relations when applied to self-concepts and ideal concepts basically imply ranking. The form of the distribution and the sorting of the items into nine piles represent the somewhat arbitrary introduction of a set number of ties into what is essentially a ranking situation. Since our concern was with the correlation between sorts, it is believed that neither the number of ties nor the form of distribution is a matter of serious concern as long as the joint distribution is normal. Indeed, we are of the opinion that the prescribed conditions are an advantage. Psychophysical considerations lead one to expect that forcing a sort leads to finer differentiations than uncontrolled sorting, whereas forcing a nontied ranking of as many as one hundred items might lead to fatigue and carelessness.

1. This is "Q-technique" as developed by Stephenson (5). To the best of our knowledge the first studies using Q-technique to assess counseling are those by Margaret W. Hartley in an unpublished Ph.D. dissertation, "A Q-Technique Study of Changes in the Self-concept during Psychotherapy" (University of Chicago, 1951), and an unpublished analysis by Thomas E. Jeffrey of data collected by Haigh entitled "A Quantitative Analysis of the Effect of Client-centered Counseling" (1949).

The Rationale of the Hypotheses

The hypotheses of this study may be stated very briefly, but it may be well to preface them with a statement of their rationale. We hold that a discrepancy between the self-concept and the concept of the desired or valued self reflects a sense of self-dissatisfaction, which in turn generates the motivation for coming into counseling. Such a discrepancy ordinarily exists when an individual comes for help. It is our hypothesis that this self-dissatisfaction is reduced as a result of counseling. Self-ideal discrepancies in an individual are a product or outcome of experiences which indicate to him that his self-organization is unsatisfactory. Also, the reduction of such discrepancies, consequent upon counseling, is based theoretically on the disorganization and reorganization of both self and ideal structures under the conditions of counseling. The immediate goal of the counselor is to create conditions under which the client can relax his defenses and assimilate experiences into new conceptual patterns. These new patterns are consistent with a wider range of experiences than the conceptual patterns which existed when the client came in. The reduction of discrepancies between self and ideal, therefore, is a result or outcome of fundamental experiences in relationship with a counselor. During the counseling process itself such discrepancies may become greater before they become less. Our basic hypothesis is, then, that a reduction of self-ideal discrepancies is a consequence of the self-concept and the ideal concept coming to rest on a broader base of available experience than before. It is in this way that they become more consistent with each other.

The Q-technique used in this study, with its sortings for the self-characteristics and their perceived values, is clearly in harmony with this theory of the dynamics of inner reorganization. Hence it seems justifiable to regard an increase in the correlation between self and ideal sorts as an operational indication of an increased congruence between the concept of self and the concept of the valued person.

It is recognized that in one respect the method used may not always reflect accurately this fundamental change which is hypothesized. It is possible for a client, either prior to or following therapy, to sort the cards so as to indicate a small self-ideal discrepancy, when, as judged by other criteria, a large discrepancy exists. He may, in other words, be sufficiently motivated by defensive needs that he pictures himself as being very much like the self he values, when, at a deeper level, he feels that he does not resemble his ideal self. The reverse—that is, the picturing of a discrepancy between self and ideal where no such discrepancy exists—is less likely to occur. While recognizing this possibility of a "defensive" type of sorting, it is our hypothesis that the changes indicated in the foregoing paragraph will be evident operationally in the group as increased self-ideal correlations.

It is a part of our theoretical expectation that self-concepts will change as a function of counseling more than ideal concepts. By their very nature it seems probable that ideal concepts are largely general societal concepts, whereas self-concepts may be more idiosyncratic. This notion is borne out by pilot studies which indicate that the correlations between the self-concepts held by different clients are low (of the order of .20), whereas the correlations between the ideal concepts held by different clients are higher (of the order of .50). However, ideal concepts can be expected to show change to the extent that they are introjected (4, chap. 11). As one client put it after a twentieth-interview sorting of his ideal self: "I am just realizing there are a lot of things I want to be that others [parents] wouldn't approve of. Until now I've acted on the basis of what I ought to be; I've wanted to be what I ought to be. Now I want to be what *I* want to be." It is clear that his concept of the desired self is undergoing change in an idiosyncratic direction.

Hypotheses

On the basis of the preceding considerations, we hypothesize that (*a*) client-centered counseling results in a decrease of self-ideal discrepancies and that (*b*) self-ideal discrepancies will be more clearly reduced in clients who have been judged, on experimentally independent criteria, as exhibiting definite improvement. The first hypothesis is without restriction. The second, in being restricted to the subclass of clients evaluated as "successful," does not require a generalized effect of counseling upon the client population.

II. FINDINGS FROM THE CLIENT GROUP AS A WHOLE

We will consider now the evidence from the client group which bears on the first hypothesis. The design of the research and the method of data collection have been described previously (see chap. 3). The correlations were computed between the self-sorts and the ideal sorts for the twenty-five clients in the first block (Block I) who had completed six or more counseling interviews and for whom follow-up tests (administered six months to one year after completion of counseling) were available. This group will hereafter be referred to as the *client group*. We will be concerned, in this study, with the sortings made by each client for self and ideal at each of three points—pre-counseling, post-counseling, and follow-up. Table 1 gives the self-ideal correlations for these clients at these three points.

The Self-Ideal Relationship before Counseling

From Table 1 it can be seen that the pre-counseling self-ideal correlations range from −.47, a very marked discrepancy between self and ideal, to .59, a considerable degree of congruence. The mean z of the array, using Fisher's method (6, p. 176) is −.01, and the corresponding r is the same, −.01. This is obviously not a significant correlation, and the calculation of the t ratio confirms this. The standard error determined from the observed distribution of z is .07, and the t ratio for testing the hypothesis that the mean z of the client population is zero is −.14, a statistically nonsignificant result.

It is a question, however, whether this zero-order correlation means that there is nothing but a random relationship between self and ideal, or whether there might be significant association between self and ideal, which is for some clients positive and for some negative, with a resulting mean in the neighborhood of zero. In order to test this possibility, which appears probable from inspection, we use the chi square, which, according to Tippett (6, p. 179), is a proper test of association for a group of correlations. We use the formula

$$\chi^2 = \Sigma \left(z \sqrt{N-3} \right)^2 ,$$

with *n* degrees of freedom, where *n* is the number of clients and *N* is the number of items sorted in each Q-sort. For these pre-counseling self-ideal correlations of the client group the value of chi square for magnitude of association is 245.5, which is well beyond the value at the 1 per cent level of significance, 44.31. This result indicates both that there is association between self and ideal in the client group and that there are significant individual differences in self-ideal correlation in this population. The latter conclusion may be also stated as indicating that there are distinct subpopulations in the client population.

Thus our finding in regard to the pre-counseling status of our client group may be stated as follows: The relationship between

TABLE 1

SELF-IDEAL CORRELATIONS IN THE CLIENT GROUP

Client	Pre-counseling *r*	Post-counseling *r*	Follow-up *r*
Oak	.21	.69	.71
Babi	.05	.54	.45
Bacc	−.31	.04	−.19
Bame	.14	.61	.61
Bana	−.38	.36	.44
Barr	−.34	−.13	.02
Bayu	−.47	−.04	.42
Bebb	.06	.26	.21
Beda	.59	.80	.69
Beel	.28	.52	−.04
Beke	.27	.69	−.56
Bene	.38	.80	.78
Benz	−.30	−.04	.39
Beri	.33	.43	.64
Beso	.32	.41	.47
Bett	−.37	.39	.61
Bico	−.11	.51	.72
Bifu	−.12	−.17	−.26
Bime	−.33	.05	.00
Bina	−.30	.59	.71
Bink	−.08	.30	−.20
Bira	.26	−.08	−.16
Bixy	−.39	−.39	.05
Blen	.23	.33	−.36
Bajo	.16	.29	.47
Mean *z*	−.01	.36	.32
Corresponding *r*	−.01	.34	.31

self and ideal, prior to counseling, is of a zero order, but this lack of correlation is not randomness of association but is due to the fact that there is a wide range of significant associations between self and ideal in the individuals or subpopulations composing the group.

It is interesting to speculate, in passing, as to the relationship between the self-ideal congruence and "adjustment" or "integration." There might be a temptation to see this as a direct relationship. It is unlikely that this is the case and more likely that certain subclasses of individuals will be found who, exhibiting certain types of high and low items in their sortings and certain magnitudes of correlations between self and ideal, will have a specifiable relationship to "adjustment" or "integration." In brief, certain patterns of the self-ideal Gestalt may be discovered to indicate certain patterns or types of personality integration. It is possible that factor analysis of the self-ideal sortings may isolate such fundamental patterns. Such studies are now under way.

The Self-Ideal Relationship at Follow-up

The self-ideal relationship of the client group at follow-up may also be observed in Table 1. The range now is even wider, from −.56 to .78, from a very sharp discrepancy to a very substantial similarity. The mean z is now .32, and the corresponding r is .31. The ratio of the mean z to its standard error, obtained from the observed values of z, is 3.39 and is well beyond the 1 per cent level of significance for 24 degrees of freedom.[2]

To test again for the significance of individual differences, we use the formula suggested by Tippett (6, p. 180) for use when the mean correlation has been found to be significant, namely,

$$\chi^2 = (N-3)\,\Sigma\,(z-\bar{z})^2\,,$$

with $n-1$ degrees of freedom, where n and N have the same meaning as before, and $\bar{z}$ denotes the mean value of z. The value

2. One-tailed tests are used for all tests of directional hypothesis in this study. Thus one-tailed tests are used for comparing pre-counseling and follow-up results on the clients and for comparisons of mean gains as between controls and clients. Two-tailed tests are used for comparing controls with controls.

of chi square so obtained is 518.7, which is far beyond the 1 per cent level of 42.98. This latter result is similar to the result obtained at the pre-counseling testing in suggesting that there are true individual differences in the magnitude of self-ideal correlations. However, these individual differences are now found in terms of a deviation around an estimated mean z of .32 instead of a hypothesized mean z of zero.

Thus we may say of our clients at the time of the follow-up study: There is now a significant degree of congruence between the perception of the self and the perception of the valued self. There is also a wide and significant range of individual differences in the degree of self-ideal similarity which exists.

A Comparison of the Pre-counseling and Follow-up Results

We come now to one of the crucial aspects of the evidence bearing upon the first hypothesis, the question as to whether there has been a significant decrease in the discrepancy between the self-concept and the wanted self over the period from pre-counseling to follow-up. The mean pre-counseling self-ideal correlation was —.01, and the follow-up correlation, .31—a mean difference of .32. Expressed in terms of z, the mean difference is .33. The ratio of the mean difference z to its standard error of .11, based on observed z's, is 3.0, which is well beyond the 1 per cent level of significance for 24 degrees of freedom. This would indicate a significant change in the hypothesized direction.

It is of interest, though it does not bear directly upon the hypothesis, that there has also been a marked increase in the degree of variation of correlations over this period. The variances of the pre-counseling and follow-up correlations, when transformed to z's, are .11 and .22, respectively. The t ratio for comparison of related variances (7, p. 190) is approximately 1.84 and is significant at the 5 per cent level.

Since there might be some question as to whether the data meet the assumptions necessary for using the t test for paired differences, it was decided to use a nonparametric statistic as well. The sign test (7, p. 431) was run on the differences. There were nineteen increases (positive differences) in self-ideal correlations and six decreases (negative differences). This result is significant at better than the 1 per cent level, thus confirming the findings from the t test.

From these results it seems doubtful that the number of increases in self-ideal correlation from pre-counseling to follow-up, the amount of such increase, and the increase in the variance are based on random changes. Rather it appears that directional changes of a significant sort are evident and that these provide confirmation of the hypothesis that the discrepancy between self and ideal will be reduced over therapy.

The Post-counseling Findings

It will have been noted that the foregoing comparisons have been made between the pre-counseling and the follow-up correlations. It was felt that the sortings made at the conclusion of counseling might be considered by some to be contaminated by the "hello-goodbye" effect described by Hathaway (3).

Consideration of the results at the end of counseling, however, only confirms the other picture. The mean post-counseling correlation for the total client group is .34 (see Table 1), which is close to the mean of .31 at follow-up. Thus the increase in congruence over counseling was from an r of $-.01$ to .34—a difference of .35, as compared to a difference of .32 over the whole period from pre-counseling to follow-up. The number of increases in self-ideal correlation from the pre-counseling to the post-counseling testing was twenty-three and, of decreases, two. This result is significant at the 1 per cent level of significance. Over the period from post-counseling to follow-up there were twelve increases in self-ideal correlation, twelve decreases, and one tie, indicating no trend during the follow-up period.

If the "hello-goodbye" effect was a factor in the behavior of these clients, it did not seem to affect their self and ideal sorts to an appreciable degree unless one wishes to postulate that it persisted during the six- to twelve-month follow-up period.

III. FINDINGS FROM THE CONTROL GROUPS

We now turn our attention to the equivalent-control group. This control group was selected to be roughly equivalent to the client group with respect to age, sex, socioeconomic status, and student-nonstudent status. Control-group subjects were tested at the same intervals as clients. At the time this analysis was begun, only sixteen of the controls had completed their testing, and these subjects comprise our group. It will be recalled that the rationale of the research design in regard to this group is as follows: The test scores of these individuals will indicate whether there is change as a result of the passage of time, the experience with the test, and the influence of random variables in a group which is in age, sex, and status similar to the client group.

This rationale leaves untouched the question of whether motivation for counseling rather than counseling itself produces congruence between self and ideal measurements. To answer this question, the own-control procedure was used, in which half the clients underwent a sixty-day control period prior to counseling. The test scores over this sixty-day period will indicate whether test results of clients change as a result of motivation for counseling per se. Obviously, if change occurs in the client group which is greater than that which occurs in the equivalent-control group or in the own-control period, then it is reasonable to attribute this degree of change to our experimental variable, client-centered counseling.

The Self-Ideal Relationship at Pre-counseling

The data from the equivalent-control group are given in Table 2. It will be seen that at the pre-counseling point the self-ideal correlations range from $-.01$ to .86. The mean z of the array is .66, with a corresponding r of .58. The ratio of the mean z to its standard error, based on the observed distribution, is 6.4. This is significant beyond the 1 per cent level. It is obvious that there is, on the average, much more congruence between self and ideal in the controls than was found in the clients. This is in accordance with theoretical expectations.

In order to determine whether there were significant individual differences in the magnitude of the self-ideal correlations, the chi square was utilized in the same way as with the client group. The value of chi square was 247.06—far above the 1 per cent value, which is 30.58. We therefore conclude, as in the case of the client group, that there are distinct subclasses of individual self-ideal relations in the control population. Whether these subclasses are the same as those in the client population cannot be ascertained from the data here presented. However, studies designed to provide answers to this question are now in progress.

The Self-Ideal Relationship at Follow-up

For the follow-up testing of the controls the range of the self-ideal correlations is from −.03 to .89. The mean z of the array is .68, with a corresponding r of .59. The standard error of the mean z, based on the observed distribution, is .11, and the t ratio is 6.3, which indicates a 1 per cent level of significance. The chi square for individual differences in magnitude of self-ideal correlations is 272.28, with the 1 per cent value being 30.58.

The variances of the pre-counseling and follow-up correlations, when transformed to z's, are .17 and .19, respectively. The t ratio for comparing related variances is .28 and is not significant for 14 degrees of freedom.

The picture at this final testing point is, it is evident, very similar to what it was at the pre-counseling point.

TABLE 2

SELF-IDEAL CORRELATIONS IN THE CONTROL GROUP

Client	Pre-counseling r	Follow-up r
Aban	.80	.50
Abor	.00	.30
Acro	.86	.89
Agaz	.75	.83
Akim	.84	.86
Akor	.48	−.03
Ajil	.49	.45
Afit	.73	.71
Abul	.58	.77
Adis	.42	.65
Abri	.35	.30
Abbe	.35	.36
Acme	.80	.65
Abco	.65	.76
Abet	−.01	.43
Adir	.30	.07
Mean z	.66	.68
Corresponding r	.58	.59

Inspection of the data from pre-counseling to follow-up in these control individuals shows a considerable degree of consistency, though there are some sharp individual changes which indicate that alteration in self-ideal congruence does occur at times in the absence of therapy. The over-all findings are, however, clear, as is indicated in the following paragraphs by both the t ratio and the Wilcoxon sign test, both showing that no significant change has occurred in the control group.

The differences between the mean z's of the pre-counseling and the follow-up correlations of the controls is .02, with the standard error of the difference being .08. The t ratio is .25, which is not significant. Therefore, there is no reason to believe that the control correlations, pre-counseling and follow-up, are from populations with different means and variances.

There were nine increases and seven decreases in self-ideal correlations from the pre-counseling to the follow-up testing. The Wilcoxon signed ranks test (7, p. 433) was used to test the paired differences, since it is sensitive to the magnitude of differences. The sum of the ranks corresponding to the negative differences is 63.5. The sum of the negatively signed ranks for the 5 per cent level of significance is 30, and the obtained sum is, therefore, not significant.

A Comparison of Change in Clients and Equivalent Controls

We have established that there are nonrandom increases in the self-ideal correlations of the client group from pre-counseling to follow-up and that similar increases cannot be regarded as established for the control group. The results for the comparisons of variances are similar. Nevertheless, the results are ambiguous, since it might be held that there is a combined effect of testing and counseling leading to a conclusion of definite increases where none exists. To test this possibility, we must ask whether the increase in the self-ideal correlations in the client group is significantly greater than the increase found in the control group. The mean gain in z for the client group is .33 and for the control group .02; the mean difference is .31, with a standard error of .13. The t ratio is 2.38 and is significant at the 2.5 per cent level of significance.

When the nonparametric Mann-Whitney test (7, p. 434) is

applied to the paired differences of *r*'s for the pre-counseling and the follow-up testing of the control and client groups considered together, the sum of the ranks for the control group is 245.5. This sum is significant at the 1 per cent level, indicating a true change in the client group over and above the change found in the control group.

Findings from the Own-Control Group

Do clients motivated for counseling show alteration in the relationship between self and ideal simply as the result of the passage of time? The data on this point come from the own-control group, the findings from which are presented in integrated fashion by Grummon in a later chapter. We will simply take from his data the two facts which are relevant to our present concern.

The fifteen members of the client group who formed the own-control group were tested at the time they requested counseling and again at the pre-counseling point. They then went into counseling and, like the others, were tested at the post-counseling point and at follow-up. The relationship between self and ideal sortings for these fifteen clients at the pre-wait point is indicated by a mean z of $-.01$. At the pre-counseling point the relationship is still the same, $-.01$, It is clear that no change has occurred during the control period.[3]

The Testing of the First Hypothesis

We are now in a position to assemble the findings which relate to our first hypothesis—that client-centered counseling results in a decrease of self-ideal discrepancies. It has been shown that:

1. Both clients and controls exhibit significant individual differences at each point tested. The degree of self-ideal congruence has wide range in each group.
2. The mean correlation of self and ideal in the client group at pre-counseling is $-.01$, which is not a significant degree of congruence.
3. The mean correlation of self and ideal in the client group at follow-up is .31, a significant relationship. This is a significant increase in self-ideal congruence, whether judged by the t test or by the sign test.
4. The finding is similar at the post-counseling point.
5. The mean correlation of self and ideal in the equivalent-control group at pre-counseling is .58, a significant congruence.

3. The finding is quite different for those applicants who did *not* continue in therapy after the sixty-day period, as will be seen by consulting chap. 14.

6. The mean correlation for this group at follow-up is .59, indicating no significant change over time.
7. The own-control group has a mean correlation of self and ideal of −.01 at pre-wait and −.01 at pre-counseling, indicating no change during the control period.
8. The change in the client group is significantly greater than the change found in the equivalent-control group or in clients in the own-control period. The difference is significant at the 2.5 per cent level in terms of the *t* test and at better than the 1 per cent level in terms of the sign test.

These findings lead us to infer that significant increases in the self-ideal correlations in the client group are consequent upon client-centered counseling.

IV. FINDINGS REGARDING DEFINITELY IMPROVED CLIENTS

We turn now to our second hypothesis—that the self-ideal discrepancies will, as a result of counseling, be more clearly reduced in those clients who have been judged, on independent criteria, as showing definite improvement. In terms of its rationale, this hypothesis states that, if the relationship between the self-concept and the ideal concept exists as theorized, the changes in this relationship should be more marked in a group in which the process of therapy has clearly occurred.

The Selection of the Improved Group

The client group was classified by using two criteria of success which were experimentally independent of each other and of the self-ideal correlations. One criterion was an over-all rating of success by the counselor of each client made at the conclusion of counseling; the rating was on a nine-point scale, with the highest scale value being 9 (see chap. 7). Another criterion was a judgment based on blind analyses of Thematic Apperception Test (TAT) protocols (see chap. 8). The TAT-derived judgments were on a seven-point scale. Those clients were selected for the "improved" group who received counselor ratings of 5 with an improvement shown in TAT ratings or who received ratings of 6 or above and whose TAT ratings were no lower for the follow-up protocol than for pre-counseling. There was general positive agreement between the TAT and the counselor rating, since, of the sixteen clients chosen by these criteria, eleven showed improvement from pre-counseling to follow-up on the TAT ratings. One additional client included in the improved group has a counselor rating below 5. He was included because, although the counselor made a low rating on the basis of a judgment that the absolute level of inner adjustment was low at termination, the counselor had also predicted that the adjustment level would rise, since an integrative process had definitely been set in motion. Since the client's TAT rating exhibited a rise in scale value, he was included in the improved category. This gave a group of seventeen clients, who will be termed "definitely improved."

Of the eight remaining clients, none showed improvement on the TAT, and only two had counselor ratings above 5. These two showed a decrease on the TAT scale.

A Comparison with the Control Group

Before counseling, the improved group (see data in Table 3) has much the same statistical characteristics as the total group. The mean z between pre-counseling selves and ideals is .02, with the corresponding r having the same value. The mean z is not significantly different from zero for the pre-counseling correlations. As before, the chi-square value for association and for individual differences is highly significant, being 164.03, with 17 degrees of freedom. At the follow-up testing the mean r between self and ideal is .44, the corresponding z being .47. The t ratio for testing the hypothesis that the population mean correlation coefficient is zero is approximately 4.7, far beyond the 1 per cent level of significance. The chi-square value for individual differences is 277.32 for 16 degrees of freedom and again is greater than the 1 per cent value of chi square. It will be seen that the total picture is similar to that found in the client group as a whole, except that the increase in the mean correlation is greater.

Let us look at this group in relation to the equivalent-control group. One would expect, if the independent criteria of success and improvement were at all valid, that a significant difference would obtain between the mean gain for this client subgroup, selected on the basis of success and improvement, and the mean gain for the control group. This, indeed, is the case. The difference between the mean gain in z's for the improved client group (.45) and the control group (.02) is .43, with the standard error being .13. The t ratio is 3.31 and is significant at the 1 per cent level. The Mann-Whitney test is also significant at the 1 per cent level. We conclude that, for clients judged on experimentally independent bases as improving in adjustment, the correlation between measured self and measured ideal increases between pre-counseling testing and follow-up testing and that the increase is a product of the counseling situation.

A Comparison with the Unimproved Group

Another comparison is that between the definitely improved group and the subgroup which is not definitely improved. One would expect that, if the criteria of success and improvement were

TABLE 3

SELF-IDEAL CORRELATION IN THE IMPROVED CLIENT GROUP

CLIENT	PRE-COUNSELING r	FOLLOW-UP r	COUNSELOR'S RATING	TAT RATING	
				Pre-counseling	Follow-up
Oak	.21	.71	8	3	4
Babi	.05	.45	8	4	5
Bacc	−.31	−.19	6	3	4
Bame	.14	.61	6	4	4
Barr	−.34	.02	6	4	4
Bebb	.06	.21	6	2	2
Beda	.59	.69	6	4	6
Beel	.28	−.04	7	2	4
Bene	.38	.78	9	4	5
Benz	−.30	.39	7	3	5
Beri	.33	.64	7	2	3
Beso	.32	.47	5	5	6
Bett	−.37	.61	7	4	4
Bico*	−.11	.72	7	....	....
Bime†	−.33	.00	4	4	5
Bina	−.30	.71	7	2	5
Bink	−.08	−.20	7	4	6
Mean z	.02	.47	....	....	....
Corresponding r	.02	.44	....	....	....

* Blind TAT ratings are not available, but a complete TAT analysis yielded a judgment of improvement.

† Counselor rated absolute adjustment level as low but held that an integrative process had begun in counseling which would result in post-counseling improvement.

related to the level of self-ideal correlation, the improved subgroup of clients could be distinguished from the less improved group by comparing them on the follow-up self-ideal correlations. This was tested by means of the Mann-Whitney test, and it was found that the sum of ranks of the less improved group was 65.5, which is significant at the 1 per cent level against a one-sided hypothesis. Thus the distribution of self-ideal correlations in the subgroup classified as improved is not from the same population as the distribution of correlations in the subgroup classified as less improved. The same test was applied to the pre-counseling self-ideal correlations classified according to whether the individual was judged as improved or less improved. The sum of ranks for the less improved group was 89, a nonsignificant result. Thus we may say that the improved group is not significantly different from those judged as less improved at the pre-counseling point. At the follow-up point, however, the difference is significant, the improved group showing a greater self-ideal congruence.

Curiously enough, when we compare magnitude of the increases in the self-ideal correlations from pre-counseling to follow-up, we do not find a significant difference between the two groups. The Mann-Whitney test was applied to the differences in the self-ideal correlations between the pre-counseling and follow-up testings when classified as improved and less improved. The sum of ranks for the negative differences was 83.5, which is not significant at the 12 per cent level.

Improvement, then, is related to final level of self-ideal correlations but not to increase in self-ideal correlations. This puzzling finding seems, on examination of the data, to be due to a defensive sorting of the cards by individuals whose final adjustment was no better or even worse than at the pre-counseling period. For example, gains of 44, 82, and 89 correlation points were made by three of the eight individuals classified as less improved. It appears that in some instances where both counselor ratings and TAT ratings give evidence of little or no improvement, defensive mechanisms are set in operation which produce sharp increases in self-ideal congruence—increases which are similar to those achieved by clients whose improvement is confirmed by evidence from other sources.[4] In spite of these exceptions, the mean changes are in line with those hypothesized.

This finding also raises interesting questions about the relationship between the adjustment of an individual and the correlation between self and ideal. It is quite certain that a correlation of unity between self and ideal would not indicate perfect adjustment. Indeed, the only self-ideal correlation above .90 was achieved by an individual (in another study) who was clearly paranoid. Tentatively the speculation would seem warranted that extremely high self-ideal correlations are likely to be products of defensive sortings.

The Testing of the Second Hypothesis

The following evidence bears on the second hypothesis. A group selected as definitely improved, by criteria independent of the self and the ideal sorts, was found (1) to exhibit a more marked increase in congruence of self and ideal than the total client group; (2) to exhibit a significantly greater increase in such congruence than the equivalent-control group; (3) to be significantly different from the less improved subgroup at the follow-up point, though not at the pre-counseling point; and (4) to show no significant difference in magnitude of increases from the less improved subgroup.

All these findings except the last give definite confirmation to the hypothesis that a more improved group of clients exhibits a greater decrease in self-ideal discrepancies than a group of less improved clients or a group of controls. The final finding suggests that we are dealing with a complex rather than a simple relationship.

V. SUMMARY

In this chapter we have reported our investigation of the hypothesis that client-centered counseling results in an increase in congruence between the self and the self-ideal concepts in the client. It was also part of our hypothesis that this reduction would be especially marked in those cases judged independently as exhibiting improvement.

4. See chap. 13 for a similar finding in the measurement of behavior changes and chap. 17 for a further discussion of this general problem.

The total client group shows, at the outset, a generally large discrepancy between self and ideal, as these concepts are measured by Q-sorts under the associated conditions of instruction. The relationship approximates a zero correlation, indicative of low self-esteem and a decided degree of internal tension. By the end of counseling the discrepancy between self and ideal had decreased for a majority of clients, and the mean correlation was .34. At the follow-up point this reduction in the discrepancy had remained constant, suggesting that it was not due to a temporary "hello-goodbye" effect.

A comparison of the self-ideal discrepancy of the clients at the pre-counseling point and at the follow-up point indicates a statistically significant change. The variance within the group has also increased during this period, indicating, perhaps, a differental reduction in self-ideal discrepancies.

The control group at the outset exhibits a small discrepancy between self and ideal, relative to the client group, represented by a mean correlation of .58. There is no significant change in this discrepancy over time, and at the follow-up point the mean correlation is .59. The differences between the changes in the client group and in the control group are so large as to be clearly non-random in character.

An own-control group of fifteen of the clients were tested before and after a sixty-day period of no counseling, prior to the beginning of counseling. The relationship between self and ideal was approximately zero, and the motivation for counseling and personal reörganization produced no change during this control period, the correlation at the end of the period being again zero.

In order to test the second hypothesis, a group of seventeen "definitely improved" clients was selected on two criteria which were experimentally independent of each other and of this study. For this group the reduction in self-ideal discrepancy from pre-counseling to follow-up is even more marked than for the client group as a whole. The gain was also significantly greater than for the controls and for the "not definitely improved" group. Even at follow-up time, however, this group still showed a discrepancy between self and ideal greater than that found in the controls, suggesting that self-esteem and degree of internal comfort were still less than optimal.

Some evidence was presented suggesting that defensiveness may, under certain conditions, bring about an increase in self-ideal congruence not confirmed by other evidence.

In our opinion the results discussed here indicate that low correlations between self and ideal are based on a low level of self-esteem related to a relatively low adjustment level and that a consequence of client-centered counseling for the clients in this study was, on the average, a rise in the level of self-esteem and of adjustment.

REFERENCES

1. Cattell, R. B. "On the Disuse and Misuse of P, Q, and O Techniques in Clinical Psychology," *Journal of Clinical Psychology*, VII (1951), 203–15.
2. Cronbach, Lee J., and Gleser, Goldine C. *Similarity between Persons and Related Problems of Profile Analysis*. (Technical Report No. 2.) Urbana: Bureau of Research and Service, College of Education, University of Illinois, 1952.
3. Hathaway, S. R. "Some Considerations Relative to Nondirective Counseling as Therapy," *Journal of Clinical Psychology*, IV (1948), 226–31.
4. Rogers, Carl R. *Client-centered Therapy*. Boston: Houghton Mifflin Co., 1951.
5. Stephenson, William. *The Study of Behavior: Q-Technique and Its Methodology*. Chicago: University of Chicago Press, 1953.
6. Tippett, L. H. C. *The Methods of Statistics*. London: Williams & Norgate, 1937.
7. Walker, H., and Lev, J. *Statistical Inference*. New York: Henry Holt & Co., 1953.

CHAPTER 5

Adjustment Changes over Therapy from Self-sorts

ROSALIND F. DYMOND

This chapter will deal with the development of an external criterion of adjustment for the SIO Q-Sort instrument (see chaps. 3 and 4) and with the results of this measure on the experimental and control groups.

In the preceding chapter Butler examined the changes in the Q-sorts of both the experimental and the control groups over time. He reports that the clients in the experimental group at the time they applied for therapy showed a high degree of self-dissatisfaction. This conclusion is based on the fact that the correlations of the sortings of the one hundred self-referent statements to describe themselves and their sortings of the same statements to describe the person they would like to be were extremely low. These correlations increased markedly after therapy had been completed. The self-ideal correlations of the control group, on the other hand, showed high self-esteem at both the beginning and the ending test points, which covered a time interval matched to that of the therapy group. One of the questions that could be raised about this finding is that these changes are based entirely upon the subject's own frame of reference. If, after therapy, they sort the statements to describe themselves and to describe their ideal so that these correlate reasonably well, they may be more comfortable with themselves, but can we also assume that they are now "better adjusted" in terms of a psychologist's standard? To answer this question requires that we introduce an external criterion of adjustment against which any particular Q-distribution can be scored. Such a measure would be useful in assessing the adjustment status of any particular person before and after therapy and the degree and direction of the change. It also would make possible the comparison of the major groups involved in this research, the experimental or therapy group, and the control or no-therapy group, in initial adjustment status and change over the testing time. It would also help us to look into the question of the extent to which a group which feels the need of help will improve over a period of waiting for therapy when no help is given. This question of spontaneous recovery will be taken up in detail in chapter 14.

I. THE Q-ADJUSTMENT SCORE

The Q-sort adjustment score was devised to provide an external criterion of adjustment level. It was based on the Q-sort test, which has already been introduced in chapters 3 and 4, in which the subject is asked to sort a hundred statements into nine piles, putting a prescribed number of cards into each, thus making a forced normal distribution. The instructions are that he put the cards most descriptive of him at one end, those least descriptive at the opposite end, and those about which he is indifferent or undecided around the middle of the distribution. Actually the required distribution looked like this:

		"Least Like Me"					"Most Like Me"		
Pile No.	0	1	2	3	4	5	6	7	8
No. of cards	1	4	11	21	26	21	11	4	1

To obtain the adjustment criterion, the entire group of one hundred statements was given to two well-trained practicing clinical psychologists from outside the client-centered orientation. They were asked to sort these into two piles: those the well-adjusted person should say are unlike him and those the well-adjusted person should say are like him. Since both these judges felt that there was a group of items which were irrelevant to one's adjustment status, they were permitted to throw these items out of their sortings. The two distributions made by these two judges agreed remarkably well, differing on only two of the one hundred items. Next, the twenty-six statements that these judges agreed did not differentiate on adjustment were put aside, and four new judges were given the remaining seventy-four to sort. They were asked to make two equal piles, so that there would be thirty-seven items that the well-adjusted individual would say are like him and thirty-seven he would say are unlike him. Again the agreement among the judges' sortings was very high. The largest discrepancy between any two judges was four items. The composite picture of the self-description of the well-adjusted person was then tabulated as thirty-seven positive indicators which should be on the "like me" side of the distribution (anywhere from scale position 5–8) of the well-adjusted person, and thirty-seven negative indicators which should be on the "unlike me" side (between 3 and 0). Table 1 lists these items.

Any person's resemblance to this ideal type can be computed very simply by counting the number of these seventy-four items which he places on the same end of the distribution when he sorts to describe himself as the hypothetically well-adjusted person would. This tally was called the "adjustment score." The optimal score that any one person could attain is, of course, 74 if he places thirty-seven items indicating good adjustment on the "like me" side at scale positions 5, 6, 7, and 8 and all thirty-seven items representing poor adjustment on the "unlike me" side at positions 3, 2, 1, and 0.

II. GROUP RESULTS

In Table 2 there is a comparison of the Q-adjustment scores of the experimental clients who waited sixty days before beginning their therapy and their controls over the waiting period.

A comparison of the mean adjustment score of the experimental wait group at the pre-wait testing time and the mean adjustment score of the matched control group that was not motivated for therapy shows that the therapy group describe themselves as significantly poorer in adjustment. (The t test is significant at the 1 per cent level.) The table also shows that the mean adjustment score of neither of these groups changes significantly over the waiting period and that the two groups remain significantly different at the pre-therapy testing point (also at the 1 per cent level using t). Thus the motivation of the experimental group to improve, as evidenced from the fact that they had applied for therapy, was not sufficient in itself to produce a significant increase in the adjustment score in the absence of therapy. The fact that there was also no change in the control group's mean score over this sixty-day period seems to show that an increase in familiarity with the test does not lead to an increase in the adjustment score.

Now let us look at what happens to the adjustment scores after

TABLE 1

ADJUSTMENT SCORE ITEMS

Q-Sort Item No.	Statement	Q-Sort Item No.	Statement
	Negative: Contribute to Score if Fall on "Unlike Me" Side (0–3)		*Positive:* Contribute to Score if Fall on "Like Me" Side (5–8)
2......	I put on a false front.	4......	I make strong demands on myself.
6......	I often feel humiliated.	5......	I often kick myself for the things I do.
7......	I doubt my sexual powers.	9......	I have a warm emotional relationship with others.
13......	I have a feeling of hopelessness.	11......	I am responsible for my troubles.
16......	I have few values and standards of my own.	12......	I am a responsible person.
18......	It is difficult to control my aggression.	15......	I can accept most social values and standards.
25......	I want to give up trying to cope with the world.	19......	Self-control is no problem to me.
28......	I tend to be on my guard with people who are somewhat more friendly than I had expected.	22......	I usually like people.
32......	I usually feel driven.	23......	I express my emotions freely.
36......	I feel helpless.	26......	I can usually live comfortably with the people around me.
38......	My decisions are not my own.	27......	My hardest battles are with myself.
40......	I am a hostile person.	29......	I am optimistic.
42......	I am disorganized.	33......	I am liked by most people who know me.
43......	I feel apathetic.	35......	I am sexually attractive.
49......	I don't trust my emotions	37......	I can usually make up my mind and stick to it.
50......	It's pretty tough to be me.	41......	I am contented.
52......	I have the feeling that I am just not facing things.	44......	I am poised.
54......	I try not to think about my problems.	47......	I am impulsive.
56......	I am shy.	51......	I am a rational person.
59......	I am no one. Nothing seems to be me.	53......	I am tolerant.
62......	I despise myself.	55......	I have an attractive personality.
64......	I shrink from facing a crisis or difficulty.	61......	I am ambitious.
65......	I just don't respect myself.	63......	I have initiative.
69......	I am afraid of a full-fledged disagreement with a person.	67......	I take a positive attitude toward myself.
70......	I can't seem to make up my mind one way or another.	68......	I am assertive.
71......	I am confused.	72......	I am satisfied with myself.
73......	I am a failure.	74......	I am likable.
76......	I am afraid of sex.	75......	My personality is attractive to to the opposite sex.
77......	I have a horror of failing in anything I want to accomplish.	78......	I am relaxed, and nothing really bothers me.
83......	I really am disturbed.	79......	I am a hard worker.
84......	All you have to do is just insist with me, and I give in.	80......	I feel emotionally mature.
85......	I feel insecure within myself.	88......	I am intelligent.
86......	I have to protect myself with excuses, with rationalizing.	91......	I am self-reliant.
90......	I feel hopeless.	94......	I am different from others.
95......	I am unreliable.	96......	I understand myself.
99......	I am worthless.	97......	I am a good mixer.
100......	I dislike my own sexuality.	98......	I feel adequate.

the experimental group has completed therapy. The control group, of course, has had no therapy, but an equal period of time has elapsed before their "post-therapy" tests. In Table 3 the mean scores at pre-therapy, post-therapy, and follow-up times for the total experimental group, both waits and no-waits, are reported and compared to the mean scores of the total control group. Only twenty-three of the experimental group and seventeen of the control group have completed the follow-up testing at this writing. Using a t test for correlated means, the experimental group is found to increase its adjustment-score mean significantly at the 1 per cent level over the therapy period. A glance at the table shows that the control group does not. A t test (for uncorrelated means) reveals that the difference between the two groups in adjustment score is significant before therapy but is not at post-testing time or at the follow-up time.

TABLE 2

ADJUSTMENT SCORES OF THE WAIT GROUPS DURING THE NO-THERAPY PERIOD

Group	Experimental ($N=11$) Q-Adjustment Scores		Control ($N=11$) Q-Adjustment Scores	
	Mean	Range	Mean	Range
Pre-wait	29.54	16–36	47.00	25–58
Pre-therapy	30.18	15–41	47.40	27–58

TABLE 3

ADJUSTMENT SCORES OF THE TOTAL GROUP OVER THE THERAPY PERIOD

Group	Experimental Q-Adjustment Score		Control Q-Adjustment Score	
	Mean	Range	Mean	Range
Pre-therapy ($N=25$)	28.80	11–42	44.96	27–60 ($N=23$)
Post-therapy ($N=25$)	39.80	18–54	45.12	27–56 ($N=23$)
Follow-up ($N=22$)	38.36	17–53	44.52	25–58 ($N=17$)

In sum, the subjects who were presumably motivated to change in some way, in that they had applied for therapy, described themselves as poorer in adjustment than a group that was not so motivated. After a time interval in which the motivated group received therapy and the others did not, the two groups described themselves at about the same level of adjustment.

An interesting sidelight showed up when the group was divided into the two sex groups. Table 4 shows that, although both males

TABLE 4

SEX DIFFERENCES IN Q-ADJUSTMENT SCORE CHANGES OVER THERAPY

GROUP	EXPERIMENTAL		CONTROL	
	Males ($N=15$)	Females ($N=10$)	Males ($N=14$)	Females ($N=9$)
Pre-therapy.........	27.46	31.10	45.38	46.16
Post-therapy........	35.86	46.10	45.69	44.41

and females in the experimental group change significantly at the 1 per cent level over the therapy period, the females showed a significantly larger change in favor of increased adjustment than did the males. Also the difference in adjustment of the sexes as measured by this test, while not significant before therapy, is significant after therapy. These sex differences do not occur in the control sample, suggesting that something in the therapy situation itself was responsible for this difference.

This sex difference in improvement in favor of the female clients is also found on the counselor's rating of success of the therapy as reported by Seeman in chapter 7 and on the change in adjustment as judged from the Thematic Apperception Test (TAT) records reported by Dymond in chapter 8.

III. SUMMARY OF GROUP RESULTS

From Tables 2 and 3 we can say now that scoring for adjustment of the self-descriptive sorts of the clients who waited for therapy show them to be significantly poorer in adjustment than their matched control group. They do not improve during their sixty-day waiting period and remain at pre-therapy time significantly lower in score than the controls who were also retested after the two-month interval. The mean adjustment score of the total experimental group after therapy was significantly higher than their pretherapy score and now not significantly different from the scores of the controls. This improvement is maintained over the six-month to one-year follow-up period. The fact that the control-group mean stays practically constant over all testing points seems to show that neither familiarity with the test nor the passage of time has any appreciable effect on these scores.

It is reasonable that we ask at this point whether there are other possible explanations of the significant improvement in the scores of the therapy group before attributing it to therapy. First to be cleared out of the way is the question of the tendency of low scores to regress toward the mean on repeated testing. Plotting the initial adjustment scores against the degree of change over therapy in these scores gives a completely random distribution. Therefore, the regression explanation can be ruled out.

Next there is the problem of the possible influence on these scores of the fact that, after all, they are based on *self*-descriptions. Perhaps the client's post-therapy sorting reflects a need to please the therapist: to demonstrate to him how much profit has been derived from the counseling. Or, perhaps, the client may have a need to convince himself that he has not wasted his time in therapy. If the gains from therapy were really minimal or superficial and the adjustment-score increase spurious, the self-description done at the follow-up point might be expected to show some regression in that it is probably less influenced by the "hello-goodbye" effect (1). The fact that the follow-up mean score of the therapy group is almost identical to the mean score at post-therapy seems to indicate some lasting improvement.

IV. RELIABILITY AND VALIDITY

The reliability of this test was estimated by the test-retest method. Since the experimental group was expected to change over time and the controls were not, the reliability is based on the stability of the control-group scores. The post-therapy to follow-up period was chosen, since this represents a fairly constant interval of six months to one year, whereas the pre- to post-therapy interval varies a good deal. The reliability of the control group scores over this period is .86.

How valid a criterion of adjustment this Q-score is depends to a large extent on the degree to which it agrees in its ordering of the subjects with other measures of improvement on which they were also tested. In many of the chapters that follow, the correlation of this test with others is reported. Rather than cite these figures here before the other tests have been introduced, let us look at just two of these: first, its agreement with the ranking on the self-ideal correlations (see chap. 4); second, the agreement with the counselors' ratings of success of therapy.

The rank-order correlation between the self-ideal correlations and the Q-sort adjustment score of twenty-three therapy subjects at pre-therapy was .83, and the rank order of these same twenty-three at post-therapy was .92, showing a high degree of agreement.

The counselor rating scale is described fully in chapter 7. For present purposes we will simply note that each therapist rated his cases on a nine-point scale from 1 (complete failure) to 9 (marked success). Table 5 shows the relation of high and low post-therapy

TABLE 5

THE RELATION OF Q-SORT ADJUSTMENT SCORE AND COUNSELOR RATING OF SUCCESS

Q-Adjustment Score (Post-therapy)	Success of Therapy Rating	
	Low (1–5)	High (6–9)
Low (17–40)	8	4
High (41–54)	2	11

adjustment scores to high and low success ratings. Using the exact method of Yates (2) for determining the significance of this relationship, it is found to be significant at better than the 5 per cent level.

V. CONCLUSION

The group entering therapy produced less well-adjusted self-descriptions as measured against a standard set up by expert clinicians than the group that did not wish therapy. After therapy there was a significant improvement in the experimental group which did not occur in the control group. The status of the experimentals as a group at post-therapy did not differ significantly from the matched controls. These therapy gains in adjustment were maintained over the follow-up period. The concurrence of these post-therapy scores with the counselors' ratings of success of therapy makes it possible for us to conclude that those who appeared to be most successful in therapy also described themselves on their Q-sort in ways which agreed best with an eclectic criterion of adjustment.

Although we now have a rather consistent picture being built up of clients coming into therapy with low self-esteem and low adjustment as compared to controls, leaving therapy with significant increases in both, and these improvements being confirmed by the counselor ratings, we are still speaking of changes as described by the client himself and his therapist. It may be argued that these two are not really independent of each other and that neither is a valid measure of adjustment. The counselor's rating of the success of the therapy may be influenced by the client's use of "well-adjusted" self-references in his closing interviews, and the therapist's attitude of satisfaction with the progress of the case may be communicated to the client, who then reflects these in his self-description. In subsequent chapters we will report changes on other measures which are not suspect on these grounds, particularly the TAT study to be found in chapter 8, and find the same pattern of results: low adjustment at pre-therapy for the experimental group and significant increase at post-therapy, no change in the control group, and no change in the therapy group during the no-therapy waiting period.

REFERENCES

1. Hathaway, S. R. "Some Considerations Relative to Nondirective Counseling as Therapy," *Journal of Clinical Psychology*, IV (1948), 226–31.
2. Yates, F. "Contingency Tables Involving Small Numbers and the χ^2 Test," *Journal of the Royal Statistical Society* (London), Suppl. 1 (1934), pp. 217–35.

CHAPTER 6

A Comparative Study of the Changes in the Concepts of the Self, the Ordinary Person, and the Ideal in Eight Cases

ESSELYN C. RUDIKOFF

The purpose of this study was to compare, in a small group of clients, the changes in their concepts of the self, the ordinary person, and the ideal during a no-therapy control period, therapy, and a follow-up period and to compare these changes with the theoretical expectations. The self-concept is defined as the self the individual himself perceives, that is, his own attributes, feelings, and behavior as observed subjectively and admitted to awareness. The concept of the ordinary person is defined as the individual's recognized perception of the attributes, feelings, and behavior of people in general. The ideal is defined as the attributes, feelings, and behavior the individual admittedly would like to possess.

Progressively greater consideration is being given to the development of these concepts and to their dynamic relationship to the adjustment of the individual. In regard to the concept of self, for example, it is a part of the theory of client-centered therapy that one of the most marked concomitants of therapy is change in the client's perception of himself in the direction of becoming a self which seems more comfortable, more confident, less anxious, with valued goals seeming more achievable. It appeared possible to test some aspects of this theory in the present data.

In regard to the interrelationship of the three concepts, certain additional theoretical expectations may be given. Taking into account the healthy desire to improve, we might expect the well-adjusted person to describe his ideal as somewhat "higher" (more integrated or adjusted) than his self-concept and "higher" than his concept of the ordinary person. Considering realistic individual differences, we might expect some variation between the concepts of the self and of the ordinary person. However, great differences among any of these concepts within the same individual would seem to reflect psychological discomfort and strain. Also, great discrepancy between any of these concepts and an external criterion of good adjustment would indicate a lack of psychological well-being.

I. HYPOTHESES

As is implied in the foregoing paragraphs, certain hypotheses may be drawn from theory. If therapy results in more improvement in psychological well-being than do other experiences in general, then:

1. The concept of the self should change more during therapy than during a no-therapy period and should change more over therapy than the concepts of the ordinary person or of the ideal.
2. The concepts of the self and the ordinary person should become more like each other and more similar to the ideal over therapy than over a no-therapy control period.
3. The adjustment value of the concepts of the self and the ordinary person, as measured by an external criterion, should increase more over therapy than over a control period.

II. INSTRUMENTATION AND METHODS OF DATA COLLECTION

Data from Clients

The basic instrument for this study was the SIO Q-Sort instrument devised by Butler and Haigh (see chap. 4). For the self-concept the clients were asked to sort the items "so as to yield a picture of yourself as you perceive yourself today"; for the concept of the ordinary person, "to express your own opinion of people in general"; and, for the ideal concept, "as the person you would most like to be."[1] The sorts used in this study were those produced by the eight own-control or wait group of clients for whom full data were available. There are four time samples of each sort: that done soon after the clients requested therapy (pre-wait); approximately sixty days later, just prior to therapy (pre-therapy); soon after therapy was completed (post-therapy); and approximately six months later (follow-up).[2]

1. This approach to the study of these variables was introduced by Hartley (1).
2. See chap. 3 for a full statement of the research design.

The Adjustment Index[3]

The thirty-seven items regarded as representative of good adjustment by a group of clinical judges were given a positive adjustment-score value if sorted as "like" the self (or ideal or ordinary person, as the case might be), and the thirty-seven items regarded as representative of poor adjustment by these judges were given a positive score value if sorted as "unlike" the concept under consideration. Thus the maximum possible score is 74.

III. SUBJECTS

The eight own-control cases who subsequently completed therapy and follow-up tests made up the population for this study. They are described in Table 1. It will be seen that there are five

TABLE 1

THE SUBJECTS

Client	Sex	Age	Student (S) or Nonstudent (NS)	No. of Interviews	Counselor's Rating
Babi.........	F	29	NS	6	8
Bame........	M	28	S	38	6
Bayu........	M	24	S	15	2
Bebb........	M	24	S	9	6
Beso.........	F	36	S	12	5
Bett.........	F	23	S	64	7
Bixy.........	M	22	NS	16	4
Blen.........	M	27	NS	31	5
Range.......	......	22–36	....	6–64	2–8
Median......	......	25.5	....	15–16	5

male and three female clients, that in age they are characteristic of the group as a whole, and that in the counselor's judgment they run the gamut from marked failure in therapy to a high degree of success. The number of interviews per client is somewhat less than for the therapy group as a whole.

IV. FINDINGS

Stability and Change in the Concepts

In order to test the first hypothesis, it was necessary to determine the degree of stability and change in the concepts. Table 2

3. See chap. 5 for a description of this index.

shows the variation in stability which occurred differentially among the concepts and among the time periods. From the material in this table, the following findings have been calculated:

1. The self-concept was more stable (<.001) over the control period than over therapy.
2. The self-concept was more stable (<.02) than that of the ordinary person over the control period.
3. The concept of the ordinary person tended to be more stable than that of the self over therapy.
4. The ideal was more stable (<.01) than the concepts of the self and of the ordinary person over all periods.
5. The ideal showed a greater tendency toward stability over the control period than over therapy.

The Testing of the First Hypothesis

Apparently, then, the greatest changes of all occurred in the self during therapy. The first hypothesis is supported in the fact both that the self changed more during therapy than during the control period and that it changed more during the therapy period than the ordinary or the ideal. The directions and nature of the changes underlying the variations in stability will be analyzed in the remainder of this chapter.

TABLE 2

STABILITY OF INDIVIDUALS' CONCEPTS OVER THE WAIT, THERAPY, AND FOLLOW-UP PERIODS
(Test-Retest Reliability)

CLIENT	WAIT			THERAPY			FOLLOW-UP		
	Pre-wait and Pre-therapy Correlations			Pre-therapy and Post-therapy Correlations			Post-therapy and Follow-up Correlations		
	Self	Ordinary	Ideal	Self	Ordinary	Ideal	Self	Ordinary	Ideal
Babi.......	.78	.77*	.83†	.63*	.72	.88†	.79	.76*	.82†
Bame......	.69	.61*	.90†	.61*	.62	.86†	.81	.68*	.85†
Bayu......	.57†	.50*	.56	.30*	.60	.63†	.13*	.58	.68†
Bebb......	.63*	.65	.77†	.41*	.52	.67†	.49	.24*	.72†
Beso.......	.62	.57*	.69†	.50*	.51	.66†	.46*	.54	.70†
Bett.......	.57	.34*	.88†	.25*	.25*	.68†	.18*	.23	.64†
Bixy.......	.77	.72*	.87†	.63	.62*	.89†	.49*	.73	.90†
Blen.......	.71	.53*	.88†	.61*	.74	.83†	.33*	.72	.86†

* Indicates the concept having the least stability for each subject over the particular period.
† Indicates the concept having the greatest stability for each subject over the particular period.

THE DEGREE OF CONGRUENCE BETWEEN THE CLIENTS' CONCEPTS

There were very wide discrepancies among the concepts of the self, the ordinary person, and the ideal for members of this group when they sought counseling. The mean pre-wait self-ideal correlation was −.03; the ordinary-ideal correlation, .15; and the self-ordinary correlation, .09. These scores reflect, according to the theoretical views mentioned at the outset, much psychological discomfort. Let us now examine the changes within each period from Table 3.

TABLE 3

INTERRELATIONSHIPS BETWEEN CONCEPTS OF THE SELF, THE ORDINARY PERSON, AND THE IDEAL

Client	Self and Ideal Correlations				Ordinary and Ideal Correlations				Self and Ordinary Correlations			
	Pre-wait	Pre-therapy	Post-therapy	Follow-up	Pre-wait	Pre-therapy	Post-therapy	Follow-up	Pre-wait	Pre-therapy	Post-therapy	Follow-up
Babi	−.01	.05	.54	.45	−.20	.24	−.02	−.02	.25	.33	.33	.39
Bame	.32	.15	.61	.61	.46	.29	.20	.40	.50	.47	.55	.73
Bayu	−.32	−.47	−.04	.42	.52	.35	.32	.58	−.29	−.03	.07	.46
Bebb	−.18	.06	.26	.21	.06	−.11	.01	.04	−.42	−.49	−.20	.02
Beso	.19	.32	.41	.47	.38	.50	.47	.44	.16	.24	.50	.54
Bett	−.22	−.36	.37	.61	.09	−.49	−.04	.28	.14	.30	.43	.09
Bixy	−.12	−.39	.05	−.39	−.19	−.36	−.08	−.47	.18	.41	.51	.50
Blen	.07	.24	.33	−.36	−.04	.43	.45	.58	.18	.41	.49	.03
Mean *Z* score	−.03	−.06	.33	.28	.15	.11	.17	.25	.09	.21	.35	.37
Significance of diffs.*		Not sig.	< .01	Not sig.		Not sig.	Not sig.	Not sig.		.05	< .01	Not sig.

* Using *t* for correlated means.

THE CONTROL OR WAIT PERIOD

1. The mean self-ideal and ordinary-ideal correlations decreased somewhat, but not significantly.

2. The concepts of the self and of the ordinary person became significantly (< .05) more similar.

At both pre-wait and pre-therapy testing the mean correlation for the concept of the ordinary person in relationship to the ideal was higher than the self-ideal mean correlation. Although the majority of the individuals regarded the ordinary person as more like the ideal than they themselves were, depreciation of the ordinary person is reflected by the low ordinary-ideal correlations. There were only three individuals whose opinions of the ordinary person improved at all over the control period, and these also showed somewhat improved attitudes toward the self. Although these clients were motivated to improve, the group as a whole did not improve on these measures without therapy.

THE THERAPY PERIOD

1. The self and ideal became significantly (< .01) more similar.

2. There was a small, but not significant, gain in the mean ordinary-ideal correlation.

3. The concepts of the self and of the ordinary person became significantly (< .01) more alike.

At post-therapy the mean self-ideal correlation was considerably higher than the mean ordinary-ideal correlation. Every person in this group showed increased congruence of the self-concept and the ideal over therapy. Those whose pre-therapy ordinary-ideal correlations ranked highest tended to show decreases at post-therapy, and those whose pre-therapy ordinary-ideal correlations were inclined to rank lowest tended to show increases at post-therapy.

THE FOLLOW-UP PERIOD

1. None of the changes for the group over the follow-up period was statistically significant.

2. The mean self-ideal correlation was decreased slightly, and the mean ordinary-ideal correlation showed a slight increment. There was a slightly higher mean self-ordinary correlation at follow-up than at post-therapy.

The mean self-ideal remained higher than the mean ordinary-ideal correlation. Most of the gains over therapy were maintained.

DIFFERENCES IN CHANGES BETWEEN PERIODS

1. The movement in the self and ideal relationship over therapy was significantly greater than that over the control period (< .05) and significantly greater than that over follow-up (< .01).

2. No other differences in changes between periods were significant.

The Testing of the Second Hypothesis

There were wide individual differences in initial psychological status and in outcomes for members of this group. However, every individual showed a higher self-ideal or ordinary-ideal correlation at follow-up than at pre-therapy testing. For the group as a whole, all three concepts showed more similarity to one another at follow-up than at pre-therapy testing. The increase in correlations between concepts was greater over therapy than over the control period.

In general, then, our second hypothesis was largely supported. The concepts of self and ordinary became more congruent during the control period, a trend which is somewhat contrary to the hypothesis. However, in strict terms, the hypothesis was entirely upheld, since the similarity between self and ordinary, self and ideal, and ordinary and ideal increased more significantly during the therapy than during the no-therapy control period.

THE EXTERNAL ADJUSTMENT INDEX APPLIED TO THE CLIENTS' CONCEPTS

Dymond's adjustment index (see chap. 5) was used to answer the validity question and to test the third hypothesis. Were the changes found in this population changes toward better adjustment as established with this instrument by expert clinicians?

In the analyses which follow, values of plus (good adjustment), zero (irrelevant), or minus (poor adjustment) were given each item in accordance with the adjustment index. The thirty-seven items assigned positive values should have the highest ranks, and the thirty-seven with negative values should have the lowest ranks in a distribution descriptive of a hypothetical "perfectly" well-adjusted person. Such a distribution would have an adjustment score of 74. Table 4 shows that there was much individual variation in adjustment scores among individuals for each concept and at each time of testing.

Comparisons of the clients' sorts with the adjustment index corroborate the trends manifested when the clients' concepts were compared with each other.

THE CONTROL PERIOD

1. The self-concept showed movement toward greater maladjustment at the 10 per cent level of significance.

2. Changes in the concept of the ordinary person were not significant.

3. The ideal showed a trend toward a closer approximation to the adjustment index.

TABLE 4

INDIVIDUAL ADJUSTMENT SCORES FOR EACH DISTRIBUTION

Client	Self				Ordinary				Ideal			
	Pre-wait	Pre-therapy	Post-therapy	Follow-up	Pre-wait	Pre-therapy	Post-therapy	Follow-up	Pre-wait	Pre-therapy	Post-therapy	Follow-up
Babi	29	27	45	39	15	18	21	9	55	61	59	55
Bame	38	36	48	47	47	33	37	39	62	64	54	62
Bayu	21	15	30	47	49	40	42	45	52	56	57	54
Bebb	23	26	33	27	41	34	33	36	53	54	54	51
Beso	33	30	41	45	38	47	37	37	58	55	52	56
Bett	35	31	51	41	32	17	36	33	53	53	58	50
Bixy	30	20	35	21	23	18	38	23	55	59	60	61
Blen	33	33	39	27	27	44	40	49	61	61	57	62
Mean	30	27	40	37	34	31	36	34	56	58	56	56
Significance of diffs		< .10	< .001	Not sig.		Not sig.	Not sig.	Not sig.		< .20	Not sig.	Not sig.

TABLE 5

SUMMARY OF DIRECTIONS OF CHANGES IN ADJUSTMENT BY INDIVIDUALS

Period	Self			Ordinary			Ideal		
	Increased	Decreased	No change	Increased	Decreased	No change	Increased	Decreased	No change
Wait	1	6	1	3	5	0	5	1	2
Therapy	8	0	0	5	3	0	3	4	1
Follow-up	3	5	0	4	4	0	3	4	1
Therapy and follow-up combined	7	1	0	6	2	0	3	5	0

THE THERAPY PERIOD

1. Improvement in the self-concept was significant at greater than the one-tenth of 1 per cent level.

2. Changes in the concepts of the ordinary person and the ideal were not significant.

THE FOLLOW-UP PERIOD

There were no significant changes in any of the concepts.

DIFFERENCES IN CHANGES BETWEEN PERIODS

1. Changes in the self-concept over therapy were greater than those over the control period and over the follow-up period at greater than the 1 per cent level of significance.

2. There were no significant differences in changes between periods for the other concepts.

The Testing of the Third Hypothesis

In general, the most significant change is again the change in the concept of self over therapy, a highly significant change in the direction of better adjustment, with a slight but not significant regression during the follow-up period. Every individual showed an increase in the adjustment score for self from pre-wait to post-therapy, and six of the eight from pre-wait to follow-up. The concept of the ordinary person shows a trend toward better adjustment over the therapy period, but this is not statistically significant.[4]

The ideal remains relatively constant throughout. However, over the control period, four of the five individuals whose ideals rose showed decreased self-adjustment scores. The four individuals whose ideals decreased over therapy tended to have the best self-adjustment scores after therapy. There seems to be an inverse relationship in the direction of movement of the self and the ideal.

4. A more refined method of deriving the adjustment score for each actual distribution equals the number of positive items rated as like the concept (weights of 5–8), minus those rated as not like the concept (weights of 0–3), plus the number of negative items rated as not like the concept, minus those rated as like the concept. With this more inclusive method of scoring for adjustment, there was a trend ($<.20$) toward gradual improvement in the concept of the ordinary person over therapy and follow-up.

The third hypothesis is thus upheld in part, since the concept of self increased very significantly in adjustment during therapy and decreased during the control period. It is not confirmed in its expectations of an improved adjustment value for the concept of the ordinary person, this increase falling short of statistical significance. There is the further suggestion that an improvement in self-adjustment may be associated with a lowering of the ideal goal.

V. ITEM ANALYSES

Changes in the placement of the items over the various times are in keeping with Rogers' (3) theory of personality and psychotherapy. The interpretations which follow are based on those items which showed a minimum gain or loss of eight points from one testing point to the next for the group. Eight was selected arbitrarily on the basis of one point per person. Group weights were based on the summation of individual weights for each item. For example, the item "I understand myself" showed a gain of sixteen points over therapy. Pre-therapy weights of individuals for this item were: 0, 2, 3, 3, 3, 4, 4, and 5, or a total of 24. Post-therapy weights were: 3, 3, 4, 4, 5, 6, 7, and 8, or a total of 40. The post-therapy total was sixteen points higher than the pre-therapy total.

Changes in the Self-concept

OVER THE CONTROL PERIOD

1. There was more admitted resistance to facing things.
2. There was a greater projection of blame on others.
3. There was a greater rejection of social values and standards.
4. There was also decreased emotional control.

OVER THERAPY

1. There was an improvement in self-understanding and attitudes toward the self.
2. Increased inner comfort was evidenced.
3. There was a more optimistic general outlook.
4. Increased self-responsibility and initiative were shown.
5. There was greater comfort in relationship with others.
6. Over this period there was less felt need to hide the self from self or from others.

OVER FOLLOW-UP

1. There was continued improvement in attitudes toward self and society.

2. Finally, there was also somewhat less feeling of ability to cope with both the world and themselves than that immediately after therapy.

Changes in the Concept of the Ordinary Person

There were fewer and less systematic group changes in items for the concept of the ordinary person than for the self-concept. Specific changes in the perception of others are best understood in relationship to the self-concept on an individual basis. However, some interesting group trends occurred.

OVER THE CONTROL PERIOD

With the increased defensiveness, projection of criticism, and decreased emotional control which occurred in the self, changes in the perceptions of the ordinary person were in the direction of (1) less self-understanding; (2) less likableness; (3) greater guilt feelings; and (4) less freedom to express emotions.

OVER THERAPY AND FOLLOW-UP COMBINED

With the greater feelings of comfort and security which accompanied increased understanding and acceptance of the self, the ordinary person gradually came to be perceived as (1) more understanding of self, less disturbed; (2) more of a separate individual with his own standards and values; (3) less threatening, having his own insecurity; (4) more of a responsible person; and (5) less guilty.

Changes in the Ideal Concept

Changes in items in the concept of the ideal were not so substantial as those in the other concepts. Over the control period and over therapy, no item showed a group change of as many as eight points. Over follow-up, the item "I feel inferior" remained in the not-to-be-desired group but was somewhat more acceptable to the concept of the ideal than it had been previously. The item "I feel emotionally mature" remained as desirable but was deemed somewhat less important than previously. At follow-up the scores for these items in the ideal were more like those in the self-concept than they were at pre-therapy. These are the most obvious examples of a lowering of the ideal toward a closer approximation to the self-concept. Forty-five of the one hundred items showed a change in the follow-up ideal from their pre-therapy scores toward those of the follow-up self. Of these, forty-five, the scores for all the items indicating good adjustment, according to Dymond's index, were rated as less like the ideal, and most of the items indicating poor adjustment were rated as more like the ideal. It seems that the desire toward perfection was lessened. Conversely, over therapy and follow-up combined, most of these forty-five items representing good adjustment were rated as more like the self, and most of those representing poor adjustment were rated as less like the self. The self-concept became better adjusted according to the index.

These findings are in agreement with Horney's (2) theory of the reciprocal relationship of the self-concept and the self-ideal in psychological disturbances and recovery. In essence, she proposed that the well-adjusted person accepts his real self on which he focuses and which he tries to actualize, while envisioning an ideal toward which he realistically can move. This realistic ideal can be raised gradually as the individual approaches it. Lack of acceptance of the real self results in a kind of compensatory, unrealistic glorification of the idealized self. The individual then tends to focus on and tries to actualize this idealized self. Being unrealistic, this results in failure, causing still further rejection of the real self with even greater need for elevation of the ideal. Consequently, the self and the ideal become more and more disparate, and discomfort increases. As the self becomes better accepted there is less need for the glorified ideal, and it becomes more realistic. In brief, as certain kinds of disturbance increase, the self and ideal move away from each other; as such disturbance decreases, the self and ideal move toward each other. By the self-ideal, Horney refers to a current level of aspiration, which might be quite flexible over time. The instructions given to our clients when sorting for the ideal have no temporal restrictions. Such ideals might not be expected to change much. Yet, our findings give support to Horney's theory. She points out further that, after good adjustment is reached, the ideal may be raised gradually and that the self-concept may move toward the gradually elevated ideal with further growth. It would be interesting to follow up this last aspect after a longer period of time.

VI. DISCUSSION

In setting up the original design for this research as a whole, it was decided to restrict the control (wait) period to sixty days in the best interests of the clients, despite the possibility that some clients might have a shorter period of waiting than of therapy. Both concerns were justified. Psychological disturbance did increase somewhat for the group, and the control period was approximately half as long as the median length of time for therapy. Furthermore, in order to test the effects of therapy over time, and since the administration of the entire test battery required many hours, it was decided not to burden the clients by follow-up tests until six months after post-therapy testing. The median follow-up period actually was almost twice as long as the median number of days over therapy.

We do not know what changes might have occurred over the wait period had it been extended. We do know that greater change occurred over therapy than over the shorter control period or the longer period of follow-up. The nature of the changes over therapy and follow-up shows so much systematic relationship to client-centered theory that it is highly doubtful that they can be attributed to time alone. The variations in outcomes are related more to differences in initial psychological status than to length of therapy. Finally, the equivalent-control group, not experiencing therapy, was tested at the same intervals of time as individuals with whom they were matched in the experimental group. The changes in the equivalent-control group are not comparable to those of the experimental group over the same intervals of time.

Many previous studies of client-centered therapy have investigated changes in the perception of the self, of others, and, most recently, of the ideal. Thus far, the nature and the extent of these changes have been shown to be related to the degree of success of the therapy. The latter has been measured by client or counselor judgment or by research instruments regarded as objective criteria for evaluation. This study has the advantage of more objective means of quantification than those based on analysis of interview protocols. The findings for change over therapy are in agreement with those of preceding investigations (3, pp. 131–96). The treatment of the data presented here does not answer important questions regarding individual differences. Factorial studies investigating the relationships between individual differences in pre-therapy psychological status and the outcomes of therapy are under way.

VII. SUMMARY

This chapter has dealt with an investigation of changes in the concepts of self, the ordinary person, and the ideal over a no-therapy control period, therapy, and follow-up. The population was a group of eight individuals who differed from one another in initial adjustment status, length of therapy, and change. Despite the counterbalancing effects of individual differences, definite trends are revealed by the total group.

Findings for the concepts of self, the ordinary person, and the ideal in relationship to one another and to clinicians' judgment of the adjusted person showed the same trends. The self-concept disclosed somewhat decreased adjustment over the control period, a very significant improvement over therapy, and a slight loss over follow-up. The perceptions of the adjustment of the ordinary person revealed a slight decrement over the control period and gradual but not significant improvement over the therapy period. The concepts of self and of the ordinary person became more and more similar over each period. The ideal was raised somewhat over the control period, but during the therapy and follow-up period it was somewhat lowered in the direction of the self, thus becoming a more achievable type of goal.

REFERENCES

1. Hartley, Margaret W. "A Q-Technique Study of Changes in the Self-concept during Psychotherapy." Unpublished Ph.D. dissertation, University of Chicago, 1951.
2. Horney, Karen. *Our Inner Conflicts*. New York: W. W. Norton & Co., 1945.
3. Rogers, Carl R. *Client-centered Therapy*. Boston: Houghton Mifflin Co., 1951.

CHAPTER 7

Counselor Judgments of Therapeutic Process and Outcome

JULIUS SEEMAN

The therapist's judgment about a case is probably the most frequently used criterion of therapeutic outcome. Not only is it a readily available criterion, but also on logical grounds it is a sensible one to use. For the counselor is a close and constant witness to the therapeutic process and, further, a person whose training should equip him to select the appropriate kinds of data on which to base his judgment. Whether this is actually so remains to be seen in cross-validation studies; in any case, the logical arguments make counselor judgment a likely candidate for study as another criterion measure of therapeutic change. This chapter will report counselor judgments of therapeutic process and outcome for twenty-three of the research clients of the first block (Block I) who have completed counseling at this writing. The characteristics of this group have been described in chapter 3. Other chapters will compare these counselor judgments with other criteria and provide some basis for assessing the validity of these judgments. Here we are concerned in a descriptive sense with the kinds of judgments counselors report about their clients. We are in effect moving from measurements of movement from the clients' own frame of reference to movement as seen by the therapists.

I. PREVIOUS STUDIES

Previous studies of counselor judgment fall into two main groups: those which compare counselor judgment with internal measures of therapeutic process and those which compare counselor judgment with other measures of therapeutic outcome. The process measures show consistently positive relationship with counselor judgment. Raimy's study (7), for example, revealed significant correspondence between counselor rating of success and a rising ratio of positive attitudes as therapy proceeded. Raskin (8) summarized the results of five therapy process studies and reported a composite correlation of .70 between counselor ratings and extent of change in these measures. Thus the results indicate clear agreement between process measures and counselor judgments.

We can argue from these results that counselors can make accurate shorthand descriptions of client process in their ratings, but we cannot make validity arguments from these data alone. For such evidence we need to turn to studies showing correspondence between counselor judgment and independent evidence of therapeutic outcome. Here we find more equivocal but, on the whole, promising results. Mosak (5) found significant correlation between Minnesota Multiphasic changes and case rating. Jonietz (4) analyzed the Rorschach as a perceptual instrument and found correspondence between extent of perceptual change and counselor rating. In Muench's study (6) the correlation of Rorschach change with case rating was significant at the 10 per cent level. Rorschach studies by Haimowitz (3), Mosak (5), and Carr (1) showed no correspondence between case rating and extent of change.

II. CONSTRUCTION OF THE PRESENT SCALE[1]

The results quoted above taken together suggest enough promise for further study of counselor judgment as a criterion measure of therapeutic change. In the foregoing studies counselor rating consisted of a single global rating of the case. Since we are here concerned with refinement of counselor judgment, the approach in this study has been to construct a rating scale which assessed in more specific terms the counselor's judgments about the events of therapy. The choice of items was based on implicit hypotheses about the variables which were pertinent to therapeutic change. The scale appears in Table 1. Table 2 gives some of the results which we shall discuss presently. A reading of the scale indicates the questions which seemed important and includes such questions as the following: Was the therapeutic process primarily an intellectual or emotional one? Did the client-counselor relationship receive explicit attention as a factor in therapy?

1. The scale was constructed jointly by Nathaniel J. Raskin and the present writer in consultation with members of the Counseling Center staff. The writer wishes to acknowledge the valuable assistance of Gerald Gratch in analyzing the scale data.

TABLE 1

CASE RATING SCALE

Name or Code Name of Client...Counselor..........................

Date..............................

Directions:

We should like to have two ratings for each item of this scale. Place a *B* in the box appropriate for the beginning phase of the case and an *E* at the point appropriate for the end of the case.

The Process

1. Degree to which therapy was an intellectual-cognitive process for the client.

1	2	3	4	5	6	7	8	9
☐	☐	☐	☐	☐	☐	☐	☐	☐
Little or none								*Maximally or exclusively*

2. The degree to which therapy was an emotional-experiential process for the client.

1	2	3	4	5	6	7	8	9
☐	☐	☐	☐	☐	☐	☐	☐	☐
Little or none								*Maximally or exclusively*

3. The degree to which the client perceived therapy as a process of personal exploration or as specific analysis of life-situations.

1	2	3	4	5	6	7	8	9
☐	☐	☐	☐	☐	☐	☐	☐	☐
Situational								*Personal exploration*

The Relationship

4. The degree to which the client has used the relationship itself as a focus for therapy.

1	2	3	4	5	6	7	8	9
☐	☐	☐	☐	☐	☐	☐	☐	☐
Negligible extent								*Maximally*

5. Estimate of the client's attitude toward you during the course of therapy.

1	2	3	4	5	6	7	8	9
☐	☐	☐	☐	☐	☐	☐	☐	☐
Strong dislike								*Strong liking or respect*

6. Estimate of your feeling toward the client.

1	2	3	4	5	6	7	8	9
☐	☐	☐	☐	☐	☐	☐	☐	☐
Strong dislike								*Strong liking or respect*

The Outcome

7. The degree of personal integration of the client.

1	2	3	4	5	6	7	8	9
☐	☐	☐	☐	☐	☐	☐	☐	☐
Highly disorganized or defensively organized								*Optimally integrated*

8. The life-adjustment of the client.

1	2	3	4	5	6	7	8	9
☐	☐	☐	☐	☐	☐	☐	☐	☐
Low								*High*

See note below.*

9. Degree of satisfaction of the client with the outcome of therapy.

1	2	3	4	5	6	7	8	9
☐	☐	☐	☐	☐	☐	☐	☐	☐
Strongly dissatisfied								*Extremely satisfied*

10. Your rating of the outcome of therapy.

1	2	3	4	5	6	7	8	9
☐	☐	☐	☐	☐	☐	☐	☐	☐
Complete failure								*Marked success*

* Please mark an × in the appropriate box for Nos. 9 and 10.

General evaluation or comments:...

....

....

What was the personal organization of the client? How did the counselor rate the outcome?

The reader will note that for the first eight items both the beginning phase and the ending phase of therapy were rated, so that for these items the difference between beginning and end ratings constituted a "movement" score for the variables, although both these ratings were made at the end of therapy. Each item was rated

TABLE 2

JUDGMENTS DERIVED FROM THE CASE RATING SCALE

Item (1)	Mean Beginning Rating (2)	Mean End Rating (3)	Mean Movement Rating (4)*	Correlation with Success Rating (5)*
The Process				
1. Degree to which therapy was an intellectual-cognitive process. Little or none (1) to maximal (9)	6.5	4.6	−1.9	−.58
2. The degree to which therapy was an emotional-experiential process. Little or none (1) to maximal (9)	3.4	5.1	1.7	.67
3. The degree to which the client perceived therapy as a process of personal exploration or as specific analysis of life-situations. Situational (1) to personal exploration (9)	3.5	6.1	2.6	.63
The Relationship				
4. The degree to which the client has used the relationship itself as a focus for therapy. Negligible extent (1) to maximal (9)	3.1	4.2	1.1	.20
5. Estimate of the client's attitude toward you during the course of therapy. Strong dislike (1) to strong liking or respect (9)	4.8	6.8	2.0	.78
6. Estimate of your feeling toward the client. Strong dislike (1) to strong liking or respect (9)	5.6	7.1	1.5	.65
The Outcome				
7. The degree of personal integration of the client. Highly disorganized or defensively organized (1) to optimally integrated (9)	3.1	5.5	2.4	.89
8. The life adjustment of the client. Low (1) to high (9)	3.8	6.3	2.5	.74
9. Degree of satisfaction of the client with the outcome of therapy. Strongly dissatisfied (1) to extremely satisfied (9)	....	6.2	....	.73
10. Your rating of the outcome of therapy. Complete failure (1) to marked success (9)	....	5.7	....	....

* All means in column (4) and all correlations in column (5) are significant at the 1 per cent level of probability, except for the mean and correlation for item 4. These are significant at the 5 per cent level.

on a nine-point scale. In general, the lower end of the scale means that the attribute existed to a minimal degree. It should be noted as a caution that all ratings were made by the counselor concerned with the particular case at the time the case closed. The data on which the ratings were based were, therefore, his own impressions and memory of the therapy as a whole. However, the ratings were made solely on the basis of the experience in the counseling hours. The counselor had no knowledge of any of the results of the tests which had been administered. Likewise, he had no knowledge of what the follow-up period might hold for the client. These limitations have both advantages and disadvantages.

In order to check on the reliability of the counselor judgments, seven of the cases were re-rated after a mean interval of five months. This is undoubtedly too long a time interval; it protects against memory of the earlier performance on the scale, but, in doing so, it may also obscure memory of the phenomena which need to be judged. However, the mean correlation between the judgments (using Fisher's normalizing transformation) was .81, indicating a fair degree of stability of the judgments.

III. THE RESULTS

The results of the counselor judgments will be presented in two ways. We shall first discuss the status scores and movement scores for the items and then present the data regarding intercorrelations between items and between other variables. The intercorrelations should be particularly helpful in finding out which aspects of process and relationship the counselors judge most relevant in their global "success" rating. Table 2 presents the beginning, end, and movement scores for each item. From the table we can make the following statements, remembering that at all times we are talking about counselor judgments:

1. For all items except item 4 (relationship) there was statistically significant movement. The result for item 4 indicates that there is relatively less probability of a change in the extent to which the client-counselor relationship is a focal point in therapy. However, even for this item there is some indication of change ($P < .05$).
2. At the beginning of therapy there is a much stronger emphasis on intellectual-cognitive processes than on emotional-experiential processes. By the end of therapy there is much closer balance between the two.

3. The most pronounced shift occurs in item 3—that is, the client was judged to see therapy more in terms of personal exploration and less in terms of situational analysis as therapy proceeded.
4. The items which rated highest at the end of therapy (items 5 and 6) indicate that a high degree of mutual liking and respect between counselor and client is judged to be characteristic of the end phase of therapy.
5. The sigma value of 2.0 for item 10 (success rating) indicates a considerable variability in judgment of success clustering around the mean value of 5.7. Actually, the ratings spanned the entire range of judged success from 1 to 9.

In the following section we shall use item 10 (success rating) as a criterion item and consider the correlates which may have a bearing on this rating. In effect we are asking, "What variables are related to the counselor's rating of success?" In addition to examining the correlation of item 10 with other items, we shall also consider the factors of age, sex, and length of therapy.

The relationship between judged success and the other items on the scale will indicate the factors which counselors consider relevant to their judgments. These correlations will be found in the last column of Table 2. All the correlations are significant at the 1 per cent level of probability except item 4. We can paraphrase the meaning of these correlations as follows: When a client is rated high in outcome, it is likely that *(a)* he has used therapy as emotional experience; *(b)* he has used therapy for personal rather than situational exploration; *(c)* he has liked and respected his therapist; *(d)* he has moved in the direction of both personal integration and situational adjustment; and *(e)* he is satisfied with the outcome of therapy. The result for item 4 was somewhat surprising, especially in view of the recent emphasis upon relationship in client-centered counseling. Our own informal prediction was that, where the client used the relationship itself as a focal point for therapy, greater change would be more likely. However, this turns out not to be the case. It should be pointed out that there is no implication that the relationship is not important, since the item deals only with explicit use of the relationship as a focus for therapy. The correlations for items 5 and 6 actually indicate that a positive relationship between counselor and client is related to judged success.

We shall consider now the relationship between judged success and the variables of age, sex, and case length. In order to test the relationship of age to judged success, the total sample was divided into "younger group" (age twenty-one to twenty-seven) and "older group" (age twenty-eight to forty). The mean success ratings for the subgroups were exactly equal, thus indicating that age within these limits has no bearing upon judged success. Regarding the variable of sex, the mean success rating for men was 5.0 and the mean for women was 6.7. This difference is significant at the 5 per cent level of probability and leads to a strong presumption that rated success for the women is significantly higher than that for the men ($P < .05$).[2]

For the judgments about case length, there is a trend in favor of higher success rating for longer cases. Further analysis shows that the shorter cases spanned the entire range of success ratings from 1 to 9, while the longer cases were judged to fall on two high points of the scale (points 7 and 8). The variability of ratings was significantly lower for the long-case group ($P < .01$). If these findings can be confirmed in further studies, they mean that, if a client is in therapy for at least twenty interviews, there is a strong assurance, as judged by the counselor, of gain from therapy.

2. Analysis of other outcome measures, Thematic Apperception Test (see chap. 8), and a self-description Q-sort measure (see chap. 5) confirm this finding. Two possibilities are raised as explanation of this outcome. Since all the counselors were men, the possibility must be considered that a heterosexual therapeutic relationship has a bearing on these results. This question cannot be answered here, but it must be tested by the use of a balanced design in which both men and women therapists counsel men and women clients.

A second possibility concerns the relative "therapeutic readiness" of men and women. In this connection, Dymond (2) found that women secured higher average scores than men on a test of empathy. Further, an armchair analysis of our culture suggests that, though women are held to stronger taboos than men in some respects, our society does accept emotional expression more readily in women than in men (*q.v.* the stereotype of the "strong silent man"). One can only conjecture as to whether these factors bear on the present results, but they point to the possibility at least that in our culture emotional expressivity and understanding are more readily available to women than to men.

One incidental question which may arise from the present results refers to the possibility of "transference cure," where changes might be ascribed to current client attitudes and needs in the relationship but are dependent upon continued relationship. The possibility finds little support in the results; the follow-up tests given six months to a year after therapy indicate that for the most part gains are maintained or increased during the interval where therapy has no longer continued.

This fact seems to make all the more important the search for the factors which militate against the client's continuation in therapy. Is it primarily a selective factor of motivation and/or personality organization, or a function of the early client-counselor interaction, or both? Studies now in progress on failure to help clients may later contribute answers to this question. Meanwhile it is still possible to make some analysis of this question in terms of counselor judgment by using item 7, which deals with personal integration of the client. Here we can ask the question, "Is rated success correlated with the client's initial status with regard to personal integration?" The correlation for this analysis for the experimental group is .08, indicating that the client's initial status makes no difference in the judged outcome of therapy. This absence of correlation is all the more striking in view of the large proportion of significant correlations throughout the scale.

There is a further analysis which yields more definite results. In addition to case ratings for our experimental group, we have case ratings for a group of thirteen clients who began therapy but who left before they had six interviews, the minimum for inclusion in the experimental groups. We compared the counselor judgments of initial personal integration for this "attrition" group and the experimental group and found that the attrition group was judged significantly higher in this respect. This analysis suggests that, for the range of clients which the Counseling Center receives, a client who is judged to be less optimally integrated is more likely to stay in therapy. In evaluating this result, we must bear in mind that the counselors had less opportunity to become acquainted with the attrition group and that the judgments were thus made on less evidence than for the experimental group. How this affects the accuracy of the judgments we cannot yet say.

IV. THE PROBLEM OF CROSS-VALIDATION

When a variable has been selected as a criterion measure, it remains to validate the measure through an independent estimate of the same phenomenon. In this sense we probably do not yet have a validity study of therapist judgments. The studies quoted earlier, which compare counselor judgment with other outcome measures of therapy, can be used as crude approximations of validity evidence, but they were not really designed to validate counselor judgment. Usually, as in this research, counselor judgments have been used as part of a series of criterion measures of therapy, and the only factor which the measures have shared in common is the fact that they were measuring aspects of the construct we call "personality." But this is a very inclusive construct, and it is probably multidimensional in nature. Thus if the counselor attended to one aspect of personality and a test to another, we might very well expect a low correlation between the two measures; and this fact would not provide us with validity information.

Conversely, the correlations which we do have are undoubtedly an underestimate of actual validity. What is required for a validity study is that we specify particular components of personality and behavior for which we wish to seek counselor judgment and then use independent measures of these variables. It is only when we have such comparable variables that we can check the validity of counselor judgment. Even this design assumes that we have checked the validity of the validating measure. Actually, we have so few instruments of known characteristics that, if we take this design seriously, we set in motion a regress of validation studies. Usually we must be content with congruence between measures as an indication that we are measuring a real phenomenon. The congruence of counselor judgments and other criteria has been pointed out in chapters 4 and 5. It will also be used in the following chapters.

V. SUMMARY

This study has examined counselor judgments of therapy for twenty-three of our research clients. It was noted that all ranges of judged success were present in the group and that as a group significant movement in therapy was rated on all items but one. Age and initial personality organization were uncorrelated with success rating within the experimental group; a group of clients who did not stay in therapy were judged to be more optimally integrated at the beginning of therapy than was the experimental group. Sex and, to some extent, length of therapy were differentiating variables in the success ratings, females and longer cases being relatively more successful.

REFERENCES

1. Carr, Arthur C. "An Evaluation of Nine Nondirective Psychotherapy Cases by Means of the Rorschach," *Journal of Consulting Psychology*, XIII (1949), 196–205.
2. Dymond, Rosalind F. "A Scale for the Measurement of Empathic Ability," *Journal of Consulting Psychology*, XIII (1949), 127–33.
3. Haimowitz, Natalie Reader. "An Investigation into Some Personality Changes Occurring in Individuals Undergoing Client-centered Therapy." Ph.D. dissertation, University of Chicago, 1948.
4. Jonietz, Alice K. "A Study of the Phenomenological Changes in Perception after Psychotherapy as Exhibited in the Content of Rorschach Percepts." Ph.D. dissertation, University of Chicago, 1950.
5. Mosak, Harold. "Evaluations in Psychotherapy: A Study of Some Current Measures." Ph.D. dissertation, University of Chicago, 1950.
6. Muench, George A. "An Evaluation of Nondirective Psychotherapy by Means of the Rorschach and Other Tests," *Applied Psychological Monographs*, XIII (1947), 1–163.
7. Raimy, Victor C. "Self-reference in Counseling Interviews," *Journal of Consulting Psychology*, XII (1948), 153–63.
8. Raskin, Nathaniel J. "Analysis of Six Parallel Studies of the Therapeutic Process," *Journal of Consulting Psychology*, XIII (1949), 206–20.

CHAPTER 8

Adjustment Changes over Therapy from Thematic Apperception Test Ratings

ROSALIND F. DYMOND

The problem of criteria measures for research in psychotherapy has already been discussed in chapters 2 and 3. The conclusion was drawn that for this project global ratings of the cases as "successful" or "unsuccessful" would be used but that they would not be the sole or most important ones. In contrast, specific changes, to be expected if therapy had taken place, would be hypothesized and tests designed for each. This paper will deal with the use of the Thematic Apperception Test (TAT) material as a criterion of adjustment and change in adjustment in therapy as compared to no-therapy cases.

Chapter 5 described the results obtained with an adjustment criterion derived from the self-descriptive Q-sorts. This study showed that the self-descriptions of those presenting themselves for therapy were significantly less well adjusted than those produced by the no-therapy control group. After therapy had been completed, the adjustment scores of the experimental subjects were significantly higher than their scores before therapy and not significantly different from those of the control group. The control group's adjustment scores showed no change over a period of time matched in length to that taken in therapy by the experimentals.

These results are, of course, open to all the usual objections to self-descriptive data: perhaps the clients *say* they are better, but are they "really"? The fact that the adjustment scores are significantly related to the counselor's rating of the success of the therapy does not fully answer this objection, since neither therapist nor client can be called an objective judge. The TAT study to be reported below was designed to check whether therapy cases are initially less well adjusted than the control sample and whether positive changes take place in the therapy group which do not occur without therapy and to get a more objective measure of the degree of adjustment or maladjustment of these subjects at the various testing points. This is a general study which is being followed by a very detailed investigation of the TAT records which is still in process.

I. METHOD

The regular twenty-card TAT, to which was added an additional picture of a group situation, was administered to all subjects in the first block (Block I) as part of the regular test battery. The experimental, or therapy, group took these tests before therapy began, at the close of the course of therapy, and six months after therapy had been concluded. The no-therapy control group was tested at the same time intervals to provide matched time samples. It was hypothesized that there were a number of scorable dimensions in these TAT records which should differentiate the experimentals who had applied for therapy from the controls who had not, as well as differentiate the records before and after therapy. Six of these variables were used in this study:

1. The ability of the hero to solve his own problems versus dependence on others or magical forces to do this.
2. The degree and quality of the creativity; well-developed fantasy and well-structured stories versus inability to form a story, sticking rigidly to the stimulus, or bizarre fantasy.
3. The quality of the emotions attributed to the characters; pleasant versus unpleasant, and the degree of control of these affect states displayed by the characters.
4. The kinds of interpersonal relations the subject depicts in his stories; constructive versus destructive interaction.
5. The degree of comfort versus disturbance of the heroes and the appropriateness of these states to the situational context.
6. The logic and mood tone of the story outcomes; happy, successful, or hopeful versus despair, failure, or indecision.

These six were not treated independently, however. A single composite rating was made for each record based on a seven-point scale with the following notations for the scale positions:

1. Severe disturbance bordering on psychotic or psychotic.
2. Severe neurotic problems with disorganization.
3. Acute neurotic problems but reality contact tenuously preserved.

4. Discomfort from problems severe enough to require therapy but ability to carry on.
5. Particular problems of some difficulty but social effectiveness maintained.
6. Only mild problems in essentially well-functioning person.
7. Well-integrated, happy person, socially effective.

Ninety-two records, coded so as to remove all identifying material, were included in this study. This made a group of records from which the rater could not tell whether they were tests of an experimental or a control person or whether they were taken at pre-therapy or post-therapy or follow-up time. This group actually included twenty-five pre-therapy, twenty-five post-therapy, and twenty-two follow-up records from experimental subjects and ten pre-therapy and ten post-therapy records from control subjects. These twenty-one story records were read and assigned a score from 1 to 7, holding the six variables in mind.

After these scores had all been entered, the tests were re-rated to provide an intrajudge reliability check. Only nine test ratings were changed one or more category. The reliability coefficient was .936.

When the records were decoded, it was found that there were nine experimental subjects and seven controls who received the same ratings at pre- and post-therapy times. The pile within which the two records of such a case fell was reread in an attempt to make a differentiation between the two ratings. For example, if a subject received a 4 rating on both his pre-therapy and his post-therapy TAT's, these were reread in the context of all the four ratings. Then if one of these fell at the high end of the 4 pile, it was assigned a 4+; if it fell at the low end of the 4 pile, it was assigned a 4−. Although these cases maintained the same score, a plus or minus was given where possible to show if any movement at all was discernible.

II. AN ILLUSTRATION

To illustrate how the ratings were made, three responses to card 11 are given below. They were all produced by the same experimental subject. The first is from the pre-therapy test, the whole of which was rated 4; the second is from the post-therapy test, which was rated 5; and the third is from the follow-up test, which was given a rating of 6.

Pre-therapy:

I'm not quite sure what this little figure is down here in the corner, but I'll call it a . . .[1] looks like a sort of a bug but with a face and a head. I imagine this has been, if this is supposed to be a fairy tale, I'll say this little figure down here has . . . at one time was a princess, and because she could not comply with the wishes of the kingdom—she refused to marry a man that the king, her father, wanted her to—a spell was cast over her, and she was put down in this cavern, canyon. Something in the background looks a bit like a tree, and yet on this side there is something that looks like a building or an edifice. We'll presume it's a cavern with trees growing in it and also a sort of housing situation to the right. The creature sticking its head out was at one time the man she wanted to marry, and he is . . . well, he's a sort of serpent-like person in appearance. Looks as though he might have a body though. In other words, not simply elongated. He's got webbed feet. And he is doomed to stay in this little cave and just look at her. He has rather a longing expression on his face. She must just sit there. Sounds as if I might have been influenced by Dante's *Inferno*. (*Laughs.*) Well, there they are, both spend the rest of their life that way. But, uh, there is somebody who is going to help them—being, optimistic maybe, but, uh, at some point, circumstances in this other world, that is, the world where their, her father is and the person who had done this to them, somebody there above this canyon, somebody up there, above this canyon, is going to do away with the king and find the magic hocus-pocus that will transform them back into, uh, garb that we call the garb of the human being, and let them get together.

Post-therapy:

Here we have a rocky road with a drop of many feet into some sort of chasm. Evidently . . . there's a slight . . . little bridge there in the archway, that leads to a, this castle. And, uh, this grasshopper or some sort of a cross between an animal or bug and, uh, (pause) might as well make it a woman, (pause) is attempting to get home. (Pause.) This creature coming out of the cave is watching and is very inter-interested, in a very interested fashion, because, uh, if this little bug gets home she will (pause) be able to claim the, uh, throne, she will become a human being. And, uh, he has been put under a spell of enchantment and is . . . this spell is not able to be broken until this particular princess gets reseated. It has been a long trip back for her, there have been many hardships in her way; and she is now about twenty feet from the door of the castle. Consequently he is very anxious about this, because before they were turned into these particular figures (pause) they had loved each other, (pause) and, uh, evidently he has retained his human being brain, because he is able to think about all this. (*Laughs.*) So he is rooting for her to get there, yet he is powerless to do anything about it. But, uh, (she'll) turn herself around and, uh, make these last twenty feet, and, uh, there'll be a wedding, uh, very shortly (*laughing*).

1. Three-dot ellipses (. . .) indicate a hesitation or very brief pause, while a longer pause is indicated in parentheses "(pause)."

Follow-up:

Today I seem to see this as a male and female symbol probably always had but it wasn't as promising before. (*Laughs.*) Well, this is some nice little serpent sort of animal, probably not so little, who is eyeing the rose bed for what he can see coming along. And a charming little beetle happens to be out for a stroll that day. The little beetle hears him whistle at her, looks over the situation. He seems to have a nice protected house; looks fairly intelligent; looks like he knew a good thing when he sees it. She decided to accept the whistle. However, she must somehow or other get herself changed into a . . . something more compatible for him to live with. So she takes a quick trip to a witch-craft village, gets herself transformed—there's a great symbol in this, after all (*laughs*)—comes back, and she is really just what he has been waiting to whistle at all these years. And what other conclusion is there but that they live happily ever after? (*Laughs.*)

In contrast we have the following story for the same card taken from a record which was rated 1.

Well, looks like Grand Canyon. Well, it looks like a mess. . . . I didn't really mean that. (*Laughs.*) Well, the reason I said that is simply because I could make a wonderful story with buildings. I all of a sudden looked at this little object here. Looks like there were two, possibly one or possibly two small figures like humans, males, bending over something like an oil can or something. But if that's the case it throws the proportion out completely. And this would have to be something huge. I mean, and it would have to be an immense bridge, and it looks like this is a small archway for a person of average height to go through. I mean, these would have to be two midgets or something, and this reminds me of a hair cut the Romans would wear, or something. I don't know what that's doing up there. But how could this be? I'll say that this is a huge wall with a moat. This could be a huge wall that a man could walk on. And these are two human figures here. There's an explosion in the background. There's a lot of rubble. This of course is reflected against this side of the wall. I don't know how it got there, but it's there. (*Laughs.*) This looks like the fin of a fish. And this looks like a galleon with men on it, or it could pass for a hat. Oh, there's a figure of a man there. I think he's running away too. That one standing still. There was a huge explosion in the background. Rubble here. Of course, this is from some previous explosion.

(Test Administrator: Could you make up a little story about it?)

Yah, well, big story or a little one? . . . (*Laughs.*) There was a little war. (*Laughs.*) And this is a siege of this particular place. Abou ben Adhem's harem. Oh, its just a terrible fight here. And rubble is flying all around and huge clouds of smoke rising. And they got the ammunition stock. (*Laughs.*) 'Course, I don't know how they got an ammunition dump in his time, but there was one. (*Laughs.*) And these two people here are . . . they've got the remnants of a cannon on the wall. Oh, it blew up or something. And they're just hiding behind it. This figure here is running across, and all of a sudden a flash and the ammunition comes. And it looks like it will be very bloody. And it looks like they're storming the fortress, so I think it will fall, and if you have floating ships, I guess when you have things like that, you usually can't help it in a war. (*Laughs.*) Because I don't know what that is. And it's just that . . . track it down. Well, that's enough. I'm glad I did it. That picture always confuses me. I'm trying to figure out, and I can't even seem to figure out what's in it.

III. RESULTS

Table 1 gives the distribution of the rankings for the two groups at the different times. It will be noted that only twenty-two of the twenty-five experimental cases had follow-up tests at the time this analysis was done.

TABLE 1

TAT RATINGS OF EXPERIMENTAL AND CONTROL GROUPS

Group	Ratings							Mean
	1	2	3	4	5	6	7	
Experimental:								
Pre-therapy	1	5	4	13	2	....	....	3.4
Post-therapy	1	3	3	9	6	3	....	4.0
Follow-up	1	2	3	8	5	3	....	4.0
Control:								
Pre-therapy	....	....	1	4	....	5	....	4.9
Post-therapy	....	....	2	1	2	5	....	5.0

The differences between the means were then tested for significance. The difference between the experimental and the control group means at pre-therapy was significant at the 1 per cent level using *t*, although it is interesting to note that there was some overlap in these two groups. If position 4 is taken as the place at which the problems, as seen by the TAT reader, were severe enough to require therapy, two of the pre-therapy experimental group were above this point, and five of the controls were at or below it. The difference between the experimental and control groups at post-therapy time was not significant, the probability being 10 per cent that this was a chance difference. The difference between the pre- and post-therapy means of the experimental group was significant at the 1 per cent level using *t* for correlated means. Obviously there was no significant change from post-therapy to follow-up, nor was there any difference from pre- to post-therapy in the control group. The difference between the pre- to post-therapy change in the experimental group as against this change in the control group is also significant at the 1 per cent level.

Since the increase in adjustment of the experimental group involves a movement from a low pre-therapy average toward the mean of the scale at post-therapy, the question might be raised: Can this result be attributed to regression? This question does not seem to be a defensible one, as the ratings of all the tests were made at the same time. In this way, if nothing but regression were at work, an extremely low post-therapy score has as much chance of regressing toward the mean at pre-therapy as an extremely low pre-therapy has of regressing at post-therapy. Therefore, these two possible effects would cancel out. In fact, though, the proportion of the total group receiving low ratings (1–3) on the pre-therapy tests who moved one or more points in a positive direction was 54.5 per cent. This was not significantly different from the proportion who moved one or more points in a plus direction whose initial ratings were high (4–7), 41.6 per cent.

In sum, then, the TAT records of those presenting themselves for therapy were judged blindly to be more disturbed than those of a control group. Over the course of therapy there was a significant change for the experimental group as a whole in a positive direction, which does not occur in a control group over a matched time interval. This change cannot be accounted for by regression of the low scores to the mean.

To turn briefly now from the group to individual changes, twenty of the twenty-five experimental subjects were given higher ratings on their post-therapy than on their pre-therapy records. (This included the plus ratings within the same category as well as the actual positive category changes.) In contrast the number of control subjects who changed positively is four out of ten. The proportion of changes from lower to higher ratings is significant for the experimental group only.

It seems that the two criterion measures, the Q-adjustment score and the TAT ratings, gave similar results. How are these two related? A product-moment correlation of the Q-adjustment and the TAT ratings on the thirty-five subjects at pre-therapy was .63 and at post-therapy .47, both of which are significant. Table 2 compares the degree of change on the two measures from pre- to post-therapy. A chi-square test correcting for small numbers is significant at better than the 5 per cent level, showing that the two criteria demonstrate change of the same extent and direction.

Another confirmation of these changes comes from the Q-studies. Taking the correlation of the subject's self-descriptive sorting and his sort to describe the person he would most like to be as a measure of his internal tension (see chap. 4), there is a marked tendency for this correlation to be very low before therapy, showing dissatisfaction with self to be high. This correlation typically increases after therapy has been completed. Plotting the changes in self-ideal correlation and TAT adjustment (see Table 3), we find marked congruence in change on these two indexes. Twenty of the

TABLE 2

COMPARISON OF CHANGE ON THE Q-ADJUSTMENT AND TAT SCORES FROM PRE- TO POST-THERAPY
($P = .05$)

Q-ADJUSTMENT CHANGE	TAT CHANGE	
	Low (−1 and 0)	High (+1 and +2)
Low (−19 to +4)	13	4
High (+5 to +23)	6	12

TABLE 3

CHANGE IN SELF-IDEAL CORRELATION AND TAT SCORES FROM PRE- TO POST-THERAPY
($N=34$; $E_x=24$; Control$=10$)

SELF-IDEAL CHANGE	TAT CHANGE		
	Negative	Zero	Positive
Negative	2	0	0
Zero (not more than + or − .10)	1	5	2
Positive	0	11	13

thirty-four cases show similar change in the two measures. The proportion of agreement is significantly greater than that anticipated on the basis of chance.

The correlation of the post-therapy TAT ratings and the counselor's rating of the success of the therapy was .40. However, the correlation of the TAT ratings at follow-up and the counselor's rating was .49. This finding suggests that the test picture of the subject lags slightly behind the therapist's view of him as reflected in his rating of the case. It is also demonstrated in a slightly different analysis using a chi-square technique with Yates's correction, as seen in Tables 4 and 5.

It seems that the counselor's rating of the case is a better predictor of how the client will appear in six months on the TAT than how he appears at the close of therapy and also of how much he will change over the total period, not just during the pre- to

TABLE 4

COUNSELOR JUDGMENT OF SUCCESS AND TAT RATING CHANGES FROM PRE- TO POST-THERAPY

($P = .10$)

Counselor Judgment	TAT Changes	
	No Change and Negative Change	Change of +1 and +2
Low success (1–6)	9	6
High success (7–9)	2	8

TABLE 5

COUNSELOR JUDGMENT OF SUCCESS AND TAT RATING CHANGES FROM PRE-THERAPY TO FOLLOW-UP

($P = .05$)

Counselor Judgment	TAT Changes	
	No Change and Negative Change	Change of +1 and +2
Low success (1–6)	8	4
High success (7–9)	2	8

post-therapy interval. One possible explanation of this is that the processes of reorganization which are set in motion during the course of therapy do not cease with the close of the formal interviews. The estimate of these ongoing processes of reorganization seems to be one of the components in the counselor's judgment of the success of the case.

It has been reported in chapter 7 that there is a significant difference in counselor ratings of success of the therapy of male and female clients, the female clients being judged as having more successful therapy, and in chapter 5 that female clients change more on the Q-adjustment score. Are these results corroborated by a difference in improvement and end-of-therapy status on the

TABLE 6

SEX DIFFERENCES ON TAT RATINGS

Sex	Pre-therapy Mean Rating	Post-therapy Mean Rating	Follow-up Mean Rating
Male ($N=12$).....	3.0	3.5	3.3
Female ($N=10$)...	3.7	4.7	4.9

TAT? Table 6 compares the mean TAT ratings of male and female clients at the different testing points.

The difference in the male and female mean score is not significant at pre-therapy time using t. However, the differences between male and female mean scores is significant at the 5 per cent level at post-therapy and at the 1 per cent level at follow-up time. Both the male and the female group means increase in adjustment significantly over the therapy period though, and neither increases from post-therapy to follow-up. If the entire test period from pre-therapy through follow-up is taken as a unit, the females as a group improve significantly, and the males do not. While it would be amusing to speculate about possible explanations of this finding, it must be recalled, before rushing to any conclusions, that all but one of these subjects were counseled by men. If this result holds when female clients are counseled by females, the explanation would be of one character, whereas, if it develops that men counseled by women show more improvement than men counseled by other men, quite a different hypothesis would be demanded. In a subsequent block of research (Block IV) there will be a sufficient number of each of these four combinations to give some possibility of handling this puzzle.

IV. SUMMARY

This chapter has reported an over-all look at the comparative changes in the TAT's of twenty-five experimental subjects who had therapy and ten controls who did not. From the blind rating of the ninety-two records reported above, the following general statements can be added to our pool of knowledge about these clients.

1. The pre-therapy records of the therapy group were rated significantly lower on a seven-point scale of mental health than those of the no-therapy control group.
2. The post-therapy records of those who had therapy were rated significantly higher than their pre-therapy tests.
3. The post-therapy records of the control group were not rated as significantly different from their pre-therapy tests.
4. The post-therapy tests of the experimental group were not significantly different from the post-therapy records of the control group.
5. The TAT and the Q-adjustment measures were found to be significantly related in terms both of level of adjustment score and of degree of change evidenced on the two.
6. The TAT change was also paralleled by the change in self-ideal Q-sort correlations.
7. The post-therapy TAT ratings were significantly related to the counselors' judgment of the success of the cases. Also the change in adjustment on the TAT from pre-therapy to follow-up was significantly related to the counselors' success ratings.
8. The significant sex difference in favor of female clients found on the counselor judgment of success of therapy and in change on the Q-adjustment score was confirmed by a significant difference in favor of females on the TAT ratings at post-therapy.

V. CONCLUSIONS

The clients who took part in this research have now been found to be less well adjusted before therapy than after on several different kinds of measures—their own self-descriptions (see chap. 4), a scoring of these by an external adjustment criterion (see chap. 5), the judgment of the therapists (see chap. 7)—and now this is again found on a blind rating of their TAT records. In this study the no-therapy control group was again discovered to be significantly better adjusted than the client group before their therapy and not significantly different from them after their therapy had been completed. The TAT ratings agreed with the counselors' estimation of the success of the therapy, with the adjustment scoring of their self-descriptive Q-sorts in terms both of score and of degree of change in adjustment, and with the change in the correlation of their self and ideal sortings.

CHAPTER 9

Changes over Client-centered Therapy Evaluated on Psychoanalytically Based Thematic Apperception Test Scales[1]

DONALD L. GRUMMON AND EVE S. JOHN

The title of this chapter may seem puzzling to some. Why would instruments based upon psychoanalytic theory be used to examine the outcomes of client-centered therapy? This study, as it evolved, departs from the original plan followed by the other studies carried out on the first block (Block I) of cases. The initial plan was to assess changes in personality and integration in terms of concepts imbedded in client-centered theory, and one such study using the Thematic Apperception Test (TAT) has been reported in the preceding chapter. However, it is also of interest to know whether client-centered therapy brings about the type of changes which psychoanalytic theory hypothesizes should occur when therapy is successful. The opportunity for throwing light on this question seemed favorable, since the junior author of this chapter is psychoanalytically oriented and is accustomed to thinking in psychoanalytic terms. It was this author who constructed the instrument used in the study about to be reported—an instrument based upon classical psychoanalytic theory.

I. SUBJECTS AND PROCEDURES

The design for this project was the same as that of the other Block I studies (see chap. 3). The TAT records of both experimental and control subjects were used.

Overview of the Design

The stories told by the subjects were recorded and transcribed and then coded so that both the subjects (control or experimental)

1. The writers appreciate the considerable help they have received from Galatia Halkides, Edward Katz, and Jack Saporta.

and the point of administration (wait, pre-therapy, post-therapy, or follow-up) were concealed.

To provide a quantitative measure of mental health status, a series of twenty-three seven-point rating scales were constructed that could be used by a trained clinician in evaluating the TAT. These scales enable the clinician to quantify his judgments and yet leave him free to examine the TAT in pretty much the usual clinical fashion. A later section describes the scales in detail.

Two judges did all the ratings of the TAT protocols. However, all the judgments for the experimental group were made by one judge—Judge J. Both judges worked on the remaining protocols.

Subjects

Our *experimental (E) group* consists of twenty-three clients who remained in therapy for at least six interviews and usually much longer. For the most part the experimental group was randomly selected from the larger group of clients seeking help at the Counseling Center of the University of Chicago; however, several factors operated to eliminate some of our experimental subjects: (*a*) incomplete data due to technical or clerical errors; (*b*) failure to obtain post-therapy measures; and (*c*) the necessity of beginning the statistical analysis before some of the clients had completed their therapy. The first factor eliminating experimental subjects is unselective. The second factor tends to eliminate subjects who probably gained less from therapy than the average client; but the third factor may eliminate clients who are more successful than the average.

Nine of our experimental subjects form a subgroup called the *own-control (O-C) group*. These are the subjects who received the test battery, waited sixty days, retook the test battery, and then began their therapy.

A control group, here called the *equivalent-control (E-C) group*, consists of persons who were not seeking psychotherapy but who were paid as subjects for "a research investigating personality." Each equivalent-control subject took the test battery at intervals comparable to those of a matched (crudely so) experimental subject.

Unfortunately, there was a considerable time lag in collecting the equivalent-control data, since the selecting and testing of an equivalent-control subject did not begin until the experimental subject had completed his therapy. Therefore, we can here report data for only sixteen equivalent-control subjects through the post-tests and for only nine equivalent-control subjects through the follow-up tests. The sixteen subjects will be referred to as the *E-C-1* group and the nine subjects as the *E-C-2* group.

II. THE RATING SCALES USED TO ASSESS MENTAL HEALTH

Description of the Scales

The rating scales were constructed to meet the need for a quantitative measure of mental health which would be directly related to psychoanalytic concepts and which could be applied to TAT materials. Twenty-three scales were devised for use by the rater, and from these scales two additional measures are derived, bringing the total number of measures to twenty-five:

Attitudes toward relations with significant people:
1. Attitude toward mother
2. Attitude toward father
3. Attitude toward siblings
4. Attitude toward mate
5. Attitude toward offspring

Self-attitudes:
6. Self-concept
7. Ideal self
8. Insight into self and others

Attitudes toward society:
9. Attitude toward superiors
10. Attitude toward subordinates
11. Attitude toward peers

Attitudes toward major areas of life:
12. Attitude toward sexual activities
13. Attitude toward work
14. Attitudes toward social and community activities
15. Attitudes toward intellectual activities

Psychodynamics:
16. Level of satisfaction source
17. Level of threat
18. Level of defense

Additional dimensions of personality:
19. Intellectual endowment level
20. Functional intelligence level
21. Energy level

Summary descriptions:
22. Degree of adjustment
23. Diagnostic impression

Derived measures:
24. Average of Scales 1–18
25. Scale 20 *minus* Scale 19

For the moment, we will not consider Scales 19, 20, 21, and 22. All the remaining scales are based on the assumptions that (*a*) the means of viewing and relating to various people or things are limited in number and that (*b*) these means are primarily derived from the behavior patterns which were established during growth through the seven stages of psychosexual development: estranged from reality (autistic), dependent (oral-sucking), idealizing and grasping (oral-biting), destructive (anal-expulsive), conservative and possessive (anal-retentive), competitive (phallic), and realistic (genital).

Thus each scale is a seven-point rating scale, with each point being described in terms of the characteristic attitudes found in one of the stages of psychosexual development. A lengthy manual (3) was prepared which outlined the kinds of behaviors that were intended to be described by each point on the scale. We cannot reproduce the entire manual, but illustrative material will be helpful to the reader.

SCALE 1. RELATIONSHIP TO MOTHER

1. Views mother in an acceptant fashion, forming his judgment of her on the basis of her actual characteristics, i.e., on the basis of her actions toward him in the reality of today. Has some recognition of her close ties to him but essentially is independent and mature in his relations with her. Where she is dependent upon him, he assumes responsibilities for her care in a manner which does not endanger his own freedom or happiness.
2. Views his mother as a sexual object, a competitor on equal par with other women he knows. Consequently, he vies for her recognition of him as a man, as a masculine sex object. This may take the form of using her as a club over his wife's or other women's heads, e.g., "My mother still weighs the same as she did when she got married, darling. Why don't you see if you can just cut out candies for a while." Where the subject is a woman, she views her mother as a competitor with her for the attention of her male peers, or she feels that only by cooking better than her mother, having prettier children, etc., can she ever win out in the competitive struggle she sees as taking place between the two. Essentially this is the tie so frequently referred to as the "unresolved Oedipus complex."
3. Views the mother as someone who desires to possess him or control him in his decision and actions, or he attempts to control and possess her. Here is the nagging mother who is "only thinking of her child's welfare," or the child who doesn't permit the mother any freedom because of an attitude of: "I'd be utterly lost if anything ever happened to you, mother dear, through my neglect."
4. Views his mother as someone who's "out for blood," or else as someone whom he'd like to rip apart and destroy. In denial of this enmity there may appear to be only milder affections expressed between the two; however,

where other attitudes derived from the other stages are not manifested, it must be assumed that such quasi-love is only what is left when hate is denied.

5. Views his mother as his "ideal." This is not as a sexual competitor with other women, as in stage 2, but rather as a portrait of the "perfect woman." She is dichotomized into either the Madonna type or the Magdalene, and each aspect, the sacred and the profane, is kept well isolated from the other. Essentially, the mother is the earliest identification of the subject, the first basis of his own ideal self, and he still retains this earliest identification without modification. The Madonna is the good mother who is always perfectly giving and kind. The bad mother is a witch who never gives, who always seduces and then doesn't gratify, who can be forced to give nothing other than poisonous milk, pain, and frustration.
6. Views his mother primarily in terms of dependency. He may see her only as rejecting his dependency wants or as the font of all milk and honey from whom he may drink. He views her rejection of his dependency wants as punishment for *his* worthlessness; this is therefore different from stage 5, where she rejects him because *she* is a witch.
7. The subject is utterly estranged from his mother and conceives of her only as an omnipotent figure within his own megalomanic fantasies. Here the indifference is true barrenness and sterility—to be contrasted with the repression of sexuality in stage 2 or the denial of hostility as in stage 4. The subject truly perceives nothing outside his own fantasy world, and the mother is never related to in reality.

The directions just presented are in many ways typical of the directions for the first fifteen scales. Scales 16, 17, and 18 are somewhat different, and so we present another illustration.

SCALE 16. LEVEL OF SATISFACTION SOURCE

The rater, in judging the subject on this scale, is attempting to answer the question: "Which needs are being met by reality for this individual; what constitutes the major proportion of his satisfactions?"

The rater is rating the subject only on the basis of the satisfactions he does get in reality. He will not be judging the subject's aspirations, which have already been dealt with on Scale 7, the self-concept.

Where a particular satisfaction serves as a defense against some threat or even serves as a threat to the individual, it will nevertheless be here viewed as a satisfaction. Subsequent scales provide for the rating of threats and of defenses.

1. The preponderance of satisfactions gained by this individual involve the subject's having attained a genital psychosexual organization, high self-esteem from his own integrity, and respect for the integrity of those with whom he associates. Direct satisfaction comes from interpersonal relations which express love and respect and from work and other activities which serve as adequate release for both aggression and sex. Direct discharge of sexual impulse into a partner of the opposite sex is possible only in a setting of mutual love and respect. His satisfactions serve to give him a sense of self-continuity and of continuity with his culture by permitting him to be creatively productive. His creativity involves a supportive attitude toward his products, and he is able to extend his attitude toward his offspring and toward other people around him who are less mature than he. Satisfactions of earlier needs are permitted but do not constitute the end-of-being for the individual. When reality demands that needs not be gratified, temporary suppression or sublimation can defend the individual against the emergence of the impulse.
2. The major satisfactions for this individual come from the physical, motoric, and intellectual exercises which serve to increase his self-esteem by allowing a feeling of successful mastery of self and of environment. It is the mastery pleasure which is paramount, and the display of such mastery—not the more adult comforts and joys which such mastery enables the individual to gain later in maturity. Education, relaxations, and heterosexual and homosexual contacts are heavily loaded with competitive strivings and are pleasurable only for the joy of victory in meeting this competition successfully and in exhibiting such success. Interest in aesthetics, athletics, dancing, acting, and "being on the make" are all forms of gaining satisfactions for the needs of this period.
3. The major gratifications for this individual come from possessing and owning. He collects; he is extremely concerned with questions of ownership, cleanliness, order, etc.; and he is happy when viewing his possessions, when making order, when implementing and following the rules of the game. This score will be rated when the TAT indicates that possession and control by possession are the major sources of gratification for the subject.
4. The major source of joy and gratification for this individual is found in being able to express aggression. His need is to keep himself from being belittled, and thus satisfaction comes from destruction of the threatening object which seeks to make the self smaller. This score will be rated where the solutions of stories take the form of aggressive destruction of the immediate impediments in the way of the hero, or where manual destructive activities, interest in the plastic arts, or actual temper outbursts are seen as satisfaction sources.
5. The major gratifications for this individual are gained from satisfaction of the need to possess an object by introjection of its image. Such sources are witty sarcasm, argumentation, thirst for knowledge, etc. Gratifications come from obtaining an object after aggressively seeking for it, identifying one's self with it, and then pulling it inside of the self in imagery. No longer is the object viewed as outside of the self. The basic drive is to increase the part of the world which can be called "self," and thus satisfactions are any introjected

objects. It follows from this that anything which appears as the embodiment of these introjected images will also serve as a satisfaction; therefore, anything which may serve as an ideal is always a source of satisfaction.

6. The major gratifications for this individual come from being given succorence and nurturence, being allowed to cling to other people for support, being warmed and stimulated and generally taken care of without having to make any effort to gain these ends. Smoking, epicureanism, singing, etc., may all be forms of satisfactions which involve giving to the self those things which are really desired from others.
7. This individual gains no *real* satisfactions—rather his joy comes from acting out his fantasies of omnipotence or from being allowed to engage in autism. Acting out may provide some actual reality satisfactions, but the subject only accepts the gratifications as proof of his omnipotence. Writing highly autistic literature, stock-market maneuvers, some executive positions, etc., allow for such acting-out. Active delusions and hallucinations also are sources of satisfaction. The essence of this level is that reality is negated—only fantastic gains are appreciated as satisfactions.

The first eighteen scales are looked at individually and also as a unit by computing the average rating on these scales. Another way of summarizing this material is to let the clinician make a subjective summary judgment, as in Scale 23. Scale 23 is a continuum of psychiatric diagnoses which are given explicit meanings in terms of the psychoanalytic conceptions of psychopathology. The rater is answering the question, "Which of the following diagnostic terms best describe this individual in view of his present conflicts and their etiology?"

1. Situational conflict in a healthy adult
   Anxiety state
2. Anxiety hysteria
   Conversion hysteria
3. Compulsion
   Phobia
4. Obsession
   Rumination
5. Involutional psychosis
   Paranoia
   Paranoid psychosis
6. Manic psychosis
   Drug addictions
   Psychosomatic disease
   Depressive psychosis
7. Catatonic psychosis
   Hebephrenic psychosis
   Simple schizophrenia

A misunderstanding may arise on Scale 23 about the meaning of points 5, 6, and 7, which, for the most part, define psychotic conditions. A rating on, say, point 7 means that the psychodynamics are of the schizophrenic variety; the rating does not necessarily mean that the subject is psychotic in the sense of requiring custodial care in an institution.

The remaining scales (19, 20, 21, and 22) do not deal directly with psychoanalytic concepts. Scales 19, 20, and 21 assess on a seven-point continuum certain features of personal make-up that have relevance to adjustive capacities. Scale 19 rates intellectual endowment as it would be defined by the Wechsler-Bellevue. Scale 20 rates functional intelligence, and of course the difference between the ratings on 19 and 20 is of interest in our study. Scale 21 rates energy level.

Scale 22 is a summary scale like No. 23, but here the rater attempts to answer the question, "How well adjusted is this individual in terms of *overt* behavior aimed at meeting the demands of the society about him?" This scale takes into account that an individual may live out, say, delusions of grandeur in such a way that society considers him well adjusted. Conversely, a person who is nosologically neurotic, not psychotic, may be unable to maintain good health, marry, hold a job, etc.

In concluding this general description of the scales, we want to comment on the mathematical properties of our measures. We can rank subjects relative to their mental health status, but we have no sound basis for assuming equal intervals between each of the seven points of the scales. That is, it cannot be assumed that the growth represented by the distance between autism and dependency is equivalent to the growth represented by the distance between competitiveness and maturity. To meet this difficulty, we have made liberal use of nonparametric statistics in analyzing our data. At other times, we have used statistical procedures which rest on assumptions not fully met by our data (e.g., the t test and the average of ratings on Scales 1 through 18). By way of justification for the latter procedures, we can cite practical considerations and an empirical finding of no essential difference in results on several occasions when both parametric and nonparametric procedures were used.

Reliability

We have a threefold problem of reliability: interjudge reliability, intrajudge reliability, and the stability over time of the picture presented by the subject taking the TAT. Information about stability as it interacts with judge reliability is contained in the data presented for the equivalent-control group in Section III, "Results." Interjudge and intrajudge reliability will be considered here.

Twelve clinical psychologists, including the two psychologists serving as judges for the research proper, were given the TAT protocols of a stratified sample of five persons who formed part of the clinical population at a psychiatric clinic in a large Chicago hospital. All twelve judges made independent ratings on Scales 22 and 23, but, for reasons of personal convenience to the co-operating clinical psychologists, as few as five judgments were used for some of the remaining scales. The coefficient of concordance (W) was computed for each scale, together with S and its appropriate confidence level (4). The agreement between judges was significant at the 1 per cent level or better for all scales except Scale 11, where agreement was significant at only the 5 per cent level.

The percentage of ratings falling at the mode was also computed for these data. Out of a total of 459 judgments, 59 per cent fell at the mode, 79 per cent deviated from the mode by one point or less, and only a small percentage deviated by more than two points.

An additional reliability study was undertaken for the two judges used in this research. These two judges re-rated twenty-three protocols after an interval of at least six months and for most of the protocols after a year. The rank-order correlations[2] between the judgments on the three summary measures are: Scale 22, .33; Scale 23, .77; and the average of Scales 1 through 18, .77. Clearly, their judgments on Scale 22 were so unreliable as to be of little value; therefore, we have made less use of this scale than was originally planned. The reliability coefficients for the other two summary measures are roughly of the same magnitude as those reported for other scoring systems applied to the TAT.

A summary of all the reliability data available for the two judges used in the study indicates that about 80–90 per cent of their ratings (considering both inter- and intrajudge reliability) will not vary more than one scale point. However, some differences are found between the scales and between the two judges. For example,

2. All the correlations computed for this study use the standard formula for rho except that Kendall's (4) *b* formula was used when many ties were present.

Judge J (who did all the ratings on the experimental group) is very unreliable on Scale 22 but does quite well on Scale 23; however, Judge K is more reliable on Scale 22 than on Scale 23.

The reliability findings are essentially the same as those reported for other scoring systems applied to the TAT. Our reliability is not very satisfactory, but it does seem sufficient to make the study worth while.

Validity

One sometimes wonders if a research of the kind undertaken here is not as much a validity study of the projective technique as it is an investigation of therapeutic outcomes. Nevertheless, we do have some independent evidence regarding the validity of the TAT rating scales.

The five patients from the psychiatric clinic of a Chicago hospital had been in psychotherapy with a psychiatrist for at least a year. The psychiatrist employed the rating scales to describe these persons, using all the information he had about them, including complete medical histories and intelligence-test scores. The pooled judgments of the clinical psychologists were then correlated (using rho) with the psychiatrist's judgments. Perfect agreement was found on fifteen of the scales, a correlation of .90 on an additional six scales, and a correlation of .60 on the remaining two scales (Nos. 3 and 7). Because of the extremely small N, a correlation of .90 is required to reach the 5 per cent level of confidence.

Correlations were also obtained between the psychiatrist and Judge J (the judge who did the ratings on the experimental subjects). Rho was 1.0 for fifteen scales, .90 for one scale, and .70 or less for seven scales. In this analysis Judge J again showed an inability to use Scale 22 as indicated by a rho of .50; however, the correlation was 1.0 on the other summary scale, No. 23.

Another question to be raised about validity is whether the different points on the scales are properly ordered along a continuum of mental health; that is, does, say, point 4 indicate better mental health than point 6. This question is of some significance, since several persons (including one of the writers) with a nonpsychoanalytic orientation have argued that a different ordering is appropriate for some of the scales. In this study, however, we are assessing mental health as it is defined by psychoanalytic theory, and we do have evidence that the ordering of the scale points is in accordance with this viewpoint. Three psychologists of established reputations, holding essentially the psychoanalytic orientation, agreed with the ordering used in this study.

III. RESULTS

The presentation of results will be divided into four sections: (*a*) the direction of changes for each individual scale; (*b*) comparisons between the experimental and the equivalent-control groups with respect to the difference in their mean changes on the two reliable summary measures (Scale 23 and the average of 1–18); (*c*) comparison of the changes over the wait and the therapy periods for the own-control group; and (*d*) the correlations between the mental health ratings and other measures of therapeutic outcome available for these same subjects.

Direction of Change on Each Scale

Our first treatment of the data looks at the direction of change over therapy for each of the twenty-five different measures. To assess the significance of these changes, we have employed the sign test (1, chap. 17) which makes no mathematical assumptions not justified by the data.[3]

Table 1 presents for both the experimental and the control groups the number of subjects making favorable, unfavorable, or no change over the therapy period. Table 2 presents the same results for the changes between the pre-therapy and the follow-up points. In interpreting the tables, the reader should bear in mind that a decrease in scale value represents an increase in mental health status.

From the *P* values presented in these tables it can be seen that the therapy has brought about in the experimental group a favorable change in mental health that is significant at the 5 per cent level of confidence, or better, for a majority of the scales. This find-

3. The *P* values reported throughout this study are based upon one-tailed tests. The one-tailed test is appropriate for the experimental group because previous research in the area justifies a directional hypothesis. The one-tailed test is not appropriate for the control data, but we have used it as an aid to the reader in comparing the experimental and the control groups.

ing holds whether we consider just the therapy period or the period between pre-therapy and follow-up.

These positive findings take on additional significance when we examine those scales which show only minimal change. In most instances these are the measures on which change might least be expected: intellectual endowment, energy level, life-adjustment (because of low reliability), functional intelligence, and functional intelligence minus intellectual endowment. If we eliminate these

TABLE 1

DIRECTION OF CHANGES ON ALL SCALES BETWEEN PRE-THERAPY AND POST-THERAPY

Scale	E Group (N=23)				E-C-1 Group (N=16)			
	No. Changing			*P* Value of Difference	No. Changing			*P* Value of Difference
	0	+	−		0	+	−	
1. Mother	9	3	11	.05	4	5	7	*
2. Father	10	3	10	.05	7	3	6	*
3. Siblings	13	1	9	.025	4	4	8	*
4. Mate	12	5	6	*	6	3	7	*
5. Offspring	9	4	10	.125	7	3	6	*
6. Self-concept	9	3	11	.05	5	3	8	.125
7. Ideal self	13	2	8	.125	2	5	9	*
8. Self and others	13	1	9	.025	4	5	7	*
9. Superiors	10	2	11	.025	6	4	6	*
10. Subordinates	12	3	8	.125	6	2	8	.125
11. Peers	12	2	9	.05	6	2	8	.125
12. Sexual activities	9	7	7	*	6	2	8	.125
13. Work	10	1	12	.005	6	4	6	*
14. Social and community	10	3	10	.05	4	4	8	*
15. Intellectual activity	9	3	11	.05	6	3	7	*
16. Satisfaction source	11	4	8	*	4	4	8	*
17. Threat level	12	2	9	.05	10	2	4	*
18. Defense level	10	2	11	.025	6	3	7	*
19. Intellectual endowment	20	1	2	*	11	3	2	*†
20. Functional intelligence	15	3	5	*	8	3	5	*
21. Energy level	11	5	7	*	4	3	9	*
22. Life adjustment	11	5	7	*	3	3	10	.125
23. Diagnostic impression	12	1	10	.025	6	3	7	*
24. Average of Scales 1–18	0	5	18	.025	0	7	9	*
25. Scale 20 *minus* Scale 19	17	2	4	*	12	0	4	.125

* *P* value larger than .125.

† Change shows decrement in mental health status.

five measures, about three-fourths of the remaining scales show changes that are favorable at the 5 per cent level or better.

Also supporting the value of these findings is the fact that the changes are in the predicted direction in every instance save for Scale 21, energy level, on the pre-therapy to follow-up comparison.

Looking at the control group, we find, as expected, little evidence of change. This is particularly true of the period from pre-therapy to follow-up (Table 2), where the changes are completely random.

TABLE 2

DIRECTION OF CHANGES ON ALL SCALES BETWEEN PRE-THERAPY AND FOLLOW-UP

Scale	E Group ($N=23$)				E-C-2 Group ($N=9$)			
	No. Changing			*P* Value of Difference	No. Changing			*P* Value of Difference
	0	+	−		0	+	−	
1. Mother	9	3	11	.05	3	3	3	*
2. Father	10	4	9	*	3	3	3	*
3. Siblings	12	2	9	.05	2	3	4	*
4. Mate	12	5	6	*	4	4	1	*†
5. Offspring	10	4	9	*	1	4	4	*
6. Self-concept	9	3	11	.05	5	2	2	*
7. Ideal self	10	3	10	.05	3	3	3	*
8. Self and others	10	1	12	.005	3	4	2	*†
9. Superiors	9	2	12	.025	2	4	3	*†
10. Subordinates	9	3	11	.05	1	4	4	*
11. Peers	12	2	9	.05	3	2	4	*
12. Sexual activities	10	3	10	.05	3	4	2	*†
13. Work	10	3	10	.05	3	3	3	*
14. Social and community	6	3	14	.025	4	2	3	*
15. Intellectual activity	8	6	9	*	2	4	3	*†
16. Satisfaction source	8	4	11	.125	1	4	4	*
17. Threat level	8	3	12	.05	3	4	2	*†
18. Defense level	10	2	11	.025	3	5	1	.125†
19. Intellectual endowment	20	1	2	*	6	2	1	*†
20. Functional intelligence	14	4	5	*	5	4	0	.125†
21. Energy level	10	8	5	*†	4	4	1	*†
22. Life-adjustment	7	6	10	*	1	4	4	*
23. Diagnostic impression	11	1	11	.005	2	5	2	*†
24. Average of Scales 1–18	2	7	14	.125	1	5	3	*†
25. Scale 20 *minus* Scales 19	16	3	4	*	4	3	2	*†

* *P* value larger than .125.

† Change shows decrement in mental health status.

A further examination of the tables reveals that, even though the changes are generally significant for the group considered collectively, still on nearly all the scales almost half of the clients fail to evidence change. However, we doubt that this finding can be taken at face value even though it must be given some weight. There is little reason to expect that every client would make gains in all the areas covered by the many separate scales. Another factor which could account for this finding is the insensitivity of the measuring instrument. That is, ties between pre- and post-therapy ratings may conceal small gains. Some support is found for this interpretation by examining the average of Scales 1 through 18, a measure on which ties occur infrequently.

In interpreting these tables, the reader should bear one precaution in mind. The *P* values cannot be combined as though they were derived from separate, independent measurements, because there is little doubt that the different scales are correlated. The separate scales are of interest because they suggest the wide scope of the changes that have occurred in these clients. We see from Tables 1 and 2 that client-centered therapy can bring about changes in many different phases of personality and interpersonal relationships, but looking at one of the summary measures alone (diagnostic impression or the average of Scales 1 through 18) provides a more cautious basis for assessing the over-all changes in mental health status. Either of these summary measures, but particularly the diagnostic impression scale, strongly supports the hypothesis of this study.

Clinical observation and some empirical data collected at the Counseling Center have often suggested the hypothesis that client-centered therapy starts a process of constructive change within the client which continues long after the client actually leaves his therapy. The data in Table 3 showing the changes over the follow-up period offer little support for this hypothesis. Considering the group as a whole, there was some tendency for continued improvement to occur during the follow-up period, but the differences are far from statistically significant. And on a few of the scales the changes are actually contrary to the hypothesis of continued change after therapy. It may still be, however, that some clients do continue to make substantial improvement and that the process of therapy for them is somehow different than it is for those clients who fail to evidence continued change.

The question can be raised as to whether there is a relationship between favorable change over therapy and the level of initial rating at pre-therapy—for example, do clients with initial ratings of 6 and 7 tend to improve, while clients with initial ratings of 2 and 3 fail to improve. The data in Table 4 help to answer this question. Here we have plotted the direction of change over the therapy

TABLE 3

DIRECTION OF CHANGES ON ALL SCALES BETWEEN POST-THERAPY AND FOLLOW-UP

Scale	E Group ($N=23$)				E-C-2 Group ($N=9$)			
	No. Changing			*P* Value of Difference	No. Changing			*P* Value of Difference
	0	+	−		0	+	−	
1. Mother	12	5	6	*	1	3	5	*
2. Father	15	4	4	*	3	3	3	*
3. Siblings	15	3	5	*	2	4	3	*†
4. Mate	11	5	7	*	3	4	2	*†
5. Offspring	13	6	4	*†	2	4	3	*†
6. Self-concept	14	4	5	*	4	3	2	*†
7. Ideal self	14	4	5	*	3	4	2	*†
8. Self and others	13	3	7	*	4	3	2	*†
9. Superiors	16	3	4	*	1	5	3	*†
10. Subordinates	14	2	7	.125	3	3	3	*
11. Peers	15	2	6	*	3	3	3	*
12. Sexual activities	10	3	10	.05	1	6	2	*†
13. Work	16	4	3	*†	4	3	2	*†
14. Social and community	16	2	6	*	3	3	3	*
15. Intellectual activity	13	7	3	*†	2	5	2	*†
16. Satisfaction source	10	5	8	*	4	3	2	*†
17. Threat level	12	5	6	*	1	5	3	*†
18. Defense level	13	4	6	*	1	5	3	*†
19. Intellectual endowment	22	0	1	*	5	3	1	*†
20. Functional intelligence	13	5	4	*†	3	6	0	.025†
21. Energy level	13	7	3	*†	3	6	0	.025†
22. Life-adjustment	10	5	8	*	2	6	1	.125†
23. Diagnostic impression	15	2	6	*	2	4	3	*†
24. Average of Scales 1–18	3	9	11	*	1	5	3	*†
25. Scale 20 *minus* Scale 19	14	6	3	*†	5	4	0	.125†

* *P* value larger than .125.

† Change shows decrement in mental health status.

period against the level of scale rating at pre-therapy. Because the *N*'s in each cell are small, we have attempted no further statistical analysis.

In Table 4 we see that positive changes over therapy are fairly well distributed over the entire range of ratings at pre-therapy, and thus we conclude that client-centered therapy can be helpful throughout the entire range of mental health sampled in this study. However, we note some tendency for less frequent improvement among those clients with initial ratings at levels 5, 6, and 7 as compared with those clients showing better mental health at the pre-therapy point. This suggests that client-centered therapy is

TABLE 4

DIRECTION OF CHANGE BETWEEN PRE- AND POST-THERAPY ON THE SUMMARY SCALES PLOTTED AGAINST LEVEL OF RATING AT PRE-THERAPY

Rating at Pre-therapy	E Group				E-C-1 Group			
	Total	No. Changing			Total	No. Changing		
		0	+	−		0	+	−
	Scale 23							
1	0	0	0	0	0	0	0	0
2	1	0	0	1	3	1	2	0
3	9	3	1	5	5	2	1	2
4	1	0	0	1	5	1	0	4
5	1	1	0	0	0	0	0	0
6	5	3	0	2	0	0	0	0
7	6	5	0	1	3	2	0	1
	Average of Scales 1–18							
1.0–1.49	0	0	0	0	0	0	0	0
1.5–2.49	1	0	0	1	2	0	2	0
2.5–3.49	9	0	1	8	8	0	3	5
3.5–4.49	1	0	0	1	0	0	0	0
4.5–5.49	3	0	1	2	3	0	0	3
5.5–6.49	6	0	2	4	2	0	1	1
6.5–7.00	3	0	1	2	1	0	1	0

relatively less effective with more disturbed clients, although the *N*'s are too small for much confidence to be placed in this finding.[4]

Direct Comparisons between the Therapy and the Equivalent-Control Groups

In the previous section we have shown that significant changes occur in the experimental group and not in the control group. However, a more rigorous analysis of the data calls for a direct comparison of the changes made by the two groups—that is, are the mean changes occurring in the experimental group significantly different from the mean changes occurring in the control group? To answer this question, we have made a further analysis of the two reliable summary measures: diagnostic impression and the average of Scales 1 through 18.

Two parallel statistical treatments have been employed. One of these, a nonparametric treatment, is the Mann-Whitney *U* test (5, 6). Here the differences between the pre- and the post-therapy ratings of each subject are the scores to which the *U* test is applied. The other treatment is a special application of the *t* test which is outlined by Edwards (2, pp. 284–85). Here the mean change over therapy and its standard error are computed for each group, taking into account the correlational factor. The standard error of the difference between the mean changes of the two groups is obtained by using

$$\sqrt{S\bar{x}_1^2 + S\bar{x}_2^2}\,.$$

The remainder of the treatment follows the usual procedures except that the test of significance is made against $(n_1 - 1) + (n_2 - 1)$ degrees of freedom.

The mean scale values at pre- and post-therapy and follow-up are given in Table 5. Table 6 presents the direct comparisons be-

4. Although we have no concrete evidence to present, clinical observations suggest that these findings would hold for most types of psychotherapy and not just client-centered therapy. That is, most therapies can be effective throughout the range of personality disorders, but the therapy is less frequently effective as the severity of disturbance increases.

tween the control and the experimental groups, with respect to the differences in their mean changes.

Without exception, the trend in the data is in the predicted direction of greater improvement in the therapy group relative to the control group. Statistically significant differences, however, occur only for the pre-therapy to follow-up comparisons. Here the diagnostic impression scale yields *P* values of .05 and .02 based upon

TABLE 5

MEANS OF SCALE 23 AND AVERAGE OF SCALES 1–18 AT PRE- AND POST-THERAPY AND FOLLOW-UP FOR EXPERIMENTAL AND EQUIVALENT-CONTROL GROUPS

GROUP AND SCALE	MEANS		
	Pre-therapy	Post-therapy	Follow-up
E group:			
23	4.78	4.13	3.91
1–18	4.58	3.99	3.92
E-C-1 group:			
23	3.88	3.5	....
1–18	3.87	3.4	....
E-C-2 group:			
23	3.44	3.44	3.78
1–18	3.39	3.12	3.66

TABLE 6

COMPARISON BETWEEN THE EXPERIMENTAL AND THE EQUIVALENT-CONTROL GROUPS WITH RESPECT TO THEIR DIFFERENCES IN MEAN CHANGES OVER THE THERAPY AND FOLLOW-UP PERIODS

Period and Scale	Difference in Mean Changes	*t*	*P*	U	*P*
Pre- to post-therapy:					
23	.28	1.34	*	197	*
1–18	.13	1.06	*	195	*
Pre-therapy to follow-up:					
23	1.20	1.81	.05	153	.02
1–18	.92	1.47	.10	137.5	.08
Post-therapy to follow-up:					
23	.55	.67	*	†	†
1–18	.60	.85	*	†	†

* *P* value larger than .10. † Not computed.

the *t* test and the *U* test, respectively. The average of Scales 1 through 18 shows marginal significance.

The failure to find significant differences for the post-therapy to follow-up comparisons was anticipated by the data presented in the previous section. Again the findings failed to support the hypothesis of significant improvement during the follow-up period.

Wait and Therapy Periods Compared for the Own-Control Group

While the equivalent-control data just considered are quite useful, a still sounder control feature is provided by examining the changes over the wait period in the own-control group: the own-control technique comes very close to controlling all variables that might conceivably influence change.

The own-control group consists of the nine experimental subjects who took the tests before and after a sixty-day wait period. The median length of time between the pre- and post-therapy tests for these nine subjects is about three months—one month longer than the wait period. This provides a satisfactory basis for comparison, although ideally the wait and the therapy periods should be equivalent for each individual client.

Using the sign test, we first examined for each measure the direction of change over both the wait and the therapy periods. These data are presented in Table 7. We see that the changes over the wait period are random; no change reaches the 15 per cent level of confidence, and the direction of change is toward a decrement in mental health on about half the scales. Over the therapy period, however, no changes are in the direction of decreasing mental health, and for about half the scales favorable changes are significant at the .125 level or better. Considering the inefficiency of the sign test with an *N* this small, these results offer considerable support for the hypothesis of improvement over the therapy period.

Table 8 uses the *t*-test procedures to make a direct comparison between the difference in mean gains over the wait and the therapy periods. Only the two summary measures, diagnostic impression and the average of Scales 1 through 18, have been examined. Table 8 reveals that there has been a decrement in mental health status over the wait period and an improvement over the therapy period; however, the *P* values resulting from this analysis, while approaching statistical significance, do not reach the 5 per cent level of confidence.

As pointed out previously, the assumptions necessary for the *t* test are not fully met by the data; we have therefore used a non-parametric procedure to make an additional direct comparison between the wait and the therapy periods. This was done with the sign test by giving a plus to each subject whose change over ther-

TABLE 7

DIRECTION OF CHANGES ON ALL SCALES BETWEEN WAIT AND PRE-THERAPY AND BETWEEN PRE-THERAPY AND POST-THERAPY, OWN-CONTROL GROUP ONLY

Scale	Wait to Pre-therapy				Pre- to Post-therapy			
	No. Changing			*P* Value of Difference	No. Changing			*P* Value of Difference
	0	+	−		0	+	−	
1. Mother	5	3	1	*†	3	1	5	.125
2. Father	3	4	2	*†	3	1	5	.125
3. Siblings	5	2	2	*	3	1	5	.125
4. Mate	3	4	2	*†	2	3	4	*
5. Offspring	3	4	2	*†	2	1	6	.125
6. Self-concept	4	4	1	*†	3	1	5	.125
7. Ideal self	2	4	4	*	5	0	4	.125
8. Self and others	2	5	2	*†	4	0	5	.05
9. Superiors	3	4	2	*†	3	1	5	.125
10. Subordinates	4	2	3	*	3	1	5	.125
11. Peers	4	3	2	*†	4	0	4	.125
12. Sexual activities	4	3	2	*†	3	3	3	*
13. Work	2	4	3	*†	3	0	6	.025
14. Social and community	4	3	2	*†	4	1	4	*
15. Intellectual activity	4	3	2	*†	3	1	5	.125
16. Satisfaction source	2	2	5	*	5	1	3	*
17. Threat level	5	2	2	*	6	1	2	*
18. Defense level	1	5	3	*†	2	1	6	.125
19. Intellectual endowment	7	1	1	*	6	1	2	*
20. Functional intelligence	3	2	4	*	6	1	2	*
21. Energy level	3	3	3	*	3	3	3	*
22. Life-adjustment	5	2	2	*	3	3	3	*
23. Diagnostic impression	5	2	2	*	4	1	4	*
24. Average of Scales 1–18	0	5	4	*†	0	4	5	*
25. Scale 20 *minus* Scale 19	4	1	4	*	8	0	1	*

* *P* value larger than .125.

† Change shows decrement in mental health.

apy was greater than his change over the wait period. The trend was in favor of the therapy period for both summary measures but was not significantly so. On the average of Scales 1 through 18, seven of the nine clients showed more improvement in the therapy period relative to the wait period, a difference which is significant at the .125 level of confidence.

Summarizing the findings for the own-control group, we find the evidence all pointing to greater improvement over the therapy period than over the wait period, but we cannot firmly rule out the possibility of this being a chance occurrence.

TABLE 8

COMPARISON BETWEEN MEAN CHANGES OVER THE WAIT AND THE THERAPY PERIOD FOR THE OWN-CONTROL GROUP

SCALE	MEAN CHANGE				
	Wait to Pre-therapy	Pre- to Post-therapy	Difference	*t*	*P*
23....................	+.22	−.78	1.00	1.04	.15
Average of Scales 1–18..	+.53	−.67	1.20	1.21	.12

Correlations between the TAT Scores and Other Measures Assessing Therapeutic Change

In planning this study, we had intended to devote considerable attention to the correlations between the TAT measures and measures for these same subjects derived from the Willoughby Emotional-Maturity Scale (E-M Scale) (chap. 13), from the Self-Other Attitude Scale (S-O Scale) (chap. 11), from the Q-adjustment index (chap. 5), and from counselor judgments (chap. 7). We now find we have little to report.

After computing nineteen different correlations, we found only one large enough to be significant at the 5 per cent level of confidence, and this could be expected by chance alone. The other rhos were all small and sometimes positive, sometimes negative.

Since we are not at all clear as to the meaning of these correlations, we merely point to the obvious conclusion that there is no relationship between mental health status as measured in this project and the measures developed for the other projects reported in this volume. To complicate matters still further, most of the several measures show that therapeutic progress has occurred in the therapy group considered collectively. Vargas has computed the correlation of four of these scales with other outcome measures on ten subjects. He reports these together with his interpretations of them in the next chapter.

Dymond also reports a TAT study in chapter 8 in which she examined the TAT protocols with a set of criteria quite different from those used here. Dymond supplied us with some correlations between her TAT scores and those found in this report. These correlations provide an exception to the above conclusion, since there does seem to be a moderately positive relationship between the two TAT measures. The correlation between Dymond's ratings and the ratings on Scale 22 (degree of adjustment) was .40 for the pre-therapy TAT's of twenty-two experimental and ten control subjects, and .65 for the ratings made by both analysts on these same cases at post-therapy. Correlating the Dymond ratings with those made for this study on Scale 23 (diagnostic impression) on the same thirty-two cases at pre-therapy gave an r of .47 and of .72 at post-therapy.

IV. SUMMARY

This study examines the changes in mental health status that occur over client-centered therapy in twenty-three clients. Mental health was defined in terms of psychoanalytic theory and was assessed by means of twenty-three specially constructed rating scales. The rating scales were used to make blind analyses of TAT's administered at pre-therapy, at post-therapy, and at follow-up. Mental health status was also determined at comparable points in time for a control group of persons not seeking or receiving therapy. An additional control feature was employed for nine of the experimental subjects. Here changes over a sixty-day no-therapy period were compared with changes over the therapy period.

The major findings of this study are as follows:

1. Using the sign test to examine the direction of changes over the two periods of (*a*) pre-therapy to post-therapy and (*b*) pre-therapy to follow-up, we find for a majority of the scales that client-centered therapy brings about a significant improvement in mental health status. In the control group favorable changes occur on a few scales over the therapy period, but over the pre-therapy to follow-up period the direction of change is essentially random.

2. The trend on most of the scales is for continued improvement over the follow-up period; however, this trend is slight and so offers little support for the hypothesis that client-centered therapy starts a process of constructive change within the client which continues after the termination of therapy.

3. Our findings indicate that client-centered therapy can be helpful throughout the entire range of mental health sampled in this study. More explicitly, clients with either neurotic or psychotic features in their personality make-ups show improvement over the therapy period. Still, there is some tendency for more frequent improvement to occur in those clients receiving the better mental health ratings at pre-therapy.

4. When the mean changes in the experimental group are compared directly with the mean changes in the control group, the experimental group does not show a significant improvement over the therapy period on the two summary measures used in this study. But we do find significant gains over the pre-therapy to follow-up period. We conclude that the data support but do not prove the hypothesis that a therapy group makes constructive gains in mental health status relative to a no-therapy group.

5. When the changes over a therapy and a no-therapy control period (using the own-control technique) are compared, the evidence strongly suggests that greater improvement occurs in the therapy period.

6. The psychoanalytic conception of mental health as measured in this study shows no relationship with the several other measures of therapeutic progress described in other chapters of this volume. It does show a positive relationship with the TAT measure presented in chapter 8.

REFERENCES

1. Dixon, W., and Massey, F. *Introduction to Statistical Analysis*. New York: McGraw-Hill Book Co., 1951.
2. Edwards, A. L. *Experimental Design in Psychological Research*. New York: Rinehart & Co., 1950.
3. John, Eve S. "Mental Health and the Principle of Least Effort." Ph.D. dissertation, University of Chicago, 1953.
4. Kendall, M. G. *Rank Correlation Methods*. London: Charles Griffin & Co., 1948.
5. Mann, H., and Whitney, D. "On a Test of Whether One of Two Random Variables Is Stochastically Larger than the Other," *Annals of Mathematical Statistics*, XVIII (1947), 50–60.
6. Moses, L. "Nonparametric Statistics for Psychological Research," *Psychological Bulletin*, XLIX (1952), 122–43.

CHAPTER 10

Changes in Self-awareness during Client-centered Therapy

MANUEL J. VARGAS

I. INTRODUCTION

This chapter will report another of the "special studies," that is, one not originally planned as part of the first block (Block I) group of projects, but one which grew out of the research as it progressed. It is a study of the process of therapy which draws on several of the outcome measures reported in the preceding chapters for its criteria of successful therapy and so relates one aspect of the process of therapy to several different measures of outcome. The particular phase of the process of therapy upon which it focuses attention is the emergence of new self-perceptions into awareness and their presumed assimilation into the self-concept.

Client-centered therapists have been interested in the self-concept as a theoretical construct that (*a*) orders the behavior of the client and that (*b*) orders the therapist's interaction with the client. Part of the client-centered therapist's definition of self is that he tries to perceive his client's problems and his client's self as he, the client, perceives them. As a result of this sharing of the client's self-perceptions, various therapists have formed opinions about what changes characteristically tend to occur in the client's self-concept during therapy.

Raimy (6) made the first objective study of change in the self-concept. He formulated a picture of the self-concept which has been basic to many of the later studies:

> The self-concept is the more or less organized perceptual object resulting from present and past self-observation. Self-perception is a process which is more than an activation of internal or distance receptors. In agreement with textbook definitions, there is in self-perception an organization which involves memorial and situational factors as well as the sense data themselves. . . . What we perceive in ourselves may have only partial correspondence with what other people

see in us or the so-called objective personality. Yet, as always, we behave in accordance with our own perceptions even though the opinions of others and the urgencies of our biological make-up interact to influence our perception of ourselves [p. 154].

Using this definition, Raimy discovered that clients in therapy tend to move from a predominantly negative evaluation of the self to a predominantly positive evaluation. Curran (1) investigated one case intensively and found a positive relationship between exploration of the self and self-insight. Snyder (10) and Seeman (8) verified these findings of Raimy and Curran as a part of their research. Sheerer (9) defined another variable of the self—self-acceptance. Sheerer in that study and Stock (12) in another found that acceptance of the self correlated positively with acceptance of others. Raskin (7) isolated another variable of the self—dependence—as expressed in the "locus of evaluation." He found that in therapy the client becomes more self-dependent.

There are several other studies which are related to our understanding of the changes in the self-concept during therapy. Hogan (4) made a significant theoretical contribution in his definition of defensiveness as having to do with those experiences which are perceived as incongruent with the structure of the self. Using such a definition, he was able to show objectively that therapy correlated negatively with defensiveness. Haigh found much to support Hogan's theory in a broader study of ten cases (2) and in a study measuring visual perception of threatening words (3).

In studying the process of therapy itself, Seeman (8) and Snyder (10) found that the category of "statement of problem" tended to decrease during the interviews, while statements of insight and self-understanding increased. By studying both successful and failure cases, Steele (11) and Wolfson (14) not only verified the positive relationship between self-exploration and insight, mentioned above, but also showed that restatements or repetitions of the problem decreased concurrently with therapy. These various studies have thus supplied us with some information as to the type of changes which occur in the self-concept during therapy and some of the changes in the client's mode of expression during the interviews.

The present study (13) attempts to push farther along this pathway, by concerning itself with still another variable of the self-concept. It is hypothesized that, when a person is in process of changing established psychological patterns (patterns of feeling, thinking, perceiving, acting), his awareness of himself increases in at least three ways: (*a*) he thinks of, or perceives, himself more often than when he is not engaged in that process of change; (*b*) as he resolves or loses one established pattern of self-perception, he ceases to be concerned with and aware of that pattern but becomes concerned with and aware of other previous patterns in himself; and (*c*) as established patterns are lost, he discovers new feelings, concepts, percepts, and experiences arising in himself, that is, he becomes aware of emerging aspects of himself. This threefold hypothesis as stated is applicable not only to the psychotherapeutic interview but also to any other situation in which a person is in process of changing his previous psychological patterns.

If the notion of increases in self-awareness of the three kinds outlined above is a reasonable one for people in process of changing established psychological patterns, then these changes should occur in people in therapy. Further, if these changes occur in clients, it follows that clients experiencing different degrees of success in therapy should experience different degrees of increase in self-awareness, the more successful clients having greater increases in self-awareness than the less successful clients.

II. PURPOSE OF THIS STUDY

The purpose of this study was to discover whether the two variables "self-awareness" and "success of therapy" were related. The working hypothesis was: *Judged success of therapy correlates positively with self-awareness during therapy*. Self-awareness was measured in the following three ways: (*a*) change from non-self-description to self-description; (*b*) change from previously described self to previously undescribed self (decrease in repeated self-perceptions); and (*c*) change from description of familiar aspects of self to description of previously unknown aspects of self (increase in emergents). This threefold change can be considered as being related to a decrease in defensiveness. This is perhaps particularly true of the second, which would seem to be related to a rigidity of defenses.

III. THE CRITERIA

Four criteria of successful therapy were used. The first of these was the counselor rating of his own case on the Case Rating Scale devised by N. J. Raskin and Julius Seeman at the Counseling Center and which has already been described in chapter 7. Two of their scales were used in this study: No. 7, "Degree of Personal Integration of the Client," which reads "highly disorganized or defensively organized" at point 1 and "optimally integrated" at point 9, the other extreme; and No. 10, "Your Rating of the Outcome of Therapy," which starts at "complete failure" at point 1 and goes to "marked success" at point 9. The cases analyzed for this study were ranked into two orders, one for each continuum.

The second criterion of success was Dymond's Q-sort adjustment score (see chap. 5) obtained from each client's self-descriptive Q-sort. These Q-adjustment scores were calculated for the pre-therapy, post-therapy, and follow-up point for each client. To get a measure of the *change* in adjustment from one sort to another, one merely subtracted one score from the succeeding one. The subjects for this study were ranked on the basis of the *degree of change* in the Q-adjustment score from pre- to post-therapy and again from pre-therapy to follow-up status.

The third criterion of successful therapy was the judgment of a Thematic Apperception Test (TAT) analyst, Eve S. John, based on the TAT record and expressed on four of her scales.[1] The Freudian theory of psychosexual development was the frame of reference within which each TAT was evaluated and rated on the scales by this TAT analyst. John, the author of these scales, expressed their theoretical basis thus:

> The principal characteristic modes by which an individual may relate to other individuals and to societal or abstract objects may be classified into seven categories corresponding to the seven stages of psychosexual development: estranged from reality (autistic), dependent (oral-sucking), idealizing and grasping (oral-biting), destructive (anal expulsive), conservative and possessive (anal retentive), competitive (phallic), and realistic (genital) [3, p. 5].

The four scales which were used in the study to be reported here were: (*a*) "Attitudes toward Self," (*b*) "Insight into Self and Others," (*c*) "Level of Defense," and (*d*) "Degree of Adjust-

1. See chap. 9 for a complete account of this study.

ment." Each scale had seven points from the least favorable to the most favorable condition. Each client's pre-therapy, post-therapy, and follow-up TAT record was used as the basis for rating him on each scale at each of these points. The amount of *change* on each scale was obtained by subtracting the pre-therapy rating from the post-therapy, and from the follow-up rating. Again the subjects were ranked on the *degree of change* from pre- to post-therapy and from pre-therapy to follow-up points.

The fourth criterion of successful therapy was a "blind" mental health rating of the TAT records by Dymond (see chap. 8) and expressed on a seven-point scale from 1 (severe disturbance bordering on psychotic or psychotic) to 7 (well-integrated, happy person, socially effective).

A rating on this scale is a composite of evaluations made on the following six variables: (*a*) self-dependence versus dependence on others or on magical forces to solve problems; (*b*) well-structured stories versus inability to form a story, sticking rigidly to stimulus or bizarre fantasy; (*c*) pleasant versus unpleasant emotions and the degree of their control; (*d*) constructive versus destructive interaction; (*e*) degree of comfort or disturbance in heroes and appropriateness of this state to context; and (*f*) happy, successful, or hopeful outcomes of stories versus despair, failure, or indecision.

IV. THE METHOD OF THE STUDY

The essential method of this study was to analyze the transscribed therapeutic interviews of ten cases by means of the self-description instrument described below and to compare the results of this independent analysis with each of the four criteria.

Definition of the Concepts

The following definitions were made:

1. Self-awareness is here used to mean the total field of self-percepts, all the percepts a person feels to be "I" or "me."
2. At any given time, self-awareness is focused on a given percept of self:
   a) A percept of self alone as a self-characteristic, or
   b) A percept of self-in-relation to someone or something else.
3. This narrow, focused self-awareness is a *self-perception*. All perceptions not of self are of *non-self*.

The following categories of client statements were then made:

1. A verbalized non-self-perception is called a *non-self-description.*
2. A verbalized self-perception is called *self-description.*
3. When a self-perception is first verbalized in therapy, it is called an *original self-description.*
4. When the same self-perception reappears, it is called a *repeated self-description.*
5. When the same self-perception reappears but is presented in another new instance (as in recurring symptoms), that is called *another instance of previous self-description.*
6. The original self-descriptions may be well known to the client, called *familiar original self-descriptions.*
7. The originals may be descriptions of self-percepts emerging during counseling or since counseling began, called *emergent original self-descriptions.*
8. When an original does not belong clearly in the familiar or in the emergent categories, it is classified as *undetermined original self-description.*
9. A simple agreement or denial of a counselor's statement is an *agreement-denial.*[2]

These definitions, expanded, illustrated, and with directions for their use, composed the self-description instrument to categorize the recorded case material.

The Statistical Hypotheses

The following hypotheses were set up to be tested by statistical measures:

1. Client statements can be reliably identified and classified with the self-description instrument.
2. The proportion of self-descriptions to all client statements will have a positive rank-difference correlation with counselor rating of outcome, with favorable change in counselor rating of client integration, with the Q-sort adjustment score, with favorable change on each of the four scales of the John TAT rating, and with the Dymond TAT rating.
3. The proportion of repeated self-descriptions to all client statements will have a *negative* rank-difference correlation with each of the criterion measures.
4. The proportion of original self-descriptions to all client statements will have a positive rank-difference correlation with each of the criterion measures.

2. Since agreement-denial statements are "Yes," "No," etc., they are not considered a significant part of client statements and so are not included with "all client statements." Hypotheses 2, 3, 4, and 5 do not mention agreement-denials, but it is to be understood that they mean "all client statements minus agreement-denials" when they say "all client statements."

5. The proportion of emergent self-descriptions to all client statements minus undetermined originals will have a positive rank-difference correlation with each of the criterion measures.
6. The proportion of emergent self-descriptions to original self-descriptions minus undetermined originals will have a positive rank-difference correlation with each of the criterion measures.
7. The proportion of emergent self-descriptions to all self-descriptions will have a positive rank-difference correlation with each of the criterion measures.

Subjects

The subjects for this study were all the experimental cases in Block I who had, at the time the study was begun, all their interviews and TAT protocols recorded, transcribed, and available for analysis. Nine cases satisfied these requirements. Another case was added that lacked only a follow-up TAT and a Q-sort. The comparison of the self-awareness measures and John's TAT ratings could be made only with nine cases, because she did not judge the case that had no follow-up TAT. The comparison with Dymond's TAT ratings could only be made in eight cases, because this judge omitted the same case that lacked a follow-up TAT and also the case of Mrs. Bico, whose records she knew too well to rate them "blindly." Summary information on the subjects is presented in Table 1.

TABLE 1

THE CASES USED IN THIS STUDY

Post-therapy Counselor Rating of Outcome*	Client	Counselor Code Name	No. of Interviews	Student (S) or Non-student (NS)
9	Miss Bene	A	10	S
8	Mrs. Oak	B	40	NS
7	Mrs. Beel	C	11	S
7	Mrs. Bico	D	33	NS
6	Mr. Bebb	B	9	S
6	Miss Bacc	E	9	S
6	Mr. Barr	F	41	S
4	Miss Bime	G	13	NS
4	Mr. Bajo	D	11	S
1	Mr. Bann	F	16	NS

* The range of the scale was from 1 through 9; the higher the rating, the higher the degree of success (see chap. 7).

Procedures

The interviews of the ten subjects were analyzed by the investigator with the aid of the self-description instrument already described. To obtain a reliability measure, one of the cases he had categorized was also categorized by a second judge who was first trained in the use and meaning of the self-description instrument. This supplied a test of the first hypothesis.

To test Hypotheses 2 through 7, the cases were:

1. Ranked according to degree of *change* from pre- to post-therapy and again on change from pre-therapy to follow-up, as expressed on (*a*) each of John's four TAT scales; (*b*) the Q-sort adjustment score; and (*c*) the Dymond TAT ratings.
2. Ranked according to counselor's rating on (*a*) change in client integration from pre- to post-therapy and (*b*) success of therapy.

This resulted in fourteen rank orders.

The various categories resulting from the content analysis were totaled for each case, and the proportions called for by the hypotheses were determined. The cases were then ranked according to these proportions.

Rank-difference correlations were computed between each category proportion and each of the rank orders of the criterion measures. To see whether the criterion measures agreed among themselves, rank-difference correlations were computed between each of the four criterion measures.

V. ANALYSIS OF DATA

Hypothesis 1

Agreement on units.—The investigator and the judge had 96 per cent agreement on the units found. The self-description instrument was used reliably to identify the units to be categorized.

Agreement on categories.—The agreements obtained were:

	Per Cent
Self-descriptions	96.0
Repetitions of self	75.7
Another instance of self	56.6
Original self	86.7
Familiar original self	75.7
Emergent original self	84.4
Agreement-denials and undetermined original self-descriptions	100.0

Each of the above agreements was statistically significant at the 1 per cent level of confidence. The category of non-self-descriptions had so few items in the test case that no statistical computations would be meaningful. Both the investigator and the judge felt that this category was more clearly defined than the others. Since they had very little difficulty in identifying these statements, the investigator assumed that this category had been used reliably. Hypothesis 1, that clients' statements can be reliably identified and classified with the self-description instrument, was confirmed.

Hypotheses 2 through 7

Since *change* on the criterion scales most often was a matter of zero, one, two, or three points, there were bound to be many ties in these rank orders. The resulting rank-difference correlations were crude statistics but nevertheless served to point out some meaningful relationships. Tables 2 and 3 present the correlations

TABLE 2†

CORRELATION OF SELF-AWARENESS MEASURES WITH CRITERION MEASURES

Criteria	EOS/S	EOS/ OS−UOS	EOS/ ALL−UOS	OS/ ALL−AD	RS/ ALL−AD	S/ ALL−AD
Counselor ratings:						
Outcome	.88**	.99**	.88**	.83**	−.64*	.65*
Integration	.79**	.86**	.82**	.79**	−.53	.67*
Q-adjustment:						
Pre- to post-therapy	.19	.32	.27	.21	.05	.35
Pre-therapy to follow-up	−.27	.00	−.28	−.31	.60	.13
Dymond TAT ratings:						
Pre- to post-therapy	.45	.74*	.51	.43	−.37	.24
Pre-therapy to follow-up	.38	.55	.46	.32	−.21	.10

† EOS/S = the proportion of emergent self-descriptions to all self-descriptions.

EOS/OS−UOS = the proportion of emergent self-descriptions to all original self-descriptions minus the undetermined originals.

EOS/ALL−UOS = the proportion of emergent self-descriptions to all statements minus the undetermined originals.

OS/ALL−AD = the proportion of original self-descriptions to all statements minus agreements and denials.

RS/ALL−AD = repeated self-descriptions in proportion to all statements minus agreements or denials.

S/ALL−AD = the proportion of all self-descriptions to all statements minus agreements and denials.

All correlations significant at the 5 per cent level are marked with a single asterisk (*). All correlations significant at the 1 per cent level are marked with a double asterisk (**). The same notation is used in all tables in this chapter.

between the self-awareness measures and each of the criterion measures. These tables reveal some striking correlations between the rank orders.

The following conclusions can be drawn from these tables. From Table 2:

1. There is a *positive* correlation between counselor judgments of outcome of therapy and integration of the client and the ratios of client self-description, original self-description, and self-emergence, but a *negative* correlation with client self-repetitions. Hypotheses 2, 3, 4, 5, 6, and 7 are all supported by the counselor judgment criteria.

TABLE 3†

CORRELATION OF SELF-AWARENESS MEASURES WITH MEASURE ON JOHN'S FOUR TAT SCALES

Measures	EOS/S	EOS/ OS−UOS	EOS/ ALL−UOS	OS/ ALL−AD	RS/ ALL−AD	S/ ALL−AD	Name of Scale
Change from pre- to post-therapy, TAT Scale 1	−.75*	−.63*	−.67*	−.67*	.78*	−.38	"Attitude toward Self"
Change from pre-therapy to follow-up, TAT Scale 1	−.75*	−.59	−.70*	−.70*	.80**	−.34	
Change from pre- to post-therapy, TAT Scale 2	−.68*	−.68*	−.62	−.64	.54	−.45	"Insight into Self and Others"
Change from pre-therapy to follow-up, TAT Scale 2.....	−.64	−.64	−.74*	−.74*	.73*	−.51	
Change from pre- to post-therapy, TAT Scale 3	−.47	.34	−.40	−.59	.86**	−.13	"Level of Defense"
Change from pre-therapy to follow-up, TAT Scale 3.....	−.38	−.05	−.23	−.20	.76*	.00	
Change from pre- to post-therapy, TAT Scale 4	−.53	−.53	−.53	−.53	.63	−.33	"Degree of Adjustment"
Change from pre-therapy to follow-up, TAT Scale 4	−.58	−.35	−.68*	−.68*	.48	−.56	

† See footnote to Table 2.

2. There are no significant correlations between the self-awareness measures and the change in Q-sort adjustment except the high positive correlation between the change in Q-sort adjustment from pre-therapy to follow-up and the change in proportion of repetitions. This is contrary to Hypothesis 3.

3. There are low positive correlations between all the self-awareness measures but one and the Dymond TAT ratings. There is a low negative correlation between these ratings and the proportion of repetitions. These findings support Hypotheses 2 through 7.

From Table 3 it follows:

4. There is a *negative* correlation between change on John's TAT Scales 1, 2, and 4 and the proportions of self-, original, and emergent descriptions, but a *positive* correlation between change on these scales and repetitions. These findings are contrary to Hypotheses 2 through 7. The correlations of the self-awareness measures with Scale 3, "Level of Defense," were very low but consistently negative except for the high positive correlation between the increase in repetitions (thought to be a crude estimate of defensiveness) and the degree of favorable change on the "Level of Defense" scale. Therefore, as defensiveness increased, as measured by the self-descriptive instrument, it decreased as measured by the John scale.

It seemed that therapy set in motion processes which were evaluated positively by the counselor, negatively by one TAT analyst (John), and positively by the other (Dymond), and which bore a low positive relation to the Q-adjustment measure.

Intercorrelations of the Criterion Measures

The somewhat contradictory findings, particularly the striking negative results when using John's TAT analysis, raises the question of the relationship between the criteria. The rank-difference correlations of all the criterion measures are presented in Table 4.

The correlations in Tables 2, 3, and 4 show a good deal of overlap between some of the measures evaluating therapy. The self-awareness ratios and the counselor ratings have the most similarity in perspective, followed by the Dymond TAT, which correlates fairly highly with both. The Q-adjustment overlaps to some extent with the counselor rating and the Dymond TAT ratings but has minimal relation to the self-awareness measures. The correlations between the change on the John ratings and the self-awareness measures are strikingly negative. They are also negatively related to the counselor ratings, are unrelated to the change on the

TABLE 4

Rank-Difference Correlations of Criterion Measures

Criteria	Counselor Rating: Outcome	Counselor Rating: Integration	Q-Adjustment		Dymond TAT		Scale 1, "Attitude toward Self"		Scale 2, "Insight into Self and Others"		Scale 3, "Level of Defense"		Scale 4, "Degree of Adjustment"	
	Pre- to Post-therapy	Pre- to Post-therapy	Pre- to Post-therapy	Pre-therapy to Follow-up	Pre- to Post-therapy	Pre-therapy to Follow-up	Pre- to Post-therapy	Pre-therapy to Follow-up	Pre- to Post-therapy	Pre-therapy to Follow-up	Pre- to Post-therapy	Pre-therapy to Follow-up	Pre- to Post-therapy	Pre-therapy to Follow-up
Outcome	......	......	.49	.10†	.62	.51	−.45	−.35	−.59	−.49	−.40	−.08	−.50	−.29
Integration	......	......	.51	−.10	.79**	.62	−.20	−.14	−.36	−.40	−.13	−.04	−.35	−.33
Q-adjustment (pre- to post-therapy)	......	......	......	......	.37	−.11	.23	.30	−.03	.00	.43	.58	−.19	−.09
Q-adjustment (pretherapy to follow-up)	......	......	......	......	.71**	.00	.32	.36	.04	.36	.50	.80**	.00	.39
Dymond TAT (pretherapy to post-therapy)	......	......	......	......	......	......	−.02	−.02	−.05	−.32	.08	−.05	−.13	−.37
Dymond TAT (pretherapy to follow-up)	......	......	......	......	......	......	.07	.07	.09	.01	.18	.12	.04	−.37

† Counselor ratings were not obtained at follow-up, so these comparisons are based on counselor ratings at post-therapy.

Dymond TAT ratings, and have some positive correlations with change on the Q-adjustment score.

It seems that the self-awareness measures and the counselor ratings, on the one hand, and the John TAT measures, on the other, represent two contradictory frames of reference from which to evaluate the changes occurring in client-centered therapy. The other two criteria occupy intermediate positions between these two extremes.

Before interpreting this difference further, the question of the reliability and the validity of these two instruments should be looked into. These questions are both answered for the counselor rating scales in chapter 7. John established the reliability of her scales by having a number of judges rate five patients' TAT protocols and the validity by comparing the pooled TAT ratings of these judges with the ratings of the psychiatrist (not client-centered) in charge of each case on the same scales (see chap. 9). Her reported correlations are well beyond chance expectation.

Comparison of the Individual Cases

Because of the positive correlation of the self-awareness measures and the criteria, excepting the John scales, it may be interesting, leaving aside the difference for the moment, to discover what *changes* occur in the emergent proportion, EOS/S, from one-fifth of therapy to the next in each case.

Figure 1 is a graphic representation of the proportion of emergents to all self-descriptions, changed into percentages, for each fifth of therapy for each of the cases. The counselor success ratings are also given.

Presumably, the percentage of emergents would be greater in those cases and within those fifths of cases where the process of therapy was most intense. It has already been shown that the changes in self-awareness which are indicated by the proportion EOS/S for the total case correlates highly but contrarily with both counselor ratings and change on the John scales. An inspection of Figure 1, showing the movement of EOS/S from one fifth to the next, seems to support the correlations of the total EOS/S with the counselor rating. However, one case seems to move in its proportion of EOS/S far below the range where one finds others of similar success ratings. This is the case of Mrs. Bico.

One, two, or all three of the following possibilities may be true: (*a*) the case of Mrs. Bico may be much less successful than the others with a similar rating; (*b*) the process of therapy as verbalized may have been quite different for this case from what

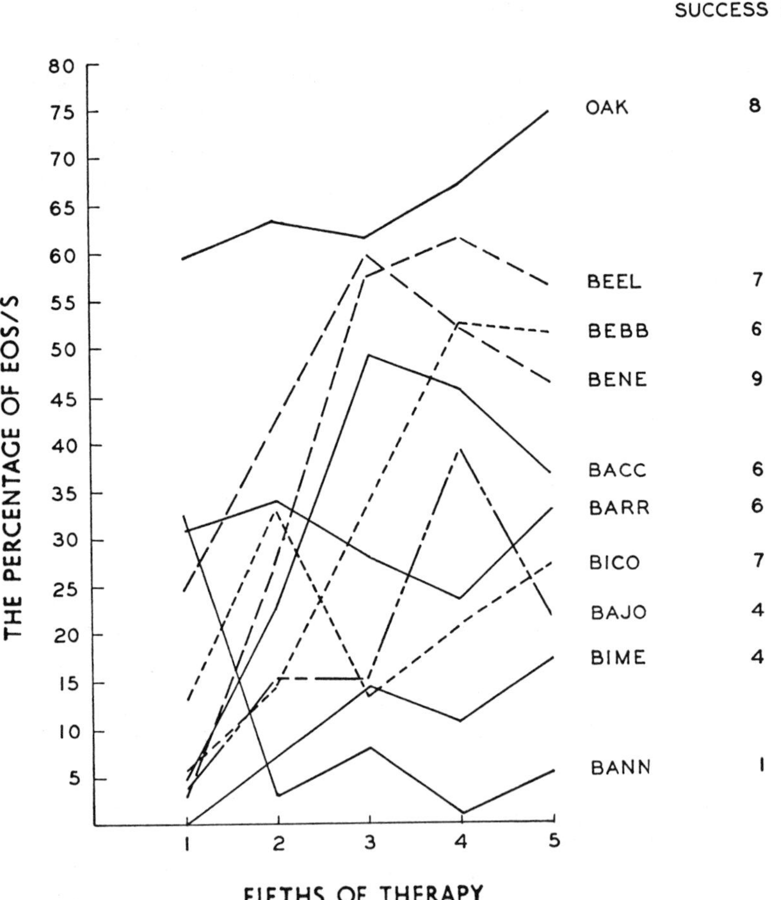

FIG. 1.—The percentage of EOS/S by fifths of therapy for each case, with the counselor rating also given.

it was for all the other cases; or (*c*) the proportion of EOS/S is not adequate as a measure of the success of therapy.

It became evident to the investigator as he categorized the case of Mrs. Bico that the process of therapy as evinced during the counseling sessions was in some important way different for Mrs. Bico than it was for the other cases. Mrs. Bico came in to "report" her troubles or her achievements. She tended to make of the interview an opportunity to report what had occurred to her during the past week outside the therapy sessions. In some interviews she had so little to report that she left early. Even some major insights occurred outside the sessions, and, when she reported them, she did not explore them much further. All the other cases did some of this reporting but tended increasingly during the therapy session to explore themselves in a gradual, formative process. Mrs. Bico tended to bring in preformed percepts and to stick to clear percepts. The others, particularly Mrs. Oak, brought in fewer ready-made percepts but rather gradually created new percepts in a process of experiencing and formulating vague aspects of self. Mrs. Bico and Mrs. Oak are at opposite ends of the continuum of "reporting life—experiencing life" in therapy.

To the investigator, and to the counselor as he reported when this question was discussed with him, Mrs. Bico's changes appeared as saltatory (each instance of change was of sudden and great emotional significance), whereas the changes in the other cases more often could be seen forming gradually. Perhaps Mrs. Bico's perceptions, including her self-emergent aspects, appeared as saltatory only because we were not able to observe her more often when she was experiencing the process of change. Perhaps Mrs. Bico did not typically break and reform feelings and Gestalts suddenly, but a slower formative process may have occurred during her living between sessions.

If we accept the theory that Mrs. Bico's therapy was saltatory, that she tended to stick to clear percepts, and that the therapy of the others was much more gradual and formative, then it would follow that the number and proportion of emerging perceptions of self would not be a strictly comparable indicator of the amount of change between these two types of cases. In Mrs. Bico's case the changes would be like leaps, less frequent but more distant from each other. In Mrs. Oak and the others the changes would be like steps, more continuous with smaller distances between them. Consequently, the units of emergents are not strictly equal between these two types of cases.

This suggests that the measure of emerging perceptions of the self is a measure of the degree of self-experiencing admitted into awareness and leading to verbal self-expression. Perhaps there may be some types of clients who are relatively nonintellectual, nonverbal, nonintrospective, and not very sensitive to self, whose emotional as well as intellectual changes are relatively sudden and great. The essential point seems to be that there may be a continuum of the facility with which people in therapy break and re-form their Gestalts of perceived self. The proportion of emerging self-perceptions might be a useful measure in comparing extreme saltatory clients with each other or in comparing the extreme gradual, formative clients with each other but cannot be used equally well to compare these two types of clients.

VI. DISCUSSION

Let us turn now to the strikingly different evaluations of the client by the counselor and the John ratings. If one accepts the counselor's evaluation of the client's experience in therapy, the conclusions would be that: As success in therapy increases, and as the client integration increases, there is a change from discussion of non-self to discussion of self, there is a change from repetitious discussion of self to discussion of original aspects of self, and there is change from discussion of familiar aspects of self to expression of emerging aspects of self.

If one accepts John's evaluations of the client's experience, the conclusions would be that: As the client has a more desirable attitude toward himself, has a greater insight into self and others, and has a better degree of adjustment, he discusses less the emergent aspects of self and more the familiar aspects of self, explores less the original aspects of self and repeats himself more, and discusses less about self and more about non-self.

The conclusions based upon the correlation with counselor ratings are in accord with self-theory as to what should occur in therapy and are supported by the Dymond TAT ratings. The conclusions based on the correlations with the John scales are contrary to this theory.

It is obvious that the consistently contradictory nature of the correlations obtained in this study indicates two consistently opposite perspectives of viewing and evaluating the same or intimately related phenomena. The writer suspects that this contradiction may arise from two current contradictory concepts of adjustment.

One concept would be that growth toward adjustment is like physical growth: the person grows and finally reaches the mature status. He attains a given end status beyond which he does not grow. From this point of view, "adjustment" means a relatively fixed pattern of behavior and of personality organization.

A similar emphasis to the relatively fixed pattern of personality is also given by the psychoanalytic concept that good adjustment is attained when a patient leaves his pattern of socially unrewarded defenses for a pattern of socially acceptable defenses. A person holding this view would then say that the patient has a more favorable "level of defense." Good adjustment seems to depend upon the "level of defense" or the point in psychosexual development at which one is fixed or organized. Briefly, this concept of adjustment emphasizes a relatively fixed organization, an adjusted state.

The first TAT analyst, John, whose work was used in this study, was employing a psychoanalytic orientation. Her TAT Scale 3 was titled "Level of Defense." Her introduction to and description of her scales contain many statements which appear to value stability of structure. Whether this positive evaluation of stability of structure grows out of her primary concern with diagnosis rather than therapy or out of her psychoanalytic orientation is not clear. Certainly many analytic therapists would probably not place this positive value on stability.

Another concept of adjustment, held by many clinicians, would be that a "well-adjusted" person would have a certain type of personality organization that would leave his awareness open to any experience and his feelings sensitive to react fully, and he would be able to consider any idea about himself or other people. In other words, this person would not have defenses. This ideal of no defense is never attained, and, properly speaking, a person is never adjusted but is constantly adjusting. This type of personality organization is very responsive to change in the outside world and within himself. Therefore, some meaning or meanings are always in process of change, either being enriched or being radically altered. Such a person would experience himself as being in a state of flux, in a relatively unfixed condition. A person with this type of organization is free to experience anxiety, fear, joy, shame, love, enthusiasm, and any other emotion or feeling which circumstances may arouse. Briefly, this concept of adjustment emphasizes the changing factors in adjustments and looks at the constant disorganizing and reorganizing in adjusting.

Both concepts imply some constancy and some change, but each concept emphasizes more one aspect than the other.

When the client-centered counselor sees a client's pattern of feeling and of behaving starting to change, perhaps even if the client experiences a high degree of disorganization or loss of control over some emotion, the counselor might think, "This client is moving; this is a sign of progress." The client who most shows this fluid process would be evaluated most favorably. A person who valued positively a state of relatively fixed organization might perceive in a client some loss of conscious control, a free play of emotion, and he might say, "This person is disorganized; he is in a bad condition." A client evaluated favorably by one would be evaluated unfavorably by the other.

The apparently static concept used by John and the apparently fluid concept used by the counselor would result in consistently contradictory evaluations of the changes occurring in therapy. The measures of self-emergence were designed to capture the fluid aspects of the client's experience. Therefore, these measures would correlate very highly but negatively with this TAT analyst and highly but positively with the counselor evaluations.

Although these concepts, if they exist as described, appear contradictory, they can both be applied to the same person, each in its own way, without contradiction. Successful clients achieve a freedom from past fears and establish a new and stable pattern of behavior which they feel to be sufficiently adequate and socially rewarding. Some seem to attain a relatively stable pattern of both public behavior and private experiencing. At this more or less happy state therapy is terminated. Other successful clients also attain a relatively stable and satisfactory pattern of public behavior, but inwardly they are not at rest. They feel a constant activity, a continuous integration of new experiences; they feel very susceptible to change.

Outwardly, perhaps, all successful clients have a relatively stable pattern of behavior, but inwardly some have an equally stable pattern of experience, whereas others feel a continuous reintegration. There is a possibility that the continuous flux is characteristic of such creative people as inventors, composers, writers, etc. On this basis one could value more positively those clients who exhibit this fluid process than those who do not. Whether one values positively the internal flux or not would depend upon whether one feels this process to be creative or destructive. It may be more of one than the other in any given instance. At any rate, it is sound to distinguish between these internal dynamics and public behavior. Internal flux does not necessarily lead to equally continuous change or disorganization of public behavior.

In the case of Mrs. Bico the writer found that the counselor ratings, John's TAT ratings, and the Q-sort adjustment score agreed more than on any other case. (The second TAT analyst did not rate this case.) On the other hand, the proportion of emergents did not rank this client as highly as those measures. The investigator has given his and the counselor's impression that this client did not evince a gradual process of change but changed rather suddenly to new patterns or new insights. He suggested that this client evinced a saltatory rather than a formative process of therapy. The changes in this client to new and relatively stable patterns would be evaluated positively by one holding the fixed concept of adjustment. The counselor would value these changes positively also if he sensed with his client the progress made. In this case, then, these raters would agree on the evaluation. On the other cases, which showed a freer flow of emotion, the evaluations would be contradictory.

It has appeared that the most discriminating of the self-awareness measures were the proportion of emergents and the proportion of repetitions. Emergents capture the fluid process; repetitions capture the fixed status. On these extremes the two concepts would lead to the most strong contradiction. This is what is found in the data.

Both of these bits of evidence support the previously given explanation for the contradictory correlations.

VII. SUMMARY

The investigator set himself the task of measuring increase in self-awareness during therapy. The working hypothesis was: Judged success of therapy correlates positively with increasing self-awareness during therapy. The self-description instrument was developed to define categories of self-awareness so that units of client self-perception could be counted in a content analysis of the recorded case material. Four different criteria of successful therapy were employed: two counselor rating scales; TAT ratings on four scales, ordered according to psychoanalytic theory; the Q-sort adjustment score; and a second independent TAT rating on another scale.

The conclusions from the analysis of the data were:

1. According to the counselor-judgment criterion, there is a positive correlation between success of therapy and increasing self-awareness; the change in self-awareness is evinced in an increasing proportion of descriptions of self, decreasing repetition of old self-perceptions, and increasing emergence of new (previously unknown or unacceptable) aspects of self.
2. According to the psychoanalytically oriented TAT analyst, there is a negative correlation between success of therapy and the threefold movement toward increasing self-awareness.
3. According to the Q-sort adjustment score, there is no correlation between success of therapy and the threefold movement toward increasing self-awareness.
4. According to the second TAT ratings, there is a low but consistent correlation between success of therapy and the threefold change toward increasing self-awareness.
5. The first TAT ratings and the counselor ratings seem to represent two contradictory frames of reference in evaluating the client. The Q-sort adjustment score appears to represent a frame of reference different from these two, which overlaps slightly with the first TAT analyst and more with the counselor. The second TAT ratings seem to represent another frame of reference which is generally congruent with the counselor frame of reference and with the Q-sort adjustment but shows no correlation with the first TAT rater's frame of reference.

It seems that the criterion measures are ordered in their relation to the self-awareness measures along a continuum. The closer the criterion is to client-centered theory, the better the correlation with the self-awareness measures. The counselor judgments were closest both theoretically and statistically. The Dymond TAT ratings follow next in order. The Q-adjustment score, which was based on the judgment of nonclient-centered eclectic clinicians, correlates minimally. John's TAT scales were based on a completely different theory, the psychoanalytic, and gave inverse correlations with the self-awareness measures. The conclusion which seems to follow from these observations is that the hypothesis—increasing self-awareness during therapy correlates with success in therapy—is confirmed when success is measured by instruments which rate highly those changes and states deducible from client-centered theory.

REFERENCES

1. CURRAN, CHARLES A. *Personality Factors in Counseling*. New York: Grune & Stratton, 1945.
2. HAIGH, GERARD V. "Defensive Behavior in Client-centered Counseling," *Journal of Consulting Psychology*, XIII (1949), 181–89.
3. ———. "The Role of Value and Threat in Perceptual Orientation." Ph.D. dissertation, University of Chicago, 1950.
4. HOGAN, RICHARD A. "The Development of a Measure of Client Defensiveness in the Counseling Relationship." Ph.D. dissertation, Department of Education, University of Chicago, 1948.
5. JOHN, EVE S. "Mental Health and the Principle of Least Effort." Ph.D. dissertation, University of Chicago, 1953.
6. RAIMY, VICTOR C., "Self-reference in Counseling Interviews," *Journal of Consulting Psychology*, XII (1948), 153–63.
7. RASKIN, NATHANIEL J. "An Objective Study of the 'Locus of Evaluation' Factor in Psychotherapy." Ph.D. dissertation, University of Chicago, 1949. (Published in W. WOLFF [ed.], *Success in Psychotherapy*, chap. 6. New York: Grune & Stratton, 1952.)
8. SEEMAN, JULIUS. "A Study of the Process of Nondirective Therapy," *Journal of Consulting Psychology*, XIII (1949), 157–68.
9. SHEERER, ELIZABETH T. "The Relationship between Acceptance of Self and Acceptance of Others," *Journal of Consulting Psychology*, XIII (1949), 169–75.
10. SNYDER, WILLIAM U. "An Investigation of the Nature of Nondirective Psychotherapy," *Journal of General Psychology*, XXXIII (1945), 193–223.

11. STEELE, BETTY LOUISE. "The Amount of Exploration into Causes, Means, Goals, and Agent: A Comparison of Successful and Unsuccessful Cases in Client-centered Therapy." A.M. thesis, University of Chicago, 1948.
12. STOCK, DOROTHY. "An Investigation into the Interrelations between the Self-concept and Feelings Directed toward Other Persons and Groups," *Journal of Consulting Psychology*, XIII (1949), 167–80.
13. VARGAS, MANUEL J. "Changes in Self-awareness during Client-centered Counseling." Ph.D. dissertation, University of Chicago, 1952.
14. WOLFSON, KATE S. "Clients' Exploration of Their Problems during Client-centered Therapy." A.M. thesis, University of Chicago, 1949.

CHAPTER 11

The Effect of Psychotherapy upon Certain Attitudes toward Others[1]

THOMAS GORDON AND DESMOND CARTWRIGHT

The findings from research in psychotherapy are fairly convincing with regard to demonstrating that clients learn in therapy to accept and live more comfortably with themselves. It is still to be demonstrated conclusively that clients learn to accept and live more comfortably with others. In fact, one popular conception of clients who have undergone therapy is that they are more "self-centered," more outspoken and aggressive toward others, or perhaps even contemptuous and antisocial. On the other hand, there is some reason to favor the hypothesis that clients learn to accept, value, and respect other people as a result of successful psychotherapy. For support of this view we can turn to clinical data, certain psychological theories of personality, and findings from a handful of research studies.

The theories of Fromm, Horney, and Fromm-Reichmann all state that one can love others only to the extent that one loves one's self. Rogers (6), too, states this relationship explicitly:

> When the individual perceives and accepts into one consistent and integrated system all his sensory and visceral experiences, then he is necessarily more understanding of others and is more accepting of others as separate individuals.

Rogers then attempts to explain how such acceptance of others tends to develop during therapy:

1. Although co-authorship of this paper is indicated, the writers carried out different functions in the research and in the preparation of the paper. The senior author conceived the problem, developed the instrument and the procedures, and supervised the data collection and tabulation. The second-named author did all the computations and contributed numerous original ideas for analyzing and interpreting the data. The senior author assumed major responsibility for the preparation of this paper. Daniel Bergman and Gerald Gratch provided assistance during the stage of tabulating the data.

The person who denies some experiences must continually defend himself against the symbolization of these experiences.

As a consequence, all experiences are viewed defensively as potential threats, rather than for what they really are.

Thus in interpersonal relationships, words or behaviors are experienced and perceived as threatening, which were not so intended.

Also, words and behaviors in others are attacked because they represent or resemble the feared experiences.

There is then no real understanding of the other as a separate person, since he is perceived mostly in terms of threat or nonthreat to the self.

But when all experiences are available to consciousness and are integrated, then defensiveness is minimized. When there is no need to defend, there is no need to attack.

When there is no need to attack, the other person is perceived for what he really is, a separate individual, operating in terms of his own meanings, based on his own perceptual field.

We would add one further element to Rogers' theoretical formulation. The individual who perceives the behavior of others as potentially threatening may try to adjust to this situation by attempting to change or to control others in such a way that the threat is minimized. This need to change or to control others, then, becomes the polar opposite of accepting others as they are.

A number of research studies provide support for the relationship between acceptance of others and acceptance of self. Sheerer (7) found that clients who experienced successful client-centered therapy became more accepting of self and that this change was accompanied by an increase in acceptance of others. Stock (8) also found a relationship between clients' positive and negative feelings toward themselves and toward others. Phillips (5) converted Sheerer's descriptions of self-other attitudes into a questionnaire which was then administered to groups of high-school and college students. Relatively high correlations were found between self-attitudes and attitudes toward others along the dimension of acceptance-rejection. A more carefully constructed questionnaire was developed independently by Berger (3), whose findings supported the original hypothesis as well as the previous studies of Sheerer, Stock, and Phillips. Pearl (4) found a definite positive relationship between high ethnocentrism and low "self-esteem and self-reliance" and "lack of awareness, and anxiety concerning impulse and hostility control." His findings also showed a "decided trend" in the direction of a relationship between increased self-awareness and a reduction of ethnocentrism as a consequence of therapy, though this result was not conclusively demonstrated.

The findings from all these studies seem to justify the following conclusions:

1. There is a relationship between *self-acceptance* (or self-esteem and self-awareness), whether inferred from a person's verbal expressions or judged by the person himself, and *acceptance of others*, inferred or self-rated. This relationship holds when the attitudes toward others refer to people in close personal relationships as well as to certain classes of people, such as specific ethnic groups.
2. An experience in some types of psychotherapy produces significant changes in clients' attitudes toward themselves in the direction of increased awareness and acceptance of self, as measured both by inferences from client statements and by self-ratings.
3. Changes in clients' attitudes toward self during therapy are accompanied by changes in attitudes toward others in the direction of increased acceptance of others, although these changes may not be as great in all types of therapy. Furthermore, attitudes toward particular kinds of "others" may change more than attitudes toward other kinds of "others."

I. THE PROBLEM

The present study is a further investigation of the effect of psychotherapy upon clients' attitudes toward others. It incorporates some of the features of previous studies and adds certain other features. The principal hypothesis under investigation can be stated in a very general way as follows:

> Client-centered individual psychotherapy produces changes in clients' attitudes toward others in the direction of greater acceptance of and respect for others.

In order to formulate this hypothesis in the most testable form, certain operational definitions were developed to make more explicit the terms in the statement of the hypothesis. Some of these operational definitions were developed by the entire research staff as a basis for formulating all hypotheses involved in each of the principal studies in the first block (Block I) of cases of the research program and have already been described in chapter 3. Inclusion of these specific definitions in our hypothesis makes it read as follows:

Clients who complete a minimum of six therapeutic interviews with a therapist of at least moderate experience and claiming a client-centered orientation will demonstrate changes in attitudes in the direction of greater acceptance of and respect for others.

The problem was to determine if a change in attitudes toward others, which one would predict from certain theories of personality, occurred as an outcome of client-centered therapy. Although a similar hypothesis had been supported by two previous researches, it seemed important to resubmit the hypothesis to a test in order to take advantage of the opportunities provided by the total research program and design for utilizing (*a*) a larger sample of clients; (*b*) more rigorous methods of experimental control; (*c*) more precise definitions of the experimental conditions; and (*d*) the additional post-therapy data provided by follow-up measures.

In addition, a different criterion measure of acceptance of others was to be used, one based upon a more extensive definition than those used in previous studies. Sheerer (7) and Stock (8) had relied on the statements of clients during the interviews, whereas in this study an "out-of-therapy" measure of attitudes was desired. Second, rather than employ an instrument made up of direct and relatively undisguised statements of attitudes toward others, as in the questionnaires of Berger (3) and Phillips (5), it was thought desirable to have a more disguised and indirect instrument to minimize the possibility of clients' answering questions the way they thought the therapist wanted them answered. Third, the investigator wanted an instrument that would be more appropriate for measuring attitudes toward "generalized others," as opposed to close, personal "others" (family and social relationships). In other words, the present study called for an instrument that would test the extreme limits of generalization of acceptance of others.

Another reason for wanting to define acceptance of others more broadly was the investigator's interest in the relationship between psychotherapeutic outcomes and democratic attitudes. Many therapists of a client-centered orientation have expressed the opinion that successful client-centered therapy seems to alter the personality of the client in the direction of his becoming more like the kind of person ideally suited to behave effectively in a democratic society. For example, one of the outcomes of therapy appears to be a decreased dependence upon authority. This also seems to be one of the requirements of a democracy—that its citizens be relatively free from dependence upon authority. Not only is freedom from dependence a necessary attribute of the citizen in a democracy but there is also a relationship between dependence and "placing a cheap value on one's self," or lack of self-acceptance and respect. Following this logic, if client-centered therapy increases one's feelings of self-acceptance and self-respect, it also decreases submissiveness and dependence upon authority. If it can be demonstrated further that placing a higher value on the worth of self is accompanied by placing a higher value on the worth of others, a second requirement for the "democratic personality" would seem to be fulfilled. This study then is attempting to investigate whether successful client-centered therapy fosters the development of certain attitudes and values generally associated with a "democratic personality."

II. THE METHOD

Description of Instrument

The search for an appropriate measure of "democratic attitudes toward others" naturally led to the instrument devised in the California studies of prejudice and authoritarian attitudes. These important studies, reported by Adorno *et al.* (1), were undertaken chiefly for the purpose of discovering the roots of prejudice within the deep layers of the personality structure of the individual. To accomplish this, these investigators developed a series of attitude scales to measure both prejudicial attitudes and certain other social attitudes thought to be associated with prejudice.

The instrument developed by the California group, therefore, seemed particularly appropriate for the present study. Although their instrument did not seem ideally suited in all respects for the present study, it was "ready-made," it had been carefully constructed and field-tested on thousands of subjects, its split-half reliabilities were relatively high, it was easy to administer and score, it had been shown to have adequate power to differentiate among people with a wide range of degrees of authoritarian attitudes, and it had demonstrated sufficient validity to correlate with many of the findings from the clinical interviews and projective tests. For these reasons the decision was made to use the three subscales developed in the California study. These made up part of our operational definition of acceptance of and respect for others.

The search for additional measures of acceptance of others led to an instrument devised by David H. Jenkins.[2] Because his "Sentiments Inventory" was constructed as a measure of certain attitudes considered consistent with effective group membership behavior in democratic groups, many of the items in the scale seemed particularly appropriate for the present study. While Jenkins' inventory had not been so rigorously tested as the California instrument, its items were of a similar nature to those of the latter. Inclusion of parts of this inventory in the present study was based upon the expectation that this would supplement the California instrument and thus give a broader and more complete definition to our concept of democratic attitudes toward others.

All the items from whatever source were combined for easy administration and scoring into one inventory, henceforth to be designated as the Self-Other Attitude Scale (S-O Scale). Illustrations from its eight subscales are given below.[3]

ETHNOCENTRISM SCALE (E-SCALE)

The E-scale provides a measure of ethnocentrism, which, as defined by Levinson, is "a tendency in the individual to be 'ethnically centered,' to be rigid in his acceptance of the culturally 'alike' and in his rejection of the 'unlike.' " The scale is identical to the E-scale in Form 60A of the California study, reported by Adorno *et al.* (1). Their scale focuses on attitudes toward three groups: Negroes, Jews, and other American minorities. Sample items from the E-scale are:

Anti-minority

3. Zoot-suiters prove that, when people of their type have too much money and freedom, they just take advantage and cause trouble.

2. An unpublished inventory made available to the authors by David H. Jenkins, Research Director and Editorial Planner, *Adult Education*, Chicago.

3. A complete copy of this test can be obtained from the Counseling Center.

Anti-Semitic

9. One trouble with Jewish businessmen is that they stick together and prevent other people from having a fair chance in competition.

Anti-Negro

6. Negroes have their rights, but it is best to keep them in their own districts and schools and to prevent too much contact with whites.

POLITICAL-ECONOMIC CONSERVATISM SCALE (PEC-SCALE)

The PEC-scale is designed to measure political-economic ideology along a liberalism-conservatism dimension. It is identical with the PEC-scale, Form 60A, developed by the California group. The rationale for its inclusion in that study was that conservatism was associated with ethnocentrism. An illustrative item is:

4. It is up to the government to make sure that everyone has a secure job and a good standard of living.

THE FASCIST SCALE (F-SCALE)

The F-scale attempts to measure implicit antidemocratic (or fascistic) trends in attitudes. Adopted directly from Form 60A of the California study, this scale attempts to tap some of the more unconscious or the deeper forces that make for an antidemocratic "potential" in the personality of an individual. An illustrative item is:

1. Human nature being what it is, there will always be war and conflict.

AUTHORITARIAN DEPENDENCY SCALE (A-SCALE)

The A-scale contains items intended to measure attitudes suggestive of dependency upon experts (authorities), of desires for authoritative statements, of reluctance to accept the validity of group-determined values or ideas. Eight of the items were borrowed from Jenkins' "Sentiments Inventory," and two were devised by one of the writers (T. G.). Inclusion of this scale was based upon the theory that acceptance of the worth and uniqueness of others would be related to group-centered values rather than to leader-centered or authority-centered values. One sample item is:

61. Many times discussions are stimulating, but greater progress is usually made if there is a specialist who knows the answers present in the group.

THE LEADERSHIP SCALE (L-SCALE)

Items in the L-scale are intended to measure attitudes related to the acceptance or rejection of democratic leadership and the notion of leadership as a set of functions that can be performed by the group rather than exclusively by the leader. All the items in this scale were borrowed from Jenkins' "Sentiments Inventory." An item from this scale is:

65. In cases of disagreement among group members, the group leader should be the final judge or arbitrator.

ACCEPTANCE OF DIFFERENCES OF OPINION (D-SCALE)

The D-scale consisted of ten items selected from Jenkins' inventory which aimed at measuring acceptance of and desire for differences of opinion in group discussion and a willingness of the group to review decisions and consider new evidence. Placing a high value on fostering and admitting differences of opinion in group discussion seemed consistent with the dimension of "acceptance of others." One sample item is:

62. Dissenting opinions should be regarded as a valuable contribution to the group's solution of a problem.

ACCEPTANCE OF DEMOCRATIC MEANS AND METHODS (M-SCALE)

The M-scale consisted of ten items from Jenkins' inventory which were designed to measure attitudes suggesting a belief in the need for democratic means if democratic ends are to be achieved and suggesting an acceptance of individual responsibility to abide by the decisions of the group. Again an illustrative item is:

63. When disciplinary problems arise in a group, it is usually necessary to abandon democratic procedures.

DESIRE TO CHANGE OTHERS (C-SCALE)

The C-scale consisted of items devised by the senior author for the purpose of measuring the tendency to change, reform, or direct the lives of others. Such a tendency seemed related to a lack of acceptance of others. A typical item is:

64. If you have a friend who you feel doesn't have good moral and ethical principles, it is your duty to try to influence him to adopt better ones.

Experimental Design

The design for this study is identical with the over-all design of the Block I studies, described previously in chapter 3. The only difference is that some of the results reported here will be based upon a somewhat smaller number of clients than originally planned for Block I, inasmuch as at the time of writing this report a few of the clients had not yet completed the post-therapy and follow-up tests.

Administration and Scoring Procedures

The S-O Scale was administered individually, and with only a few exceptions the same examiner did each of the repeated administrations for each subject. There was no time limit for the S-O Scale. The subjects indicated their answers on a separate IBM answer sheet by placing a check on a five-point scale, ranging from "Strongly agree" to "Strongly disagree."[4] Most of the items were stated in such a way that a "Strongly agree" received a score of 7 and a "Strongly disagree" a score of 1: Intermediate points on the scale were assigned scores of 5, 4, and 3. Scores were tabulated for each item, for each subscale, and for the total S-O Scale. High scores indicate lack of acceptance of others (antidemocratic); low scores, the opposite. Therefore, a decrease in score from one administration to another represents the predicted direction in this study.

III. RESULTS

Group Equivalence on First Scores

To determine if groups differed, in spite of the matching procedure, in terms of total scores on the first administration of the S-O Scale, Student's *t* test was calculated for the difference between related means of the experimental (E) and control (C) groups. Table 1 shows that the two groups were not significantly

4. This procedure differs from that of the California study where a seven-point scale was used. Since the Jenkins inventory employed a five-point scale, this procedure was adopted for the total S-O Scale. This now seems unfortunate in retrospect, for, had a seven-point scale been used, direct comparisons between some of our results and those of the California study could have been made without conversions.

different, thus permitting the conclusion that the experimental and control groups were equivalent with regard to first scores on the S-O Scale.

A similar test of significance was calculated for the difference between unrelated means of the experimental wait or own-control group and the no-wait group, this difference proving nonsignificant, as shown in Table 2.

Further indication of the equivalence of the different groups was provided by the fact that males (N = 16) and females (N = 11) did not differ significantly on first scores.

Change during the Wait (No-Therapy) Period

Having first established that all the groups were equivalent in terms of total scores on first administration of the S-O Scale, the

TABLE 1

DIFFERENCES BETWEEN FIRST-SCORE* MEANS OF EXPERIMENTAL AND CONTROL GROUPS

	E Group†	C Group	
N	26	26	
Mean	311.31	340.33	
S.D.	71.77	79.63	t = 1.35 P > .10

* For the wait group of E and the wait group of C, first scores are the pre-wait scores; for the no-wait groups of E and C, first scores are the pre-therapy scores.

† One client is omitted because no matched control was available.

TABLE 2

DIFFERENCES BETWEEN FIRST-SCORE MEANS OF OWN-CONTROL AND NO-WAIT GROUPS

	E-Wait Group	E-No-Wait Group	
N	10	17	
Mean	307.00	316.47	
S.D.	80.3	48.5	t = .326 P >.10

next step was to determine whether any change in attitudes occurred in the period during which a portion of the experimental group waited for approximately sixty days before beginning therapy. It will be recalled that this procedure was adopted in order to control for the factor of motivation for therapy. The equivalent-control group, though serving as a control for no-therapy, consisted entirely of persons who presumably were not intending to go into therapy. Thus, so that there would be a *client* group who experienced a no-therapy period, almost half of the clients in the experimental group were tested, asked to wait for sixty days, and tested again immediately before entering therapy. Table 3 shows

TABLE 3

DIFFERENCES BETWEEN MEANS OF PRE-WAIT AND PRE-THERAPY TOTAL SCORES FOR THE E-WAIT GROUP

	Pre-wait	Pre-therapy	
N.	10	10	
Mean.	307.0	304.4	
$S.D._{Diff.}$	28.91		$t=$ .27 $P > .10$

that no significant change in the attitudes of clients occurred during the wait period.

Change during a Therapy Period as Compared to an Equivalent No-Therapy Period

Having established that clients motivated for therapy do not change over a period of no therapy, we are thus permitted to compare the change of clients during therapy with the change of the matched controls during an equivalent time period of no therapy. This calls for a comparison of the experimental group and the control group with regard to differences in scores between the pre- and post-therapy administrations. Table 4 shows these differences with regard to total scores on the S-O Scale. The difference between the means of the two groups was not statistically significant.

Table 5 shows the comparison between the experimental group and the control group with regard to differences between pre- and post-therapy scores on each of the subscales of the S-O Scale. None of these differences was significant even at the .10 level of confidence.

From the results shown in Table 4 and 5 we can conclude that there were no significant changes in total scores or subscale scores during the therapy period.

TABLE 4

COMPARISON OF DIFFERENCES BETWEEN PRE- AND POST-THERAPY TOTAL SCORES OF EXPERIMENTAL AND CONTROL GROUPS

	E Group	C Group	
N	27	23	
Mean diff. (pre- to post-therapy)	− 9.1	− 4.2	
$S.D._{Diff.}$	37.55	29.42	$t = .45$ $P > .10$

TABLE 5

COMPARISON OF DIFFERENCES BETWEEN PRE- AND POST-THERAPY SCORES ON SUBSCALES OF EXPERIMENTAL AND CONTROL GROUPS

SUBSCALE	MEAN DIFFERENCE BETWEEN PRE- AND POST-THERAPY SCORES		
	E Group (N=27)	C Group (N=23)	P
E-scale	−0.63	+0.32	>.10
PEC-scale	+1.41	+0.32	>.10
F-scale	−2.82	+1.59	>.10
A-scale	−0.59	−1.84	>.10
L-scale	−1.81	−1.04	>.10
D-scale	−1.04	−0.45	>.10
M-scale	−1.89	+0.55	>.10
C-scale	−1.76	−0.59	>.10

Change from Pre-therapy to Follow-up

Perhaps a more severe test of the effect of psychotherapy upon clients' attitudes toward others is to measure the amount of change during the period from the pre-therapy administration to the follow-up administration. Previous studies of certain outcomes of therapy have demonstrated that during the follow-up period some clients continue to show changes that were initiated during the therapy period. It is also important not to overlook the possibility that some clients may not begin to change until after the therapy has been terminated. Table 6 shows the comparison between the

TABLE 6

COMPARISON OF DIFFERENCES BETWEEN PRE-THERAPY AND FOLLOW-UP MEAN TOTAL SCORES OF EXPERIMENTAL AND CONTROL GROUPS

	E Group	C Group	
N	22	11	
Mean diff. (pre-therapy to follow-up)	− 8.54	− 6.45	
$S.D._{Diff.}$	41.5	20.0	$t = .15$ $P > .10$

experimental group and the control group with regard to changes in total scores from the pre-therapy point to the follow-up point of six months to one year.

This comparison is made less sharp by the small number of cases in the control group. At the time of writing, however, the required time had not elapsed after the post-therapy administration of the S-O Scale for some of the control cases. Nevertheless, the results shown in Table 6 demonstrate that there was no significant difference between the experimental group and the control group with respect to changes in total scores from pre-therapy to follow-up.

In order to determine if during this same period changes occurred in the scores of any of the subscales, the experimental group pre-therapy and follow-up scores were compared for significance of differences on each of the eight subscales. From the summary of these comparisons in Table 7, it can be seen that there were no significant differences between the pre-therapy and follow-up scores of the experimental group on any of the subscales.

Comparison of Changes of Successful Clients and Less Successful Clients

For the purpose of determining whether success in psychotherapy is associated in any way with changes in attitudes toward others during and following therapy, a multiple criterion of success was constructed for the purpose of differentiating clients in the experimental group on the basis of the degree of success of their therapy experience. Changes in S-O Scale scores could then be related to this criterion of success.

TABLE 7

COMPARISON OF PRE-THERAPY AND FOLLOW-UP SCORES FOR THE EXPERIMENTAL GROUP ON EACH OF THE SUBSCALES ($N = 22$)

Subscale	Mean Differences Pre-therapy to Follow-up	$S.D._{Diff.}$	t	P
E-scale.......	−0.91	9.3	0.45	>.10
PEC-scale....	+0.41	6.2	0.30	>.10
F-scale.......	−3.77	16.1	1.06	>.10
A-scale.......	−0.77	7.4	0.48	>.10
L-scale.......	−1.40	5.9	1.08	>.10
D-scale.......	−1.82	5.1	1.63	>.10
M-scale.......	−1.14	5.6	0.95	>.10
C-scale.......	+0.55	6.4	0.39	>.10

Construction of the multiple criterion.—It was considered desirable to include in the multiple criterion estimates of client success from the counselor, from the client himself, and from a diagnostician.

1. *Counselor estimate.*—Each counselor at the conclusion of therapy had filled out the Case Rating Scale (see chap. 7, Table 1) containing a global rating of the outcome of therapy ranging from complete failure to marked success. It was this over-all rating that was utilized in computing the multiple criterion.

2. *The client's own estimate.*—An index based upon the degree of resemblance of the client's post-therapy self Q-sort distribution to a criterion Q-sort distribution obtained by asking "experts" to judge items indicating good adjustment and items indicating poor adjustment (see chap. 5).

3. *The TAT analyst's estimate.*—An index based upon a blind rating of the Thematic Apperception Test (TAT) protocols of both experimental and control groups. A single rating on a seven-point scale of adjustment was given to each TAT record (see chap. 8). The final index was one which combined the separate indexes: (*a*) the rating of the post-therapy TAT and (*b*) the difference between the pre- and post-therapy TAT ratings (an index of change during therapy).

Clients in the experimental group were ranked on the basis of each of these three adjustment criteria, henceforth called "counselor rating," "Q-adjustment score," and "TAT rating." Intercorrelations between these three rankings were as follows:

	ρ
Counselor rating and Q-adjustment score..	.60
Counselor rating and TAT rating..........	.46
Q-adjustment and TAT rating...........	.36

These correlations indicate that no one of the three adjustment indexes was sufficient alone, inasmuch as each was contributing an estimate on some dimension of adjustment not measured, or measured considerably less, by the others.

The next step in constructing the multiple criterion was to compute ranks by summing each client's ranks on the three separate criteria and dividing by three. The final step involved converting the *ranks* on the multiple criterion to a simple *rating scale* whose range was identical to the range of the counselor's original ratings (from a rating of 2 to a rating of 9), so that comparisons might be made between different criteria of success.

Comparison of successful and failure cases with respect to change from pre-therapy to follow-up.—The clients in the experimental group were divided into two groups on the basis of multiple criterion ratings, those with ratings from 5 to 9 designated as the "successfuls" and those with ratings from 2 to 4 designated as the "failures." These two groups were compared with respect to the mean changes in total score from pre-therapy to follow-up. The results of this comparison are presented in Table 8, where it can be seen that clients rated as successfuls tended to change in the predicted direction of greater acceptance of others, while those rated as failures tended to change in the opposite direction, although the difference between these two group means is significant at only the .10 level. Furthermore, these results must be interpreted with caution, inasmuch as it is not possible to contrast these findings with those from a similar analysis of the no-therapy control (C group) for the obvious reason that they cannot be divided into success and failure groups. However, by examining the mean total score change from pre-therapy to follow-up of those control group cases who at time of writing had completed their follow-up testing, a rough comparison can be made between their change over this period and the changes of the success cases in the therapy group (E group). The mean pre-therapy to follow-up change for the eleven completed control group cases was found to be −6.45, as has been shown in Table 6. This finding detracts considerably from the obtained difference between the successes and the failures with

TABLE 8

DIFFERENCES BETWEEN SUCCESSES AND FAILURES WITH RESPECT TO CHANGES FROM PRE-THERAPY TO FOLLOW-UP

	Successes	Failures	
N	16	6	
Mean changes (pre-therapy to follow-up)	−17.62	15.67	
$S.D._{Diff.}$	48.11	20.98	$t=1.719$ $P=.10$

respect to their changes, for it indicates that changes in the predicted direction may occur over time with no therapy. Although this control group change is not so great as that which occurred in a "successful" therapy period, it is greater than that which occurs in an "unsuccessful" therapy period! Since none of these differences is statistically significant, such findings are at best only suggestive.

Contrasting trends between the success and failure clients.—Although no significant differences were found between the successfuls and failures with respect to changes either during therapy or during the period of therapy plus follow-up, contrasting trends can be observed in the changes of these two groups of clients. Those few successfuls who formed a part of the wait group showed a slight decrease in scores during this period of no therapy; the total success group showed a somewhat larger decrease in scores during the therapy period and an even larger decrease during the period including both the therapy and the follow-up times. In contrast to this trend, those failures who were in the wait group showed a slight increase in scores during the period of no therapy; the total failure group showed almost no change in scores during therapy and a fairly large increase during the period including both therapy and the follow-up.

Although none of these changes approaches the .10 level of significance, the trend is of interest, for it appears that successful clients become slightly more accepting of others even during the period of waiting to begin therapy and continue to change more in this direction during therapy and even more in this direction after completing therapy. Failure clients become slightly less accepting of others while waiting to begin therapy, change very little during therapy, and become even less accepting of others after completing therapy.

The Relationship between First Scores and Subsequent Changes in S-O Scale Scores

The hypothesis that changes in attitudes toward others during therapy might be related to the degree of initial acceptance of clients as indicated by their first scores was suggested by a study reported by Barron (2) and by the findings of a study by Tougas, reported in chapter 12. These studies demonstrated a relationship between first scores on the E-scale and subsequent success in therapy. It seemed logical to infer that where a client starts in terms of his first score on the total S-O Scale might be related to the direction and amount of subsequent change in score during therapy, since in the two previous studies first scores (at least on the E-scale) had been shown to be related to counselors' judgments of relative success of therapy.

The first test to determine if this relationship existed involved the computation of Spearman rho correlations between total scores on the first administration of the S-O Scale and subsequent changes in total scores during both the wait period and the therapy period. For this purpose the highest total score on the first administration was given a rank of 1; similarly the highest increasing change was assigned a rank of 1, and the highest decreasing change the bottom rank for each group. Table 9 summarizes the results of this test. The various groups were treated separately, inasmuch as the first administration for the two wait groups (own-control wait group and equivalent-control wait group) occurred at pre-wait, while for the other two groups (no-wait experimental group and no-wait control group) the first administration occurred at pre-therapy.

From Table 9 it can be seen that the no-wait experimental group, unlike its matched control group, showed a significant negative relationship between initial scores and direction of subsequent

TABLE 9

CORRELATIONS BETWEEN FIRST TOTAL SCORES AND SUBSEQUENT CHANGES IN TOTAL SCORES

Group	Rho Correlations between First Scores and Changes From			
	N	Pre-wait to Pre-therapy	N	Pre-therapy to Post-therapy
No-wait experimental	14	....	14	−.544*
No-wait control	14	....	14	+.156
Own-control experimental	9	+.317	8	+.500
Wait control	9	−.113	8	−.090

* Significant at less than the .05 level of confidence.

change—that is, initial high scorers tended to decrease their scores during therapy, and initial low scorers tended to increase their scores. We can infer that the experience of therapy is associated with a *de-emphasizing* of attitudes toward others, at least for the no-wait therapy group but, interestingly enough, not for the own-control group. Although significant only at the .09 level of confidence, the rho of +.500 indicates that the wait group became *more extreme* or emphatic in their attitudes; similarly this tendency prevailed even during the wait (no-therapy) period, as indicated by the rho of +.317 ($P > .10$). This is supported by the low negative rho coefficients for the control wait group. This interesting finding will be treated separately in a subsequent section.

The Relationship between Success in Therapy and De-emphasis in Attitudes

Having discovered a tendency for the no-wait experimental group of clients to de-emphasize their attitudes over the period of therapy, the investigators became interested in examining whether a relationship existed between this tendency and success in therapy. Do successful clients show more de-emphasis of attitudes over therapy than do less successful clients? For this purpose rho correlations were computed between total scores on first administration and changes in total scores from pre- to post-therapy and from post-therapy to follow-up for the *entire no-wait client group*. Then rho correlations were computed between the same two variables for this *no-wait group minus those clients rated as failures* and for the *no-wait group minus clients rated as either failures or moderate successes* (rating of 5 or 6). Similar correlations were computed for the matched control group. This procedure provided a comparison of four different groups (control group, experimental group, successful experimental group, and most successful experimental group) with respect to their tendency to de-emphasize attitudes during therapy and during therapy plus the follow-up period. These results are summarized in Table 10.

TABLE 10

RHO CORRELATIONS BETWEEN FIRST SCORES AND SUBSEQUENT CHANGES FOR CONTROL GROUP, EXPERIMENTAL GROUP, EXPERIMENTAL GROUP MINUS FAILURES, EXPERIMENTAL GROUP MINUS FAILURES AND MODERATE SUCCESSES

GROUP	RHO CORRELATIONS BETWEEN FIRST SCORES AND CHANGES FROM			
	N	Pre- to Post-therapy	*N*	Pre-therapy to Follow-up
Control	23	−.099	11	+.052
Experimental	24	+.082	22	−.005
Experimental minus failures	18	−.231	16	−.259
Experimental minus failures and moderate successes	11	−.325	10	−.721*

* Significant at the .02 level of confidence.

Although only one rho coefficient is significant beyond the .05 level of confidence, it can be seen from Table 10 that there is a consistent relationship between clients' success in therapy and the tendency to de-emphasize their attitudes during and after therapy. The more successful the therapy, the more the tendency toward de-emphasis of attitudes.

The relationship between success in therapy, initial scores, and subsequent changes can be presented more clearly graphically. Consequently, in Figure 1 the changes between pre-therapy and follow-up have been plotted separately for each client in the experimental group. Successes, moderate successes, and failures are also differentiated. Figure 1 allows us to obtain a visual picture of the scores of each client at each of two points—before therapy and at the follow-up point. These general trends are apparent: (*a*) Initial high scorers and initial low scorers tend to be failures or moderate successes, and they tend to intensify their attitudes from pre-testing to follow-up. If they were high initially, their scores increase; if they were low initially, their scores tend to decrease. (*b*) Initial medium scorers tend to be successes and tend to *de-emphasize their attitudes*—that is, the higher scorers within this middle range decrease their scores from pre-testing to follow-up; the lower scorers increase them from pre-testing to follow-up.

The Relationship between First Scores and Success in Therapy

In the following chapter Tougas reports significant differences between the marginal successes and both the failures and the successes with respect to mean first scores on the total S-O Scale. In that study clients were grouped as to degree of success on the basis of counselor ratings alone. Inasmuch as in this study we consistently used a multiple criterion of success, it was considered important to check Tougas' findings by a similar analysis in which clients would be grouped on the basis of our multiple criterion of success. Means of the first scores were calculated for each of the three groups: successes (ratings of 7, 8, 9), moderate successes (ratings of 5, 6), and failures (ratings of 2, 3, 4). In contrast to the nonlinear relationship found by Tougas, a slight but nonsignificant linear relationship was found between first scores and success in therapy, when the degree of success was based upon our

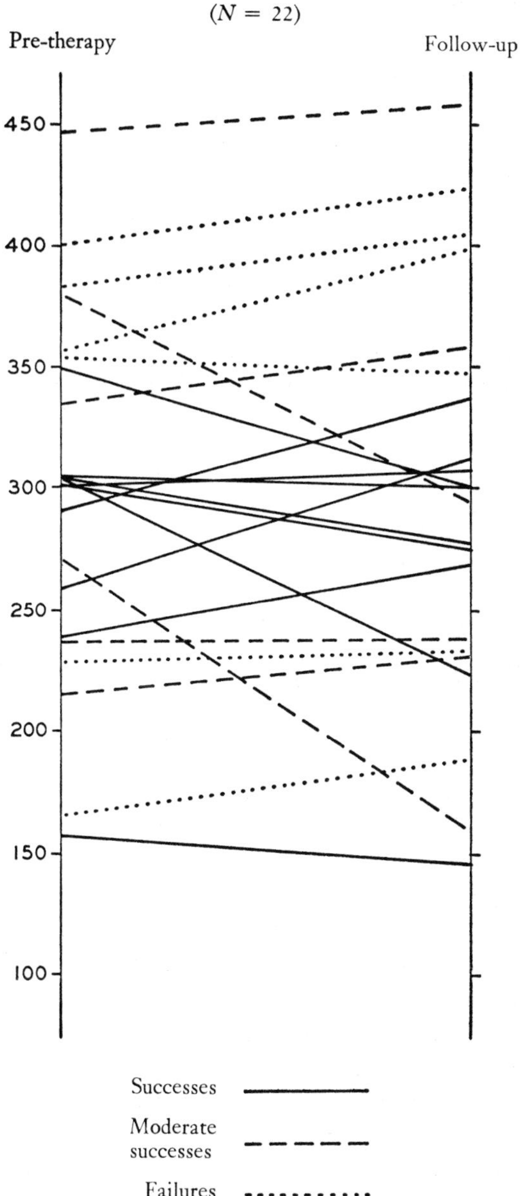

Fig. 1.—Changes in S-O Scale total scores from pre-therapy to follow-up for successes, moderate successes, and failures.

multiple criterion. However, as shown in Table 11, the differences between the three groups were too small to be significant, a finding which detracts somewhat from Tougas' findings based solely upon the counselor's rating.

It would appear that no conclusive statement can be made about the relationship between first scores on the S-O Scale and success in therapy, inasmuch as different results are obtained when different criteria of success are employed. Additional studies may show that the relationship is nonlinear, as is suggested by Tougas' findings, in which case one could predict moderate success but not differentiate between successes and failures. Or the relationship may turn out to be linear, as suggested in Table 11, in which case

TABLE 11

COMPARISON OF SUCCESSES, MODERATE SUCCESSES, AND FAILURES WITH RESPECT TO MEAN FIRST SCORES ON TOTAL S-O SCALE

	Success Group	Moderate Success Group	Failure Group
N..............	11	7	6
Mean first scores..	293.0	308.0	314.2

one could predict all degrees of success. Or, finally, additional studies may find there is no statistically significant relationship at all, as was demonstrated in the present study.

The Effect of the Wait Period

It will be remembered that the purpose of including a wait group in the design of the present study was to provide a control for the factor of "motivation for therapy"—that is, to see if any changes would take place in a group of clients motivated for therapy during a period of no therapy. This control feature supplemented the control provided by the equivalent or nonclient control group. Some interesting differences between the wait group and the no-wait group of clients were discovered, as indicated earlier in this chapter. Specifically it was found that the wait group tended to increase the intensity of its attitudes both during the wait period and during therapy, in contrast to the trend of the no-wait group toward a de-emphasis of attitudes (see Table 9). In other words, wait-group clients whose first scores were high tended to have even higher scores on second and third administration, and those scoring low tended to register even lower scores.

This interesting finding suggested the hypothesis that clients who had to wait sixty days before beginning their therapy developed certain feelings—perhaps of hostility and resentment—toward the Counseling Center or the research.[5] It seems possible that they felt they were being perceived as research subjects rather than as clients or as objects rather than as persons. Were they not being asked to delay getting help for themselves in favor of helping the Center conduct a research study? Such feelings and attitudes might have shown up as a tendency to express their attitudes more intensely, more extremely—agreeing more strongly where they previously had agreed and disagreeing more strongly where they previously had disagreed.

Certain deductions may be made from this hypothesis. One might deduce that (*a*) the wait-group clients would like their counselors less than those clients who did not wait; (*b*) they would take some of their hostility out on themselves in the form of lower ratings of their own adjustment than those of the no-wait group; (*c*) more of the original wait group would drop out of the research, and those who dropped out would do it sooner than the drop-outs from the no-wait group; and (*d*) the wait-group clients would benefit less from the therapy than clients in the no-wait group.

All four of these deductions were tested in one way or another, and all were confirmed, even though none was confirmed with a high degree of statistical significance. Tables 12, 13, 14, 15, and 16 summarize the findings from the tests of these four deductions.

From Table 12 it can be seen that at the beginning of therapy counselors of the wait group felt that their clients liked them less than did the counselors of the no-wait group. The fact that there was no difference between the two groups after therapy is a reasonable reflection of the modification of hostile attitudes through close and prolonged acquaintance.

5. This hypothesis and the subsequent statistical tests were developed by Desmond Cartwright.

From Table 13 it is apparent that the wait group's evaluation of their own adjustment was lower than the no-wait group's at each point, though there is a slight tendency for the wait group to approach the adjustment level of the no-wait group immediately after therapy.

Although none of the differences in Tables 14 and 15 is large enough to be statistically significant, the percentage of clients who had to be dropped from the experimental group because they failed to complete the required number of interviews for inclusion in that group was larger for the wait group than for the no-wait group. Also, those in the wait group who dropped out did so earlier than those in the no-wait group.

Although the chi square in Table 16 is significant at only the .15 level of confidence, the general hypothesis is borne out that wait-group clients did not benefit as much from therapy as the no-wait clients, as judged by the multiple criterion of success.

To summarize the findings relating to differences between those who waited for therapy and those who did not, all four of the deductions were confirmed by independent measures, though no single deduction was confirmed at an acceptable level of statistical confidence. We must conclude that more rigorous demonstration of the general hypothesis is necessary. Our findings suggest, however, that, when clients are asked to wait for a period of sixty days before entering therapy, something happens to these clients which intensifies their social attitudes, and this intensification of their attitudes seems psychologically consistent with an increase in hostility or resentment which manifests itself in a number of different ways—less liking for their counselors, a greater tendency to drop out of therapy and to drop out sooner, lower evaluation of their own adjustment, and less benefit from therapy as judged by several independent criteria. The present study does not permit a more rigorous test of this general hypothesis, nor does it allow us to determine what specific factors are operating to produce the effects suggested by our findings. The present study does suggest that the wait-group technique for controlling the factor of motivation for therapy should not be employed without serious consideration of the nontherapeutic effect upon the clients who are required by the procedure to delay their entrance into therapy.

TABLE 12

COUNSELOR RATINGS OF DEGREE OF LIKING FOR COUNSELOR BEFORE AND AFTER THERAPY (Extreme Liking = 9; Extreme Dislike = 1)

Group	N	Mean Counselor Rating	
		Pre-therapy	Post-therapy
Wait...........	9*	4.56	6.44
No-wait.........	17	5.06	6.42

* One wait-group client was not rated.

TABLE 13

CLIENT EVALUATIONS OF OWN ADJUSTMENT AS MEASURED BY THE Q-ADJUSTMENT INDEX

Group	N	Mean Q-Adjustment Index		
		Pre-therapy	Post-therapy	Follow-up
Wait.............	9	27.1	38.8	33.9
No-wait..........	15	31.3	39.8	39.8*

* Based on $N = 12$.

TABLE 14

ATTRITION FOR WAIT GROUP AND MAIN GROUP

Group	No. Originally Assigned to Experimental Group	No. Failing To Complete Six Interviews	Per Cent Attrition
Wait.........	21	11	52.4
No-wait.......	30	13	43.3

IV. SUMMARY AND DISCUSSION

The results of this study do not support the hypothesis as originally formulated, namely:

> Clients who complete a minimum of six therapeutic interviews with a therapist of at least moderate experience and claiming a client-centered orientation will demonstrate changes in attitudes in the direction of greater acceptance of and respect for others.

When all such clients taken as a group were compared with an equivalent no-therapy control group with respect to changes in attitudes toward others, no statistically significant differences were found.

The findings suggest that three additional factors, other than an experience in therapy, are operating to effect changes in scores during therapy and including the follow-up period: (*a*) the original

TABLE 15

MEAN NUMBER OF INTERVIEWS FOR ATTRITION CLIENTS IN WAIT GROUP AND IN MAIN GROUP

Attrition Clients	*N*	Mean No. of Interviews
Wait group	11	1.55
No-wait group	13	2.39

TABLE 16*

COMPARISON OF WAIT GROUP AND NO-WAIT GROUP WITH RESPECT TO MULTIPLE CRITERION RATINGS OF SUCCESS IN THERAPY

Group	*N*	No. of Clients with Multiple Criterion Rating of		
		Success	Moderate Success	Failure
Wait	9	4	1	4
No-wait	15	7	6	2

* $\chi^2 = 3.960$; $P = .15$.

(pre-therapy) position of a client on a continuum of acceptance of and respect for others; (*b*) the degree to which a client's experience in therapy is judged successful; and (*c*) whether or not a client was in the wait group. How these three factors operate in combination cannot be accurately determined from the results of this study, yet certain hypotheses for future investigation are suggested by some of the present findings: (*a*) Clients who fall roughly into a middle range of initial scores tend to change in the direction of becoming less extreme in their attitudes toward others, and they in turn tend to benefit most from therapy. (*b*) Clients who fall either above or below a middle range of initial scores tend to become more extreme—in the direction of becoming less accepting of others if they were initially high scorers and more accepting of others if they were initially low scorers. Such clients also tend to benefit less from their therapy experience.

These general trends must be viewed in relation to the effect of a client's being in the wait or own-control group, for having to wait for a period of sixty days seems to be associated with both lack of success in therapy and becoming more extreme in one's attitudes toward others.

Further caution is required when interpreting the results of this study, inasmuch as the sample of clients (as well as the sample of controls) proved to be one characterized by rather accepting and democratic attitudes even before therapy. For example, as contrasted with a theoretical total score of 436, which would be obtained by marking each of the 109 items at the midpoint of 4 on the scale 7–5–4–3–1, the mean total score (before therapy) for our sample of clients was 311.31. Furthermore, the highest (most antidemocratic) scorer obtained a pre-therapy total score of only 492, which is much less than one standard deviation above the theoretical mean of 436. In other words, as a group the sample of clients in this study was already fairly accepting and democratic in attitudes. Consequently, the present study does not answer the question of what therapy does to the attitudes of extremely antidemocratic and unaccepting clients.

In view of the fact that the original hypothesis was not supported by the findings, one could ask: (*a*) Was the hypothesis a poor one? (*b*) Was the criterion employed in this study inappropriate for the variable being investigated? Each of these questions will be considered separately.

With regard to the adequacy of the original hypothesis, the findings suggest that a better hypothesis would have been one which included the dimension of "success in therapy." This study demonstrated that the experience of therapy was not the same for all the clients—that is, clients utilized the therapy with varying degrees of effectiveness, as measured by several different independent criteria (i.e., the counselors' judgments, the TAT adjustment index, and the Q-sort adjustment index). Furthermore, the findings indicate that clients whose therapy was most successful, as judged by these criteria, tended to change their attitudes more than clients whose therapy was not successful, though this difference was not highly significant. Nevertheless, a more fruitful hypothesis for future studies would be one which predicted changes in attitudes in clients whose therapy reached some minimum level of success.

The findings also suggest that a better hypothesis would have been one which predicted that clients experiencing "successful" therapy would become less extreme in their attitudes toward others rather than the hypothesis that all clients become more accepting and democratic. When therapy is most successful, it may tend to "liberalize" one's attitudes toward others, whether these at first be strongly democratic or strongly antidemocratic. Psychologically, this may be the equivalent of the concept of reduction in defensiveness—that is, clients after therapy may not have as much need to indorse strongly either highly democratic or highly antidemocratic attitudes. We may also use the concept of "openness to experience" to explain such an effect, postulating that therapy enables the client to admit to awareness past experiences which previously have been denied because they were inconsistent with his extreme attitudes. Thus, after therapy a client may modify his attitudes in such a way as to make them more consistent with his new reality.

Whatever the theoretical basis for this tendency to de-emphasize one's attitudes during therapy is, should it be demonstrated more conclusively in future studies, we may have to revise some of our psychological notions about liberalism and conservatism. *Extreme* liberalism may be found to be associated with some of the same personality characteristics as extreme conservatism or authoritarianism. The militant liberal may be equally as inflexible, defensive, and perhaps insecure or unstable as the authoritarian.

Returning to consideration of the S-O Scale as a criterion for our concept of "acceptance," there is some justification for doubting its adequacy. It is likely that therapy has a measurable effect upon clients' attitudes toward significant others in their lives, such as parents and friends, and we have the studies of Sheerer (7) and Stock (8) to support this. Yet, where the attitudes are those toward more generalized others, such as leaders, minorities, sexual deviates, group members, and the like—then perhaps personal therapy does not result in more acceptance on the part of all clients. Cultural stereotypes and the absence of personal contact with such "others" may be operating against the potential effect of therapy, as in the case of attitudes toward minorities. To change such attitudes as these, more than personal therapy seems required—perhaps experiences involving close interaction with "others." If this is true, then group therapy may have a greater effect upon attitudes toward others, as suggested by Pearl (4).

REFERENCES

1. ADORNO, T. W.; FRENKEL-BRUNSWIK, ELSE; LEVINSON, D. J.; and SANFORD, R. N. *The Authoritarian Personality*. New York: Harper & Bros., 1950.
2. BARRON, F. X. "Psychotherapy as a Special Case of Personal Interaction: Prediction of Its Outcome." Ph.D. dissertation, University of California, 1950.
3. BERGER, E. M. "The Relation between Expressed Acceptance of Self and Expressed Acceptance of Others," *Journal of Abnormal and Social Psychology*, XLVII (1952), 778–82.
4. PEARL, DAVID. "Ethnocentrism and the Concept of Self." Ph.D. dissertation, University of Chicago, 1950.
5. PHILLIPS, E. L. "Attitudes toward Self and Others: A Brief Questionnaire Report," *Journal of Consulting Psychology*, XV (1951), 79–81.
6. ROGERS, CARL R. *Client-centered Therapy*. Boston: Houghton Mifflin Co., 1951.
7. SHEERER, ELIZABETH T. "An Analysis of the Relationship between Acceptance of and Respect for Self and Acceptance of and Respect for Others in Ten Counseling Cases," *Journal of Consulting Psychology*, XIII (1949), 169–75.
8. STOCK, DOROTHY. "An Investigation into the Interrelations between the Self-concept and Feelings Directed toward Other Persons and Groups," *Journal of Consulting Psychology*, XIII (1949), 176–80.

CHAPTER 12

Ethnocentrism as a Limiting Factor in Verbal Therapy[1]

ROLLAND R. TOUGAS

The present study was designed to study factors which might throw some light on the nature of failure cases in therapy. It was not one of the projects originally planned for the first block (Block I) of cases, but, as it seemed likely that the presence of ethnocentric attitudes in the client might be related to some of the causes of failure, it appeared desirable to look into this. Both the measures necessary for such a study were readily at hand: a rating of the success or failure of the therapy (see chap. 7) and a measure of ethnocentrism in the clients from the Self-Other Attitude Scale (S-O Scale).[2]

Before proceeding to this, let us review a few pertinent researches, particularly those exploring the influence of ethnocentrism on interpersonal relations and on perceptual functioning within the individual. The term "ethnocentrism" is used throughout these studies as defined by Adorno (1): "[Ethnocentrism] is based on a pervasive and rigid ingroup-outgroup distinction; it invokes stereotyped negative imagery and hostile attitudes regarding

1. This research was undertaken during the author's internship at the Counseling Center, University of Chicago. Sincere thanks are due to the Center's staff for their generous co-operation in making the data available and to Desmond Cartwright, Rosalind Dymond, Eugene Gendlin, Robert Lipgar, William Littlewood, and Carl R. Rogers for invaluable suggestions.

2. The California Scale of Ethnocentrism (E-scale) (1) was included in its entirety as part of the S-O Scale reported on in the preceding chapter by Gordon and Cartwright. The E-scale, devised as an indirect measure of ethnocentrism, is composed of twenty items of social stereotypes to which the subject indicates agreement or disagreement. Scores may range theoretically from 20 to 140. Since all the statements are worded negatively, agreement (and, therefore, a high score) is presumed to be an index of ethnocentrism. The reliability of this scale for different groups has ranged from .69 to .90. Its validity has been established through interview ratings and questionnaires.

outgroups; and stereotyped positive imagery and submissive attitudes regarding ingroups; and a hierarchical, authoritarian view of group interaction in which ingroups are rightly dominant, outgroups subordinate."

Considering first the influence of ethnocentric attitudes on interpersonal relations, Barron (2), in an unpublished dissertation, has shown that the degree of ethnocentrism in a client was prognostic of rated success or failure in therapy of Sullivanian orientation. Clients "low" in ethnocentrism were generally rated as being good therapeutic risks. It could be inferred that these same clients were better able to explore interpersonal relations with their therapists. The possibility of altering ethnocentric attitudes through therapy was studied by Pearl (15), who showed that high degrees of ethnocentrism were essentially refractory to individual therapy but slightly modifiable under a combination of intensive individual and group therapy. Both studies employed the E-scale as a measure of ethnocentrism. Both were suggestive of difficulty in interpersonal relationships in ethnocentrics and of the tenacity of ethnocentric ideology.

Turning now to studies of perceptual functioning in relation to measures of ethnocentrism, only a sample of the most relevant of recent researches will be touched on. Block and Block (3) demonstrated that "high" scorers on the E-scale tended to the rapid establishment of a norm in an experiment on autokinetic phenomena. "Low" scorers were individualistic and resisted not only early closure but also those suggestions by the experimenter which seemed arbitrary. They suggest that ethnocentrism, rapid norm establishment, and submission to authority may all reflect a compulsive structuring approach to a somewhat unpredictable environment.

Fisher (7), in exploring the relation between ethnocentrism and memory changes, found that "high" scorers on the E-scale showed greater distortion in successive reproductions of asymmetrical test figures than did "low" scorers. The latter were better able to alter the course of "*pragnanz*" and to preserve the idiosyncrasies of the original designs. On a similar dimension, Korchin *et al.* (8) showed reduced accuracy and greater primitivation or tendency toward symmetry in a group of subjects who were asked to reproduce a series of sample designs before and after a frustrating task. The demonstration of perceptual regression even under mild frustration would seem related to a similar phenomenon in ethnocentric subjects.

Rokeach (10) showed a significant correlation between E-scale scores and three distinguishable types of cognitive organization. "Low" scorers used what was termed a comprehensive approach, middle scorers favored an isolated approach, and "high" scorers a narrow one. Bronfenbrenner (4), in reviewing this study, alluded to the strong similarity of these types to W, D, and Dd functioning in Rorschach terms, but this cannot be considered demonstrated.

Finally, the studies on rigidity and the related ones on the influence of anxiety on the higher mental processes seem highly relevant. Cowen's (5) as a representative paper has shown the tendency of rigidity in problem-solving to be a generalized personality variable. Thus, the phenomena of perseveration, distortion, concreteness, premature closure—in short, the bringing of *old* responses to *new* situations—would seem to be likely concomitants of ethnocentric functioning as well as of behavior under stress.

The studies that have employed the E-scale as a base upon which to assess either therapeutic progress or intra-individual functioning indicate quite clearly that increasing degrees of ethnocentrism (as measured) are correlated with decreasing probabilities for change in therapy. Important differences in perceptual and general psychological functioning within the individual would also seem involved. The presence of ethnocentric attitudes would then seem to point to impaired functioning and possibly maladaptive behavior in the sense of not being able to "shift" appropriately under changing environmental conditions. Conditions of ambiguity and uncertainty would further exaggerate these effects and would probably be most clearly evidenced in social contexts.

The therapeutic relationship is a social one in a limited sense. It is also an environment in which unpredictability is consciously reduced to a minimum. Thus, the assessment of change within the clients in the relatively controlled social context of verbal therapy could then be an index of the client's plasticity, on the one hand, or of the effectiveness of the particular environmental conditions, on the other. If an individual does not or cannot change in what is considered an optimal environment, it is generally held that the limiting conditions are within the individual. Only the possible limitations within the clients will be examined through this study.

The probability that some failures in therapy may be due to the presence of ethnocentric attitudes and their related psychological concomitants has been implied by Barron's (2) research. To test further this hypothesis was one of the purposes of the present investigation. If an independent group of clients with varying degrees of ethnocentrism are again rated on a scale of success and failure in a manner systematically related to the degree of ethnocentrism measured, possible limitation to verbal therapies may be revealed. To put it somewhat differently, the degree of ethnocentrism in a client would then be seen as a limiting factor on his plasticity in a therapeutic setting. A basis for studying failure cases in therapy would likewise be established.

Thus, to seek to isolate "good therapeutic risks" from those who are not would seem to be a worth-while step in the direction of studying the conditions which seem to lead to failure in therapy. This constituted the second aim of this investigation: to define failure cases more clearly, preparatory to a more detailed research on their intra-individual organization. With this end in view, the differentiation of clients with varying degrees of rated success relative to their measured expression of ethnocentric attitudes would be attempted. For this purpose, two sets of comparable data were available. Ratings of success and failure in therapy of Sullivanian orientation for twenty-five clients had been paired with their E-scale scores in the study made by Barron (2). A similar set of ratings and scores was obtained for a group of twenty-seven clients seen at the Counseling Center, University of Chicago.

The specific hypotheses to be tested with the available data, then, were: (*a*) there is no difference in the range of optimal functioning between Sullivanian and Rogerian therapies with respect to varying degrees of ethnocentrism in clients and (*b*) "good therapeutic risks" are statistically differentiable from those who are not with reference to their E-scale scores when paired with ratings of success and failure in therapy.

I. PROCEDURE

Subjects

Two groups of individuals who presented themselves for psychotherapy constituted the sample upon which this exploratory study was based. The first of these, Barron's (2), was at the Langley Porter Clinic, University of California, and the second at the Counseling Center of the University of Chicago. Both were part of research studies, the sampling for which was restricted only by regular intake procedures at both institutions and the client's willingness to participate in an experiment. It was assumed that each group was fairly representative of the client population in general. Heterogeneity of composition would seem to be one essential feature extending through age, sex, degree of maladjustment, motivation for therapy, and range of functional intelligence. The California group of clients included twenty-five men and women, seen by six Sullivanian psychiatrists, four of whom were male and two female. The Chicago client-centered group consisted of twenty-seven clients, sixteen men and eleven women. There were ten therapists involved, all of whom were male.

Method

Two sets of data were available from each group and for each client. A rating of "improved" or "unimproved" was related in each instance to a particular client's E-scale score.

The ratings themselves admittedly could vary in so far as they might reflect different goals of therapy and/or a margin of error in estimating therapeutic gains. For purposes of this study it was assumed that the ratings were comparable. For the California group, ratings on a scale of improvement were made by psychiatrists other than the therapists, whereas the Chicago therapists rated their own clients on a nine-point scale varying from "complete failure" to "marked success"[3] (see chap. 7).

An additional set of scores was available for the Chicago group

3. Wherever the California group was compared to the Chicago group, the ratings used were as follows: for the California group, ratings were scaled with top half considered improved, other half unimproved; for the Chicago group, ratings of 5 through 9 were considered improved, whereas ratings of 1 through 4 were considered unimproved (see Tables 1 and 3 and Fig. 1).

from the S-O Scale (see chap. 11), of which the E-scale is but one part. The S-O Scale generally extended the range of social attitudes and stereotypes assessed and was seen as being useful in reflecting the pervasiveness of ethnocentric functioning.

In all instances the data related to the *first* contact the client had with the test, whether this was the pre-wait for the wait group or the pre-therapy for the no-wait group (see chap. 3 for the design of this research). The first part of the analysis involved a comparison of Sullivanian and Rogerian therapy along the dimension of ethnocentrism in the clients. The second part assessed intergroup differences for purposes of future selection of experimental subjects. The statistical analysis was thus directed at attempting to differentiate between the degree of "good therapy risk" in a sample of clients *prior* to therapy.

II. RESULTS

An estimate of the range of effectiveness of therapy conducted under Sullivanian and Rogerian orientations with respect to ethnocentrism, as measured by the E-scale, may be gained through inspection of Figures 1 and 2 and Table 1.

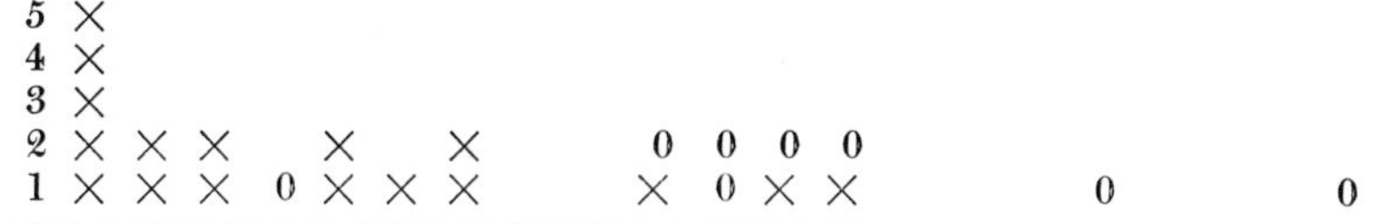

20 25 30 35 40 45 50 55 60 65 70 75 80 85 90 95 100 105 110 115 120 . . . 140

FIG. 1.—Frequency of improved and unimproved in relation to E-scale scores (ratings by other an own psychiatrist). California group ($N = 25$). × = improved; 0 = unimproved.

E-SCALE SCORES

5 ×
4 × × × 0
3 0 × × × 0
2 × × × × × × 0
1 × × × × × 0 × 0 × ×

20 25 30 35 40 45 50 55 60 65 70 75 80 85 90 95 100 105 110 115 120 . . . 140

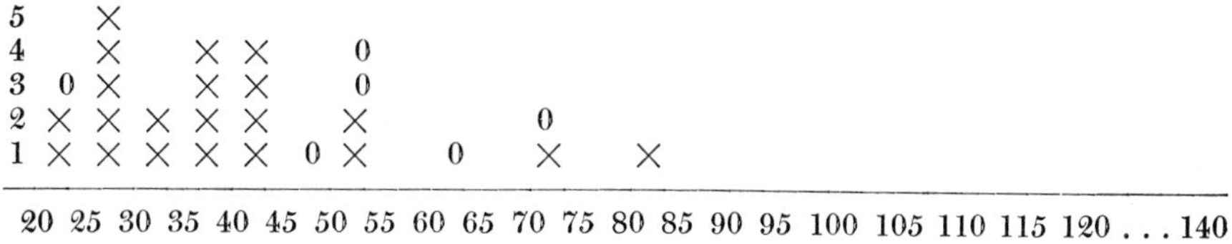

FIG. 2.—Frequency of improved and unimproved in relation to E-scale scores (own counselor tings). Chicago group ($N = 27$). × = improved; 0 = unimproved.

E-SCALE SCORES

There is a marked concentration of instrumentally rated success at the lower end of the scale. Unimproved cases are almost exclusively at the higher levels, that is, above the mean. In each group a few scattered successes are evident beyond a certain range. A chi square of these two frequencies yielded a score of .60 (or .23, applying Yates's correction). For 1 degree of freedom the probability that a difference as large as the one obtained could occur by chance alone lies between .50 and .30 (corrected to .70, following Yates). The hypothesis that the range of effectiveness for Sullivanian therapy is no different from that found under the Rogerian approach cannot be rejected by the present findings.

TABLE 1

CHI-SQUARE COMPARISON OF THE FREQUENCY OF IMPROVED AND UNIMPROVED IN THE CALIFORNIA AND CHICAGO GROUPS

	Improved	Unimproved	χ^2	P
California (N = 25)...	17	8	.60 (.23)*	.50 – .30 (.70)
Chicago (N=27)......	21	6		

* Using Yates's correction.

The evidence thus far seems to indicate the possibility that there may be an optimal range of functioning for verbal therapy, be it Sullivanian or Rogerian, with respect to ethnocentrism. The possibility that some individuals may be "good therapeutic risks" and some not seems to be indicated. That the E-scale scores seem so intimately related to this probability warrants closer scrutiny of this variable.

Within Block I of the research program at the Counseling Center of the University of Chicago, E-scale scores were available for twenty-seven clients as well as for twenty-six selected control subjects. The norms from this larger sample of N = 53 could thus serve as background for evaluating particular group scores.

From a statistical point of view, the Chicago therapy group and its control group form a homogeneous population, there being no difference as to either means or variances between them. The t test yielded .92 and the *F* test 1.84, neither value approaching the 5 per cent level of confidence. Using the mean of the combined group ($N = 53$) as a reference point to estimate the range of effectiveness of the particular therapies concerned, Figures 1 and 2 make it fairly clear that, up to and including the group mean of 45 on the E-scale, one could predict a fair degree of success and that, beyond this point, the probability of improvement decreases to the level of chance or less. As to the probability of success or failure at the higher levels of the E-scale, the present data give little information. The total range of the scale is from 20 to 140. Only 9 per cent of the California and Chicago samples combined exceeded the mid-

TABLE 2

COMPARATIVE DATA FOR THE CHICAGO THERAPY AND CONTROL GROUPS ON THE E-SCALE (FIRST CONTACT): MEANS, STANDARD DEVIATIONS, STANDARD ERROR OF THE MEANS, "T" AND "F" TESTS

Group	*N*	Mean	Standard Deviation	Standard Error	*t*	*P*	*F*	*P*
Therapy.....	27	41.55	16.41	3.16				
Control......	26	46.57	22.06	4.33	.92	>.05	1.84	>.05
Total...	53	44.01	19.50	2.68				

point of 80 on the test. Further, there were only two cases scoring beyond 85, both of which were rated unimproved. These data were considered insufficient to assess the effectiveness of therapy at the upper reaches of the scale for the samples employed.

A study by Pearl (9) would seem to confirm the decreasing probability of success at the higher levels of the E-scale. For a group of twelve hospitalized patients experiencing both individual and group therapy, an E-scale mean of 74.41 was obtained. Only three patients were rated as improved, two as marginally improved, and seven as failures. These data are not directly comparable to those used in this study but are added here to indicate an apparent trend.

To this point there has been established a statistical frame of reference within which to compare the two groups of clients on the E-scale to their rated progress in therapy. Now, utilizing the group mean as a cut-off point to dichotomize arbitrarily improved from unimproved therapy cases, Table 3 shows that a difference as large as that obtained for the California group could occur by chance alone less than 5 times in 100. For the Chicago group the probability is at something less than the 2 per cent level of confidence. Combining the two obtained chi squares of 4.06 and 6.03 yields a value of 10.09, which for 2 degrees of freedom indicates that results such as these could occur by chance alone at something less than 1 in 100 samplings. We may now reject with some confidence the hypothesis that the obtained pairings of instrumentally rated success or failure and their related E-scale values were due to chance.

TABLE 3

CHI-SQUARE† COMPARISON OF THE FREQUENCY OF IMPROVED AND UNIMPROVED RATINGS IN THE CALIFORNIA AND CHICAGO GROUPS USING THE MEAN E-SCALE SCORE (44.01) AS A DICHOTOMY POINT

SAMPLE	E-SCALE SCORE		χ^2‡	*P*
	20–45	46–140		
California improved.......	11	6	4.06	<.05*§
California unimproved.....	1	7		
Chicago improved........	17	4	6.03	<.02*
Chicago unimproved......	1	5		

† Attention is drawn to a shortcoming in the use of chi square as a test of significance of difference in the frequencies of success and failure in the samples available. Though obviously inadequate in that cell frequencies and theoretical expectancies do not reach minimum limits, Table 3 was included for the following reason: pooling the data from the California and Chicago samples raised the theoretical frequencies above minimum limits and still yielded a highly significant chi square of 12.40 ($P < .01$). Despite this, however, caution is urged in the acceptance of the results.

‡ Using Yates's correction.

§ A single asterisk (*) is used to denote significance at the 5 per cent level and a double asterisk (**) at the 1 per cent level throughout this chapter.

While the present data offer no possibility of clarifying this problem further, we may assume that something within the therapists, or within the clients, or in the interaction between them accounts for the obtained results. Though the therapy ratings may be considered as the most likely source of bias,[4] the independence of

4. A multiple criterion, as against the unitary one of counselor ratings used in this study, was developed by Cartwright (chap. 11) and was applied to twenty-four of the twenty-seven Chicago clients. Three clients rated on the single dimension criterion were retained in this new distribution. This effects some shuffling in the actual clients rated as successful or as failing to profit from therapy. Using the same dichotomy point as above, the chi square obtained was now 4.09, which, for 1 degree of freedom, is a value significant at between the .05 and the .02 level of confidence.

sampling, the fact that sixteen therapists were involved, the relative independence of some of the ratings, the fact that therapists of different orientations were involved and that the research projects from which the data were obtained were not designed for the present purpose—all lend some support to their reliability. On a more objective basis, and restricted to the Chicago group of clients, Dymond's study (see chap. 5) indicates a high degree of reliability between counselor ratings of success in therapy and measured adjustment ratings on the part of the clients. There remains, then, the possibility of re-examining the clients' E-scale scores for further clarification of the nature of success and failure groups in relation to this measure of ethnocentrism. The results and comments that follow pertain to the Chicago group exclusively.

The twenty-seven clients in the Chicago group were rated as to improved or unimproved on a nine-point scale. For purposes of this study ratings of 7–9 shall constitute the "improved group," ratings of 5 and 6 shall be termed "marginally improved," and ratings of 1–4 shall be termed "unimproved."

Referring now to Table 4, it may be seen that the subgroups

TABLE 4

TABLE OF E-SCALE MEANS AND STANDARD DEVIATIONS OF THE IMPROVED, MARGINAL, AND UNIMPROVED CHICAGO THERAPY SUBGROUPS (BASED ON THE SINGLE CRITERION OF OWN COUNSELOR RATINGS)

Counselor Ratings	*N*	Mean	*S*
Improved (7–9)	11	45.45	17.66
Marginal (5–6)	10	31.40	16.85
Unimproved (1–4)	6	51.33	14.67
Total group	53	44.01	19.50

thus formed fall below, at, and above the mean for the normative group. It should also be noted that the marginally improved group is below the mean, the improved group at the mean, and the unimproved above it. From Table 5, the improved group is significantly different at less than the 5 per cent level of confidence from the marginal group (t of 2.16 for 19 degrees of freedom) but not differentiable from the unimproved group (t of .65, P = .65 for 15 degrees of freedom). However, the marginal group is different as to means from the unimproved group at the 1 per cent level of confidence (t of 3.18, $P < .01$ for 14 degrees of freedom). The F test for homogeneity of variance proved insignificant in all instances. This then assures the obtained differences as being due to differences in the means of the respective groups.

So far in this study, evidence has been presented which supports the hypothesis that there may be an optimal range in the effectiveness of some verbal therapies with respect to ethnocentrism. The range of effectiveness may be defined operationally as between the lower limit (20) and the group mean (45) on the E-scale. Also it

TABLE 5

TABLE OF "T" TEST COMPARISONS OF IMPROVED, MARGINAL, AND UNIMPROVED CHICAGO THERAPY SUBGROUPS ON THE E-SCALE (BASED ON THE SINGLE CRITERION OF OWN COUNSELOR RATINGS)

	Control (N = 26)	Improved (N=11)	Marginal (N=10)	Unimproved (N=6)
Therapy group (N=27).............	t .92 $P>.05$ F 1.84 $P>.05$	t .63 $P>.05$ F 1.15 $P>.05$	t 1.82 $P>.05$ F 1.05 $P>.05$	t 1.31 $P>.05$ F 1.31 $P>.05$
Improved..........	....	....	t 2.16 $P<.05$* F 1.09 $P>.05$	t .65 $P=.65$ F 1.44 $P>.05$
Marginal..........	....	....	....	t 3.18 $P<.01$** F 1.31 $P>.05$

was shown that, within the Chicago sample, subgroups of improved, marginally improved, and unimproved could be differentiated. Despite the limitations of very small samples, the improved group could be reliably differentiated from the marginal and the latter from the unimproved. Though the unimproved group could not be differentiated from the improved, examination of the tables and raw data indicate a clear trend toward failure as E-scale scores increase beyond the group mean. Pending further research with more adequate sampling, it may be said that there is a progression in the effectiveness of some verbal therapies with respect to ethnocentrism from minimal to maximal to failure as scores on the E-scale move from their lower limit to the mean and beyond.

Finally, a duplicate analysis was made of the Self-Other Scale[5]

5. Acknowledgments are due to Thomas Gordon for his helpful discussions and suggestions on his Self-Other Scale, for a fuller description of which the reader is asked to see chap. 11.

in an attempt to gain corroborative evidence for the above findings. The E-scale, it will be remembered, is one part of the total scale of social attitudes. Similar findings would tend to confirm the generality and pervasiveness of ethnocentric functioning.

From Table 6 and with reference to Table 5, it may be seen that the same relationships are again demonstrated. The improved group is clearly differentiable from the marginal group, which in turn is reliably different from the unimproved group with respect to means on both the E-scale and the entire S-O Scale. Again, the improved group is not distinguishable from the unimproved, but

TABLE 6

TABLE OF "T" TEST COMPARISONS OF IMPROVED AND UNIMPROVED ON THE SELF-OTHER SCALE (SUBGROUPS DERIVED FROM OWN COUNSELOR RATINGS)

	Control ($N=26$)	Improved ($N=11$)	Marginal ($N=10$)	Unimproved ($N=6$)
Therapy group ($N=27$)	t 1.29 $P>.05$ F 1.22 $P>.05$	t 1.03 $P>.05$ F 1.18 $P>.05$	t 1.91 $P>.05$ F 1.81 $P>.05$	t .99 $P>.05$ F 1.25 $P>.05$
Improved	....	....	t 2.73 $P<.02$* F 1.53 $P>.05$	t .16 $P=.85$ F 1.06 $P>.05$
Marginal	....	....	....	t 2.57 $P<.05$* F 1.44 $P>.05$

the same trend appeared, with failures getting scores above the mean.[6]

Operationally, and for purposes of selection, differing degrees of therapeutic risk could be defined by limits of the improved group on the S-O Scale, 339.63 ± 66.03. For scores below 273.60, marginal success is most probable. Those scoring above 405.66 are very likely not to succeed. This suggested operational definition of the optimal range of some verbal therapies with respect to ethnocentrism, and now of social attitudes generally, is subject to the limitations of the present small sample and to further investigation as to its reliability.

6. The reader's attention is drawn to the finding that, when a multiple criterion of success or failure in therapy is employed, the groups are no longer differentiable (see chap. 11).

III. DISCUSSION

The present study has confirmed the general notion that the degree of ethnocentrism present in a client is prognostic of rated success or failure in some forms of individual therapy where the rating is done either by the client's own counselor or by an independent therapist. While only two groups of clients, and consequently two verbal therapies, were directly comparable on the basis of available data, Pearl's study (9) would tend further to substantiate the decreasing probability of success in verbal therapy with pervasive ethnocentrism in the client. Thus, research results from independent sources tend to support those advanced by the California group and particularly the contention that "the main traits of the ethnocentrist are precisely those which, when they occur in the setting of a clinic, cause him to be regarded as a poor therapeutic risk" (1, p. 974). The implied limitation this imposes on individual therapy generally is an important problem, especially since ethnocentric attitudes have also been shown to be widespread in the population and their influence on interpersonal and group relations anything but salutary.

With reference to the two samples of clients in this study, it would seem that self-referred individuals are generally *not* highly ethnocentric, if it may be assumed that the E-scale scores adequately reflect the presence of ethnocentrism in the general population of clients. Not only did 92 per cent of the fifty-two clients involved score below the scale's midpoint of 80, but there was a marked concentration at the lower end of the scale. This is reflected by the group mean of 41.55 for the Chicago clients, where the range of the scale is from 20 to 140. Distributionally, all but one of this group scored below the E-scale midpoint. This is to say that in the Chicago group there were no high scorers in the sense given to that category by Adorno *et al.* (1), that is, 102–140. There were only two "highs" in the California sample (see Figs. 1 and 2); in Pearl's group there was but one. This would seem to confirm the anti-ethnocentric trend in the Chicago sample in particular and possibly of self-referred clients in general. This is further supported by the findings of the California group (1), where a consistent relationship was demonstrated between degrees of ethnocentrism and educational level, functional intelligence, social class, and age. In contrasting E-scale means, of therapy clients and other specialized groups, the anti-ethnocentric trend of the former is highlighted. For example, hospitalized veterans (organics) score 100 on the average; male San Quentin prisoners, 92; Maritime Union men, 86; Langley Porter Clinic patients, 73; working-class men and women, 66. The above averages are extrapolations from scores obtained on a shorter and earlier form of the E-scale but are statistically comparable within reasonable limits. Pending further evidence to the contrary, it may thus be held that self-referred clients may be expected to be generally anti-ethnocentric.

Despite the fairly definitive anti-ethnocentric character of the clients in this study, there were among those who remained in therapy for an extended period of time a number of failure cases. The only distinguishing sign permitted by the present results was that failure cases were generally above the group mean on the E-scale. In so far as this scale does not necessarily indicate increasing degrees of maladjustment but rather a dynamic interplay of several uncontrolled factors subsumed under the category of ethnocentrism, it does not seem possible to say more than that failure cases are probably different from those who are successful in terms of their respective psychological organization.

Let us consider now the probability of there being a difference in the intra-individual organization of the failure cases, as a group, and as compared to the more successful cases. The clinical description of "high" scorers as against "low" scorers offered by Adorno *et al.* (1) suggests a basically different perceptual organization in these widely separated groups. Whereas the former *project* their feelings on a moralistic basis of good or bad and have no conscious content to their anxieties, the latter *introject* their feelings from the reactions of others to them and have much insight as to the nature of their anxieties, albeit frequently with much distortion. The maintenance of security and the means of acquiring safety and satisfaction are thus diametrically opposed in individuals deemed withdrawn (low scorers) as against those seen as projecting themselves (high scorers). For the groups under consideration here the difference in mode of perceptual functioning claimed should probably be attenuated to quite some extent in view of the narrow range on the E-scale as noted above. However, if this basic difference should be substantiated, as Block and Block's study (3) suggests, a problem of alteration in the very mode of perception would seem indicated for the failure group particularly. From perceiving people in hierarchical terms to the possibility of viewing others and self as equals is one possible description of the task of therapy as envisaged in terms of cognition.

From another point of view, the results of this study indicate a nonlinear relationship between E-scale scores and counselor ratings in therapy. The progression, as noted above, was that the lowest mean scorers were rated as marginally successful, those at the group mean as successful, while those beyond the group mean were rated unsuccessful more frequently than chance would allow. Additionally, there was evidence (2, 6) to support the hypothesis that success in therapy was related to the functional capacity of an individual to form a meaningful interpersonal relationship. The nonlinear function of measured ethnocentrism and ratings in therapy and the greater probability of success for the person who can "communicate significantly" (6) to some extent suggest that there may be here varying degrees of autism at the lower extreme of the scale, and of conventionality at the other extreme. Put somewhat differently, there seems to be a shift from a more purely idiosyncratic view of the social world and of the self to one more nearly molded by public or group expectancy as more successful clients are contrasted to failures. Autism in the present context is taken to mean the investing of highly personalized meanings into conventional symbols, words, and ideas. Thus, in extreme instances, abstract terms and many concrete ones would reflect the *personal* experience of the individual and not the more generally accepted meaning of them. Being my "self" could thus vary all the way from a highly individualized expression of feeling to the very conventionalized portrayal of a social expectancy. The particular social context in which the expression was being viewed would be violated in the former case and ritually confirmed in the latter. In both instances, however, there would be a distortion of objectivity and, in the second case, a denial of self. Consensual validation would be underplayed in "low" scorers and overrated in "higher" scorers.

Now, the nature of the E-scale and the manner in which it is scored indicate that a "low" scorer is predominantly and strongly in disagreement with what are held as stereotypes in the culture. In order to average around 31, as the marginals did, at least fifteen of the twenty items would have to be strongly disagreed with. As for the successful group, strong disagreement up to eight items, with some degree of acceptance of cultural stereotypes, would be necessary to average about 45. For the failure group, objection sinks to the level of about five items or less, with subsequently higher degrees of acceptance or neutrality toward the remaining fifteen to meet the obtained group norm. In other words, the progression seems to describe movement from a largely individualized frame of reference to one more nearly depersonalized, that is, carrying much less personal conviction if at all. In the more general sense, the descending order of disagreement, or the corresponding increasing order of acceptance, of negatively worded cultural stereotypes seems to describe the breadth and depth of social contact the individual has acquired and accepted or that he is presently capable of.

This hypothesis finds some support in the validation study (1), where, through questionnaires and interviews, it was shown that "low" scorers tended to be essentially introspective, withdrawn, social isolates, and given to depression, whereas in the high scorers increasing degrees of expressive hostility, projection, and bound-anxiety were observed. This would seem to mean that "low" scorers would tend to be more individualized and, in a therapeutic setting, more autistic and defensively isolated. Beyond the group mean, and where failure cases become more frequent than do successes, the present results would seem to imply increasing in-groupishness or conventionality and quasi-isolation but of a different quality from that of "low" scorers. Whereas the former seem withdrawn from adequate social contacts, the latter seem segregated from them. An essentially idiosyncratic frame of reference is thus contrasted to a more nearly in-group-centered one. In the face of the present evidence, both are narrow and constricted but with qualitatively different rigidity aspects inherent within them. The capacity for change and particularly the ability to withstand disorganization, which of necessity precedes change, would thus seem a possible distinguishing characteristic of anti-ethnocentric clients in comparison to those showing increasing degrees of ethnocentric functioning.

Finally, if it may be assumed that the ability to form meaningful interpersonal relationships is a crude index of "selfhood," the results of the present study seem to point to an important difference in degree of achievement or loss of "selfhood" between "low" scorers and those beyond the group mean. Too great a degree of conformity, or conformity for conformity's sake, seems to lead to progressive depersonalization. On the other hand, having too few "shared meanings" seems to lead to increasing individuation and to isolation of self. Whereas the foundation of "selfhood" seems present but possibly unintegrated in "low" scorers, it seems more diffuse and unassimilated in the "higher" scorers. In neither case does there seem to be enough of a "self" actualized, and, the less a person is a "self," the poorer a therapeutic risk he seems to be. The further suggestion that there may be a more feasible balance between individualism and conventionality seems reflected in the moderately anti-ethnocentric group who were more successful in therapy. It is planned to study the nature and direction of clients' areas of identification, as reflected in the E-scale, in an effort to further clarify the problem of failure in therapy.

IV. CONCLUSIONS

With regard to the single variable of ethnocentrism, within two groups of clients, in voluntary verbal therapy, and faced with either interpretation and focusing on interpersonal reactions or with reflection of feeling centering on "self," the following tentative conclusions seemed warranted:

1. There was no difference in the frequency of improved and unimproved clients in the two samples used in this study.
2. The probability of a client being rated as improved, if his E-scale score was at or below the mean, derived from a normative group, was significantly different from chance at less than the 1 per cent level of confidence.
3. With respect to ratings of improvement in therapy, a limited range of effectiveness was indicated for Sullivanian and Rogerian therapeutic approaches. This finding should be qualified to the extent that the exact comparability of the ratings could not be ascertained and was not considered part of this study.

4. Evidence was presented to the effect that the Chicago counselor ratings were indicative of a client's improvement in adjustment. There was no evidence available on which to assess the reliability or validity of the California sample's ratings.
5. Within the Chicago sample three subgroups were statistically differentiable on the basis of their respective ratings and E-scale scores. Thus, for purposes of a projected study, "good therapy risks" may be discriminated from those less likely to succeed at well beyond chance expectancy, at least with reference to ethnocentrism and some verbal therapies.
6. The results in paragraph 5 were somewhat more sharply delineated by analysis of the full S-O Scale, of which the E-scale is one part. Corroborative evidence for the generality and pervasiveness of ethnocentric attitudes was also indicated.

The two hypotheses being examined in this study thus seemed tenable. A limitation in the range of effectiveness of some verbal therapies was shown with respect to the degree of ethnocentrism in the clients as measured by the E-scale. There was no difference in such range of effectiveness between Sullivanian and Rogerian therapy in action. It was also shown that the E-scale alone, or the total S-O Scale, may be used for selection of subjects portraying presumably differing degrees of therapeutic risk for the purpose of a projected study. The support for this hypothesis was limited to the condition of utilizing the single dimension criterion of "own counselor" rating of client success or failure for separating the groups.

V. SUMMARY

From two independent sources data were available on a measure of ethnocentrism in clients in therapy. One group of clients was seen in a Sullivanian setting; the other was Rogerian. Ratings of improved and unimproved were also available for each of the fifty-two clients involved. It was assumed that the ratings were comparable for the present purpose.

A statistical and interpretive analysis indicated a possible limit in the range of effectiveness of the two verbal therapies under consideration with respect to degrees of ethnocentrism in clients. It was also shown that individuals could be reliably differentiated as to the probability of their being good or poor therapeutic risks within the limitations of the small samples used.

The essentially anti-ethnocentric nature of self-referred clients was discussed. The nonlinear relationship between counselor ratings of success in therapy and a client's E-scale score was proposed as being an indication of a failure to achieve a certain degree of "selfhood," or a loss of it, on the part of those less successful in therapy.

Further research on the question of "which people, in what circumstances, responding to what therapeutic stimuli" (11), would seem profitable. Thus we might extend the boundaries of verbal therapy and clarify the conditions leading to failure in the capacity to form meaningful interpersonal relationships.

REFERENCES

1. Adorno, T. W.; Frenkel-Brunswik, Else; Levinson, D. J.; and Sanford, R. N. *The Authoritarian Personality*. New York: Harper & Bros., 1950.
2. Barron, F. X. "Psychotherapy as a Special Case of Personal Interaction: Prediction of Its Outcome." Ph.D. dissertation, University of California, 1950.
3. Block, Jack and Jeanne. "An Interpersonal Experiment on Reactions to Authority," *Human Relations*, V (1952), 91–98.
4. Bronfenbrenner, Urie. "Personality," *Annual Review of Psychology*, IV (1953), 157–82.
5. Cowen, E. L.; Wiener, M.; and Hess, J. "Generalization of Problem-solving Ability," *Journal of Consulting Psychology*, XVII (1953), 100–103.
6. Dittman, A. T. "The Interpersonal Process in Psychotherapy: A Test for Three Theories." Ph.D. dissertation, University of California, 1950.
7. Fisher, J. "The Memory Process and Certain Psychosocial Attitudes, with Special Reference to the Law of *Pragnanz*," *Journal of Personality*, XIX (1951), 406–20.
8. Korchin, S. J.; Singer, J. L.; and Ballard, R. G. "The Influence of Frustration on the Reproduction of Visually Perceived Forms," *Personality*, I (1951), 54–66.
9. Pearl, David. "Ethnocentrism and the Concept of Self." Ph.D. dissertation, University of Chicago, 1950.
10. Rokeach, Milton. "Narrow-mindedness and Personality," *Journal of Personality*, XX (1951), 234–51.
11. Sanford, R. N. "Clinical Methods: Psychotherapy," *Annual Review of Psychology*, IV (1953), 317–42.

CHAPTER 13

Changes in the Maturity of Behavior as Related to Therapy[1]

CARL R. ROGERS

The purpose of this study was to examine the hypothesis that, following the completion of client-centered therapy, the individual behaves in ways which indicate a greater degree of emotional or behavioral maturity and that this alteration in behavior is evident both to the client himself and to observers. The previous chapters have gathered much complex data about the changes which occur in the client's concepts of himself and others and in the structure of his personality. This investigation tackled the question which is of more concern to the layman and to society, "Does the client's everyday behavior change in such a way that the changes can be observed, and is the nature of these changes positive?"

There have been many studies completed which examine alterations during therapy in the client's verbal behavior, his test-response behavior, his behavior in sorting cards to describe himself, and the like. These studies have been adequately presented and reviewed (2, chap. 4; 3). There has been a study of changes in the individual's physiological reactions to frustration (4). No study, however, has been attempted of any qualitative change in the maturity of behavior.

I. THE DERIVATION OF THE HYPOTHESIS

In the theory of therapy and personality which has been proposed by the author, various behavioral changes are hypothesized as occurring concomitantly with client-centered therapy (2, chap. 11). These may be listed as follows:

1. Many members of the staff played a part in the planning and execution of this research, but grateful mention should be made of the assistance of Thomas Gordon in the planning of this particular study and of the help given by Richard Jenney in the analysis of the data.

After therapy, the individual:

Is less defensive in his behavior, less concerned about self and the protection of self.

Is more likely to be accepting of others, less likely to be attacking, is better socialized.

Accepts himself more fully as being different from others.

Evaluates experience in terms of the evidence coming from his own senses and does not change this evaluation except on the basis of new evidence, his behavior being consistent with his evaluation.

Behaves in such ways as to give evidence of a socialized system of values.

In summary, the theory proposes that the individual, after therapy, will behave in ways which are less defensive, more socialized, more accepting of reality in himself and in his social environment, and will give more evidence of a socialized system of values. It is behavioral changes in these directions which might be thought of as being more mature.

The difficult question to which we then addressed ourselves was the question as to whether any operational definition could be given to our hypothesis.

II. THE SELECTION OF AN INSTRUMENT

There are few instruments purporting to measure the quality of behavior. The best of these seems to be that developed by Willoughby (5, 6) many years ago. Out of his psychoanalytic background he formulated a careful definition which fits well with the behavioral changes described in the preceding section. He says: "Emotional maturity is freedom from narcism and ambivalence; in other terminology it is release from egocentrism, the achievement of socialized impulses, of insight; emotional acceptance of the reality principle and an 'analyzed' condition are also approximate synonyms."

Willoughby constructed many items descriptive of behavior and had them sorted by a hundred clinicians into step intervals indicating varying degrees of maturity, the foregoing definition being used as a guide in their sorting. On the basis of these combined judgments he selected sixty items on which there was high agreement and which were representative of various levels of maturity. Several of the items, and their score values, are given below. The scores range from 1 (most immature) to 9 (most mature).

SCORE	ITEM
1	S (subject) characteristically appeals for help in the solution of his problems (Item 9).
2	S demands that he be punctiliously served in hotels, sleeping cars, etc. (Item 15).
3	When driving an automobile, S is unperturbed in ordinary situations but becomes angry with other drivers who impede his progress (Item 12).
4	S is scrupulously tidy, placing neatness high among his major objectives (Item 37).
5	On unmistakable demonstration of his inferiority in some respect, S is impressed but consoles himself by the contemplation of those activities in which he is superior (Item 45).
7	S organizes and orders his efforts in pursuing his objectives, evidently regarding systematic method as a means of achieving them (Item 17).
8	S chooses his course of action with reference to maximum long-time satisfaction of entire group affected (Item 27).
9	S welcomes legitimate opportunities for sexual expression; is not ashamed, fearful, or preoccupied with the topic (Item 53).

The scale (known as the Willoughby Emotional-Maturity Scale) is used by having the subject or an observer check only those items which apply to the person being rated. The total score is the mean score of the items checked, multiplied by 10.

This was the instrument chosen for the study, since in spite of its peculiar scoring system, and some other deficiencies such as its highly abstract wording, it appeared to be most nearly related to the concepts it was desired to measure.

Nine additional items were added to the scale. These were items devised by Willoughby and rated by his judges, so that the score values were known. They were added to give additional range and variety to the scale, particularly on the "immature" end of the scale.

III. OPERATIONAL HYPOTHESIS

Having selected an instrument, it was possible to restate the hypothesis in more specific and operational terms as follows: Following the completion of client-centered therapy, the behavior of the client will be rated both by himself and by others as being emotionally more mature, using the concept of emotional maturity as operationally established by expert judges.

In this hypothesis the significant terms have these definitions:

Completion.—Therapy is regarded as complete when there has been a series of at least six interviews before termination.

Client-centered therapy.—Therapy carried on by a person with training and experience in this orientation, who regards this orientation as representing many of his basic hypotheses.

Emotionally mature.—The measure of maturity of behavior is the score on the Willoughby Emotional-Maturity Scale (E-M Scale).

Expert judges.—The one hundred clinicians utilized by Willoughby in establishing his scale.

Change will be judged to have occurred if differences in scores are found which are statistically significant at the 5 per cent level.

IV. THE EXPERIMENTAL DESIGN

The clients who were the primary focus of this study were those in the first block (Block I) of cases in our total research project. A description of these clients, and of the various studies in which they participated, has been presented in chapter 3. For the present investigation the aim was to provide a central core of data by having E-M Scale evaluations prior to therapy, following therapy, and at a follow-up point at least six months after the conclusion of therapy. At each of these points the E-M Scale was filled out by the client himself and by two friends whom he designated as persons who knew him well. Neither the client nor the friends were given any information regarding the purpose of the study, and the scale filled out by each friend was mailed directly to the Counseling Center. A letter of instruction to the friends simply stated that this was a research in personality, that their co-operation was needed, that their responses were confidential, and that, because of the nature of the research, they were requested not to discuss their filling-out of the instrument with the subject.

As in any research regarding personality variables, the problem of controls was a difficult and subtle one. As has been mentioned previously, two types of controls were decided upon. Approximately one-half of the clients in Block I were given the E-M Scale (and other tests for other projects) and then requested to wait for a period of sixty days before beginning therapy. At the end of this "wait" period the E-M Scale was readministered, and therapy was begun. The E-M Scale for a client in this group was also filled out by each of his two friends at each of these points (pre-wait and pre-therapy). Thus a control period was provided in which the individual was his own control subject. In this way the question as to whether behavioral change was observed by the client himself or by observers, in an individual motivated for therapy but during a period of no therapy, could be answered.

The second control had to do both with our observers (the friends) and with individuals not in therapy. Each friend, at the time he first rated the client on the E-M Scale, was asked to choose another person and to rate this person on the E-M Scale and identify him by some code name which he (the friend) could remember. Then, on each subsequent occasion that the friend rated the client, he was also asked to rate this control individual. This plan gave us a double check. If any or all of these friends of our clients were unreliable raters, this should show up in unreliable ratings of the nontherapy controls as well as the therapy group. If they proved to be reliable raters, then we had a nontherapy group (presumably not in therapy) whose behavior was rated at the same time intervals by the same judges. From a study of the findings on this group the question could be answered: "Do ratings of control individuals differ significantly from ratings of individuals in therapy when the ratings are made by the same observers at the same time intervals?"

Having presented the general rationale behind the design of this study, an enumeration of the various steps in the collection of the data should make clear the way in which the rationale was put into effect.

V. METHOD OF THE STUDY

1. The client was requested to make a self-evaluation of his behavior on the E-M Scale.

2. The client was asked for the names of two friends who knew him well, so that they might make ratings of him. The instructions accompanying the scale stressed that this was a research in personality, that the rater should not discuss his ratings with the subject, and that the ratings should be mailed directly to the Counseling Center.

3. Each friend was requested to rate, in addition to the client, one other person who was well known to him. He should designate

this person by a name or by a code name which he would recognize several months later. (This person will be referred to in this study as a "control individual.")

3*a*. (This step applied only to the half of the total group which has been designated as the own-control group.) After a waiting period of sixty days the E-M Scale was readministered, a self-evaluation being obtained from the client, and the ratings of the client were again made by each of the two friends. Therapy then commenced.

3*b*. (This step, too, applied only to the own-control group.) After the waiting period of sixty days, each friend filled out an E-M Scale for the control individual whom he had selected.

4. Following the conclusion of therapy the E-M Scale was administered once more, being filled out by the client and by each of his two friends.

5. Following the conclusion of therapy each friend was asked to fill out an E-M Scale for the control individual whom he had designated.

6. Following the conclusion of therapy the counselor was asked to rate the outcome of therapy on a nine-point scale from 1 ("complete failure") to 9 ("marked success"). He was also asked to rate the degree of personal integration of the client at the beginning of therapy and at the end of therapy. These ratings were also made on a nine-point scale from 1 ("highly disorganized or defensively organized") to 9 ("optimally integrated").

7. Six months after the conclusion of therapy the E-M Scale was administered for the last time, to the client for self-ratings, and mailed to each of his two friends, for a rating of the client.

8. Six months after the conclusion of therapy each friend was asked to fill out an E-M Scale for the control individual whom he had designated and previously rated.

It was thus hoped that for any one client at each one of the testing points in the study there would be five E-M scales: one filled out by the client on himself, two ratings of the client by friends, and two ratings of control individuals, one by each friend.

The design obviously permitted many comparisons to be made in the data. Some of the comparisons related most closely to the hypothesis would be the following: a no-therapy period could be compared with a therapy period for half the clients; behavior of clients in therapy could be compared with control individuals not in therapy; behavioral evaluations by the client himself could be compared with evaluations made by observers; behavior during therapy could be compared with behavior during a follow-up period.

VI. DIFFICULTIES IN DATA COLLECTION

Some difficulty had been anticipated in obtaining repeated ratings of our clients from friends over a period often extending over a year or two. These friends, it will be recalled, had no contact with anyone at the Center except by mail. This difficulty proved to be greater than we had anticipated, and as a result there are numerous "holes" in our data where these observers did not mail in their ratings of the client or of the control individual whom they had designated. Sometimes this was due to failure to co-operate and sometimes to the fact that the friend had moved away or was no longer in contact with the client. Occasionally clients too, particularly at the follow-up point, failed to return their E-M Scale, thus creating further gaps in the material.

As is so frequently true in such studies, more data are missing for clients who were rated as having made relatively little progress in therapy than for those who were considered to have made more progress.

The problems created by these gaps in the data have been kept in mind in analyzing the findings, and precautions have been taken so that none of the results is distorted by this absence of material. The only comparisons made are those in which pairs of ratings were available. Hence, in the findings which follow, the number involved varies, depending upon the number of pairs of observations available for the particular comparison. The number available for each comparison may be seen from a study of Table 1, which gives much of the basic data.

VII. FINDINGS

The results of this study will be presented and briefly discussed under several different headings.

TABLE 1

Raw Data of the Study: Willoughby Evaluations of the Experimental Group

Client	Evaluation by Client				Observers' Evaluations of Clients				Counselor Rating of Therapy		
									Out-come	Personal Integration	
	Pre-wait	Pre-therapy	Post-therapy	Follow-up	Pre-wait	Pre-therapy	Post-therapy	Follow-up		Pre-therapy	Post-therapy
	Pre-Wait Group										
Babi	37	37	43	41	40 49	…… 42	…… 61	48 60	8	2	8
Bame	39	38	47	44	51 50	50 58	51 48	62 ……	6	2	5
Bayu	40	40	40	48	63 50	63 48	58 34	32 ……	2	3	2
Bebb	33	39	34	36	43 38	48 27	38 ……	53 32	6	2	4
Bink	37	35	……	……	37 ……	39 ……	42 ……	…… ……	7	7	7
Bisk	38	43	38	……	54 53	…… 64	…… 64	…… ……	……	……	……
Bitz*	41	34	……	……	42 ……	…… 52	…… ……	…… ……	……	……	……
Bira	38	38	……	……	46 33	51 ……	…… ……	…… ……	3	1	2
Bixy	42	31	36	38	56 45	59 47	…… ……	…… ……	4	4	6
Beso	44	44	50	55	53 ……	…… ……	…… ……	…… ……	5	5	6
Bett	42	42	46	50	52 ……	…… ……	47 ……	…… ……	5	6	7
Biju	52	40	……	……	42 47	49 47	…… ……	…… ……	4	3	6
Blen	56	37	39	32	60 52	46 53	53 58	45 56	5	3	5
	No-Wait Group										
Oak	……	55	63	69	…… ……	58 52	67 59	…… 65	8	4	7
Bacc	……	44	47	46	…… ……	49 45	50 43	…… ……	6	3	6
Bajo	……	58	50	51	…… ……	…… ……	…… ……	…… ……	4	4	5
Bana	……	39	51	59	…… ……	56 ……	57 ……	…… ……	5	3	6
Bann	……	39	49	……	…… ……	65 52	…… 55	…… ……	1	3	3
Barr	……	40	41	35	…… ……	36 34	50 32	…… ……	6	4	6

TABLE 1—*Continued*

Client	Evaluation by Client				Observers' Evaluations of Clients				Counselor Rating of Therapy		
									Out-come	Personal Integration	
	Pre-wait	Pre-therapy	Post-therapy	Follow-up	Pre-wait	Pre-therapy	Post-therapy	Follow-up		Pre-therapy	Post-therapy
	No-Wait Group—*Continued*										
Beda	......	60	60	57	....	56 68	71 69	67 64	6	2	6
Beel	......	47	47	43	....	41	35	35	7	4	7
Beke	......	52	52	42	....	49	....	....	7	6	8
Bipi†	......	36	......	......	....	33 28	....	....	......	......	......
Bela	......	45	46	......	....	48 54	42 58	....	5	4	5
Bene	......	68	64	64	....	62 51	55 55	 59	9	5	9
Benz	......	41	46	45	....	53 34	60 33	....	7	2	6
Beri	......	57	52	54	....	55 51	58	57 58	7	1	7
Blos*	......	42	......	......	....	35	....	....	4	......	......
Bico	......	38	55	54	....	47 52	 46	 42	7	2	5
Bifu	......	41	38	43	....	34 64	28 54	25 57	2	2	2
Bime	......	39	51	52	....	43 50	....	....	4	3	3
Bina	......	44	54	62	....	40 34	58 40	....	7	2	6

* Dropped out of therapy.

† Still active at the time the data were analyzed.

Intra-individual Consistency of Evaluations

It will be clear from the experimental design that the best approximation to a test-retest reliability of the E-M Scale was the rating by the observers (the client's friends) of control individuals not in therapy. In this situation a minimum of personality and behavioral change was hypothesized. The time intervals between ratings varied from a few weeks to more than a year, each time interval corresponding to some significant time interval for the client with whom the control was matched.

Taking then each observer's rating of a control individual, and pairing it with the following rating of the same control by the same observer, we obtained 64 pairs. The correlation between these earlier and later ratings was .85, a highly significant correlation, indicating that one individual was able to rate another on the E-M Scale with satisfactory consistency.

As a second indication of consistency we have the observers' repeated ratings of the client. Pairing each observer's rating of a client with the next following rating of the same client, we again have 64 pairs. Since some change was hypothesized in the clients, we did not expect the consistency to be as high. The correlation was .71, significant at the 1 per cent level, which was in line with this expectation.

As a third indication of consistency we have the repeated self-evaluations by clients. Pairing each client self-rating with the next following self-rating, we have 62 pairs, and an r of .70.

1. *The E-M Scale proved to have satisfactory intra-individual consistency when used by any one rater, whether an observer or the client himself.*

Inter-individual Consistency of Evaluations

To determine whether the clients were rating themselves in a fashion similar to that of the observers, each observer rating was paired with the client rating made at that time. This gave 122 pairs of ratings. The correlation was .37, which, while significant at the 1 per cent level, indicated little correspondence between the client's self-evaluation of his behavior and the evaluation made by his friends at the same time.

The correlation was then run between the evaluation by the friends. The evaluations of a given client by Friend No. 1 and Friend No. 2 at the same time were treated as a pair. There were 47 such pairs, and the correlation was .22, which was not even significant at the 5 per cent level.

2. *There was little significant relationship between the client's evaluation of his behavior and that made by friends; there was no significant relationship between the observation of Friend No. 1 and Friend No. 2 on the same client.*

It is possible that the abstruse wording of the E-M Scale might account to some small degree for this lack of congruence, with three different individuals seeing three different meanings in the same description. It does not seem likely that this could be a very important factor, however.

It appears more clear that we have here three different perspectives of observation of the client's behavior—the client himself, Friend-Observer No. 1, and Friend-Observer No. 2—and that each of these perspectives is a consistent vantage point of measurement in itself but that they have little in common. This seems to be in line with recent studies of diagnostic judgments, which tend to show that, though there may be intra-individual consistency of diagnostic judgments, there is very little inter-individual consistency. It suggests the possibility that personality and behavior actually are different when viewed from different perspectives and that the attempt to determine the "real" personality or the "real" behavior is somewhat naïve. Many issues are raised here for further research.

The Evaluations of the Controls

Do the control individuals show any change in rated behavior over the time period when the clients were having therapy? The answer to this is best given by the mean ratings on 32 control individuals at the pre-therapy point and again at the post-therapy point. These individuals were presumably not in therapy, and the intervals between ratings ranged from four weeks to over a year, depending upon the length of therapy for the client with whom the control individual was paired. The mean rating of these controls was 48.4 at the pre-therapy point and 48.8 at the post-therapy point; the change was not significant. Similar comparisons were made of ratings of control individuals during the wait period and during the follow-up period. In no case was there any significant increase or decrease in the mean rating.

3. *Control individuals showed no significant change in behavior ratings during the period in which the clients were receiving therapy or during the other periods involved in this study.*

This question can be further investigated by examining both the self-rating and the observer ratings of the thirteen clients who were part of the own-control group. During this sixty-day period the self-rating of the thirteen clients dropped from 41.5 to 38.3, which was not a significant change. There were 16 pairs of observations of these clients by their friends during this same period. The mean was 48.9 at the pre-wait point and 51.1 at the pre-therapy point; this change, in the opposite direction from the trend of the self-ratings, was not significant.

4. *Clients during a period of no therapy showed no significant change in self-ratings, and there was no significant change in the way observers saw their behavior.*

Changes as Seen by Observers

There were 33 observer judgments of the clients at pre-therapy time which could be matched with judgments by the same observer at post-therapy time. The mean was 49.6 at the pre-therapy point and 50.9 at the post-therapy point; the change was not significant.

5. *There was no significant change in the observers' ratings of the clients over the period of therapy.*

There were 15 observer judgments at the follow-up point which could be paired with judgments made at the conclusion of therapy. The mean was 52.9 at the conclusion of therapy and 51.9 at the follow-up point—a decrease which was not significant.

6. *There was no significant change in the observers' evaluations of the clients' behavior during the six-month period of follow-up.*

There were 17 comparisons possible between the observers' judgment at the pre-therapy point, with the judgment by the same observer at the follow-up point. The means were 50.2 and 51.2, respectively, a change which was not significant.

7. *There was no significant change in the observers' evaluations of the clients' behavior during the combined period of therapy and follow-up.*

The general hypothesis of the study appears not to be upheld in so far as the friends' observations of the clients' behavior was concerned.

Observer Evaluations in Relation to Counselor Ratings of Outcome

It seemed desirable to determine whether this negative finding held for all clients regardless of the movement they appeared to make in therapy.

On each case there was available the counselor's rating of the outcome, with ratings from 1 to 9, 9 being most successful (see chap. 7). When we took the changes in observer judgments of our clients and related these to the counselor judgment of outcome, the findings shown in Table 2 emerged. The number of paired E-M Scale scores on which each comparison was based is indicated in parentheses.

TABLE 2

OBSERVERS' EVALUATIONS OVER THERAPY AS RELATED TO COUNSELOR RATINGS

Counselor Rating of Outcome	Observers' Willoughby Evaluation		Diff.	*N*
	Pre-therapy Mean	Post-therapy Mean		
7–9	47.1	51.5	4.4*	(13)
6	49.3	50.2	0.9	(9)
1–5	51.8	49.7	−2.1	(10)

* Significant at the 5 per cent level.

It is clear that there was a definite relationship here which was further confirmed by calculating the correlation between changes in the pre- to post-therapy evaluation of the client by the observers and the counselor's rating of outcome. The correlation was .41, which had less than 5 per cent probability of being due to chance.

8. *Observers saw a significant increase in maturity of behavior during the therapy period in those clients rated by the counselor as being successful in outcome and a slight decrease in maturity of behavior in those clients rated as being unsuccessful.*

Let us carry this investigation through to the follow-up period. Because of gaps in our data, there are only 17 pairs of ratings which can be compared from pre-therapy to follow-up. Table 3 shows the results of this analysis.

Though the subgroups were small, the evidence here was even more definite. The successful cases showed a clear increase in maturity of behavior, while the unsuccessful cases revealed an even sharper deterioration in the quality of their behavior. When we compared the group rated by the counselors as 6 or above with the group rated 1–5, the difference was significant at the 2 per cent level. The correlation between the counselor ratings, on the one hand, and the change in observers' evaluations from pre-therapy to follow-up point, on the other, was .70, which was significant at the 1 per cent level.

TABLE 3

OBSERVERS' EVALUATIONS OVER THERAPY AND FOLLOW-UP AS RELATED TO COUNSELOR RATINGS

Counselor Rating of Outcome	Observers' Willoughby Evaluation		Diff.	*N*
	Pre-therapy Mean	Follow-up Mean		
7–9........	49.1	53.7	4.6	(7)
6..........	49.8	55.6	5.8	(5)
1–5........	52.0	43.0	−9.0	(5)

9. *During the whole period from pre-therapy to follow-up, observers saw a definite increase in the maturity of behavior of those clients whose therapy was rated as successful and a sharp decrease in the maturity of behavior of those clients rated as unsuccessful. The relationship was statistically significant.*

Observer Evaluations in Relation to Counselor Ratings of Change

As a further check upon the validity of the preceding findings it seemed wise to investigate the possibility of an even more subtle relationship. It will be recalled that, at the conclusion of therapy, the counselor rated the personal integration of the client on a scale to indicate the client's personal integration status at the beginning of therapy and his status at the end of therapy. Thus change in integration over therapy can be obtained from these ratings.

Now the question we wished to raise was as follows: Is there any relationship between the change in personal integration as observed by the counselor and the change in maturity of behavior as observed by the friends?

The correlation was first calculated between the change in counselor rating, on the one hand, and the difference between the pre-therapy and post-therapy E-M Scale scores, on the other. The number of pairs was 31, and the correlation was .50, significant at the 1 per cent level, indicating that those clients judged by the counselor to have shown the greatest change in personal integration had more than a chance likelihood of exhibiting positive change in maturity of behavior as seen by their friends.

When the change in counselor rating was compared with changes in E-M Scale scores over the whole period from pre-therapy to follow-up, the relationship was even more striking. In this calculation 17 pairs were involved, and the correlation was .67, which was also significant at the 1 per cent level.

10. *There was a significant positive correlation between the degree of change in "personal integration" as estimated by counselors and the degree of change in maturity of behavior as seen by observers over the period of therapy. This relationship was even more marked when the behavioral change from pre-therapy to follow-up was considered.*

The full significance of findings 8, 9, and 10 may not be immediately apparent. Let us review the factual situation underlying these judgments. The counselors, at the conclusion of therapy, made a judgment, admittedly global and subjective, as to the general "success" of the process which therapy had initiated in each case. The counselors also estimated the degree of change in psychological integration which had occurred, the amount of movement in therapy. The counselors undoubtedly differed to some degree in the criteria and standards which they used in making these evaluations. The counselor had no opportunity to observe the general behavior of his client but made his judgment solely on the client's verbal behavior in the interview and on the quality of the relationship.

On the other hand, friends of the client, who might or might not know that the client was in therapy, who knew nothing of the research and certainly nothing of the degree of success or movement in the therapy, made, at various points in time, evaluations of the client's general behavior on an instrument which was admittedly very crude.

It is a matter for genuine surprise, and an indication of the size of the changes which must actually have occurred, that the observers noted an increase in the maturity of the daily behavior of those clients whom the counselor subjectively viewed as showing movement in therapy and that the observers noted a decrease in the maturity of behavior of those clients whom the counselor viewed as showing little or no movement in therapy. That this was not a temporary phenomenon was indicated by the fact that the relationship continued and grew sharper during the follow-up period. We have here a confirmation of the effective influence of therapy upon daily behavior—a confirmation by many neutral and unbiased judges.

Changes as Seen by the Clients

What changes, if any, did the clients see in their own behavior? We have already indicated (finding 4) that there was no significant change during the pre-therapy waiting period of sixty days in which thirteen clients participated. From the pre-therapy to the post-therapy point there were 26 pairs of client self-ratings available. The pre-therapy mean was 44.5; the post-therapy, 47.7—an increase which was significant at the 5 per cent level.

Perhaps the most satisfactory over-all comparison may be made by taking the twenty-three clients for whom we have pre- and post-therapy and follow-up E-M Scale scores. Here the respective means were 44.8, 48.1, and 48.7. The changes from pre- to post-therapy and from pre-therapy to follow-up were significant at the 5 per cent level.

11. *The clients' evaluation of their own behavior showed a significant increase in the direction of maturity during the period of therapy.*

12. *There was no significant change in the clients' evaluation of their behavior during the follow-up period, though the trend was toward a slight further increase.*

13. *During the total period from the beginning of therapy to the follow-up point, clients evaluated their behavior in such a way as to produce a significant increase in the maturity score.*

Changes in the Maturity of Behavior as Related to Therapy

It may help to give some additional meaning to these scores to express them in terms of Willoughby's norms. His norms were based upon a student population, which was not strictly comparable to our client group. Our client group contained a majority of students, but some nonstudents as well. With this limitation in mind, we may say that the mean Willoughby score of our clients prior to therapy was at the 26th percentile according to Willoughby's norms. At the post-therapy point the mean score was at the 44th percentile, and at follow-up time at the 47th percentile.

14. *In terms of Willoughby's norms, the self-rated behavior of the clients moved from the lower quartile to approximately the mean, so far as maturity of behavior was concerned, during the total period of therapy and follow-up.*

Client Evaluations in Relation to Counselor Ratings

In order to see whether the increase in maturity scores of the clients' Willoughby scales was related to counselor judgment of outcome in therapy, correlations were calculated between changes in the clients' self-evaluations on the E-M Scale and the counselor rating of degree of success. It was puzzling to discover that no relationship existed. When changes over the period of therapy were correlated with counselor ratings, the result was a correlation of .04. When changes over the total period were used, the correlation was −.06. This seemed particularly surprising in view of the positive correlation between observer evaluation and counselor rating (findings 8 and 9).

15. *There was no relationship between the degree of change seen by the clients in their own behavior and the degree of success in therapy as seen by the counselor.*

Table 4 presents the facts which seem to throw light on the situation. Some data from the observer evaluations are repeated here in order to make the comparison more clear. It is evident that in the cases rated successful (7–9) or showing modest positive change (6) there was a positive relationship between the observers' evaluations, the clients' self-evaluations, and the counselors' ratings. But in the unsuccessful group the picture was quite different, and this was sharpest when we considered the over-all period from pre-therapy to follow-up. Here it may be said that in those cases where the counselor regarded the therapy as having shown little or no movement, and where friends observed a real deterioration in maturity of behavior, the clients themselves saw a marked positive increase in the maturity of behavior. It seemed quite reasonable to infer that we had here a clear-cut and measured instance of the operation of defensiveness. Those clients whose therapy was least successful found it necessary to report the most marked positive changes. This fitted with findings from other studies. The writer's judgment is that the facts thus far known can be generalized in this way: that negative reports of behavior, and of strain and tension,

TABLE 4

OBSERVED CHANGES AS RELATED TO COUNSELOR RATINGS

(The *N* for Each Mean Is Given in Parentheses)

Counselor Rating of Outcome	Mean Changes in Observers' Willoughby Evaluation		Mean Changes in Clients' Willoughby Evaluation	
	Pre- to Post-therapy	Pre-therapy to Follow-up	Pre- to Post-therapy	Pre-therapy to Follow-up
7–9......	4.4 (13)	4.6 (7)	4.1 (9)	3.9 (9)
6........	0.9 (9)	5.8 (5)	1.6 (5)	−0.4 (5)
1–5......	−2.1 (10)	−9.0 (5)	3.7 (11)	8.1 (9)

based on phenomenological data, tend to be supported by other evidence; positive reports of behavior, internal comfort, and the like are dichotomous, some being definitely supported by outside evidence, and others (the defensive variety) being strongly contradicted by outside evidence. It seems clear that we are approaching specific measures of defensiveness and that additional research in this area is vitally needed. To return from this speculation, the factual finding may be worded in these terms:

16. *The evidence suggested a positive relationship between client evaluation of behavior and counselor rating of therapy, in those cases which were at least modestly successful; in unsuccessful cases there appeared to be a negative relationship between the clients' evaluation of behavior, on the one hand, and the counselors' rating of outcome and the friends' observation of behavior, on the other.*

Differences between Observer Evaluations and Client Evaluations

Since we need to learn more about the relationships between evaluations from the internal and external frames of reference, it may be of interest to state the general finding in regard to client self-evaluations of behavior and observer-evaluations of the same behavior. These data are contained in Table 5.

TABLE 5

RELATION OF OBSERVER EVALUATIONS TO CLIENT EVALUATIONS

Mean of	Pre-wait ($N=13$)	Pre-therapy ($N=29$)	Post-therapy ($N=21$)	Follow-up ($N=12$)
Evaluations by observers (friends)............	48.0	48.4	50.9	50.5
Self-evaluations by clients	41.5	42.7	47.6	48.7
Diff..................	6.5	5.7	3.3	1.8

17. *At every point at which measurements were taken—pre-wait, pre-therapy, post-therapy, and follow-up—the friends rated the clients as being more mature than the clients rated themselves.*

18. *The differences between client self-evaluations and observer evaluations decreased at the post-therapy and follow-up points, the differences being significant only prior to therapy.*

It is interesting to speculate as to the meaning of these two findings. Why did friends rate the maturity of the clients' behavior higher than the clients did themselves? Were they simply being flattering to these individuals whom they knew? This seemed best answered by their willingness to describe increasingly *immature* behavior on the part of the clients in the unsuccessful cases (Tables 2 and 3). Did the answer lie in the fact that clients as a group tended to be self-depreciating? This appeared to be the more likely explanation. The data suggest that perhaps one of the outcomes of therapy was that the client came to see his own behavior at more nearly the level of maturity at which it was seen by his friends.

VIII. DISCUSSION

Meaning of the Changes

Since the E-M Scale is not well known, the meaning of some of the above findings may be made clear by giving additional illustrative items. In general, it may be said that, in the cases in which therapeutic movement occurred, both the observers and the client saw a decrease in such behaviors as are listed below in the first group and an increase in such behaviors as are listed in the second group.

IMMATURE BEHAVIORS

SCORE	ITEM
1	S evinces hostility toward his immediate family associates (Item 65).
2	S devotes much energy to recounting his achievements (Item 62).
2	S cannot give up or retain an objective completely; if he tries to give it up, he must make some gesture of retention, and if he retains it he feels the desirability of giving it up (Item 60).
2	S is conscience-ridden, anxious lest he violate the sanctioned codes (Item 44).
3	S urges a child or younger person to exhibit for group approval any abilities he may possess (Item 51).
3	S derives satisfaction from bringing to attention instances of his own usefulness, altruism, etc. (Item 46).
4	S is tolerant of most divergent opinions but feels that there are some ideas so far beyond the pale as to make their suppression an obligation on all right-minded people (Item 56).
4	S is "scientific" in conversation, appearing to regard others' points of view as specimens (Item 28).

MATURE BEHAVIORS

SCORE	ITEM
6	S disregards all but realistic, naturalistic factors in the solution of his problems (Item 52).
6	S, in conversation, inhibits his own expression for therapeutic ends (Item 24).
7	S is clear cut in his decisions; when relinquishing an objective, he relinquishes or postpones it entirely; when retaining it, he retains all of it without regret (Item 59).
7	S conducts himself in discussion as if the only objective of the discussion were the mutual discovery of truth (Item 11).
8	Being interrupted in the performance of an act, S gives attention, when resumption is possible, to the total situation and resumes or abandons the act unemotionally as the new situation makes advisable (Item 42).
8	Faced with several insistent demands simultaneously, S sorts them quickly by urgency, settles one at a time, disregards (i.e., does not react to) insistence of deferred demands (Item 47).
9	S evaluates suggestions without heat, settling the issue upon rational bases, and cannot be persuaded to alter a matured decision except on the basis of new evidence (Item 41).

The listing of these items may give more of the qualitative "feel" of the changes which have been observed in the behavior of these clients.

Suggestions for Further Research

Some of the difficulties encountered in this study are due to the crudities of the E-M Scale. With some effort it could be transformed into a Q-sort in which every item would be given some placement and thus would play its part in the comparisons and correlations. A refined instrument for behavioral measurement would have much usefulness.

A second striking need is for an instrument which would directly measure defensiveness. If such a tool were available, giving us the degree to which the individual is denying experience to awareness, then much more use could be made of data obtained directly from the subject. This phenomenological material can be incomparably richer than the reports of external observers but may have a negative meaning in the defensive individual, as has been indicated in this investigation. If we knew the degree of defensiveness, it might be possible to apply a correction to the data.

Another suggested need is for the study of behavioral disorganization during therapy. If clinical judgment is correct that the unsuccessful client is essentially one in whom therapy is incomplete, then the finding of deterioration in the behavior of such clients suggests a question about all clients. If continuing behavioral evaluations were made throughout therapy, would some degree of regression in behavior be generally found, before the behavior becomes more mature? Study of this would shed further light on the process of therapy.

One of the deepest issues raised in this investigation is that of the differences in "perspective." Is it generally true that there is intra-individual consistency of perception of an individual but little inter-individual consistency? If so, what becomes of the "real" individual whom we are supposedly studying? Would this lead us to an Einsteinian type of personality theorizing? This seems like a promising avenue for investigation.

IX. CONCLUSION

The hypothesis of this portion of our total project was that, following the conclusion of client-centered therapy, the client would be measurably more mature in the quality of his behavior, as judged by himself and his friends. The experimental group was the group of clients in therapy in Block I. Two types of controls were used: this same group during a waiting period prior to the beginning of therapy and a group of individuals not in therapy. The primary instrument was the E-M Scale. Counselor ratings of the outcome of therapy and change in personal integration were also available for the therapy group.

In a number of respects the hypothesis was upheld. A summary of the results may be quickly obtained by reading the numbered paragraphs 1 to 18 in the section of this chapter entitled "Findings."

In general, it may be said that the E-M Scale proved to be consistently used by any one rater. There was, however, little consistency of judgment among the three perspectives of measurement—the client, Friend No. 1, and Friend No. 2. There were no significant changes found in the control individuals over a period of time or in the therapy group over a period of no therapy. There were significant changes in clients whose therapy was rated by the counselor as being at least moderately successful. In these instances there was a significant increase in the maturity of the daily behavior of the client, whether the behavior was judged by the client himself or by his observer-friends who knew him well. In those instances where the counselor rated the therapy as unsuccessful, the observer-friends noted a deterioration in the maturity of behavior, but the clients (defensively?) rated themselves as much more mature.

The over-all conclusion appears justified that, where client-centered therapy is judged to have been successful, an observable change in the direction of maturity of behavior takes place in the client. Where therapy is judged not to have occurred in significant degree, some deterioration of behavior is observed.

Thus this chapter adds to our total picture of the outcome of client-centered therapy. Not only do certain inner conceptual changes occur, and certain subtle changes in personality, but the way the client makes choices, drives a car, behaves in group discussion, treats other people, acts when interrupted, etc., changes in ways that are evident both to himself and to his friends. These changes are in the direction which clinicians have designated as representing greater maturity of behavior.

REFERENCES

1. Bartlett, Marion R "A Six Month Follow-up of the Effects of Personal Adjustment Counseling of Veterans," *Journal of Consulting Psychology*, XIV (1950), 393–94.
2. Rogers, Carl R. *Client-centered Therapy*. Boston: Houghton Mifflin Co., 1951.
3. Seeman, Julius, and Raskin, Nathaniel J. "Research Perspectives in Client-centered Therapy," in O. H. Mowrer (ed.), *Psychotherapy: Theory and Research*, chap. 9. New York: Ronald Press Co., 1953.
4. Thetford, William N. "An Objective Measure of Frustration Tolerance in Evaluating Psychotherapy," in W. Wolff (ed.), *Success in Psychotherapy*, chap. 2. New York: Grune & Stratton, 1952.
5. Willoughby, R. R. *The Willoughby E-M Scale*. Stanford University: Stanford University Press, 1931.
6. ———. "A Scale of Emotional Maturity," *Journal of Social Psychology*, III (1931), 13–36.

CHAPTER 14

Personality Changes as a Function of Time in Persons Motivated for Therapy[1]

DONALD L. GRUMMON

I. INTRODUCTION AND PROBLEM

In this chapter an attempt is made to answer a question of considerable importance to all studies attempting to evaluate the effectiveness of psychotherapy, namely: "To what extent does motivation for psychotherapy tend to bring about constructive changes in personality make-up as a function of time alone?"

In recent years there have been several reviews of studies assessing the outcomes of psychotherapy. Eysenck (3) examined the literature in this area and tentatively concluded that there is no evidence that psychotherapy is of any value in the treatment of emotional disturbances. Hebb (4), Denker (1), Zubin (6), and others suggest a similar conclusion. For example, Hebb stated, "It has not been shown that any specialized psychotherapy, such as psychoanalysis, has any special value in mental illness" (4, p. 261), although he makes it clear that he is talking about "scientific proof" and not "reasonable belief."

Obtaining scientific proof about the value or worthlessness of psychotherapy presents many imposing problems—problems so imposing, in fact, that, in this writer's opinion, rigorous answers cannot be expected for years to come.

First, and of prime importance, we have a criterion problem. Many different criteria for evaluating therapy have been proposed, for example, symptom removal, deep personality reorganization, reduced anxiety, increased frustration tolerance, changes in par-

1. Numerous persons in our Research Group have made substantial contributions to the study reported here. The writer is especially indebted to John M. Butler, Rosalind Dymond, Thomas Gordon, Eve S. John, Edward Katz, Carl R. Rogers, Esselyn Rudikoff, Julius Seeman, and Jack Saporta.

ticular kinds of overt behavior, client satisfaction with the outcome, an increase in positive over negative feelings about self and others, etc. Each of these criteria has its special merits and limitations which we will not discuss here. However, it is safe to conclude that every criterion thus far proposed or used is open to criticism in one way or another. The underlying problem here is that no one can say with certainty what constitutes good psychological adjustment, and therefore there can be no fully accepted definitions of what constitutes improvement or a "cure."

In chapter 2 we pointed to a possible way out of the criterion dilemma. We suggested that the effectiveness of psychotherapy should not be thought of in terms of *success* and *failure*, because these are value terms which do not readily lend themselves to scientific examination. We suggested the necessity of an approach which examines for specific correlates of psychotherapy selected because of their relevance to personality theory. In part, this is the approach used in the study reported in this chapter, that is, specific aspects of personality make-up are measured, and, while these have relevance for a more global concept of adjustment, generalizations about total adjustment are not fully justified.

There is a second imposing difficulty encountered in determining the value of psychotherapy which forms the main argument of Eysenck, Hebb, Denker, and others. We know that spontaneous recovery can take place, that is, persons with emotional difficulties sometimes get better even though they have received no specialized treatment such as therapy. Therefore, the researcher who attempts to evaluate psychotherapy is called upon to show that any personality changes coming about during therapy would not also have occurred in the absence of therapy.

It is difficult to meet the control requirements necessary to test this. A truly rigorous study would call for perfect matching of the therapy and no-therapy group because we do not know for certain what variables are related to changes in personality make-up and adjustment status. At a minimum, it would appear necessary to to control for motivation for therapy, initial personality make-up, type and severity of disturbance, duration of disturbance, age, sex, socioeconomic status, and environmental influences. The control problem is so complicated that the researcher usually ignores it, and with justification, since, at our present level of knowledge about psychotherapy, he can perhaps expend his efforts elsewhere with more profit.

In this research program we did succeed in setting up a control feature which provides excellent matching on most variables that might influence therapeutic outcomes. I refer to the own-control technique described in chapter 3. That is, a person requesting psychotherapy is given the test battery to be used in the research, waits a period of time, and then retakes the test battery at the time psychotherapy is actually begun. In the study reported here the status of the own-control subjects on seven different measures of adjustment is examined to help answer the question: "Does motivation for psychotherapy bring about changes in personality as a function of time alone—that is, in the absence of psychotherapy?" While dealing with this specific problem, we are also making an initial attack on some of the broader issues presented by Hebb, Denker, and others.

II. SUBJECTS AND PROCEDURES

Overview of the Design

Twenty-three of the research clients were given the first block (Block I) test battery, waited for a sixty-day period, and then retook the tests before actually beginning their therapy. We have labeled these two test administrations as the *pre-wait tests* and the *pre-therapy tests*, respectively, and the interim period is called the *wait period*. We make the assumption that these persons are motivated to change, since they have requested counseling. Any personality changes occurring in this group of subjects, as shown by their pre-wait and pre-therapy tests, are compared with changes occurring over an identical time period in a control group of persons who were not seeking professional help.

Ideally we should have assessed personality changes over a much longer waiting period than the sixty days used here. However, ethical considerations influenced the design. Our research team decided that it would be unfair to penalize clients participating in our research program by having them wait longer for their therapy than is generally the case at the Counseling Center.

The Own-Control Group

The twenty-three subjects[2] who had applied for therapy will be called the *own-control group*. These people were the clients who took the test battery before and after the sixty-day wait period. The own-control group was also subdivided into the *attrition group* and the *continuers group*[3] on the basis of the number of therapeutic interviews received once therapy was begun. The eight own-control subjects who continued their therapy for five or less interviews were called the *attrition group*. For the most part these subjects did not get started in treatment at all, since they broke off their therapy after an interview or two. The *continuers group* consists of the fifteen subjects from the own-control group who remained in therapy for at least six therapeutic interviews. Most of these subjects stayed in treatment much longer, the mean number of interviews being 31.8.

There is some justification for assuming that the attrition group is less motivated for treatment than the continuers, since the attrition-group subjects failed to use their opportunity for therapy. However, other factors may also well be associated with their decision to stop therapy (e.g., a diminishing of problems or a dislike of the therapist).

The No-Therapy Control Group (Equivalent-Control Group)

The *no-therapy control group* consists of those subjects who were not seeking psychotherapy but who were paid to take the test battery at intervals corresponding to those of the continuers. There was a crude matching of these control subjects with the continuers for age, sex, student versus nonstudent status, and socioeconomic level (see chap. 3, Table 4). However, because of a time lag in testing the no-therapy controls, we have, for most of the measures, been able to use only eight subjects in this group.

2. The *N*'s for each group that we report in this section are correct for most of the measures employed in this study. However, for some of the measures the *N*'s are slightly smaller or larger, depending upon the amount of raw data available when the statistical analysis was undertaken. Each table contains the *N*'s which are exact for the results being reported.

3. See chap. 3 for a further explanation of the division of subjects into the attrition group and the continuers group.

This group of course serves as a control for the effect of retaking the tests after a sixty-day period. We made no special attempt to recruit no-therapy controls who were experiencing personal difficulties. Our test information indicates that as a group they were better adjusted than the own-control subjects, although some control subjects did evidence considerable maladjustment.

The Measures of Personality Status

A more complete description of the measures used to assess personality status and change in the no-therapy period will be given along with the presentation of results. For convenience, a listing of these measures is presented here:

1. *Correlation between the perceived self and the ideal (or wanted) self*—the degree of congruence between the subject's perceived self and his ideal self as revealed by the way he describes these aspects of self with a series of one-hundred self-referent statements. Q-technique procedures are used here. (See chap. 4.)
2. *Q-adjustment score*—an index of adjustment status derived from experts' opinions as to how the well-adjusted subject should describe himself on the one hundred self-referent statements referred to above. (See chap. 5.)
3. *Willoughby Emotional-Maturity Scale*—a scale which emphasizes the actual behavior rather than self-attitudes. Here the subject describes himself and is also described by two of his friends. (See chap. 13.)
4. *The Self-Other Attitude Scale*—measures attitudes toward other persons of, very roughly speaking, a democratic versus an authoritarian nature. (See chap. 11.)
5. *The Thematic Apperception Test (TAT)*—here we use two especially devised psychoanalytic rating scales upon which the clinician can quantify his judgments of mental health status. (See chap. 9.)

The Statistical Design

In setting up our design, we reasoned that the changes over the sixty-day period for any one group have meaning only when compared with changes made by one or more of the remaining groups. The statistical manipulation of the data, therefore, uses the *t* test to compare differences in mean changes between the following groups: (*a*) own-control and no-therapy controls, (*b*) continuers and attrition, (*c*) continuers and no-therapy controls, and (*d*) attrition and no-therapy controls. This treatment follows the procedures described by Edwards (2, pp. 284–85).

III. RESULTS

The Perceived Self and the Self-ideal

Several of our measures are derived from the Q-sort developed by Butler and Haigh (see chap. 4). One of the major hypotheses advanced by Butler and Haigh is that successful psychotherapy is accompanied by an increase in the correlation between the self and the ideal sorts. The correlations between these two sorts were computed for both the pre-wait and the pre-therapy points and then converted into *z* scores. Thus the difference between these two sets of *z* scores serves as a measure of any change in the congruence between the wanted self and the perceived self.

The results for this measure are presented in Tables 1 and 2. Table 1 gives the means for all groups at the pre-wait and the pre-

TABLE 1

CHANGES OVER THE WAIT PERIOD OF THE MEAN CORRELATIONS (EXPRESSED IN "Z" SCORES) BETWEEN THE SELF-SORTS AND THE SELF-IDEAL SORTS

Group	*N*	Pre-wait	Pre-therapy	Mean Change
Own-control.......	23	.001	.098	+.097
Attrition........	8	.013	.297	+.284
Continuers......	15	−.006	−.008	−.002
No-therapy control	8	.793	.825	+.032

TABLE 2

COMPARISONS BETWEEN GROUPS WITH RESPECT TO THEIR MEAN CHANGES IN THE CORRELATIONS BETWEEN THE SELF AND THE SELF-IDEAL SORTS

Groups Compared	Difference between Mean Changes	*t*	*P*
Own-control and no-therapy....	.065	.616	.50
Attrition and continuers........	.286	1.722	.10
Attrition and no-therapy.......	.252	1.415	<.20
Continuers and no-therapy......	.034	.300	....

therapy points, and Table 2 compares the various groups with each other with respect to their mean changes over the wait period.

Tables 1 and 2 reveal a minute gain in the mean correlation between the self and the self-ideal sorts for both the own-control and the no-therapy groups, with the gain of the own-controls being a little the larger. This trend in the data is so small as to be of negligible importance, and there is no basis for accepting the hypothesis that motivation for therapy brings about a constructive personality change as a function of time alone. This finding takes on additional significance because both Butler (chap. 4) and Rudikoff (chap. 6) have reported that client-centered therapy brings about marked increases in the congruence between the perceived self and the ideal self.

Comparing the continuers and the attrition groups brings out an interesting difference. Those clients who later continued in therapy for six or more interviews actually show a slight decrease in the correlation between the self and the self-ideal sorts. But the correlation for the attrition group increases, and the difference between the mean gains of these two groups is significant at the 10 per cent level of confidence. This suggests that those persons who broke off their therapy early (or never really started at all) may have made some constructive personality changes during the sixty-day wait period.[4]

In Table 1 it will be noted that the no-therapy controls, in accordance with theoretical expectations, have a very high correlation between the self and the self-ideal sorts, while the own-control group shows no relationship. These data are mean correlations, and, when the correlations for individual cases are considered, we find a fair amount of overlap between the two groups. However, the lowest correlation between the self and the self-ideal sorts in the no-therapy group was +.22, whereas we found many negative correlations, some of them quite high, in the own-control group. Also, the congruence between the perceived self and the wanted self was especially low for the continuers group. Here only one

4. Esselyn Rudikoff will soon report on an intensive investigation of the Q-sort data for the attrition and the continuers groups. Appreciation is expressed to Miss Rudikoff for permission to use a portion of her data in this report.

correlation above .40 was found at either the pre-wait or the pre-therapy point.

The great difference between the own-control and the no-therapy controls in the size of this correlation raises the question as to whether the no-therapy group serves as a useful control at all. As one check on this, a simple four-cell contingency table was used to determine if an increase or a decrease in the correlation between the self and the self-ideal was related to the initial strength of this relationship at the pre-wait point. Almost identical frequencies appeared in all four cells, and so the change does seem independent of the starting point.

The Q-Adjustment Score

Dymond (chap. 5) developed an adjustment score based upon the self-sort data just discussed. It should be noted that this measure is not strictly independent of the previously discussed measure, but it does treat the raw data in a quite different way and is looking at a somewhat different facet of adjustment status.

In Tables 3 and 4 it can be seen that the results for the Q-adjust-

TABLE 3

CHANGES OVER THE WAIT PERIOD OF THE MEAN Q-ADJUSTMENT SCORE

Group	*N*	Pre-wait	Pre-therapy	Mean Change
Own-control	23	30.74	34.48	+ 4.269
Attrition	8	32.13	43.00	+10.87
Continuers	15	30.00	29.93	− 0.07
No-therapy control	8	49.25	50.125	+ 0.375

TABLE 4

COMPARISONS BETWEEN GROUPS WITH RESPECT TO THEIR MEAN CHANGES ON THE Q-ADJUSTMENT SCORE

Groups Compared	Difference between Mean Changes	*t*	*P*
No-therapy and own-control	2.87	.972	<.30
Attrition and continuers	10.95	2.563	.02
Attrition and no-therapy control	10.00	2.275	<.05
Continuers and no-therapy control	0.945	....	....

ment scores are very similar to those just reported for the correlations between the self and the self-ideal sorts. The own-control group shows a slight gain, but this is far from being significantly greater than the gain of the no-therapy group. Again the attrition group accounts for all the gain in the own-control group, while the continuers show a slight decrease in their mean score. Even greater confidence can be placed in the finding of real gains for the attrition group, as evidenced by the low *P* values, when it is compared with the continuers and with the no-therapy controls. Again the no-therapy group shows better adjustment than the own-controls, and the attrition group improves so that at pre-therapy testing they are closer in score to the equivalent controls than to the continuers. Our conclusions, therefore, are the same as those reported for the changes in the self-ideal correlations.

We used a contingency table once more to see if there was a tendency for the low adjustment scores to show more improvement over the sixty-day period than did the high adjustment scores. Here we found a very slight, but far from significant, tendency for this to occur.

Maturity of Reported Behavior

Rogers (chap. 13) conducted a study of actual behavior changes in the clients and control subjects over the testing period. The instrument used was the Willoughby Emotional-Maturity Scale (E-M Scale) (5), to which Rogers added nine items to give the scale more range on the immature side. Two measures are used: Self-ratings and ratings made by close friends of the subjects.

Tables 5 and 6 present the data obtained when the subjects rate their own behavior. The findings are very similar to those reported for the previous measures. One slight difference is that the small change appearing here for the own-control group is in the direction of less mature behavior.

There was no significant tendency for either the high or the low emotional maturity scores to change more than the other over the sixty-day wait period.

To conserve space, we do not present the data for the friends' ratings of the subjects or the friends' rating of friends. However, only fractional changes occurred over the wait period on these measures, and the direction of these changes fails to support the hypothesis that motivation for therapy alone produces improved personal adjustment.

Attitudes toward Others

Another hypothesis about the outcome of client-centered counseling is that the client's attitudes will change in ways that can be generally described as more accepting of the worth and individuality of others. Gordon and Cartwright (chap. 11) reported the results of a project to test this hypothesis. The measuring instrument used here is the Self-Other Attitude Scale (S-O Scale), which is designed to measure the following attitudes: antidemocratic tendencies, ethnocentrism, political-economic conservatism, dependence upon experts, acceptance of differences of opinion, belief in democratic means, acceptance of the worth of others, and a desire to change others.

TABLE 5

CHANGES OVER THE WAIT PERIOD OF THE MEAN E-M SCORES

Group	*N*	Pre-wait	Pre-therapy	Mean Change
Own-control	23	43.52	43.47	− .043
Attrition	8	45.25	49.00	+3.750
Continuers	15	42.60	40.53	−2.066
No-therapy control	9	54.88	55.77	+ .889

TABLE 6

COMPARISONS BETWEEN GROUPS WITH RESPECT TO THEIR MEAN CHANGES ON THE E-M SCORES

Groups Compared	Difference between Mean Changes	*t*	*P*
No-therapy and own-control	.931	....	....
Attrition and continuers	5.816	1.768	.10
Attrition and no-therapy control	2.862	.741	.50
Continuers and no-therapy control	2.954	.882	.35

The findings for the S-O Scale are presented in Tables 7 and 8. Again there is no evidence that motivation for therapy plus time will bring about changes of the type predicted for successful psychotherapy. In fact, the no-therapy group changes in the favorable direction, while the own-control group changes unfavorably, and the difference here is significant at the 5 per cent level of confidence.

The S-O Scale findings differ in some ways from the pattern described by the earlier data. On the S-O Scale the no-therapy control group does not show any greater tendency than does the own-

TABLE 7

CHANGES OVER THE WAIT PERIOD OF THE MEAN S-O SCALE SCORES

Group	*N*	Pre-wait	Pre-therapy	Mean Change
Own-control	23	316.13	321.87	+ 5.74
Attrition	8	302.25	315.63	+13.38
Continuers	15	323.53	325.20	+ 1.67
No-therapy control	8	332.12	312.87	−19.25

TABLE 8

COMPARISONS BETWEEN GROUPS WITH RESPECT TO THEIR MEAN CHANGES ON THE S-O SCALE SCORES

Groups Compared	Difference between Mean Changes	t	P
No-therapy and own-control	24.99	2.232	<.05
Attrition and continuers	11.71	1.072	.30
Attrition and no-therapy control	32.63	2.489	<.05
Continuers and no-therapy control	20.92	1.757	.10

control group to possess attitudes that would be evaluated as indicative of better adjustment. Another important difference is that the attrition group changes in an unfavorable rather than a favorable direction. We can only speculate about the meaning of these differences. The first difference may possibly mean that the attitudes measured by the S-O Scale are not the kinds of issues that bring people to psychotherapy. A suggested interpretation of the second difference in pattern is even more speculative: perhaps the attrition-group subjects do feel better about themselves (as suggested by the earlier data), but this gain has a defensive element, so that it comes at the cost of more reliance upon experts and authority, more conservatism, less acceptance of the uniqueness of others, etc.

Changes in Mental Health Characteristics as Assessed by the TAT

With one exception the measures reported up to now have dealt with one kind or another of self-assessment where distortion (either conscious or unconscious) is often considered a likely possibility. We now report data based upon the Thematic Apperception Test (TAT), where this is less likely.

For a project undertaken by Grummon and John (see chap. 9), John devised a series of twenty-three psychoanalytically oriented rating scales which would enable the clinician quantitatively to record the kinds of judgments that are customarily made in the clinical evaluation of the TAT. These are all seven-point rating scales, with the higher figure indicating poorer mental health status. We here deal with only two scales which are summary impressions of all the TAT material. Scale 22 deals with overt life-adjustment to family, work, friends, etc.; scale 23 is an over-all diagnostic impression of the outstanding psychodynamic features in the personality, defined essentially in terms of the classical Freudian stages of psychosexual development.

The results for the TAT are presented in Tables 9, 10, 11, and 12. (In reading the tables, be sure to note that a *higher* score indicates a *poorer* mental health status.) The findings are essentially the same as those reported for the correlations between the self and the self-ideal sorts, for the Q-adjustment score, and for the E-M Scale. The main difference between the TAT data and the previously reported measures is that here the no-therapy control group changes in the direction of poorer mental health status. We are at a loss to explain this trend in the data except to wonder if it is due to the unreliability of the ratings themselves.

However, even with this trend in the equivalent-control group, the difference between the mean changes for the own-control and the no-therapy groups is still such that it could easily be due to chance alone. So we must again reject the hypothesis that motivation for therapy has of itself brought about a constructive change.

The TAT data again show a marked tendency for the attrition

TABLE 9

CHANGES OVER THE WAIT PERIOD OF THE MEAN SCORES ON TAT SCALE NO. 23 (DIAGNOSTIC IMPRESSION)

Group	N	Pre-wait	Pre-therapy	Mean Change
Own-control	22	4.72	4.45	− .27
Attrition	7	5.00	3.86	−1.14
Continuers	15	4.60	4.73	+ .13
No-therapy control	11	3.27	3.64	+ .36

TABLE 10

COMPARISONS BETWEEN GROUPS WITH RESPECT TO THEIR MEAN CHANGES ON TAT SCALE NO. 23

Groups Compared	Difference between Mean Changes	t	P
No-therapy and own-control	.63	1.204	.24
Attrition and continuers	1.27	1.961	.07
Attrition and no-therapy control	1.50	2.302	.04
Continuers and no-therapy control	.23	.408	.70

TABLE 11

CHANGES OVER THE WAIT PERIOD OF THE MEAN SCORES ON TAT SCALE NO. 22 (DEGREE OF ADJUSTMENT)

Group	N	Pre-wait	Pre-therapy	Mean Change
Own-control	22	3.91	3.91	0
Attrition	7	3.71	3.29	− .429
Continuers	15	4.00	4.20	+ .20
No-therapy control	11	3.27	3.82	+ .55

TABLE 12

COMPARISONS BETWEEN GROUPS WITH RESPECT TO THEIR MEAN CHANGES ON TAT SCALE NO. 22

Groups Compared	Difference between Mean Changes	t	P
No-therapy and own-control	.55	.794	.44
Attrition and continuers	.62	1.258	.23
Attrition and no-therapy control	.97	1.421	.18
Continuers and no-therapy control	.35	.514	.61

group to improve over the wait period, while the opposite condition holds for the continuing group.

IV. DISCUSSION

In summarizing all our comparisons between the own-control and the no-therapy control groups, we find absolutely no basis for accepting the hypothesis that motivation for therapy brings about constructive personality changes as a function of a sixty-day time interval. On four of the seven measures the trend was for the own-control group to improve relative to the no-therapy group, but the *P* values for the comparisons were all quite large and thus indicate that the differences could easily be a chance occurrence. On three of the measures the opposite trend occurred, and for one of these (S-O Scale) the difference between the mean changes of the two groups was significant at the 5 per cent level of confidence. Furthermore, if we consider only those subjects who later continued in their therapy (presumably the subjects who had the greater motivation to change), we find that the trend in the data for all measures except the two TAT scores is contrary to the hypothesis that motivation for therapy brings about constructive change as a function of time alone.[5]

We wish to mention some qualifications. While we cannot accept a hypothesis that change has occurred over the sixty-day period, neither can we with complete certainty reject the null hypothesis of no change. All we can say is that it is probable that no true change occurred. This difficulty of interpretation of course arises because we have used a statistical procedure that is commonly employed in situations where little value is attached to the firm acceptance of the null hypothesis and much value is attached to its firm rejection. We emphasize this difficulty of interpretation of the data only because the point at issue in this paper is of considerable methodological importance to all studies attempting to evaluate psychotherapy.

5. While motivation for therapy clearly did not bring about improvement in the continuers group, it might be argued that motivation was important in the improvement found for the attrition subjects. This argument would seem to assume that there is no essential difference between the two groups in motivation at the pre-wait point but that the attrition subjects have lost their motivation at the pre-therapy point, possibly due to gains they made over the wait period.

A second qualification is that the sixty-day wait period used here is shorter than the period over which psychotherapy usually takes place. A study using a one-year or a two-year wait period would have given a firmer basis for comparison.

Third, our results should not be used as evidence against the occurrence of spontaneous remission. At least for this writer, spontaneous remission is so commonly observed that its existence can hardly be doubted. However, "spontaneous remission" is a phrase used to label our ignorance. If spontaneous improvement occurs, it is, of course, caused—that is, the improvement must be a result of forces acting within or upon the individual. Presumably, these forces, even though unknown, are also commonly present in everyday living. Psychotherapy is said to offer unique or specialized forces (or possibly common forces occurring with greater frequency or intensity), and thus it is distinguished from spontaneous remission. The writer views the present study as a direct attack upon our ignorance about spontaneous recovery. The study suggests that motivation for change by itself is not an important force in spontaneous recovery. (Motivation for change may of course be very important as it interacts with other forces.)

It should also be noted that, when we speak of spontaneous recovery, we are usually rather vague as to what the recovery consists of. Customarily, the definition of spontaneous recovery is that the individual is now better able to adjust to his life-situation, although it may contain some specifics as "the patient has discarded his delusions" or "less anxiety is present." In Denker's (1) study of five hundred cases, recovery consisted of the individual's being able to earn enough money so that the insurance company no longer had to pay him disability benefits. In short, observations of spontaneous recovery seldom provide us with exact information about the kinds of changes that have occurred or have failed to occur. If, as is frequently suggested, the spontaneous recovery rate is to be used as a base line for evaluating the effectiveness of psychotherapy, then we need to know with more exactness the kinds of changes that occur under the two conditions. Many therapists would consider a case a failure if the only gain from treatment was the client's ability to stay off the insurance company's disability roll. To put the issue another way, would Denker's subjects have shown an increase in the congruence between their perceived selves and their wanted selves, that is, personality changes of the kind expected after successful therapy? The argument being presented here does not imply that studies such as Denker's are of no value. Quite the contrary is true. We do imply that we only scratch the surface of our problem until we begin to examine specific personality variables selected because of their relevance to theory.

We now turn to the data obtained for the continuers and the attrition groups. On every measure except the S-O Scale the attrition group gained more than the continuers, and on four measures the *P* value of the difference between mean changes was .10 or smaller. There was also a strong tendency for the attrition group to make gains that were significantly greater than the changes found in the no-therapy group, while the opposite tendency is seen for those who continued in therapy.

So the attrition subjects, those clients who *do not* later get involved in therapy, improve over the sixty-day wait period; but the continuers, those clients who *do* later get involved in therapy, do not gain over this period—in fact, they tend to get slightly worse.

This finding has some interesting implications for studies attempting to evaluate the outcomes of psychotherapy. It appears that the composition of the continuers group is influenced by a special selective factor, namely, that these subjects are less likely to improve their mental health status as a function of time alone. Furthermore, it is apparent that it is the continuers who must serve as the experimental group for any evaluation of psychotherapy itself. Thus the experimental group used to evaluate psychotherapy tends to be selectively composed of clients who, as a group, are less likely to show spontaneous recovery. In turn, this finding suggests that the proper base line for evaluating the outcomes of psychotherapy, for self-referred cases at least, is not the spontaneous remission rate as suggested by Eysenck, Denker, and others but instead is at some point below this. This finding must be considered still tentative, but it at least casts a doubt on Eysenck's implication that persons seeking and receiving psychotherapy obtain no benefits that would not also have occurred in the absence of such treatment.

There is a further implication of these findings which concerns the proper interpretation of therapeutic outcomes for those clients who break off their treatment. Such clients are frequently considered to be unsuccessful cases. However, it may well be that these clients correspond to the attrition-group subjects of this study, and, if so, cases discontinuing treatment should not necessarily be classified as unimproved. Instead, attempts should be made to determine more carefully the presence or absence of personality change.

V. SUMMARY

This study is an initial attempt to meet one of the valid criticisms that has been aimed at studies trying to evaluate the effectiveness of psychotherapy. We have tested and rejected (within the limits of our design) the hypothesis that motivation for therapy brings about constructive personality changes as a function of time alone—that is, in the absence of psychotherapy. In testing the hypothesis, we utilized seven different measures of personality make-up selected because of their relevance to personality theory. Twenty-three clients seeking help at a university counseling center were given a battery of tests, waited sixty days, and then retook the tests before actually beginning their therapy. Personality changes in these subjects over the sixty-day wait period were compared with changes over a similar period in a control group of subjects who were not seeking psychotherapy.

In addition, the experimental group was subdivided into (*a*) an attrition group composed of clients who later made little or no use of their opportunity for therapy and (*b*) a continuers group who came to therapy for an average of thirty-two interviews. The attrition group tended to show constructive personality changes over the sixty-day wait period, while the opposite held for the continuers group. The continuers group, who must form the experimental group for any evaluation of psychotherapy itself, thus tends to be differentially selected as subjects less likely to change as a function of time. This finding suggests that the spontaneous remission rate is somewhere above the proper base line to be used for studies evaluating the effectiveness of psychotherapy.

REFERENCES

1. Denker, P. G. "Results of Treatment of Psychoneurosis by the General Practitioner: A Follow-up Study of 500 Cases," *New York State Journal of Medicine*, XLVI (1946), 2164–66.
2. Edwards, A. L. *Experimental Design in Psychological Research*. New York: Rinehart & Co., 1950.
3. Eysenck, Hans. "The Effects of Psychotherapy: An Evaluation," *Journal of Consulting Psychology*, XVI (1952), 319–24.
4. Hebb, D. O. *The Organization of Behavior*. New York: John Wiley & Sons, 1949.
5. Willoughby, R. R. "A Scale of Emotional Maturity," *Journal of Social Psychology*, III (1931), 3–36.
6. Zubin, J. A. "Evaluation of Therapeutic Outcome in Mental Disorders," *Journal of Nervous and Mental Disorders*, CXVII (1953), 95–111.

PART III

Case Studies

CHAPTER 15

The Case of Mrs. Oak: A Research Analysis[1]

CARL R. ROGERS

I. INTRODUCTION

In the preceding chapters the group results for several of the projects have been given. Such presentations, however valuable from a factual point of view, are not likely to make the total research investigation come to life in the mind of the reader. Also, by being presented as separate studies, they have tended to avoid the complex problem of the way in which these diverse facts are interrelated in the life of the client. Finally, they tend to conceal the fact that counseling or psychotherapy is a warm, fluctuating, human relationship, no matter how statistically measurable the changes produced.

It is hoped that in this chapter we can remedy some of these deficiencies. What has been done, in the pages which follow, is to take one client, whom we shall term "Mrs. Oak," and illustrate in her therapeutic experience and in her performance on a variety of tests and research instruments the way we have been attempting to measure some elements of the process of psychotherapy and its results. It might be thought of as a vertical sampling of our research effort, reporting all the measures on one case, and integrating the meaning of those measures. The preceding chapters, with their reports of the results on all of the therapy cases, represent the horizontal slices which this account cuts down through in vertical fashion. In addition to thus integrating in one individual the various

1. In preparing this chapter, the author has drawn upon the data of all the preceding chapters, in addition to making special studies on this client alone. He is particularly indebted to the following staff members for their help in gathering the basic data: John M. Butler, Rosalind Dymond, Thomas Gordon, and Esselyn Rudikoff. Thanks are also due to Daniel Bergman, Carol Bowie, Jacques Boyer, Sarah Counts, Richard Farson, Gerard Haigh, and Margaret Hartley for assistance given in various aspects of the several researches.

research procedures, extensive excerpts from the recorded interviews are also given, so that the clinical meaning of the objective findings may become evident.

The Chronological Steps in the Client's Experience

We will first examine the various events in which Mrs. Oak participated during the total period with which we are concerned. These are listed below in such a way as to indicate the manner in which the data were collected for the co-ordinated investigations which will be discussed.

a) Preliminary interview. This was a fifteen-minute interview, in which she requested help for herself. She knew of the Counseling Center through a relative who had been helped. Arrangements were made for her to see a counselor twice a week, which was the frequency she preferred. She indicated her willingness to devote a number of hours to research tasks, with the understanding that these would probably be of no help to her in her own therapy but would advance our knowledge in this field.

b) The complete battery of research instruments was administered by the research psychologist carrying this responsibility (not the counselor). The battery included:
   (1) The Thematic Apperception Test (TAT).
   (2) One hundred Q-sort cards, sorted to give a picture of the self, the desired self or self-ideal, and the ordinary person.
   (3) The Willoughby Emotional-Maturity Scale (E-M Scale). In addition to filling it out for herself, she took two copies for two of her friends to fill out for her and to mail in to the Center.
   (4) The Self-Other Attitude Scale (S-O Scale).
   (5) The role-playing situational test of interpersonal situations.

c) The therapist held interviews Nos. 1–7 with the client, each interview being electrically recorded for later transcription.

d) The research psychologist made an appointment with the client and readministered the Q-sort material to obtain a new picture of self, self-ideal, and the ordinary person.

e) The counselor at this same time made three Q-sorts of the client's self, self-ideal, and concept of the ordinary person, as he thought the client would perceive these three entities.

f) The therapist held interviews Nos. 8–25 with the client, two interviews per week except where illness, holidays, etc., prevented. The interviews were recorded as before.

g) The research psychologist readministered the Q-sort material, exactly as in *d*.

h) The therapist held interviews Nos. 26–39 with the client, at which point she tentatively terminated. She wrote a note requesting one more interview, and

No. 40 was held nine days after No. 39. At this point she terminated. There had been a period of five and a half months from the first interview to the last.

i) Shortly after the conclusion of therapy, when the therapist was out of town for an extended period, the client asked if she might come in and express herself to the recording machine. There were two such sessions.

j) The complete battery of research instruments was administered by the research psychologist immediately following the termination of therapy, exactly as in *b*.

k) The therapist used the Q-sort material to predict the client's perception of self, self-ideal, and ordinary person at the end of therapy. This task was the same as in *e*.

l) The follow-up period ensued. This was a period of seven months during which there was no contact between therapist and client.

m) The complete battery of research instruments was readministered as in *b* and *j*. In addition, the client was asked to sort the Q-sort items once more to represent herself as she *remembered* herself at the beginning of therapy.

n) The research psychologist held a follow-up interview with the client to obtain her subjective reactions to the experience of therapy and its outcomes. This was the final material to be gathered, according to the general design of the research.

o) At this point, however, the client requested further interviews with the therapist, and eight interviews were held, at which point the client terminated for the second time, indicating that she felt more certain now that her therapy was concluded. These interviews extended over two months.

p) A battery of research instruments was administered once more, five months after the tests at *m*, three months after completion of the interviews in *o*. The client at this time was given the TAT; she was asked to use the Q-cards to give four pictures: herself, her self-ideal, the ordinary person, and herself as she *remembered* herself at the beginning of therapy.

II. THE CLIENT IN THERAPY

The Client as Viewed by the Therapist

This particular client was chosen as the subject of this report for two reasons. She was the first client in the research group, and the first to complete therapy, and hence the material in regard to her became available earlier than the material on other clients. In the second place, the counselor felt that a significant degree of reorganization of attitudes and personality had taken place, and thus there was a presumption that the objective measures might show some change. It would not, for example, have seemed worth while to make such a complete analysis if the indications were that nothing had occurred. We are primarily interested at the present time in a refined and objective description of what changes occur when therapy is deemed to have taken place.

It should be made clear that the selection of the case for reporting was not based upon knowledge of the results. At the time the case was selected it was known, as mentioned above, that the therapist had rated it as a successful case. A few of the Q-sortings had been correlated, and it was known that there had been some change in the self-picture, though not so great as in some other cases which had been calculated. None of the other results was known.

Although some excerpts from the recorded interviews will be used later to illustrate and illuminate some of the objective findings, it is scarcely possible to give all the material of the interviews, since the transcriptions take up more than three hundred single-spaced typewritten pages. The therapist has therefore provided this very brief and general over-all picture of the client and her therapy as he viewed it from his frame of reference. It was written before the findings from the various research studies were known.

The presenting situation was that Mrs. Oak was a housewife in her late thirties who was in a deeply discordant relationship with her husband and also much disturbed in her relationship with her adolescent daughter, who had recently been through a serious illness which had been diagnosed as psychosomatic. Mrs. Oak felt she must be to blame for this illness. She herself was a sensitive person, eager to be honest with herself and to search out the causes of her problems. She was a person with little formal education, though intelligent and widely read.

By the fifth interview any specific concentration on her problems had dropped out, and the major focus of therapy had shifted to an experiencing of herself and her emotional reactions. She felt at times that she *should* be "working on my problems" but that she felt drawn to this experiencing, that somehow she wanted to use the therapy hour for what she called her "vaguenesses." This was a good term, since she expressed herself in half-sentences, poetic analogies, and expressions which seemed more like fantasy. Her communications were often hard to follow or understand but obviously involved much deep feeling experienced in the immediate present.

She was unusually sensitive to the process she was experiencing in herself. To use some of her expressions, she was feeling the pieces of a jigsaw puzzle, she was singing a song without words, she was creating a poem, she was learning a new way of experiencing herself which was like learning to read Braille. Therapy was an experiencing of her self, in all its aspects, in a safe relationship. At first it was her guilt and her concern over being responsible for the maladjustments of others. Then it was her hatred and bitterness toward life for having cheated and frustrated her in so many different areas, particularly the sexual, and then it was the experiencing of her own hurt, of the sorrow she felt for herself for having been so wounded. But along with these went the experiencing of self as having a capacity for wholeness, a self which was not possessively loving toward others but was "without hate," a self that cared about others. This last followed what was, for her, one of the deepest experiences in therapy (between interviews Nos. 29 and 30)—the realization that the therapist *cared*, that it really mattered to him how therapy turned out for her, that he really valued her. She experienced the soundness of her own basic directions. She gradually became aware of the fact that, though she had searched in every corner of herself, there was nothing fundamentally bad but, rather, at heart she was positive and sound. She realized that the values she deeply held were such as would set her at variance with her culture, but she accepted this calmly.

I have termed these realizations "experiencings," hoping to convey something of the half-fantasy, half-trance state into which she could let herself go in the deeper aspects of therapy, when the tears, or the joy, or the hatred, or the tenderness which was the immediately present part of herself could be fully and completely experienced.

One of the outstanding characteristics of the interviews was the minimal consideration of her outside behavior. Once an issue was settled in her, the behavioral consequences were mentioned only by chance. After she had "felt" her way through her relationship with her daughter, there was little mention of her behavior toward the daughter until much later when she casually mentioned that the relationship was much better. Likewise in regard to a job. She had never worked outside the home, and the prospect terrified her, yet she thought it highly important if she were to feel independent of her husband. She finally settled the issue in her feelings to the extent that she said she thought now that she could look for or take a job. She never mentioned it again. Only through a chance outside source did the therapist learn that, at about the end of therapy, she chose an establishment in which she wished to work, applied for a position, ignored the turn-down which she received, and convinced the manager that he should give her a trial. She is still holding the position. It was the same in regard to her marriage. She decided that she could not continue in marriage but that she did not wish to break up the marriage in a battle or with resentment or hurt. Shortly after the conclusion of therapy she achieved this goal of a separation and divorce which was mutually agreed upon.

When she left therapy, it was with the feeling that a process was going on in her which would continue to operate. She felt that the relationship with the therapist had been very meaningful and in a psychological sense would never stop, even though she walked out of the office for good. She felt ready, she thought, to cope with her life, though she realized it would not be easy.

The Therapist as Viewed by the Therapist

Since therapy is a relationship, it will be well to get some view of the therapist's reactions and feelings during his contacts with Mrs. Oak. He has provided us with this statement:

My first meeting with Mrs. Oak was in the preliminary interview. At that time she seemed to me like a shy, almost nondescript person. I did not feel attracted to her or repelled by her. As therapy commenced, I felt first that she was a sensitive and interesting person, and gradually my respect for her grew. As is nearly always true with me, whenever a client goes deeply into himself in therapy, I find myself experiencing a profound respect, almost an awe—it is the closest I come to a feeling of worship—as I experience the marvelously intricate capacity of the human organism to forge ahead through turmoil and pain to integration. I felt this with unusual strength in dealing with Mrs. Oak, partly because her frequent discussions of the stirrings of the therapeutic process in herself gave me a clearer and more meaningful picture of these intricacies than one usually obtains. To me the thought of trying to guide or direct such an intricate human process is literally abhorrent, and I never felt any such impulse in regard to Mrs. Oak. To try to understand her, to go with her on the paths she was exploring, to let her feel the acceptance I experienced toward her, this seemed to be a fully satisfying task for me.

Her incoherent way of expressing herself made understanding difficult but in no way lessened it. Perhaps partly because she had such unique ways of expressing herself, and partly because of my respect for her, I concentrated with great intensity upon understanding these emotional communications. On the whole, my understanding was deep and accurate, and when it was not she corrected me—sometimes impatiently, but usually eager to have me see what was the private meaning of her expression. Since the completion of therapy I have listened to some of the recordings and have read the transcriptions of the interviews. I must say that I am at times amazed (and others who have listened are more amazed) that I was able to understand what these jumbled analogies, half-sentences, and incomplete thoughts were intended to convey. Yet I was frequently able to catch clearly the feeling which was being expressed. I can only say that the two of us were sufficiently "in tune" that the emotional communication was clear, even when the verbal production of the client almost defies ordinary language analysis.

Unlike some clients, Mrs. Oak never made me uneasy or anxious. She rarely attacked me, and then her feeling that I wasn't of much help was clear even to her as being an expression of annoyance at the resistance she found within herself. The only anxiety I experienced was at the depth of her vagueness. Could this be therapeutic? Was I right in permitting a person to explore such caverns of feeling in a verbal way which surely would have been labeled as the product of an abnormal person by any competent diagnostician? It is the anxiety I not infrequently feel when I realize that it is a hypothesis upon which I am working and that to allow the client to guide himself to integration *might* be a mistaken hypothesis for *this* client. This anxiety was not great, however, for she seemed to exhibit a high degree of ruggedness in her sensitive individuality and could frequently call the turn as to the next step of the process. Even when she felt the greatest degree of inner disturbance and disintegration, she always had, and expressed, a quiet conviction that this could only lead to something more constructive.

I often feel grateful to clients for what I have learned from them. This feeling was unusually strong in my contacts with Mrs. Oak. There have been interviews when I could have very honestly closed the interview with the statement, "Thank you very much for what you have permitted me to learn." I never did express this except in a partial way at the conclusion of therapy, but I felt it often. To me, one of the "extra dividends" of the client-centered approach is the fact that one can openly and eagerly learn from the client as he leads you into the unique complexities of himself. He is a much better instructor than books or professional colleagues, both hampered as they are by biased theories to which the facts must be distorted. From Mrs. Oak I learned much about the inner strength of the human spirit; I learned many new concepts of the process of therapy; I gained a whole new picture of the meaning of the therapeutic relationship; and a number of significant new research hypotheses have sprung into clear formulation as a result. Not one client in fifty has taught me so much. When I read the Preface of Rogers' new book, I felt that one of the last sentences expressed exactly what I might have written about Mrs. Oak. Speaking about the clients with whom we have worked, he says: "To these men, women and children who have brought themselves and their struggles to us, who have with such natural grace permitted us to learn from them, who have laid bare for us the forces which operate in the mind and spirit of man—to them goes our deepest gratitude" (3, p. xii). That describes one of the strongest feelings I had, and have, toward Mrs. Oak.

The Therapist's Rating

The counselor's judgment of the client's experience of therapy is best indicated by giving the ratings which he made at the conclusion of the series of forty interviews (not at the time of follow-up). Although this scale has been presented in chapter 7, it is reproduced here in full in order to show the ratings for the beginning and end of therapy in this case.

DIRECTIONS FOR CASE RATING SCALE

We would like to have two ratings for Items 1–8 of this scale. Place a *B* in the space appropriate for the beginning phase of the case and an *E* at the point appropriate for the end of the case. For Items 9 and 10 place an *X* in the appropriate space.

1. Degree to which therapy was an intellectual-cognitive process for the client.

Little or None						*Maximally or Exclusively*		
1	2	3	4	5	6	7	8	9
	E		B					

2. The degree to which therapy was an emotional-experiential process for the client.

Little or None — *Maximally or Exclusively*

1	2	3	4	5	6	7	8	9
						B		E

3. The degree to which the client perceived therapy as a process of personal exploration or as specific analysis of life-situations.

Situational — *Personal Exploration*

1	2	3	4	5	6	7	8	9
		B						E

4. The degree to which the client has used the relationship itself as a focus for therapy.

Negligible Extent — *Maximally*

1	2	3	4	5	6	7	8	9
			B			E		

5. Estimate of the client's attitude toward you during the course of therapy.

Strong Dislike — *Strong Liking or Respect*

1	2	3	4	5	6	7	8	9
					B			E

6. Estimate of your feeling toward the client.

Strong Dislike — *Strong Liking or Respect*

1	2	3	4	5	6	7	8	9
				B			E	

7. The degree of personal integration of the client.

Highly Disorganized or Defensively Organized — *Optimally Integrated*

1	2	3	4	5	6	7	8	9
			B			E		

8. The life-adjustment of the client.

Low — *High*

1	2	3	4	5	6	7	8	9
			B				E	

9. Degree of satisfaction of the client with the outcome of therapy.

Strongly Dissatisfied — *Extremely Satisfied*

1	2	3	4	5	6	7	8	9
								X

10. Your rating of the outcome of therapy.

Complete Failure — *Marked Success*

1	2	3	4	5	6	7	8	9
							X	

III. GLOBAL PERSONALITY CHANGE

One of the research projects was an investigation to determine whether personality change took place during and after therapy. The design of this study is reported in chapter 8. The instrument was the TAT, administered before and after therapy, and at the follow-up point six months to one year later. The general hypothesis was that "if therapy has been completed . . . the post-test and follow-up TAT's will reveal significant differences in the total personality indicative of better adjustment as compared with the pre-test."

The "Blind" Analysis

In the case of Mrs. Oak the TAT's were administered prior to therapy, five and a half months later at the conclusion of therapy, and again after the follow-up period of seven months.[2] In each case, her TAT stories were electrically recorded and then transcribed. They were then ready for analysis.

The analysis was made "blind." The three sets of TAT protocols were given, without any identifying data, to Dr. Carol Bowie, a clinical psychologist at the Municipal Court in Chicago, a person of eleven years' clinical experience who has worked extensively with the TAT. She was told that these three protocols were from the same person at different periods. She was asked to make a clinical analysis of each TAT and also to rank them in terms of degree of integration. By an oversight she was not even told the age or the sex of the client, so that the analysis was "blind" indeed!

From her study of the stories, Dr. Bowie concluded that the person was in therapy and placed the tests in the correct order from first to last. Since there are six possible orderings of the three tests, this appears significant. She judged that the first test was given prior to therapy, the second during therapy, and the third at its conclusion. This is an error, since the second test was a post-test and the third is a follow-up measure. In the following sections the analysis of each TAT is given as it was made by Dr. Bowie

2. The fourth TAT, given at the time of the second follow-up, will be presented and discussed later.

without any knowledge whatsoever of the client, or of the order of administration of the TAT's.

The First TAT

This person is a dependent, passive individual who has experienced rejection both at home and in social groups. She has a tremendous drive to achieve something "great," although there is an equally tremendous resistance to the need or drive, as *imposed upon* her, rather than as something she wants to do. Hostility toward women as a group is strong; toward the mother surrogate, decided. This hostility carries over into parent-child relationships in general. She is unsure of herself and quite insecure about her personal attractiveness. She is very lonely and unhappy, feels unaccepted, and has no real affectional ties with anyone. Such as there are, are either rebellious attachments or "duty" attachments. The individual's pattern for need gratification is escape—escape into another environment, escape into other idea—daydreams. She sees herself as a sort of ugly-duckling character—"warm and comfortable" under a camouflaging exterior of coldness and almost repulsiveness—certainly a consciously "thorny" one. This she dimly sees as a defense against being hurt, but she wants others to go all the way toward discovering her good qualities without any exertion on her part. Such excursions on her part would lead only to deep hurt.

She has been, she feels, deeply betrayed by other women. A *possible* homosexual episode or latent homosexual tendencies have sent her into a complete sexual panic. She sees heterosexual contacts as desirable but on a very unreal, romantic level, undemanding and a-physical.

She feels basically useless, formless, and is filled with anxiety and real fear, which she dares not face because of the "terrible things that lurk" beneath the surface. Her drive for achievement and high level of aspiration are thus a type of "busy work"—a method of filling up her life with a lot of things about which she can feel or express concern even though she realizes that they are rather unimportant. There is a great deal of compulsiveness in this busy-ness, and a feeling of being driven by outside forces so that relaxation becomes impossible. She feels that there is no "fun," no zest for living, and hence her desire for escape becomes a frenzied squirrel-cage kind of activity. Things must become better for her through outside agencies; there is no move toward doing anything about it herself, except running away. There are generalized suspicion, hostility, resentment, frustration, dejection, and strong guilt feelings—directed specifically toward some family member (possibly a mother or mother surrogate) and considerable confusion about her own sex role.

Happiness to her is equivalent to lack of status (or desire for it), to "relaxation," to having plenty of props to lean upon. Her guilt feelings are in large part related to denial of affectional responses and to rebellion against outwardly imposed goals.

This individual has very little insight and will demand considerable support in therapy—will be at once hostile and pleading with the therapist to see past her hostility to the "warmth and comfort" inside; will use her façade of envious criticism to mask her own feelings of inadequacy. However, much of this is very close to the surface, and possibly the individual is closer than she knows to realization that she herself has maintained the barriers which she alternately denies and parades.

The Second TAT

The individual is beginning to have some doubts as to whether striving for achievement per se is really worth the effort. Self-sufficiency is now seen as a possibility for this person, but there is still considerable self-doubt, despair, and resignation, with a strong dependency trend. The necessity for familial and/or cultural "props" is not so pressing as before, while the irritation caused by forced adherence to sociocultural mores is recognized as such in a halfhearted sort of way. There is grave conflict in the sexual area—the individual goes into a complete panic state or idealizes and romanticizes the whole sexual connotation. There is still some confusion about her own sex role. The "lurking things" are seen as wry jokes played on one's self—the patient begins to see, dimly, that her poverty of inner resources is "by choice."

There are still strong guilt feelings clustered about a constellation of family expectancy and/or her social role as she sees it. There is far less threat from people in general with little of the implied scorn, condemnation, fear, or panic expressed in the first record. Whereas the earlier record verbalized the desire to go her own way, do as she pleased, this had scarcely gone beyond a wish-fulfilment fairy-godmother stage. Now she is beginning to sense a real liking for going her own way without necessarily knowing where she will finally end. There is far less generalized pessimism as her own self-confidence grows. Positive transference is strongly inferred, for the counselor, with perhaps beginning negative transference. There is a growing tendency toward objectivity and away from identification with strongly pessimistic or disruptive forces. She is still insistent upon freedom of choice and "relaxation" as prerequisites for happiness and still feels insecure in social and/or familial groups. There is a growing tendency to express, overtly, ideas running counter to those acceptable by the group, and, while she does not quite defy the group, she can view more tolerantly outside pressures as she feels able to move away—ever so slightly—from their demands.

There is panic still, but the individual feels that now there is somewhere to turn *if she needs it*. She no longer feels that help must be forthcoming from outside or the cause is lost.

Fantasy is now depersonalized and on a more healthy level—an outlet for frustration rather than an escape; active rather than passive. There is far less abasement and submissiveness, far more ability to work co-operatively.

There is a general feeling of organization of forces within the individual rather than the disorganized "keep busy at all costs" of the first record. The individual is still strongly pessimistic and somewhat depressed, but a *possibility* of balance and harmony is sensed. She is "groping," with a lack of clarity and certainty, but no longer fear-ridden.

Her romanticizing of the male (Sir Galahad in shining armor) is overdone—sex is either completely denied, or "they all lived happily ever after" ending with Mendelssohn.

The Third TAT

The individual recognizes and accepts self-directed goals as being equal with imposed goals so far as social and/or cultural desirability is concerned. Value judgments are a personal rather than a group matter for her, and she does not mistrust her own ability to make them for herself. There is increasing freedom from the necessity to "please," and familial ties are pleasant experiences rather than threats. Less and less fearful, her despairs are now on a macrocosmic plane. There is much more objective enjoyment. She feels she *has been* through a "rugged" experience, but she also feels confident that the worst is over. There is increasing ability to accept the idiosyncrasies of others rather than to condemn or fear them, and personal threat has almost disappeared as a component of social groups. The extreme swing to pessimism and depression have leveled off—the general attitude is balanced, perhaps rather optimistic, but the feeling tone is far less intense—as she puts it, "no fanfare." She still resents sentimentality but does not see it as deliberate insincerity. There is admitted ambivalence in parental relationships as regards both herself as child and herself as parent. The advisability of some standards is admitted, but there is no longer the resentment to such standards.

Dependency needs are fewer than in previous records and are verbalized Drive for achievement is seen as a panic reaction resulting from "lack of organization" (the squirrel-cage type of activity), and accomplishment is seen as possible, even if there is still considerable tendency toward procrastination. It is no longer the *deus ex machina* who will solve her problems; she'll do it herself, although to do so may involve quite a bit of last-minute rushing around.

She still feels that she has missed a great deal of happiness of an idealized sort—that she has been "locked out of Eden" through some basic lacks in herself. The sexual area is still a very sensitive one indeed. The panic reaction is not so strong, but she is evasive and defensive here to a degree not found elsewhere in the record. She is still not quite sure whether her role is the dominant or the submissive, and, while she desires "warm" heterosexual relationships, she is rather irreal and Graustarkian about the whole thing. The earlier feeling of betrayal by women and mistrust of men lest they "hurt" her is somewhat ameliorated, but she is unsettled here. There is a feeling of real struggle for dominance with some male, while being ambivalent about the outcome. Hence the central sexual conflict has not been faced and is far from resolved—although the individual is better able to make a surface adjustment. Sex itself is "dirty" and "sordid," although man-woman association is desirable.

Ego strength is greater than in preceding records; inner resourcefulness and self-directed goals are strongly implied. The necessity for "props" has almost disappeared, and the individual accepts herself as a unique person capable of contributing her *own* share in community projects.

The Fourth TAT

As indicated earlier, the design of the research ended with the first follow-up study. Since, however, we have the information from a second follow-up study of this client, we will include these data at each appropriate point in our report.

The analysis of the fourth TAT was also made by Dr. Bowie, without any knowledge of the case. It was, however, given to her later, and hence she naturally presumed that it had been administered later than the first three. Here then is her analysis of the fourth TAT, which comes five months after the third, there having been eight additional interviews in the early part of this five-month period.

> The general impression of this entire record is that the client "sees through" the purpose of the TAT and in rather good-humored fashion goes along—not telling "stories," but directly communicating feelings and emotions, including rejections as well as acceptancies. There is in this procedure a certain amount of defensiveness, but of the type found between two good friends, when each realizes that the other is being defensive. This is the "necessary" kind of defensiveness which keeps the ego intact as an individual contribution rather than a hostile or fearful defensiveness against intrusion. The client's expressed desire, some months back, to "relax and enjoy life" seems to be coming to fruition. Her anxieties and the consequent blocking are much less turbulent. There is a constant growth in insight, and the client shows increasing ability to see herself and her activities objectively. Accompanying this is a decrease in guilt feelings when she discovers areas of tension. Interpersonal relationships with her daughter no longer provoke terror; she no longer feels the need to "be a good girl" and "do what is expected of her" by the outside world. The relaxed attitude carries over also (in addition to interpersonal relationships with a younger female and to social demands) to her attitude toward her husband. She is still not quite ready to face her rivalry with her daughter completely—but very nearly. It is close to the surface, and the client is even fairly comfortable with the situation instead of fighting it.
>
> Sexually the client is apparently doing two things. She is better able to face the *fact* of sexual demands in herself and others, but at the same time she does not quite admit this fact to emotional acceptance for herself. Her relationships with her daughter as a rival for her husband's affection in a father-daughter setting is dimly realized; what is not quite so clear is the possible rivalry on a more adult level. This awareness is fairly close to the surface—one gets the feeling that the client doesn't "see" it more because she doesn't care to than because she can't. The possibility of real satisfaction in adult heterosexual relationships is equally faced but with an undertone of wistfulness, a depersonalization which is almost "This *would* have been good for me, too." The dissolution of marriage is ac-

cepted as a thing that happens—naturally if by death—but in any case something which can be faced. She still looks upon marriage as an invasion of her privacy or an intrusion upon her "personal integrity" rather than a sharing—but sees the possibility of sharing for others. She is about ready for acceptance of the "fact" that she really married to get herself a father, that she has outgrown the need of a father, that she is ready for deeper experiences involving the "whole" person she has become.

Throughout, the client states over and over that the essence of successful therapy is the inclusion of the *whole* self into the consciousness of the person; that this state is "lonely" but not threatening. Not even the overthrow of all known value systems is fearsome. The outstanding value for her is now honesty—being true to one's self and one's own convictions and facing one's fears face-on. The terrible urgency to do things, go places, reach personal heights has slackened; she is content to see perfection and striving for it as symbolic rather than as possible personal goals.

This is a highly sensitive, highly intelligent individual who has been very deeply hurt, and whose attempts to find security were on an immature level, frequently abortive. She has felt that she has left little pieces of herself all along—and she has felt it necessary to please people in order to have their love which she desperately wanted. Now she is relaxed, the "bits and pieces" are collected within herself, and she is willing to admit fears and frustrations. The most complete "about face" is her ceasing to strive for approval on other's terms and being content to live her life on her own individual terms—and her astonishment at finding that in so doing she frees herself for fuller participation.

Comments on the Personality Change

Comment is almost superfluous. The change registered in these four analyses is striking and in many ways parallels the changes predicted by the theory of client-centered therapy. Let us examine some of these areas.

Confidence in self.—Perhaps the greatest change is in this area. In the first TAT the descriptive terms are such as the following: "passive," "dependent," "unsure," "insecure," "unattractive," "escapist," "anxious," "there is no move toward doing anything about it herself except running away." One year later, by the time of the third TAT, the descriptive phrases are quite different: "self-directing," "does not mistrust own ability," "confident," "more enjoyment," "balanced," "optimistic," "dependency needs fewer," "she'll solve her problems herself," "self-directed goals," "individual accepts herself as a unique person." This is indeed a marked change.

Anxiety and compulsiveness.—From being a driven, compulsive person, escaping from reality into daydreams, she has become a person who does not have to please others, is less intense and anxious, more realistic and objective, with fantasy as a healthy outlet. At the time of the fourth TAT, eighteen months after the first, she is primarily described as a relaxed person, no longer intense or desperate about any aspect of life.

Relationships to others.—At first hostility toward women, loneliness, lack of any real affectional ties, are said to characterize this woman. Poor relationships with family members and others exist. Social relationships are seen as potentially hurtful threats. One year later she is more accepting of others, "and personal threat has almost disappeared as a component of social groups." She sees herself as able to make her own unique contribution to group activities. Familial ties are now pleasant experiences.

Sexual conflict.—From a state judged to be "a complete sexual panic" at the time of the first TAT, there has been steady progress to a point where the possibility of real satisfaction in adult relationships is evident in the fourth TAT. It should be noted that most of this progress took place after the conclusion of therapy. This area is still not regarded as fully resolved even at the time of the fourth TAT. She has not yet shown evidence of full emotional acceptance of her sexuality, in spite of the progress made.

Integration.—The movement from the "formless" individual she feels herself to be in the first TAT to the organized "whole" self in the fourth TAT is perhaps one of the most striking changes. A realistic self-organization which is unafraid in meeting life appears to have been achieved.

A comparison of these judgments with findings from other sources will be left until a later point in our report, in order to permit the reader to make his own comparisons as he follows the different studies.

IV. CHANGES IN SELF-PERCEPTION

A second project in the research, developed particularly by Butler and Haigh, was aimed at determining the changes in the perception of the self and others during therapy. This project was described in chapter 4. Like the other clients, Mrs. Oak was asked to sort the one hundred self-referent statements in such a way as to indicate her picture of her self, of the self she would like to be, and of the characteristics of the ordinary person. This triple sorting for self, wanted self, and the ordinary person was obtained prior to therapy, twice during therapy, at the conclusion of the interviews, and at the follow-up contacts seven months and one year after the conclusion of therapy. At one point during therapy, and at the conclusion of therapy, the counselor sorted the cards as he thought the client would sort them. This was, in other words, the counselor's attempt to predict the client's perception of self, self-ideal, and ordinary person.

These sortings have supplied us with many rich data about the changes which took place in Mrs. Oak's phenomenal world and the relationship of these changes to some external criteria.

Some Illustrations regarding Self

Perhaps it will give more meaning to the statistical findings which follow if we commence with one very tiny portion of the raw data which will give the reader a more concrete basis for interpreting the objective results. In Table 1 are listed the sixteen statements perceived as most characteristic of self before therapy and the sixteen statements least characteristic. The sixty-eight items falling in between are not given here. In the right-hand half of the table are the corresponding statements from the sorting at the second follow-up contact, twelve months following the conclusion of therapy and approximately eighteen months later than the first sorting.

The qualitative change in these two sortings is rather striking. In the first place they are quite different. Only three items (33, 88, 96) are common to the first sixteen items in the two sortings, and only four items (16, 65, 40, 99) are common to the last sixteen items. The actual correlation between the two sortings is .30, though this has little meaning until we compare it with other correlations, which we will shortly do. It will be noted that at the second follow-up period she perceives herself as much more secure, more confident, more emotionally mature, more expressive, less inhibited, less disorganized, warmer in relationships, and less fear-

TABLE 1

THE CHANGE IN THE PERCEIVED SELF

SELF BEFORE THERAPY Item No. and Item	RATING OF ITEM	SELF AT SECOND FOLLOW-UP Item and Item No.
	Items Most Characteristic	
(32) I usually feel driven.	8	I express my emotions freely. (23)
(11) I am responsible for my troubles.	7	I feel emotionally mature. (80)
(21) I am really self-centered.	7	I am self-reliant. (91)
(33) I am liked by most people who know me.	7	I understand myself. (96)
(88) I am intelligent.	7	I feel adequate. (98)
(22) I usually like people.	6	I often kick myself for the things I do. (5)
(42) I am disorganized.	6	I have a warm emotional relationship with others. (9)
(85) I feel insecure within myself.	6	Self-control is no problem to me. (19)
(86) I have to protect myself with excuses, with rationalizing.	6	I usually like people. (22)
(51) I am a rational person.	6	I can live comfortably with the people around me. (26)
(53) I am tolerant.	6	I am just sort of stubborn. (30)
(55) I have an attractive personality.	6	I am liked by most people who know me. (33)
(66) I am a dominant person.	6	I am impulsive. (47)
(74) I am likable.	6	I take a positive attitude toward myself. (67)
(37) I can usually make up my mind and stick to it.	6	I feel relaxed and nothing really bothers me. (78)
(96) I understand myself.	6	I am intelligent. (88)
	Items Least Characteristic	
(1) I feel uncomfortable while talking with someone. (I feel comfortable while talking with someone.)*	2	I have few values and standards of my own. (I have some standards and values of my own.) (16)
(4) I (do not)* make strong demands on myself.	2	I (do not) feel helpless. (36)
(16) I (do not) have few values and standards of my own.	2	I (do not) often feel guilty. (39)
(28) I (do not) tend to be on my guard with people who are somewhat more friendly than I had expected.	2	I (do not) feel apathetic. (43)
(29) I am (not) optimistic.	2	I am (not) afraid of what other people think of me. (60)
(41) I am (not) contented.	2	I (do not) shrink from facing a crisis or difficulty. (64)

* In giving the items least characteristic, the item as printed on the card is given, but in parentheses is indicated the descriptive meaning which it has when placed at this end of the distribution. Thus if the item "I usually feel driven" is sorted as being one of the least characteristic, it means descriptively "I do not usually feel driven." In the table the exact wording of the item is given by reading the words not in parentheses. For the meaning of the item, read the statement as modified by the parentheses or as restated in parentheses immediately below the item.

TABLE 1—*Continued*

Self before Therapy Item No. and Item	Rating of Item	Self at Second Follow-up Item and Item No.
Items Least Characteristic—*Continued*		
(57) I (do not) need somebody else to push me through on things.	2	I just don't respect myself. (I respect myself.) (65)
(65) I just don't respect myself. (I respect myself.)	2	I am (not) confused. (71)
(78) I feel relaxed, and nothing really bothers me. (I do not feel relaxed, and things bother me.)	2	I am (not) a failure. (73)
(84) All you have to do is just insist with me, and I give in. (I do not give in when you insist.)	2	I am (not) afraid of sex. (76)
(87) I am (not) a submissive person.	2	I am (not) inhibited. (93)
(3) I am (not) a competitive person.	1	I am (not) a hostile person. (40)
(18) It's (not) difficult to control my aggression.	1	I (do not) despise myself. (62)
(40) I am (not) a hostile person.	1	I (do not) feel insecure within myself. (85)
(59) I am no one. Nothing really seems to be me. (I am someone.)	1	I am (not) worthless. (99)
(99) I am (not) worthless.	0	I don't trust my emotions. (I trust my emotions.) (49)

ful of sex. There are five items whose placement changed by four-step intervals or more. These are as follows:

(85) I feel insecure within myself. (Moved from 6, characteristic, to 1, not at all characteristic.)

(32) I usually feel driven. (Moved from 8, most characteristic, to 4.)

(3) I am a competitive person. (Moved from 1, not at all characteristic, to 5.)

(78) I feel relaxed, and nothing really bothers me. (Moved from 2 to 6.)

(98) I feel adequate. (Moved from 3 to 7, very characteristic.)

Some Illustrations regarding Self-ideal

When we examine Mrs. Oak's perception of the person she wishes to be, her self-ideal, we find no such sharp change as is exhibited in the self-picture. Examination of Table 2, which lists the "most characteristic" items in the self-ideal before therapy and at the time of the second follow-up, will show that the picture is quite similar. This impression is confirmed by a correlation of .72 between these two sortings. Hence in a general way we may say that the self-ideal has shown no radical change.

There have been some subtle changes, however, and these are of considerable interest. A number of items have been lowered in their ratings (have become less characteristic of the self-ideal), and others have been raised. Certain of the more static qualities have been given less value—intelligence (88), adequacy (98), and optimism (29) are examples. Their place has been taken by more expressive, less controlled characteristics such as free expression of emotions (23) and impulsiveness (47). There is also a shift from characteristics which essentially reside in others' judgments ("I am liked by most people who know me") to characteristics which reside within the individual ("I can live comfortably with the people around me"). When the low end of the distribution is examined, these conclusions are confirmed, and one new one is

TABLE 2

THE CHANGE IN THE PERCEIVED SELF-IDEAL

Ideal before Therapy Item No. and Item	Rating of Item	Ideal at Second Follow-up Item and Item No.
Items Most Characteristic		
(80) I feel emotionally mature.	8	I understand myself. (96)
(26) I can live comfortably with the people around me.	7	I express my emotions freely. (23)
(51) I am a rational person.	7	I am poised. (44)
(88) I am intelligent.	7	I am a rational person. (51)
(98) I feel adequate.	7	I feel emotionally mature. (80)
(9) I have a warm emotional relationship with others.	6	I have a warm emotional relationship with others. (9)
(11) I am responsible for my troubles.	6	I am a responsible person. (12)
(12) I am a responsible person	6	I can live comfortably with the people around me. (26)
(29) I am optimistic.	6	I am impulsive. (47)
(33) I am liked by most people who know me.	6	I am tolerant. (53)
(44) I am poised.	6	I take a positive attitude toward myself. (67)
(67) I take a positive attitude toward myself.	6	I am assertive. (68)
(72) I am satisfied with myself.	6	I feel relaxed, and nothing really bothers me. (78)
(78) I feel relaxed, and nothing really bothers me.	6	I am intelligent. (88)
(91) I am self-reliant.	6	I am self-reliant. (91)
(96) I understand myself.	6	I feel adequate. (98)

added. Such items as "I feel hopeless," "I feel driven," "I feel helpless," "I feel disturbed," "I feel disorganized"—all move slightly upward from the bottom of the pile. Thus it appears that the person she wants to be does not reject so fully even the very negative emotions.

All in all, then, we may say that, while the change in the wanted self is not great, there are a number of interesting changes. The self-ideal at the conclusion of the study appears to place less stress on the more absolute qualities and more on an expressive living of feelings, even when those feelings are not positive or comfortable. The criteria of the ideal tend to become inner rather than external. The total impression is of a somewhat more comfortable self-ideal.

Changes in the Perceived Self

Though we have tried to give the material more meaning by giving some of the specific items, we cannot study the data in that fashion, since some twenty-six hundred item placements were involved in this investigation. As a first step away from this mass of raw material let us examine the matrix which has been obtained by correlating each of these twenty-six sortings with every other. This matrix will be found in Table 3. In order to understand this table clearly, and the statements about it, and some of the figures and tables which follow, it will be necessary to give some attention to the simple code by which each sorting is identified.

We have in the individual Q-sortings and in the correlations a rich picture of different aspects of Mrs. Oak's phenomenal field, obtained at different times, and with the interrelationships of these different segments of the internal frame of reference expressed in objective form. We will examine some of the trends in this material which seem most significant.

Let us begin by considering simply the changes in the perceived self. The data will be found in full in Table 3 or partially illustrated in Figure 1. It will be seen that these statements can be made. (In each instance the pertinent correlations are cited.)

> The perceived self exhibits marked change during a five-and-a-half-month period of therapy and much less change during a twelve-month period following therapy (r SB · SA = .39; r SA · SF2 = .65).

TABLE 3*

CORRELATION MATRIX OF Q-SORTINGS: CASE OF MRS. OAK

	Pre-therapy			After 7th Int.			Counselor after 7th Int.			After 25th Int.			After Therapy			Counselor after Therapy			First Follow-up				Second Follow-up			
	SB	OB	IB	S7	O7	I7	CS7	CO7	CI7	S25	O25	I25	SA	OA	IA	CSA	COA	CIA	SF1	OF1	IF1	RSF1	SF2	OF2	IF2	RSF2
SB																										
OB	−10																									
IB	21	20																								
S7	50	02	46																							
O7	10	49	22	36																						
I7	25	26	76	47	25																					
CS7	15	03	−23	14	09	−13																				
CO7	27	33	35	39	35	46	17																			
CI7	21	20	69	35	16	70	−22	41																		
S25	42	13	35	54	26	36	12	19	32																	
O25	20	43	17	31	53	25	14	32	25	22																
I25	26	28	80	48	29	83	−20	35	66	45	30															
SA	39	16	61	54	24	64	−06	32	55	57	27	69														
OA	09	41	28	39	57	33	04	41	26	32	56	44	35													
IA	30	14	75	51	18	77	−14	33	67	47	26	80	69	29												
CSA	29	19	68	48	29	69	−04	45	77	42	34	66	57	39	69											
COA	10	36	01	21	41	13	33	58	04	15	29	07	12	32	00	08										
CIA	25	17	75	45	19	70	−12	41	85	38	22	71	62	30	74	86	04									
SF1	30	17	72	52	27	69	−09	41	66	53	28	76	74	32	78	63	11	71								
OF1	−02	39	09	25	47	16	13	38	15	16	41	21	14	51	10	28	26	17	08							
IF1	21	17	75	45	21	80	−23	31	66	32	17	78	64	24	79	65	−02	73	70	13						
RSF1	44	−04	−12	36	01	−07	27	14	−07	38	06	−07	26	−01	04	03	15	01	11	15	02					
SF2	30	14	70	44	14	76	−15	38	68	44	24	75	65	29	80	66	06	72	70	06	77	01				
OF2	16	48	39	39	60	47	15	39	28	35	59	51	38	66	33	43	35	28	33	53	28	09	22			
IF2	36	06	72	39	06	79	−28	27	63	41	27	76	67	20	78	63	−08	68	73	−02	76	−03	79	24		
RSF2	44	−18	−21	36	02	−16	35	02	−17	32	02	−20	14	−10	−10	−06	19	−07	−01	−04	−14	65	−13	−03	−11	

CODE

S = Self
O = Ordinary person
I = Self-ideal or wanted self
B = Before therapy
7 = Following the seventh interview
25 = Following the twenty-fifth interview
A = After therapy
F1 = First follow-up, seventh months after conclusion of therapy
F2 = Second follow-up, twelve months after conclusion of therapy
RS = Remembered self as of pre-therapy
C = Counselor's prediction of client's sorting

* Decimal points omitted.

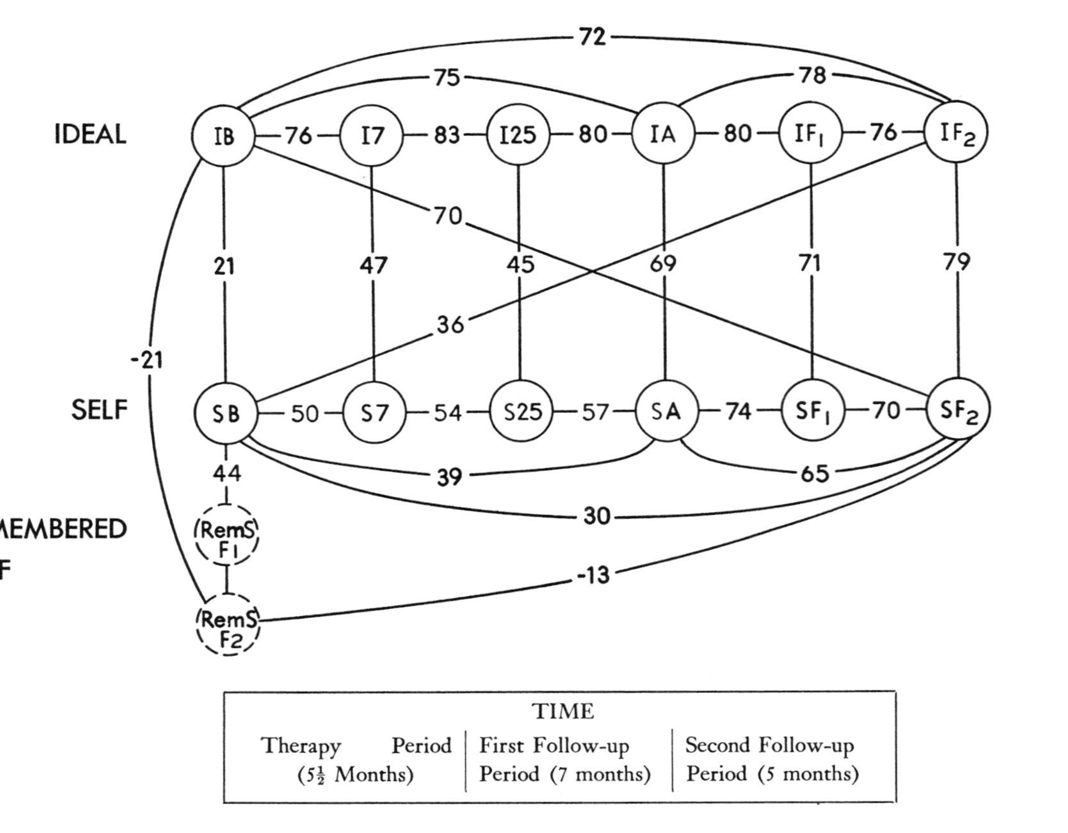

Fig. 1.—The changing relationships between self and self-ideal. (See Table 3 for code. Figures are correlations, with decimal points omitted.)

As much change occurred in the perceived self during the first seven interviews as during the remaining thirty-three (*r* SB · S7 = .50; *r* S7 · SA = .54).

A directional tendency seems to be evident in the changes in the self, which makes it increasingly discrepant from the earlier selves (*r* of SF2 with preceding selves, SF1, SA, S25, S7, and SB is as follows: .70, .65, .44, .44, .30).

There are some interesting findings regarding the "remembered" self. It will be recalled that Mrs. Oak was asked, at each of the two follow-up points, to sort the cards to represent herself as she remembered herself at the time she began therapy. There is considerable evidence that these remembered selves are less defensive pictures of the pre-therapy self than was the self-sorting made at the time. An inspection of the items shows that the five items given as most characteristic of the remembered self at the second follow-up (RSF2) are these: "I feel insecure within myself"; "I often feel guilty"; "I often feel resentful"; "I don't trust my emotions"; "I have to protect myself with excuses, with rationalizing." These statements give a much less favorable picture of self than do the items sorted prior to therapy, which were given in Table 1. They also seem more closely related to the pre-therapy diagnosis, a conclusion for which objective evidence will be given later.

Various intercorrelations justify still further the conclusion that the remembered selves represent a less defensive picture of the pre-therapy self than the client could give at the time.

The remembered selves have only a moderate relationship with the actual pre-therapy self-sorting, the discrepancy possibly representing a rough measure of the defensiveness existing prior to therapy (*r* RSF1 · SB = .44; *r* RSF2 · SB = .44).

Each of the remembered selves is more discrepant from the pre-therapy ideal and more discrepant from the final self than is the self as sorted before therapy (*r* RSF1 · IB = −.12; *r* RSF2 · IB = −.21; *r* SB · IB = .21. Also *r* RSF1 · SF2 = .01; RSF2 · SF2 = −.13; while *r* SB · SF2 = .30).

Following from these findings, the assumption will be made in some of the subsequent paragraphs that the sortings for the remembered selves approximate a picture of self prior to therapy which includes material which was not at that time in awareness or, if in awareness, was not communicable.

Changes in the Self-ideal

Certain statements may also be made about the self-ideal.

The self-ideal, or wanted self, remains relatively constant during and after therapy (*r* IB · IA = .75; *r* IA · IF2 = .78).

The slight changes which occur in the self-ideal do not bring it significantly closer to the pre-therapy self, though there is a slight suggestion of such a shift (*r* of SB with successive self-ideals, .21, .25, .26, .30, .21, .36).

The changes in the self-ideal are such as to make it more achievable. When the Q-adjustment score developed by Dymond (see chapter 5) is calculated for each successive ideal, the scores from IB to IF_2 are as follows: 56, 55, 60, 53, 52, 49. Thus the scores after therapy and at the two follow-up points are lower than the pre-therapy or in-therapy scores, indicating that the ideal is less "adjusted," less perfect, and more within reach.

Changes in the Relationship of Self and Ideal

Some of the most striking findings occur in the changing relationship between the self Mrs. Oak perceives herself to be and the self she wants to be. These are easily observed in Figure 1.

The self bears little resemblance to the wanted self at the outset of therapy. (*r* SB · IB = .21.)

During the process of therapy the congruence is somewhat greater (*r* S7 · I7 = .47; *r* S25 · I25 = .45).

At the conclusion of therapy the perceived self bears much resemblance to the desired self (*r* SA · IA = .69).

This marked congruence holds steady or increases during twelve months of follow-up (*r* SF1 · IF1 = .71; *r* SF2 · IF2 = .79).

The change in the perceived self is gradual and directional, bringing it increasingly closer not only to the self-ideal at each point but to the self which was wanted before therapy (*r* of IB with successive selves, .21, .46, .35, .62, .72, .70).

If the remembered selves are accepted as more revealing pictures of the pre-therapy self, then the increase of congruence between self and wanted self is even more drastic than has been indicated, going from a −.21 at the outset of therapy to a .79 at the conclusion of the study (*r* RSF2 · IB = −.21; *r* SF2 · IF2 = .79).

The Perception of the Ordinary Person

The findings in regard to Mrs. Oak's perception of the ordinary person are more scattered and more difficult to interpret.

The perception of the ordinary person is not very stable, showing fluctuating changes and intercorrelations usually in the neighborhood of .50 (*r* OB · OF2 = .48; *r* OB · O7 = .49; *r* O7 · O25 = .53; etc.).

The ordinary person before therapy is perceived as very different from the self, but by the seventh interview there is some degree of congruence, and this persists throughout the period of study (successive correlations of self and ordinary person are: −.10, .36, .22, .35, .09, .22).

The self, during the period of therapy and follow-up, has become slightly more similar to the ordinary person as perceived prior to therapy (*r* SB · OB = −.10; *r* SA · OB = .16; *r* SF1 · OB = .18; *r* SF2 · OB = .14).

The perception of the ordinary person maintains a low positive relationship to the self-ideal throughout the therapy and follow-up (successive correlations of self-ideal and ordinary, beginning with *r* IB · OB; .20, .25, .30, .29, .13, .24).

A Factor Analysis of the Matrix

An obverse factor analysis was made by Boyer (1) of a correlation matrix which was available at the conclusion of therapy. This included simply the client's sorts for self, other, and ideal before therapy and at three later periods ending with the conclusion of therapy. It does not include the counselor's sortings or the sortings made at the follow-up points. It is, therefore, a much less complete matrix than is included in Table 3. The factor analysis indicated three factors, as will be seen from Table 4, or more clearly from Table 5, which lists only the significant factor loadings.

The interpretation of the factors is not difficult. The first is clearly the self-factor. Following the early part of therapy the later "selves" have a decreased loading on this factor. It helps to give a better picture of the factor to note that the concept of the ordinary person has a significant negative loading on this factor. It should also be noted that the self-ideal after therapy has a loading of 17 on this factor, which, while not significant, suggests a convergence of these two factors. The elements in this self-factor have already been indicated to some extent in Table 1, which contains the extreme items (characteristic and uncharacteristic) of the self before therapy (SB), which has one of the heaviest loadings on this factor.

The second factor is clearly the concept of the ordinary person which remains remarkably stable throughout therapy and which is decidedly independent of the other ratings, none of the self or ideal sortings having a significant loading on it.

The third factor is the wanted self or self-ideal. Here again the picture is clear cut. The earlier sortings for the self-ideal have the heaviest loading, and the after-therapy ideal has a somewhat lower weighting, having become more similar to the self-factor. The outstanding element is that the self after therapy now has a significant loading on this ideal factor. The self as it exists at the conclusion of therapy has an equal loading on the self and ideal. The self before therapy had a heavy loading on the self-factor and a negative loading (−13) on the ideal factor. This indicates something of the shift which has taken place. The qualitative meaning of this third factor can be estimated by studying the items characteristic of the ideal before therapy (Table 2). The self and ideal of the follow-up period (Tables 1 and 2) also give clues to its content, though follow-up sortings were not actually included in the factor analysis.

TABLE 4

FACTOR LOADINGS

	A	B	C
SB	58	−11	−13
OB	−34	60	20
IB	00	−04	70
S7	58	04	−03
O7	−03	69	−05
I7	−02	02	71
S25	47	05	02
O25	02	64	−06
I25	04	08	66
SA	37	−02	35
OA	−06	64	06
IA	17	−09	60

TABLE 5

SIGNIFICANT FACTOR LOADINGS

	Self	Other	Self-ideal
SB	58	....	....
OB	−34	60	....
IB	....	....	70
S7	58	....	....
O7	....	69	....
I7	....	....	71
S25	47	....	....
O25	....	64	....
I25	....	....	66
SA	37	....	35
OA	....	64	....
IA	....	....	60

Although Boyer gives a somewhat more elaborate qualitative analysis of these factors, it is not regarded as necessary here, since the results of the factor analysis are largely confirmatory of the findings previously given from a study of the more complex matrix.

Boyer makes an interesting dynamic analysis and interpretation of the changing relationship between the factors through time. This indicates that during the first phase of therapy (through the seventh interview) the greatest movement was in connection with the perception of others. The ordinary person, during this period, came to be seen as considerably less like the ideal and more like the client herself. There is also some movement in the perception of the self in the direction of both the self-ideal and the ordinary person. The basis for these statements may be found in a study of the factor loadings in Table 4, through the seventh interview. They are graphically illustrated in Figure 2. It should be clear that the diagram represents the movements of the flexible aspects of a concept as these are seen through the perspective of the more stable basic structure of all three concepts.

During the second phase of therapy (eighth through twenty-fifth interviews) all the movements are quite limited. Though self and ideal converge very slightly, and also self and ordinary, these movements are very minor. During the third phase of therapy, however (twenty-sixth through fortieth interviews), the three factors show extensive changes in their relationship. Self and self-ideal mutually approach each other, and this is the most extensive change found in any of the three segments of therapy. Mrs. Oak was coming to see herself as more like her ideal, and at the same time certain aspects of her ideal were changing in a manner which made it more similar to the way she felt herself to be. But at the same time the self and the ordinary became less similar—with aspects of each moving in a direction away from the other. Yet both move toward the ideal. Thus the client has come to see other people and herself as being less alike than she had previously felt, but, in the total picture, both had become more similar to the ideal.

Two other comments grow out of this study. Observation of the self-ideal factor indicates increasing movement in each successive phase of therapy. Does this mean an increasing flexibility or decreasing rigidity in the concept of the desired self? It is also to be noted that the total amount of change in the phase of therapy is most closely proportional to the amount of change in the perception of self. Does this support that aspect of self-theory which holds that self-perception is basic to many of the percepts and concepts of the individual? At least it provides food for such speculation.

A General Comment regarding Self-changes

In concluding the presentation of the material from the Q-sorts, several comments may be made. In the first place, the measured changes in the perceived self and in the changing relationship of self and ideal are the first objective measures we have used which seem to correspond, in magnitude, with the degree of change which is subjectively judged by client and therapist to have occurred.

PRE-THERAPY THROUGH SEVENTH INTERVIEW

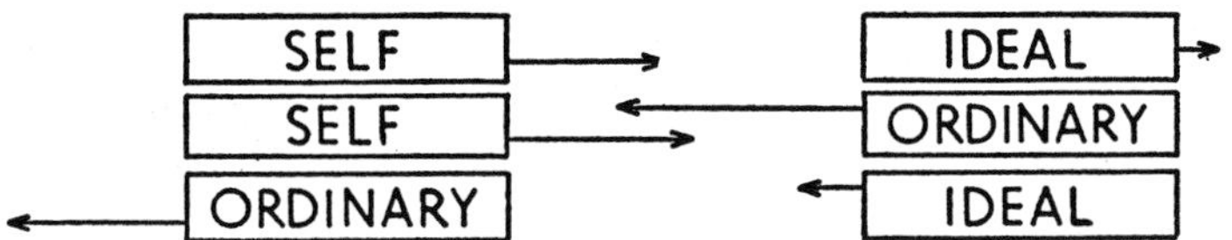

EIGHTH THROUGH TWENTY FIFTH INTERVIEW

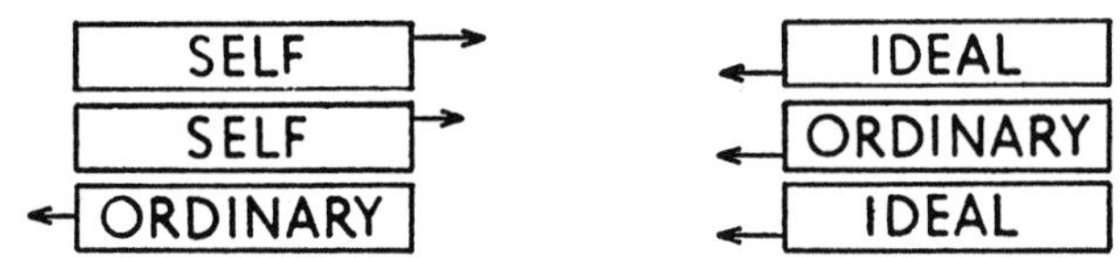

TWENTY SIXTH INTERVIEW TO POST THERAPY

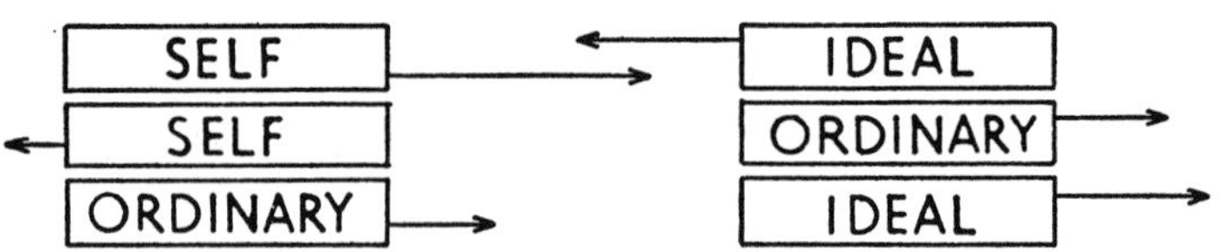

Fig. 2.—A graphic presentation of the relative movements of factor concepts. (Adapted from Boyer [2, p. 26].)

This may be important. It suggests, at least, that we have found an instrument which comes close to measuring the specific kind of change which comes about in psychotherapy.

Another comment has to do with the objectification of the client's phenomenological field through the method of Q-technique. There is much internal evidence, in the intricate web of intercorrelations, that this has provided us with a valid and promising approach to many of the subtleties of the therapeutic process, as well as to its outcomes.

On the other hand, the limitations of the material just presented are quite obvious. The statements made are accurate descriptions of therapy for this client only, and no generalizations to other cases can be made from these data alone. Another limitation is that changes in the phenomenal field, of the sort described, would have only personal psychological value, unless it can be shown that they correlate with socially observable phenomena. Evidence on this score will be made available in the next section of this report.

Within this context of limitations, then, we may say that the evidence shows that this client perceives herself as being more expressive, more mature, more self-reliant, more self-confident, more self-understanding, and less insecure, guilty, resentful, and defensive after a period of therapy. She perceives herself as having become substantially similar to the self she has wanted to be. The change which has come about is largely in the self as perceived rather than in the ideal as perceived. The change occurs primarily in the period of therapy but continues at a slower rate thereafter. The perception of others changes in some degree, others being perceived as having slightly more in common with the self.

V. THE RELATION OF THE DIAGNOSTIC PICTURE TO THE SELF

In the two research sections which have been presented, evidence has been given that there were certain personality changes in Mrs. Oak, as indicated by the TAT, and certain changes in her phenomenal self and self-ideal, as indicated by the Q-sortings. But what is the relationship, if any, between these two types of change? Is there any way in which we can bring together the TAT diagnosis, which is formulated essentially from an external frame of reference, and the self-picture, which is formulated from the client's internal frame of reference? This section describes such an attempt.

The Hypothesis

It was hypothesized that during and after therapy there would be an increasing congruence between the self as perceived by the client and the client as seen by a diagnostician. The rationale for this hypothesis grows from theory. It is assumed that a diagnostician, studying an individual by such a means as the TAT, will perceive that individual as he is both in his conscious experience and also in terms of his unconscious elements, or in those respects in which experience has been denied to awareness. But the theory of therapy is that during therapy the individual incorporates into self many previously denied aspects of experience. The conscious phenomenal self should therefore become more congruent with the diagnostic picture of the total personality. Hence the client as seen by himself and the client as seen by the diagnostician should become more similar.

The Method

The method employed to investigate this hypothesis was a novel one, based on Stephenson's Q-sort method. A judge[3] who was familiar with the TAT but who did not know the case, the research design, or the order in which the TAT's were administered was asked to study each of the four TAT's and its analysis. On the basis of this study he sorted the Q-cards—the same cards the client had used to portray herself—to give a picture of the client as she diagnostically was at the time of that TAT. Hence this procedure gives us a diagnostic picture which can be directly correlated with the client's self-picture at the same point, or with the self-ideal, or with another diagnostic picture at another point in therapy.

The reliability of the method was tested by having the judge sort the cards for one of the TAT's one month later. The correlation with the first sorting was .68, which indicates usable but not a high reliability. The modest reliability may be due in part to the

3. Mr. Richard Farson served as the judge and later made the computations for this study.

fact that the Q-sort items were chosen to be a basis for description of the phenomenal self and doubtless are not so suitable as might be for the description of a personality diagnosis.

The question as to whether other judges would be able to sort in the same fashion was also investigated. After the correlations which we are about to report had been computed, it seemed advisable to check on the degree of interjudge consistency of sortings. Two other judges who knew nothing of the case or the research design were asked to sort the cards to represent the client as she diagnostically was at the time of a given TAT. The intercorrelations of these two judges with the first judge and with each other were low, with a mean correlation of .36 for nine comparisons. It was felt that this low interjudge consistency might have been due to a lack of any training instruction. The judges might have been using different definitions of their purpose in making the sorting. Consequently, the first judge worked with a fourth judge who was familiar with the TAT, the two of them making sortings on other TAT's and comparing their sortings so as to increase the clarity of definition of their purpose. Judge No. 4, who knew nothing of the case of Mrs. Oak, then made sortings for each of Mrs. Oak's TAT's, working entirely independently on this task. The correlations of this judge with Judge No. 1 are .50, .30, .43, and .55, respectively. While all of these correlations are statistically significant, they are very modest in size. We must conclude that in this respect our findings confirm those from several other studies—that, while a diagnostician may be reasonably consistent with himself, there is only a relatively small amount of agreement between diagnosticians.

We therefore return to the sortings made by the first judge, and the remainder of the data in this section is based on his sortings. It should be stressed that the comparisons which are made are comparisons with the judgment of one diagnostician. We have however computed enough of the correlations from the other judges to know that the same major findings would have resulted had we used any other one of the four diagnosticians. The minor findings would vary with the particular diagnostician. Let us then look at the comparisons which may be made on the basis of the sortings by Judge No. 1.

The Findings

In considering the findings, let us pose the particular questions to which we are addressing our inquiry and also a more general issue. We ask two specific questions: (1) What changes are observable in the diagnostic picture of the client? (2) Is there a correspondence between the diagnostic picture of the individual and the picture of the individual as seen through self-descriptions? In this second question there is implicitly another and more general question in psychology, namely, the issue as to the place of subjective judgments in psychological measurement. We take the position here that it is just as feasible to study the parameter of subjective judgments as it is to study judgments from any other perspective. The problem in the use of any parameter is the same: to determine the lawful relationships which exist both within a given parameter of measurement and between the different parameters. Our total task is to construct a picture of the person in his total functioning and to understand more fully the meaning of each perspective of measurement. The comparison of the internal and external frames of reference is simply one aspect of this goal.

The Changes in the Diagnostic Picture

The correlations which were obtained from the data are given in Table 6. Two findings are related to the diagnostic sortings.

TABLE 6

CORRELATIONS BETWEEN DIAGNOSTIC SORTINGS AND SELF-SORTINGS

Diagnostic Sortings	Self-sortings								Ideal Sortings						Diagnostic Sortings			
	RSF2	RSF1	SB	S7	S25	SA	SF1	SF2	IB	I7	I25	IA	IF1	IF2	DB	DA	DF1	DF2
DB.....	30	14	00	00	−02	−28	−38	−36	−42	−40	−18	−48	−50	−38	....	....	....	....
DA.....	37	30	28	18	24	05	−01	−13	−09	−19	−08	−15	−12	−12	52	....	....	....
DF1....	05	12	36	43	37	52	56	50	54	41	59	50	50	53	−06	30	....	....
DF2....	−11	06	16	36	34	59	68	55	61	53	63	59	55	46	−33	15	66	....

The diagnostic picture changes very markedly. There is a negative correlation between the diagnostic picture of the client before therapy and the diagnostic picture eighteen months later (r DB · DF2 = −.33).

The sharpest change in the diagnosis occurs not during therapy but during the follow-up period (r DB · DA = .52; r DA · DF2 = .15).

The Relationship between Diagnosis and Self

Several of the findings have to do with the changing relationship between the client's self-perception and the diagnostician's perception of the client.

There is no relationship between the diagnostic picture and the self-picture at the beginning of therapy (*r* DB • SB = .00). This is also true at the end of therapy (*r* DA • SA = .05). But seven months later and twelve months later there is substantial congruence (*r* DF1 • SF2 = .56; *r* DF2 • SF2 = .55). Thus our hypothesis is not upheld for the in-therapy period but is upheld for the over-all period of study.

There is some relationship between the pre-therapy diagnosis and the pre-therapy self as remembered at the follow-up periods (*r* DB • RSF1 = .14; *r* DB • RSF2 = .30). It would appear that, when the client has become less defensive, her self, as she remembers it, changes in the direction of the diagnostic picture. This is what one would expect from the theory of therapy.

There is a substantial negative relationship between the initial diagnosis and the initial self-ideal (*r* DB • IB = −.42). At the two follow-up points there is a substantial positive relationship between the follow-up diagnosis and the follow-up self-ideal (*r* DF1 • IF1 = .50; *r* DF2 • IF2 = .46).

The orderliness of the relationship of the different diagnoses to the successive selves is notable. If we accept the remembered self at the second follow-up point as the least defensive picture of the pre-therapy self, and arrange the eight self-sortings in order, as in Table 6, then the orderliness becomes apparent. The first diagnosis has this gradually descending relationship, as expressed by the correlations: .30, .14, .00, .00, −.02, −.28, −.38, −.36. The final diagnosis has this gradually ascending relationship: −.11, .06, .16, .36, .34, .59, .68, .55.

To put these findings another way, we may say that, during the course of therapy and after it, the person as seen by herself becomes less and less like the self as seen diagnostically before therapy began. Conversely, as therapy proceeds, the client as seen by herself becomes more and more like the diagnostic picture of herself twelve months after the end of therapy.

Another way of inquiring into the correspondence between the two perspectives of measurement is to compare the order of relationship obtained by each measure with the other at comparable points in time. For example, we can take the final follow-up self-description and the final follow-up diagnostic description and compare them in terms of their relationships with the successive self-descriptions during and after therapy. The correlations and the rank orders are then arranged as shown in Table 7. It will be noted from these data that there is an almost exact correspondence in the ranks (rho = .99). This means that we have the same order of relationship whether we use the self-description as criterion or the diagnostic-description as criterion.

An example of a reverse type of correspondence may be observed when we compare self-description and diagnostic description immediately after therapy in terms of their comparative rela-

TABLE 7

	SF2	Rank	DF2	Rank
RSF2	−.13	7	−.11	7
RSF1	.01	6	.06	6
SB	.30	5	.16	5
S7	.44	3.5	.36	4
S25	.44	3.5	.34	3
SA	.65	2	.59	2
SF1	.70	1	.68	1

TABLE 8

	SA	Rank	DA	Rank
RSF2	.14	7	.37	1
RSF1	.26	6	.30	2
SB	.39	5	.28	3
S7	.54	4	.18	5
S25	.57	3	.24	4
SF1	.74	1	−.01	6
SF2	.65	2	−.13	7

tionships with the series of self-descriptions. The correlations and rank orders are as shown in Table 8. The rho for this comparison is −.93, this indicating an almost complete reversal of trend. In this comparison we note further that the highest correlations with self-description after therapy are the follow-up selves, whereas the diagnostic description after therapy correlates most highly with the remembered selves before therapy. In other words, the self-description showed the highest correspondence with the "future selves," whereas the diagnostic description showed the greatest relationship with "past selves."

The Relationship of Self-change to Diagnostic Change

Certain comments may be made on this attempt to integrate the internal and external frames of reference. Some of the comments will be most easily illustrated by Figure 3, which gives the relevant correlations.

In the first place, the change in the individual as diagnostically perceived is even greater than the change which the client perceives in herself. It is only if we bring in the remembered self, to get a less defensive picture of the pre-therapy self, that the phenomenal change, as represented by a correlation of $-.13$, begins to approach the amount of diagnostic change, as represented by a correlation of $-.33$. In view of the questions which have often been raised about data gained from the internal frame of reference, this fact is of interest. Some have thought that, if material is obtained from the client's frame of reference, it is in the same category as introspection or that, because it is susceptible to such phenomena as "faking good" or "faking bad," it cannot be useful. All the present evidence would indicate, however, that data obtained from the client's phenomenal field are extremely valuable, can be treated objectively, have their own unique advantages and disadvantages, and in this instance at least are more modest in estimating the degree of change than are the data from an external frame of reference.

A second point of significance is that change in the phenomenal self occurred primarily during therapy and that changes during the follow-up period are much less. On the other hand, less change occurred in the diagnosis during therapy than during the follow-up period. Does this suggest that change in self-perception is a forerunner of change, a predictor of change in diagnosis? If so, this is a fact with profound implications.

Another point which was surprising to the investigators is the relationship of the self-ideal to this change. Let us put this in two brief statements. (*a*) During and after therapy the client, from her own frame of reference, becomes decidedly similar to her initial self-ideal (r SB · IB = .21; r SF2 · IB = .70). (*b*) During and after therapy the client, as viewed by a diagnostician, made even more radical progress in the direction of becoming her initial self-

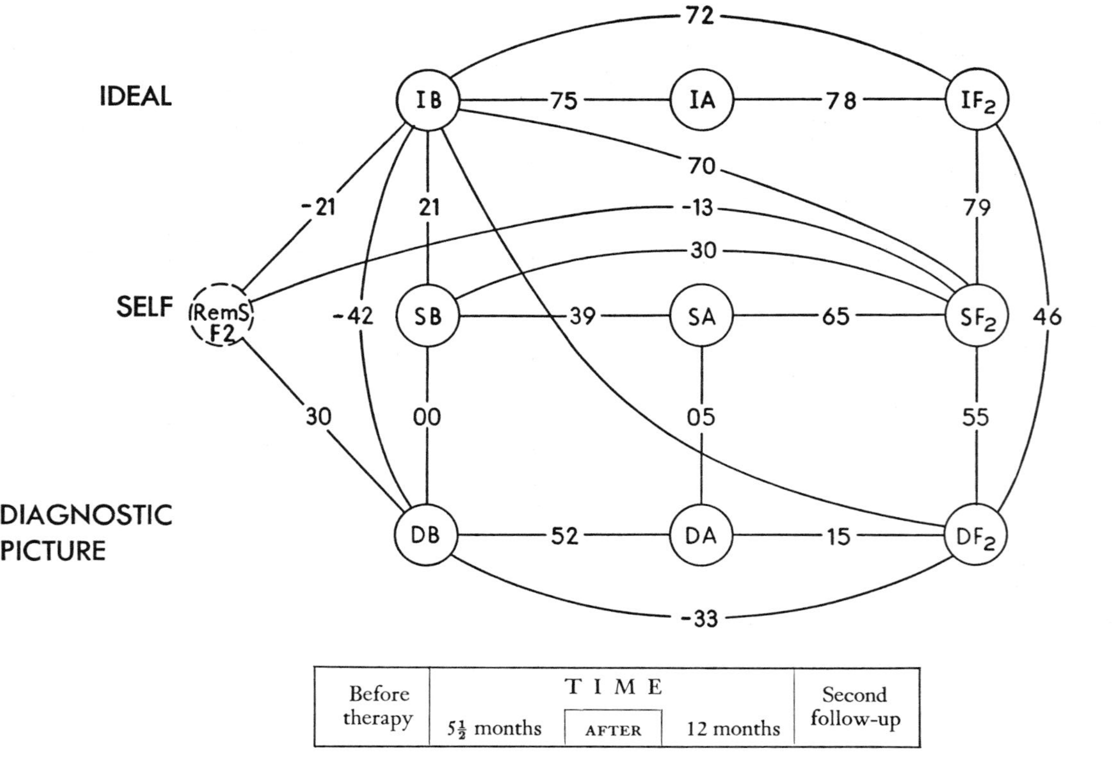

Fig. 3.—Relationship between self, self-ideal, and diagnosis. (Figures are correlations, with decimal points omitted.)

ideal (r DB · IB = − .42; r DF2 · IB = .61). It seems clear that the client, as perceived by herself, and as perceived by others, has become substantially similar to the person she wished to be at the beginning of therapy.

As a final check on the meaning of the findings presented in this section we may apply the Q-adjustment score developed by Dymond (see chap. 5) to both the self and the diagnostic sortings. This will give us a rough measure of the level of adjustment of the client as perceived by herself and by a diagnostician.

When we take the respective selves as perceived by the client, beginning with the remembered pre-therapy self, the adjustment scores are as follows: RSF2, 26; RSF1, 26; SB, 36; S7, 43; S25, 41; SA, 52; SF1, 54; SF2, 51. The increase throughout the course of therapy is apparent. The adjustment scores of the four diagnostic sorts from pre-therapy to the second follow-up are as follows: DB, 13; DA, 28; DF1, 51; DF2, 60. It is clear that the client, prior to therapy, was seen as more poorly adjusted by the diagnostician than by Mrs. Oak herself. By follow-up time, however, this discrepancy had disappeared, and the diagnostician sees her as somewhat more "adjusted" than she perceives herself. The total change in adjustment score as seen by the client is from 15 to 28 points, depending on whether one uses the remembered self or the pre-therapy self as the base line, and the self at first or second follow-up as the end point. The total change in the adjustment score of the diagnostician's picture is 47 points, a much larger figure. Thus, both in her own eyes and even more markedly in the perceptions of the diagnostician, Mrs. Oak became, during therapy, much more "well-adjusted," as this term is operationally defined by clinicians.

VI. THE THERAPIST-CLIENT RELATIONSHIP

The problem of investigating objectively the subtle aspects of the relationship between the therapist and client is one which we had not mastered at the time this study was designed. There are, however, some elements of this question which are illumined by the data from the Q-sorts, and we shall turn to this material before moving on to other kinds of data regarding Mrs. Oak.

How accurately was the therapist able to see the client from her own frame of reference, and hence reproduce her self-sortings without any knowledge as to what these had been? This is a question of general interest and is of particular interest in an orientation in which the therapist has often described his function in part as that of "achieving the client's internal frame of reference." Since the therapist sorted the Q-cards at the seventh interview and after therapy to represent the client's self as he thought she perceived it at these points, we have a certain amount of evidence. The relationship of the counselor's sorts to all the other sortings has been given in Table 3, and some of the most meaningful relationships are shown in Figure 4.

Some Findings

Examination of the above material will support the following statements.

The counselor showed little ability to predict the total self-picture of the client at the time of the seventh interview (*r* CS7 · S7 = .14).

The counselor's prediction at the seventh interview, while poor, is far from random. It is most closely related to the least defensive pre-therapy self-picture (RSF2). It shows an orderly and decreasing relationship with each of the succeeding self-pictures (*r*'s of .35, .27, .15, .14, .12, −.06, −.09, −.15).

By the conclusion of therapy the counselor showed a substantial ability to predict the client's self-picture (*r* CSA · SA = .57).

The counselor's prediction at the end of therapy has also an orderly and generally increasing relationship to the successive client selves (*r*'s of −.06, .03, .29, .48, .42, .57, .63, .66).

The change or discrepancy which the counselor perceived between the self earlier in therapy and the self at the conclusion of therapy was much greater than the change perceived by the client (*r* CS7 · CSA = −.04; *r* S7 · SA = .54).

In considering the therapist's prediction of the client's ideal, we find the correlations very marked.

By the seventh interview the counselor showed a high degree of ability to predict the client's self-ideal (*r* CI7 · I7 = .71). By the end of therapy this ability remained at about the same level (*r* CIA · IA = .74).

These high correlations probably represent in part a cultural artifact. Preliminary evidence already indicates that the self-ideals of most individuals—clients and counselors—have considerable similarity, and this no doubt helps to account for these correlations.

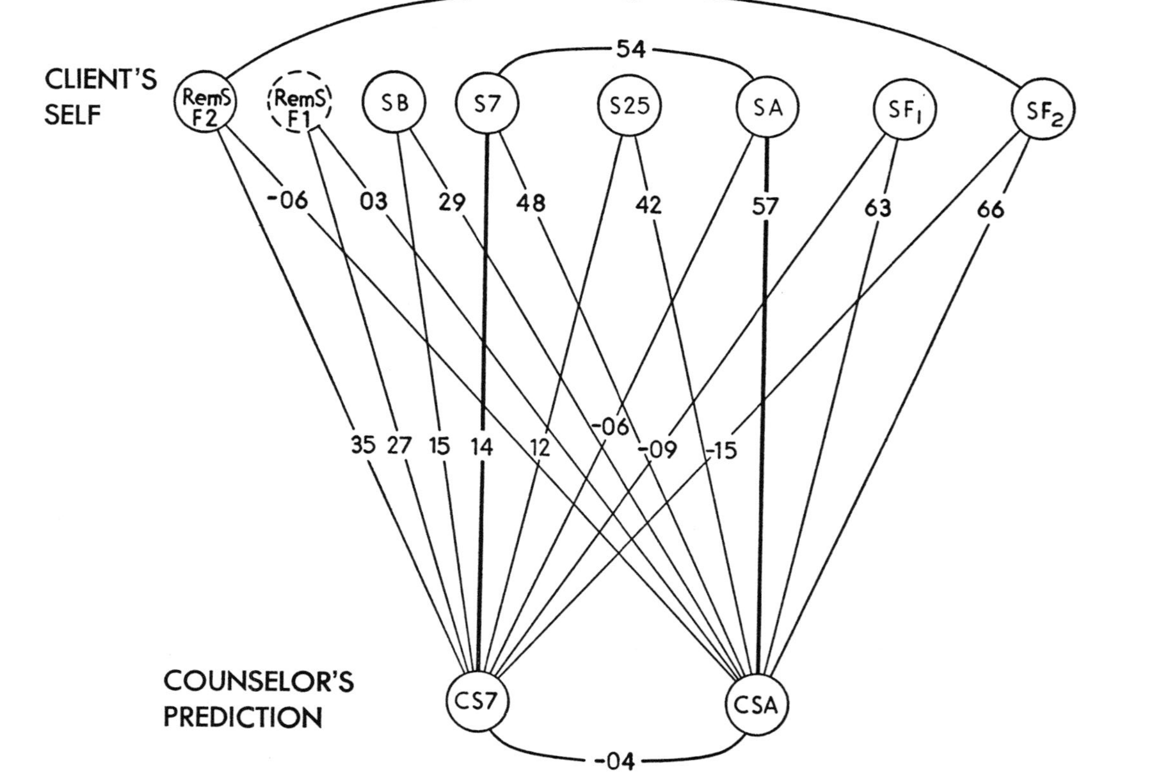

FIG. 4.—The counselor's prediction of client's self-sorts. (The designations are those used in Table 3. Figures are correlations, with decimal points omitted.)

An Interpretation

Certain of the findings appear paradoxical. The therapist's perception of the client early in therapy was most closely related to a nondefensive self-picture, which could not be given by the client until nearly a year and a half later. Likewise the therapist's perception of the client at the end of therapy was most similar to a self she was becoming during the next year but had not yet become.

Perhaps this may be summarized by saying that, though the therapist in the interviews was responding to the consciously expressed self of the client, his actual relationship appears to have been to something deeper. Early in therapy he saw the client, and thought she saw herself, as more unhappy and insecure than she could consciously admit. At the conclusion of therapy he saw her as having more integration and strength than she as yet perceived for herself. In both instances he was relating to something a bit deeper than the consciously communicated self.

Does this have any relationship to success in therapy? We do not know. Another case has been similarly studied by Hartley (2) in which the client made much progress, though the counselor's predictive sortings, even at the end of therapy, had no relationship to the client's actual sortings. We can only say that the situation is as described for this particular therapist-client relationship and that we are faced with the exciting prospect of being able to study these and even more subtle aspects of the relationship in future studies.

An Integration and a Speculation

As we mused over the fact that the therapist seemed to be relating to something deeper than the client's conscious self, some further steps suggested themselves. In following them and in undertaking what was thought to be a minor by-road of the research, some unusual findings were turned up which, combined with facts already cited, raised highly significant questions.

Correlations first were calculated between the counselor's sortings and the different diagnostic sortings mentioned in the preceding section. It was hypothesized that, if the therapist was relating to more of the person than was consciously revealed or communicated, his sortings would have a higher correlation with the diagnostic sortings than with the self-sortings made at the same time. The results are shown in Table 9. The hypothesis is not entirely confirmed, but the findings hold a real surprise. To appreciate this, let us review the facts briefly.

The counselor sorted the cards after the seventh interview to depict the client as he thought she saw herself. Previous evidence indicates that he saw her as admitting to awareness more of her experience than was actually the case. Therefore it would be theorized that the counselor's sorting would show a more substantial relationship to the diagnostic sortings than to the self-sortings done by the client. Examination of Table 9 confirms this. The diagnosis nearest in time is the diagnosis before therapy. The counselor's

TABLE 9

THE RELATIONSHIP OF COUNSELOR SORTINGS TO DIAGNOSTIC AND SELF-SORTINGS

Correlation of	Before Therapy	After Therapy	First Follow-up	Second Follow-up
CS7 with self..........	.15	−.06	−.09	−.15
CS7 with diagnosis.....	.36	.40	−.17	−.15
CSA with self.........	.29	.57	.63	.66
CSA with diagnosis....	−.30	.06	.54	.68

self-picture of the client correlates .36 with this diagnosis and only .15 with the client's own self-picture. We turn then to the counselor's sorting done after therapy. Here his picture of the client's self correlates only .06 with the after-therapy diagnosis, but .57 with the client's self-picture. This appears to be a clear contradiction of our hypothesis. But when we look at the information from the follow-up we find that the counselor's sorting correlates .68 with the final diagnosis! As we mull over this surprising finding, its meaning appears to support a statement made very tentatively in the preceding section (pp. 293–95). Let us amplify that statement to include the present material.

In this case the client's self-perception at the end of therapy and the therapist's estimate of the client's self-perception at that time are the best predictors we have. Either of them is a much better predictor of the diagnosis one year later than is the *diagnosis* made at the end of therapy (*r* SA · DF2 = .59; *r* CSA · DF2 = .68; while *r* DA · DF2 = .15).

Some may interpret this statement as casting doubt on the diagnostic test used. This does not seem to be justified, since the diagnostic sortings in general have a meaningful relationship to all the other data. The true meaning of this finding appears to cut much deeper. It suggests that the person *becomes* what he experientially perceives himself to be. If one examines Table 6 on this point, it is found that without exception each self-sorting by the client correlates more highly with the *next following* diagnosis than it does with a diagnosis made at the same time or earlier.

The implications of all this are as yet far from clear, but the consistency of the data, considering the relative crudeness of the instruments and the complete methodological independence of the sortings, is astonishing. Since much further investigation is needed of these points, perhaps the implications are best put as questions.

Does this material mean that the phenomenal self of the individual is the best predictor of his personality in the near future?

Does it mean that this is true only when a person is able to admit much of his experience to awareness? (Later selves seem to be better predictors than early selves.)

Since both the phenomenal self and the diagnostic picture seem to predict only for the short range, does it mean that personality is (potentially at least) far more changeable than psychologists have thought?

Does this mean that the emphasis on finding stable measures of personality is foredoomed to failure if the primary basic characteristic is change, not stability?

One is tempted to raise this question also, though it may seem fantastic to many. What would our society be like if it were built around the concept of personality change rather than personality fixity? To put it specifically, what would it mean if our thinking was predicated on the possibility that within a year and a half an individual's personality might change so that it would be negatively correlated with what it was at the outset?

These questions are highly speculative. They ignore for the moment some important limitations: that these Q-sorts are based on a certain set of items—that the sorting of these items may not truly represent the actual self-concept; that the sorting of these same items by a diagnostician may not truly represent the diagnostician's perception; that we are speaking here of findings in one case; etc. Yet the data do raise these questions; and, since they have important implications which run contrary to current professional and lay thinking, they demand the most thorough and complete investigation.

VII. CHANGES IN EMOTIONAL MATURITY OF BEHAVIOR

A Project for Measuring Behavioral Change

Though one of the most important social considerations in regard to psychotherapy is the degree of behavioral change which occurs, this is one of the most difficult areas to measure objectively. Briefly put, the problem is this. If a client gives up his job as a result of psychotherapy, this may indicate the achievement of sufficient independence to leave an intolerable situation, or it may indicate increased instability. If, as a result of psychotherapy, he quarrels less frequently with his spouse, this may indicate an improved adjustment, or it may indicate an unhealthy submissiveness. Thus, though behavior change may be observed, the evaluation of those observations involves many problems.

For reasons of this sort the instrument chosen for measuring alteration in behavior was the Willoughby Emotional-Maturity Scale devised by R. R. Willoughby twenty years ago. This scale, and the design of this aspect of our research, has been described in chapter 13. It will be recalled that the design required that the client rate himself on the E-M Scale before therapy, after therapy, and at the conclusion of the follow-up period. Likewise he solicited the aid of two of his friends who filled out the scale at these times and mailed the rating directly to the Counseling Center. Thus we had self-ratings of behavior and ratings by judges who knew the client well but who had no knowledge of the purpose of the instrument. At the same time that they made the ratings of the client, each friend also rated another individual who was well known to him. These ratings served as controls which provided a basis of comparison for the ratings of the client.

This was the procedure followed in the case of Mrs. Oak,[4] and Table 10 gives the pertinent data. It will be noted that the client's own rating of her behavior shows a steady increase from pre- to post-therapy, and from post-therapy to follow-up; that the ratings by friends show an almost identical increase from pre- to post-therapy and from post-therapy to follow-up (follow-up rating by

4. Since the E-M Scale was not administered at the second follow-up point, this study ends at the first follow-up point, seven months following the conclusion of therapy.

one friend was not returned); and that the change in the two control individuals, rated at the same interval by the same raters, is much less than in the client, and this small change is in the direction of decreased emotional maturity.

It may be of some interest to compare the scores for Mrs. Oak with the norms which Willoughby established. Since the scale was standardized on college students, the norms are not entirely applicable, and the comparison is suggestive only. On this basis Mrs. Oak's mean rating was at the 72d percentile at the beginning of therapy and well above the 99th percentile at the follow-up period.

TABLE 10

MATURITY OF BEHAVIOR: E-M SCALE SCORES FOR MRS. OAK

(Higher Scores Indicate More Mature Behavior)

	Pre-therapy	Post-therapy	Follow-up
Rating of Mrs. Oak by:			
Self	55.0	63.3	69.4
Friend No. 1	52.1	58.7	65.0
Friend No. 2	57.6	66.6	*
Mean rating	54.9	62.9	....
Mean difference		8.0	....
Mean of self and Friend No. 1	53.6	61.0	67.2
Mean differences		7.4	6.2
Rating of Control A by Friend No. 1	61.0	58.5	55.3
Differences		−2.5	−3.2
Rating of Control B by Friend No. 2	30.5	28.7	*
Difference		−1.8	....

* Missing.

Illustrative Items

It may give more meaning to the scores to list a few of the items which showed change. By and large, the increased score is due both to dropping behaviors which are immature and to adding to the behavior picture items which receive a high score of maturity. A few in each group will be listed, and in parentheses will be indicated the rater or raters making the change. The score value of each item is also noted, 1 indicating the extreme of immaturity, and 9 the maximum of emotional maturity. The change was made either between the pre-therapy and post-therapy tests or between the pre-therapy and follow-up tests.

ITEMS DROPPED

ITEM	SCORE	
(5)	1	S chooses his course of action with reference to his own maximum immediate satisfaction. (Mrs. Oak.)
(9)	1	S characteristically appeals for help in the solution of his problems. (Friend No. 1.)
(14)	4	S believes in democracy in principle but prefers not to associate too closely with individuals from groups widely divergent from his own. (Mrs. Oak, Friend No. 1.)
(23)	2	Faced with several insistent demands simultaneously, S is upset and fights the situation, his dominant idea being to compel order. (Mrs. Oak, Friends Nos. 1 and 2.)
(25)	2	Exposed to unsocial behavior (e.g., antagonism) on the part of an individual with whom he is closely associated, S is annoyed and seeks to escape or to drive the other individual away. (Friend No. 2.)
(57)	4	S is accustomed to achieve some of his ends by indirection, for example, by diverting the attention of important individuals to other interests. (Friends Nos. 1 and 2.)
(60)	2	S cannot give up or retain an objective completely. If he tries to give it up, he must make some gesture of retention; if he retains it, he feels the desirability of giving it up. (Friend No. 2.)
(61)	1	S tends to meet his problems by ascribing elsewhere the responsibility for them. (Mrs. Oak.)

ITEMS ADDED

ITEM	SCORE	
(38)	7	S feels that the universe is relatively impersonal and nonethical regarding his wishes and those of his group or of mankind. (Mrs. Oak.)
(42)	8	Being interrupted in the performance of an act, S gives attention, when resumption is possible, to the total situation and resumes or abandons the act unemotionally as the new situation makes advisable. (Mrs. Oak.)
(43)	8	Exposed to unsocial behavior (antagonism, etc.) on the part of an individual with whom he is closely associated, S adopts a detached attitude and is interested in the underlying causes. (Friend No. 2.)
(47)	8	Faced with several insistant demands simultaneously, S sorts them quickly by urgency, settles one at a time, and disregards (i.e., does not react to) insistence of deferred demands. (Mrs. Oak.)
(53)	9	S welcomes legitimate opportunities for sexual expression and is not ashamed, fearful, or preoccupied with the topic. (Mrs. Oak.)
(55)	7	Subjected to public criticism (e.g., a reprimand from some person in authority or open adverse criticism of his actions), S waits composedly for opportunity to reply and states his position without heat. (Friend No. 2.)

(64) 7 S's ambitions are in harmony with his capacities. His limitations are accepted by himself without emotion. He enjoys making the most of his capacities, which he also accepts realistically. (In a word, he has good insight regarding himself.) (Friend No. 2.)

A careful inspection of the item changes seems to indicate that the rating by the two friends increased primarily because of dropping immature items and only secondarily by the addition of more mature ones. In Mrs. Oak's ratings the two tendencies were more nearly balanced. This makes clinical sense, since she would probably be aware, earlier than her friends, of emerging behavior.

It is of some interest that on Item 53 (see above) both friends rated her as being sexually well adjusted, before therapy as well as after. Mrs. Oak, however, does not attribute this characteristic to herself until after therapy.

The one element which cannot be entirely controlled in this study is the question as to whether the judges know that the client is in therapy. From some chance remarks of Mrs. Oak's, it is believed that in this case they did know that she was in therapy. Did this bias their judgments? The best answer to this is the marked consistency of the raters at all three points, extending over a one-year period. Yet this consistency of score is achieved not by marking the same items but by marking different items. This lends strong weight to the likelihood of an unbiased rating, each rater making his judgment on those aspects of the client's behavior which were personally known to him.

A Comment on the Findings

The findings themselves seem clear enough. During and following psychotherapy this client's behavior, as observed by herself and by two friends, has changed in a direction defined by experts as constituting emotional maturity of behavior. Examination of the item changes would justify this description in the case of Mrs. Oak. She has become less defensive and better organized. She has also become less dependent, less inclined to blame others, less selfish, less ambivalent and conflicted in her behavior. She exhibits more acceptance of her capacities and limitations, more basically democratic behavior, and less conflict and inhibition in the sexual area.

The reality of these changes is confirmed by the fact that the ratings of another person by each of the friends, at the same intervals, show no such changes as these judges have observed in Mrs. Oak.

VIII. CHANGES IN THE ACCEPTANCE OF OTHERS

The Rationale Underlying This Project

We turn next to an investigation of the attitudes of Mrs. Oak toward others and the extent to which these attitudes changed during and after therapy. The rationale and the method for this aspect of the study have been described in chapter 11. The instrument used was the Self-Other Attitude Scale, a paper-and-pencil test compiled from instruments already developed and tested. It was hypothesized that in the process of client-centered therapy the individual would tend to show a reduction in authoritarian, ethnocentric attitudes toward others and an increase in acceptance and democratic attitudes which place a high value on the worth of the individual. Operationally these changes would be indicated by a decrease in score on the S-O Scale. Let us now examine the results in the case of Mrs. Oak.

Scores on the S-O Scale

The detailed scores obtained by Mrs. Oak prior to therapy, after therapy, and seven months later are shown in Table 11, which also describes the more specific meaning of each of the subscales. It will be observed that in every one of the subscales both the post-therapy score and the follow-up score are lower than the pre-therapy score. In other words, all these sixteen comparisons are in the expected direction. It will also be seen that the total follow-up score shows a slight regression toward the pre-therapy score and that on some scales (D, PEC, C, A) this regression is fairly marked. In general, the whole trend is markedly in the direction of more regard for the worth of others, more acceptance of others, and a more democratic attitude. For purposes of simple comparison it seems best to take the pre-therapy score and compare it with the mean of the two post-therapy scores. On this basis there has been a drop in score from 310 to 218.5, a change of 91.5 in the predicted direction. As is evident from the material in chapter 9, this change is much sharper than for most of our clients.

To give somewhat more of the "feel" of the change which occurred, several characteristic items are given below, with the alteration in Mrs. Oak's response from the pre- to the post-therapy test. The capital letter in parentheses indicates the subscale from which the item comes.

61. (A) Many times discussions are stimulating, but greater progress is usually made if there is a specialist who knows the answers present in the group. (From agree to disagree.)

TABLE 11

S-O SCALE SCORES: CASE OF MRS. OAK
(Low Scores Indicate Democratic Attitudes)

Description of Subscale	Pre-therapy (1)	Post-therapy (2)	Follow-up (3)	Mean of (2) and (3) (4)	Net Change* (5)
F-scale (30 items): Basic antidemocratic, authoritarian, fascistic tendencies	90	74	62	68.0	−22.0
L-scale (10 items): Ideology regarding leadership; acceptance of leadership role as a function of the group; acceptance of group decision rather than leader decision or control	29	22	20	21.0	− 8.0
A-scale (10 items): Acceptance of the worth of members' contributions to the group	26	14	18	16.0	−10.0
D-scale (10 items): Acceptance of differences of opinion and ideas in group discussion; willingness for the group to review its decisions and consider new evidence	29	17	25	21.0	− 8.0
M-scale (10 items): Tendency to believe in and use democratic means of achieving goals; acceptance of individual responsibility	38	24	27	25.5	−12.5
C-scale (10 items): Desire to change others versus willingness for others to be themselves	30	18	23	20.5	− 9.5
E-scale (20 items): Ethnocentrism; tendency to exalt own group above all others; antagonism to minority groups	43	29	26	27.5	−15.5
PEC-scale (10 items): Political and economic conservatism	25	16	22	19.0	− 6.0
Total	310	214	223	218.5	......
Mean change, total scale	......	......	......	......	−91.5

* Net change is calculated as follows: column (1) − $\frac{\text{Sum of columns (2) and (3)}}{2}$.

85. (A) It is more efficient in a group if experts tell the group what to do. (More strongly disagree.)
62. (D) Dissenting opinions should be regarded as a valuable contribution to the group's solution of a problem. (More strongly agree.)
68. (D) Practically, it is necessary to ignore the feelings of some members in a group in order to reach a group decision. (From agree to disagree.)
63. (M) When disciplinary problems arise in a group, it is usually necessary to abandon democratic procedures. (From agree to disagree.)
100. (M) The real criterion for judging any technique of dealing with other people is how efficiently it will get the job done. (From agree to disagree.)
64. (C) If you have a friend who you feel doesn't have good moral and ethical principles, it is your duty to try to influence him to adopt better ones. (From undecided to disagree.)
42. (E) The people who raise all the talk about putting Negroes on the same level as whites are mostly radical agitators trying to stir up conflicts. (More strongly disagree.)

Discussion of Social Attitude Changes

There seem to be several points which might be mentioned in regard to the score changes described above. In the first place, it is of interest that there is a change in attitude on the part of Mrs. Oak on topics and in areas which were never in any way touched upon in the therapeutic interviews. Attitudes toward democracy, toward democratic means, toward other groups, toward leadership, toward economic and political issues, were, with one minor exception, never touched upon in any way. She did bring up and discuss her lessened desire to change her daughter, a topic which has some relation to the C-scale. But for the most part the attitudes measured by the S-O Scale were never a part of therapy, yet they altered sufficiently to represent a very marked change on an instrument developed in the field of social psychology.

The changes which have occurred in these attitudes in this client are those predicted by the theory of the client-centered orientation. The evidence is that this client, concomitantly with her experience of client-centered therapy, changed markedly toward a greater acceptance of others as separate individuals, as individuals of worth, and that her attitudes shifted decidedly in a direction which from a philosophical point of view would be regarded as deeply democratic.

IX. SIGNIFICANCE OF THE CHANGES

I am quite sure that a number of my readers have felt annoyed (as have some of my colleagues) that, in presenting the various types of evidence in regard to Mrs. Oak, there has been no discussion of the statistical significance of these changes. There has been no mention of critical ratios, *t* tests, or other measures of significance. This has not been accidental. It has seemed to the writer that, while some of the changes might well be significant and others not, this is a most unsatisfactory way of handling the problem when one case is involved. It is the consistency with which hypothesized predictions have been fulfilled that appears to be the true measure of the significance of the findings. In this section this problem will be considered.

Let us have the logic of the method we have been using well in mind. Each of the investigations in which Mrs. Oak participated had one major hypothesis and a number of secondary hypotheses, not all of which can be tested on one case. The particular case of Mrs. Oak was selected for investigation because it was the first case in which data were complete. There was no knowledge of her performance in any of these research tasks except for some preliminary knowledge of the Q-sort data. The only specific knowledge was that the therapist had rated her as a "successful" case. It was therefore presumed that change might have occurred.

In this situation a variety of specific predictions had been made in the form of hypotheses by each of the investigators. We have been, in this report, presenting the evidence in regard to them. Let us restate them here, noting only whether they have or have not been upheld.

It was hypothesized:

That if a competent clinical psychologist, experienced in psychodiagnostics, placed the three TAT's in an order from most poorly integrated to best integrated, this order would correspond with the order in which they were administered—pre-therapy, post-therapy, and follow-up. (Hypothesis upheld.)

That the TAT's would show changes in the direction of greater self-confidence, greater integration, fewer aspects of experience denied to awareness. (Hypothesis upheld.)

That the perceived self as measured by Q-sorting would become increasingly congruent with the perceived self-ideal as therapy progressed. (Hypothesis upheld.)

That the perceived self would change more than the perceived self-ideal. (Hypothesis upheld.)

That the self as perceived at the end of therapy would be more assured, more self-directing, less divided, less inhibited, more expressive than the self at the beginning of therapy. (Hypothesis upheld.)

That the changes in the perceived self would be greater during a period of therapy than during a period of no therapy. (Hypothesis upheld.)

That the self as perceived by the client, and the client as perceived by a diagnostician, would grow more congruent during and after therapy. (Hypothesis not upheld for the therapy period but upheld for the over-all period.)

That the client's behavior, as perceived by herself, would change during therapy in a direction defined by experts as constituting greater emotional maturity. (Hypothesis upheld.)

That the client's behavior, as observed and rated by two friends who knew her well, would change in the direction of emotional maturity. (Hypothesis upheld in both instances.)

That ratings of the behavior of two control persons by these same friends, using the same instrument, would show less change in the direction of emotional maturity. (Hypothesis upheld in both instances.)

That the client's score on a standardized S-O Scale would change in a direction indicating more democratic attitudes; greater acceptance of the worth of others; greater acceptance of other racial and minority groups; less dependence upon experts; more tendency to use democratic means and democratic leadership; lessened desire to reform or change others. (Hypothesis upheld for the total score and for each one of the eight subscores on both the post-therapy and the follow-up administration.)

We may now return to the question of the scientific significance of these findings. The likelihood that they could have occurred by chance seems the best criterion. Let us take only a few items in which chance is most easily calculated on the hypothesis of random sampling:

1. The chance of three TAT's being placed in the predicted order is 1 in 6.
2. The chance that three raters using the E-M Scale (self and two friends) would all change in the predicted direction at the post-therapy period is 1 in 8.
3. The chance that all eight subscales of the S-O Scale would change in the predicted direction at the post-therapy period is 1 in 256.
4. The chance that this unanimity of change in the predicted direction on all eight scales would occur again at the follow-up period is 1 in 256^2 or 1 in 65,536.
5. The chance that all of these four described events, which constitute only a small portion of the predictions, would occur in one case is—we will stop the calculations here.

At this point it is probable that even the skeptic will agree that the series of predicted changes which have occurred in Mrs. Oak could not have occurred by chance. Even if we take our eleven hypotheses on the simplest possible basis and consider that change might be in the predicted direction or not in the predicted direction, there is only 1 chance in 2,048 that they would all move in the predicted direction. Thus we may state that the observed changes in the case of Mrs. Oak are significant and could not have come about as the result of chance factors alone.

But are these changes attributable to the forty hours of therapy? On this point we may draw upon the evidence from both the own-control and the equivalent-control groups cited in the previous chapters. In no instance have these groups shown significant changes on the measures used here. Hence we may say, with considerable assurance, that the changes exhibited in the case of Mrs. Oak are significant and appear to be related to the variable of therapy, in her case to the forty-eight therapy sessions, rather than to any other factor.

X. THE PROCESS OF THERAPY IN MRS. OAK

The research findings which have been given thus far in this report have all come from investigations which had the outcomes of therapy as their main interest. In the course of discovering outcomes, considerable light has been thrown on process. The seeming primacy of self-change as the basis of personality change is one example. Yet little understanding has been gained as to the dynamics of the process by which that change occurred. It is felt that the best description of process at the present time is found in the clients' descriptions of the "feel" of therapy. Later, of course, our researches will provide a more objective view of the elements which facilitate the learnings which occur in therapy, but the hypotheses for these studies will come from a careful analysis of the significant factors as they are experienced by client and therapist.

Mrs. Oak is an individual who gives us many clues to the process of therapy, because she, unlike many clients, often talks about the psychological events which occur in her during and between interviews. This section of the report is made up of a selection of excerpts from the interviews—excerpts which appear to have relevancy for the understanding of the process. The writer no doubt has biases which may have affected the selection, but the effort was made to select in terms of meaningfulness to the client. From this point we will attempt to let Mrs. Oak and the therapist speak for themselves, through portions of the interviews, with a minimal amount of descriptive comment. For purposes of comparison with earlier evidence, the material is grouped into segments.

First through Seventh Interviews

In the early interviews Mrs. Oak spoke rather often of specific reality problems. One excerpt will illustrate this as she speaks about herself and her daughter.

(*First interview.*) *C.*:[5] Well . . . apparently things with Peggy seem to be going well, and of course we might as well get right down to the point where it isn't Peggy. It's me. And what'll we do? Are we . . . where we find the source, I don't know, I mean, I'm confused, I'm shocked. . . I know it's this, that apparently I have made this girl my only link with life. I have a . . . I've sublimated everything. And I have—I don't know. But it isn't fair, I mean, it's a shocking situation. (Pause.) There's a kind of transference, something, I've simply identified myself with her. Of course there are these terrible tensions and the anxiety feelings. But the shocking part of it is that the-the awful part to face, I mean I'm not saying it all now, I naturally won't . . . is that it's really *me*. . . I mean it's, I'm afraid for *myself*, you see.

By the third interview Mrs. Oak is describing the full experiencing of a feeling in a way which is almost a forecast of what therapy was to mean for her. This is the way the interview started.

C.: I feel very glad to get back today. (*Both laugh.*) A couple of things just came to my mind, say in passing so to speak. The fact that once I get into this thing, as I start talking, I'm not the least bit conscious of you. And I, of course, I know ideally I shouldn't (word lost) . . . but I'll simply have to go on as it's been. And, secondly, the realization that last time I was here I experienced a-an emotion I had never felt before—which surprised me and sort of shocked me a bit. And yet I thought, I think it has sort of a . . . the only word I can find to describe it, the only verbalization is a kind of cleansing. I-I really felt terribly *sorry* for something, a kind of grief. And found myself comparing it with, with things

5. Certain conventions will be utilized in this section. "*C.*" refers to the client; "*T.*," to the therapist. Three-dot ellipses (. . .) indicate a hesitation or very brief pause, while longer pauses are indicated in parentheses "(pause)." Five-dot ellipses (. . . . .) mean that some material, irrelevant to the main point being illustrated, has been omitted.

I had felt before, I-I . . . when Peggy was ill and I had felt this terrible anxiety and what I thought was a terrible kind of grief, I realize now it wasn't. It was a kind of a hysterical feeling.

T.: You mean there, that this last was sort of somehow a pseudo-feeling. This that you felt here last time was a real, genuine emotion of deep regret.

C.: That's right. And I-I've never experienced it before. It sort of makes me wonder how many things I probably am sincerely sorry for, but just have never felt, covered up.

In the next interview we find a good expression of what she later called her "vaguenesses." All the way through therapy this type of experience and this manner of expression were very characteristic and clearly meant a great deal to her.

(*Fourth interview.*) *C.*: I have a feeling I've had since I started these sessions here, a feeling I've described of not giving a damn, that kind of thing, while it still isn't beginning to shape into something, it's-it's there. And, and I find that, I find a-a kind of-of self-centeredness that's kind of hard to put into words. It isn't selfishness. It's-it's a kind of . . . and it isn't preoccupation. But it's kind of feeling myself to the exclusion of other things. And I know what it is I want to do. I want to be able to-to feel myself in, in rather the same way, I-I . . . not with so many sharp edges maybe. And to be able to *always* feel myself, but in relationship to the . . . to-to things, and personalities which it, it seems to me at present I-I sort of want to push aside. . . . . It's as though I were to say that what I think intellectually isn't nearly as important as something I want to happen to me on a nonverbal plane. It's all very vague.

A little later this sense of an increasing acquaintance with herself is beautifully described. One gains in the following excerpt a clear picture of therapy at this point as being a full experiencing of self in all its many facets.

(*Fifth interview.*) *C.*: It's as though the-the . . . I have to fuse, somehow bring together what I am able to intellectualize with this something that I know is there. It all comes pretty vague. But you know I keep-keep having the thought occur to me that this whole process for me is kind of like examining pieces of a jigsaw puzzle. It seems to me I-I'm in the process now of examining the individual pieces which really don't have too much meaning. Probably handling the—not even beginning to think of a pattern. That keeps coming to me. And it's interesting to me because I-I really don't like jigsaw puzzles. They've always irritated me. But that's my feeling. And I mean I pick up little pieces (*she gestures throughout this conversation to illustrate her statement*) with absolutely no meaning except I mean the-the feeling that you get from simply handling them without seeing them as a pattern, but just from the touch I probably feel, "Well it is going to fit someplace here."

T.: And that at the moment that—that's the process, just getting the feel and the shape and the configuration of the different pieces with a little bit of background feeling of, "Yeah they'll probably fit somewhere," but most of the attention's focused right on "What does this feel like? And what is its texture?"

C.: That's right. There's almost something physical in it. A-a. . .

T.: You can't quite describe it without using your hands. A real, almost a sensuous sense in . . .

C.: . . . that's right. Again it's-it's a feeling of being very objective, and yet I've never been quite so close to myself.

This theme is expanded in the next interview in a passage which is logically very incoherent but psychologically quite clear. The fact that the passage is meaningful to her may be indicated by the fact that a slight speech defect is more noticeable here than in many other portions of the interview.

(*Sixth interview.*) *C.*: Uh, I caught myself thinking that-that-that during these uh, sessions, uh, I've been sort of singing a song. Now that sounds uh-uh, vague, and-and-and uh-uh, not actually singing . . . sort of a song without any music. A-a, uh, probably a kind of poem coming out. (M-hm.) And uh, I like the idea, I mean it's sort of come to me with-without anything built out of-of anything. And in . . . following that, it came, it came this other kind of-of-of a uh, feeling. Well, I s-s-found myself sort o-of asking myself uh, is that the shape that cases take? (M-hm.) A uh-uh, is it possible that I-I-I am just verbalizing and, and-and uh, at times kind of become intoxicated with my own-own, uh-uh, verbalizations? (M-hm.) And then uh, following this, came, well, am I just taking up your time? Uh . . . then a doubt, a doubt. . . (M-hm.) Then something else occurred to me. Uh, from whence it came I-I don't know, no actual logical kind of a sequence to the thinking. The thought struck me: We're (two words missing) uh, overwhelmed or uh, doubtful, or-or uh, we can show concern or, or an-a-any uh, interest when-when the, when blind people uh, learn to read with their fingers, uh, Braille. And I don't know, it-it may be just sort of-of . . . it's all mixed up . . . it may be that's something that I'm uh, uh, eg-experiencing now.

T.: M-hm. Let's see if I can get some of that "uh-uh," that sequence of feelings. First, sort of as though you're . . . and I gather that the first one is a fairly positive feeling . . . as though maybe you're kind of creating a poem here . . . uh, a song without music somehow but something that might be quite uh, quite creative, and then the-the feeling of a lot of skepticism about that. "Maybe I'm just saying words, uh, just being carried off by words that I, that I speak, and maybe it's all a lot of baloney, really." Uh . . . and then a feeling that uh . . . perhaps you're almost learning a-a new type of experiencing which would be just as radically new as for a blind person to try to make sense out of what he feels with his fingertips.

C.: M-hm. M-hm. (Pause.)

It is evident in the foregoing excerpt that she is perplexed as to why she is going about therapy this way. A moment later she discusses this point further, wondering whether she should be taking up her problems more systematically rather than proceeding in this natural fashion.

C.: Perhaps that's why I'm doubtful today of-of this whole thing. Uh . . . because it's something that's not forced. And really I-I-I'm feeling that what I-I should do is-is sort of systematize the thing. I, uh, ought to work harder and. . .

T.: Sort of a deep questioning as to what am I doing with a self that isn't-isn't pushing to get things done, solved? (Pause.)

C.: And yet the-the fact that I-I really like this, other kind of-of thing, this, I don't know, call it a poignant feeling, I mean . . . I felt things that I've never felt before. I *like* that, too. Uh-uh . . . maybe that's the way to do it. I-I just don't know today.

T.: (M-hm.) Don't feel at all sure, but you do know that you somehow have a real, a real fondness for this poem that is yourself. Whether it's the way to go about this or not, you don't know.

C.: And that thought struck me. I mean quite accidentally. I wasn't even thinking uh, about myself. And it gave me a terrific lift. Just a terrific lift. And-and I-I thought to myself, well, uh, saying, well, there's-there's just parts of me I'm never going to know. Uh, but uh, by golly I'm going to sing a song first. And it-it just gave me a-a terrific lift. (M-hm.) And then of course today, I mean, that was followed by this, well, I mean this completely, well, I mean how can I put it, how can I discuss a kind of sensate thing? I mean we just don't believe in things like that. (M-hm.) It's-it's-it's uh. . . .

T.: "After all, be practical . . ."

C.: That's right, it's-it's just, I mean what, you're just fascinated with your words. It's uh, intangible, this, this uh . . . it just doesn't make good sense.

A moment later, after debating whether she should give a complete case history of herself or proceed in this "vague" fashion, she adds:

C.: And I tell myself, now . . . well, the climate is such in here that I *have* to act in a certain way. And a certain part of me says, "Nuts, it isn't." I can act any way I want to act. (M-hm.) And yet this is how it's coming out. . . . . And then, I mean I'm-I'm-I'm utterly confused if, is it something that is just happening, is it something that I want to happen this way? And yet, I-I. . . Well, I'm, that answers it-itself . . . ac-actually. If it's something that's just happening, then it's happening because I want it to happen, I-I'm sure.

Eighth through Twenty-fifth Interviews

For the most part the excerpts which have been selected do not deal with the content of Mrs. Oak's feelings but more with the way she experienced the therapeutic process itself. We will make one exception to this, the area of sexual conflict, since this is an area in which the research findings indicate less progress. Several excerpts will touch upon this problem, and the first is from the eighth interview.

C.: You know over in this area of-of oh, sexual disturbance, I have a feeling that I'm beginning to discover that it's pretty bad, pretty bad. I'm finding out that-that I'm bitter, really. *Damn bitter*. I . . . and I'm not turning it back in, into myself. I could, I could say it's me. But I'm probably not ready for that. I'm-I'm surprised at how-how very bitter I am.

T.: When you say it's something that's pretty bad, I judge you mean that it's something you really don't like in yourself, but here is this feeling of just intense bitterness, something of a very emotional bitterness. And it's-it's not turned your way; it's turned out.

C.: I don't, I can't even bring myself to say that it's pretty bad concerning me. (Long pause.) Well, I-I think what I-I . . . I probably feel is a certain e-element of "I've been cheated." (*C.'s voice is very tight, and her throat chokes up*.) And I've-I've covered up very nicely, to the point of consciously not caring. But I'm-I'm sort of amazed to find that in the practice of, what shall I call it, a kind of sublimation that right under it . . . again words . . . there's a-a kind of passive force that's, it's pas- . . . it's very passive, but at the same time it's kind of *murderous*.

T.: So there's the feeling, "I've really been cheated. I've covered that up and seem not to care and yet underneath that there's a kind of a-a latent but very much present *bitterness* that is very, very strong."

C.: It's very strong. I . . . that I know. It's terribly powerful.

T.: Almost a dominating kind of force.

C.: Of which I am rarely conscious. Almost never. . . . . Right now that's how it is. It's sort of, how can I sum it up, a-a kind of gyp. (Pause.) And again the feeling is-is not of wanting to hurt anyone, to-to create conflicts. It's-it's kind of an abstract thing of just sort of wanting to kick back at life.

Mrs. Oak almost never expresses any feeling, positive or negative, toward the counselor. Yet in the eleventh interview there is an expression of real resentment. Mrs. Oak had said that she felt she must resolve certain situations in a way that she recognized as superficial and disregard certain other feelings. The therapist responds, and the excerpt begins with the conclusion of his response.

T.: Therefore you'll forget all this first, but it kind of refuses to stay forgotten. (Long pause.)

C.: Well it certainly refuses to stay forgotten, that's for sure. (Pause of several minutes.) You're not being very helpful.

T.: (*Laughs.*) You say I'm not being very helpful. Hardly fair to have you look at your feelings, hm?

C.: (*Pause.*) Well actually for the sake of getting . . . I was actually really sitting here just pushing feelings away, sort of catching onto little bits of nothing.

T.: Really quite busy pushing out the feelings, keeping them from flowing in.

C.: M-hm. I mean that is something that just happened now.

T.: Yeah, that's what I mean.

C.: I was feeling a mild resentment because you weren't being very helpful. (*A moment after this exchange she continues on the same theme.*)

C.: (Several minutes' pause.) This is a bad day. One of these days when (words lost) I don't want the responsibility and you won't take it.

T.: M-hm. Kind of rough going, and you feel it should be, whatever takes place should be deep. And yet here I don't take the responsibility for guiding that. And you're fearful of taking it on yourself.

C.: Yeah, I-I . . . that's a little bit mild. I don't want to take it.

T.: Don't want to.

C.: I don't want to. And I-I'm just resentful that you . . .

T.: M-hm. Really more the feeling toward me, "You *ought* to take this over."

C.: Yeah, that's right. You don't help one damn little bit.

T.: Feel really quite deeply resentful that I don't . . . (Yeah) . . . take it on.

C.: That's right. Probably do me good. I don't know. (Pause.) I think it would be very nice if I could just dump the responsibility . . . you see today I just do not *want* to accept responsibility for my own feelings. I just don't *want* to examine them.

T.: "To hell with being responsible for my feelings today. I don't want to look at them. I don't want to be responsible for them. Somebody else can do it."

C.: Well I think somebody else should. I mean I know better. That's just my feeling right now. I *know* better.

T.: Any of that knowledge doesn't prevent you from feeling that really I should take over.

C.: And I don't feel the least bit polite about it either.

T.: Nothing ladylike in that feeling.

C.: No.

At about this point in therapy she felt that she was more troubled, more neurotic, more disorganized than when she first came in. She expresses this clearly.

(*Twelfth interview.*) *C.*: I think what has happened to me is that . . . internally, emotionally, I don't know . . . I've sort of gone to pieces. That is, there have been breakdowns, not devastating ones, but it's almost as though you had a kind of physical structure, a piece of architecture, and there have been certain breakdowns, certain parts removed. And it's just not functioning well. And certainly the repair work hasn't set in yet, which. . .

T.: You feel as though at the present time your structure is more impaired or less organized perhaps than it was when you came in, and the rebuilding of any newer type of structure to take its place hasn't really gotten under way.

C.: That's right.

As part of this troubled period she faces up to the basic issue as to whether she will focus on this intangible, almost mystical exploration of self or whether she will concentrate on a plan of action, an adjustment to the world.

(*Twelfth interview.*) *C.*: (Pause: 3 minutes, 11 seconds.) It seems to me that I've reached a point where I've sort of lost touch with myself. When I take stock . . . I'm pretty well convinced that intellectually I'm sound, I mean, I know I am sane and I know I'm . . . my thinking is pretty correct, it's pretty sound, but somewhere along the way there . . . I got hold of something. I may be all wrong, I may have gone on a completely wrong tangent. But what I wanted to do was to examine intangibles. I felt that I-I really don't need to examine my thinking. It's something else, it's something else when one gives all kinds of names to it, and none of the names are it. I lost . . . sort of lost the thread.

T.: For a time you were really working in the field of these intangibles, and then somehow you lost contact with that self.

C.: That's right.

T.: But you have, I take it, a pretty strong feeling that it's . . . that the important thing lies somewhere in that realm.

C.: That's exactly the point. My feeling is, if I can't get in and examine those things, and really pick them out and . . . things, they aren't things . . . really kind of harness it, put it into shape, then it's not going to work. And I think, I think I'll find my way back, or forward. Of course you see, and then, I ask myself when I go out into the sunlight and dodge a few cars . . . well, what in the world are you looking for, what in the world are you looking for?

T.: What are you chasing cobwebs for?

C.: That's right. What are you looking . . . maybe you're off on a wrong track.

T.: Seems awfully shadowy and sort of dubious when you get out into the white light of day.

C.: M-hm. Sort of a sense of an embarrassment. Yeah. That's it, I mean, sort of a "Come take your place in this gorgeous progressive twentieth century." I mean, "stop it."

T.: Almost "What are you doing out there in that other realm?" You ought to be a little ashamed of yourself somehow.

C.: M-hm, that's right. And yet, when I listen to myself, I know that's it. So, of course, I mean, I just feel that if I could hold on to that I'll find it, that it's much more real.

T.: It may not seem like the twentieth century to you, but, when you get hold of it, you're pretty damn sure that it is something very real. The kind of thing, I take it, where you don't need someone else to tell you, "Yes, that's important"; you *know* that's important.

C.: Yeah, yeah. That's what I meant when I said that, when I, when I can just listen and sort of feel a push and that's it. (Long pause: 12 minutes.) I think this conflict of . . . what I feel should be genuine—the feeling of a sort of experiencing self and the adjustment to the world, has really always caused me trouble really.

T.: M-hm. You're saying there has always been kind of a rift between the real experiencing of yourself and the way you operate to get along in the world.

C.: Yeah. It's probably way, way back. I think . . . I think I can remember always . . . or very often having a definite feeling, a being certain that the-the values that people seem to live by and uphold were kind of unreal things.

T.: All this structure that they live by is really sort of a shell, not really the real thing.

C.: Yeah. And just in sitting here I realize, "My goodness, it goes back a long, long way."

It seems clear that at this point this concept of "listening to myself," of stopping to "listen and sort of feel a push and that's it," has a great deal of meaning to her and involves the whole issue of herself as the locus of evaluation versus the values held by others.

One of the characteristic elements of the process in Mrs. Oak seems to be the experiencing, in the interview, of strong emotions which have never been fully lived out in the ordinary life-situation. An example of this is the feeling of adolescent reactions, accompanied by very slow-paced expression, deep feeling, and weeping. The printed excerpt can hardly convey the full flavor.

(*Fourteenth interview.*) *C.*: (Long pause.) You know, actually . . . it occurs to me that . . . I probably . . . should have . . . lived through this thing when I was about sixteen years old. It's a . . . I imagine it's the kind of thing . . . young people feel . . . a-a-adolescent people feel . . . a resistance, a pulling-away from the father kind of symbol. And I never did experience that, you know. And . . . I can feel, I can sort of feel that now. "Let me be free." Which of course doesn't help, because I can . . . see what a . . . a terribly immature thing it-it-it is.

A moment later comes this expression:

C.: I wonder . . . I wonder how a child feels when they become disillusioned with their parents . . . a kind of feeling that . . . of . . . of not needing punishment. A . . . certainly finding no . . . satisfaction in it, a kind of point that . . . might be reached when it . . . isn't a satisfying kind of . . . experience to . . . perhaps . . . be the . . . the kind of a child who even . . . will do things to . . . be sure of holding the . . . attention of the . . . I mean, might even allow themselves to be punished. Of the . . . then . . . and in it is the element of . . . being disillusioned . . . a . . . and I-I feel right now . . . I somehow . . . I'm sure that very young people probably feel this.

T.: Your whole feeling is perhaps a little more akin to that of a child who might think in regard to his parents, "I see you as not all wise or all good. I do feel disillusioned. You're just not so important to me. It's neither so important to do things as you wish, nor even to do things against you in order to be sure of your interest in me." Is that a little bit . . . ?

C.: Something like that. M-hm. (Pause.) And then of course, I mean, there follows this . . . this *resentment* . . . this (pause) that I'm sure must be a very adolescent kind of thing because if I resent so much and yet most of the time feel that, well, I'm right . . . if a person is right, then why be so damn resentful. I'm . . . I-I . . . a. . . . (Pause.) It's really a pretty immature kind of thing. (Pause.)

T.: A very strong resentment, but you feel it's kind of a childish thing in its immaturity. (Long pause.)

C.: I don't know quite how one handles that kind of thing, and . . . (pause) and my feeling on that matter is just, well, let's wait; let's just wait, now, let's see.

What does it mean for the individual to become more open to his experience, more aware of elements previously denied? Mrs. Oak gives a vivid answer which seems much more sound than most of the descriptions in psychological or psychoanalytic treatises.

(*Sixteenth interview.*) *C.*: I think there's a. . . . . I think I've mentioned this before. A . . . loosening-up process taking place. Afraid (?) might . . . just get loose. (*Both laugh.*) But I feel a . . . a certain . . . a certain awareness. (Pause.)

T.: Sort of a loosening-up that means being more-more alive to yourself, more. . .

C.: Yeah. A certain kind of awareness. A . . . kind of letting things come through. A . . . (pause) and a kind of conviction that . . . (pause) what I have to do is . . . well, broadening the scope of my consciousness . . . to be able to handle these things. Which I think is . . . why I'm not really concerned too much about wanting to know why I'm impelled to face certain things. A . . . feeling of . . . well, of . . . regardless of what comes through, so to speak, from . . . bygone times . . . it's not really important. But important maybe in so far that it will help me to broaden the scope of . . . consciousness. A feeling that the . . . the answers are not to be found in the . . . subconscious, shall we say.

T.: M-hm. Sort of the feeling that if you can sufficiently broaden out this aliveness to an awareness of what comes through and what you experience, then somehow *that* is the important thing, not the things that happen to come through from the tie-up, is that . . . ?

C.: That's right. I feel that those things are only important in that they *do* come out. But they aren't the answers.

Throughout the interviews there are a number of references to the rhythm which the client feels in the therapeutic process. One of these is given below, from an interview where Mrs. Oak feels she is not very productive.

(*Seventeenth interview.*) *C.*: Well . . . course I know what's happening, I'm building. This is the strange thing; honestly, it's a pattern, you could say, a definite rhythm, I'm building, and I know it. I don't know when the words will come. I don't know from what area, from what . . . it really is.

T.: There's just a lot you don't know about it, but you do know that this is a getting ready and preparing for something.

C.: M-hm.

T.: From what direction it comes or what it'll be, you're content to wait and see. (Pause.)

C.: Course I'm beginning to understand many things that I . . . I was, that were only . . . intellectual . . . feelings before. And I think I can well understand in my own case, if there was any attempt at forcing this thing, by a . . . second . . . party, I would probably become frightened to death and just run. Well, we'll wait.

In the eighteenth interview she talks about the only way she can make progress in, for example, the sexual area. She gives an excellent picture of what it means to move ahead on this nonverbal, experiencing level which has come to mean so much to her. It is a temptation to quote at some length.

C.: But it seems to me what I-I actually have to work with here is not what I know, but it seems that the tools . . . that the only way to pull things into shape is to work with what it is I don't know.

A few minutes later, after further conversation about the sexual area, she says:

C.: But. . . . . No, the solution to this is again something on a nonverbal level. It's something that's got to take place. It's something that no amount of talking . . . or advice or . . . even a thought-out . . . a thought-out kind of behavior is going to do anything . . . much for. . . . . It's something on a nonverbal level, which I suppose is what we mean when we say, an emotional thing. (Long pause: 2 minutes, 45 seconds.) Each time I hit a . . . well, that sort of peak it's definitely the same thing. I'm vaguely conscious of a . . . a kind of shock, a . . . and when I say shock, I . . . mean it in a . . . very technical sense, not a . . . a kind of embarrassment, or a, I mean, in a sense. . .

T.: You don't mean morally shocked.

C.: No. A kind of shock that . . . if we could measure it here, I'm sure we'd find . . . it affects my whole nervous system, a . . . and it's coupled with either a feeling of pleasantness or unpleasantness. But I have this feeling, I mean, my deduction of the, what I feel takes place is that it's almost as though . . . there were impulses of new thought being somehow forced through, somehow a broadening.

T.: M-hm. At any rate, when you . . . when you hit one of these things that's very real, it seems as though it affects all of you, your whole nervous system, your whole organism. Almost as though it was creating new channels.

C.: Yes. A . . . kind . . . that's my deduction. I'm not conscious of it now. Later, I mean, I will get this feeling of a certain broadening of consciousness, a . . . not because I'm thinking of it. It'll sort of . . . of come to me fleetingly and go. I mean, a. . .

T.: Something that just happens, not a product of thinking about it, something . . . m-hm.

C.: That's right. (Pause.) In fact I hadn't even tried-tried before even in thinking to . . . to put what I feel . . . into words, but again, I mean, I'm saying what I feel impelled to say, and I . . . I felt that not in a way that seems very clear to me . . . a. . . (Pause.) I think there's a certain element of fear that has to be in experiences. Not as . . . I mean, as time goes on, as I understand them better. . . . I . . . probably not so much.

T.: That each one of these pretty vivid experiences brings a certain amount of fearfulness with it.

C.: Yeah. (Pause.) And yet I can handle them, which again implies a . . . a kind of . . . confidence in myself.

Along with the sense of rhythm which has been described goes a feeling on the part of the client that therapy cannot be forced. It is something that occurs inside.

(*Twenty-second interview.*) *C.*: I've gone into that before. This idea . . . of what one must bring *in* to a therapeutic situation. The . . . my husband's feeling that I mean, one must be . . . very sincere, very determined . . . must really *want* change. Well, the more I think about this thing, the more I'm convinced that actually, it's sort of affected to say, I am coming into this thing sincere, I want to change, I . . . I'm very determined and very honest. Because, not because they're just words. And . . . I don't know. I think maybe if you . . . just bring in yourself, and . . . just give yourself a chance, that's probably the answer. . . I feel that this is a . . . a period in my life that is kind of experimental . . . a . . . I, a feeling that I am willing to use *me*. It's just that clear.

Although Mrs. Oak very rarely mentions behavior changes on her own part, these sometimes are described. One interesting incident, in which she feels free to be angry, will illustrate this phase of the process.

(*Twenty-second interview.*) *C.*: (Long pause: 2 minutes, 15 seconds.) I think . . . really my relationship with . . . Peggy has come along on . . . almost leaps and bounds. It seems *awfully* good. I . . . as a sort of proving point, there has been a feeling, well, let's try to be as easy as possible. Let's know if the shoe pinches. And . . . at times, I mean, there has been a certain amount of . . . control on my part. But just last week end, we just both blew up at each other, and I just let her have it, and she let me have it. And I think it was very fine. I mean, no . . . hangover, no tensions, no nothing.

T.: M-hm. Somehow that seems like more proof than you'd had before that the relationship really was . . .

C.: Yeah.

T.: . . . better. That . . .

C.: Much better.

T.: . . . you didn't have to hold off from any negative feelings . . .

C.: That's right.

T.: . . . you just bring 'em out, both of you.

C.: That's right. And I mean, it was a good thing, too. I mean, it was sorta, kind of . . . her saying to me, "Now, you-you can't run my life." And me in . . . I in . . . turn saying, "No, I can't run your life, but I can certainly think my own . . . a . . . a . . . thoughts too." And I mean, it was a good *thing*. And . . . there was no hangover at all. Fact, sort of ended with both of us sort of laughing because we had become so darn dramatic over a . . . practically nothing . . . which is awfully good. I mean, that. . .

T.: Feel as though that relationship has really come a long way.

C.: Yeah. (Pause: 10 seconds.)

T.: To a point where you can either of you, I gather, be your real self in the relationship, and that is good.

Only rarely does the client refer to the process as being a living out of a normal growth, but at times this is her way of perceiving it, as is shown in the following account of the adolescent development she feels taking place within her.

(*Twenty-fourth interview.*) *C.*: . . . the . . . emotional conflict that I've felt with . . . Peggy . . . I mean, never actually felt, but apparently existed, was . . . seems to tie up . . . with what I'm led to believe and accept . . . is a part of this . . . emotional . . . well, just part of me that just didn't grow up. Immaturity doesn't quite express it.

T.: But it has to do with this adolescent view.

C.: Yeah. I'm beginning to . . . see this is . . . was probably a part. Actually I don't think I was ever aware of a real conflict until it . . . came out here. A kind of . . . competitiveness. Then I think it's of course very interesting that once it came out, it was quite shocking and . . . quite bad. It seems to be over.

T.: M-hm. That is, you mean when it came out, it was finished, almost.

C.: Yeah. But of course where it is interesting is that in the . . . the peeling *off* of that or the opening *up*, somehow . . . somehow put me in a position of . . . being able to remove the conflicts that I've felt within myself from her, and almost . . . almost begin a . . . process of acting *out* the *adolescent spurt* of growth myself. You see. I mean, I'm just beginning to see in a certain area what has happened.

A sense of the self-responsibility which she feels as well as her difficulty in dealing with the sexual area are illustrated in the following excerpt from the same interview.

C.: I think there's a lot to be done. I still think that. I mean we have this whole sexual area that I just . . . I just don't know how to . . . start. Not because of . . . reticence. But again because I have the feeling that . . . it'll, it will have to, it'll have to be worked out. That just as I . . . one area I slipped into, and made . . . pretty good progress, really. I think. Now this is an area that I have the feeling I'm . . . I've got to have to . . . there . . . well, I'm just not ready yet. I don't know.

T.: Is this the kind of thing that you're saying? That you know perfectly well that there's that whole area of sexual relationships and so on, that at some point will be . . . you'll work into it, but that it's . . . the expression of that is something that's got to happen, not something that can be forced, and that *hasn't* happened yet. Is that . . . ?

C.: That's it . . . that's it. I know it's there. I know it's a part of the whole. And it all ties in. But it's . . . let's see, it's . . . it's as though . . . well, I just haven't found the jumping-off spot yet, the . . . the way, the method.

A new note also comes into expression in this same interview, foreshadowing later feelings about the relationship.

C.: But I think that's what I meant, that in the, in the therapeutic . . . situation there are times when it's "I," and times when it's "we."

T.: M-hm. There are times when it is really a shared relationship of feeling, and there are times when it is you, with your feelings.

C.: Yeah. Never consciously, I'm sure.

The place and the meaning of therapy in a total context are well described in a very brief passage in which she weighs the relative significance of circumstance and self.

(*Twenty-fifth interview.*) *C.*: The fact *remains* that the situation is what it is and . . . maybe in a different situation, I'd have different problems. But . . . kind of feeling . . . that . . . it's really not all me.

T.: There is quite a deep feeling along that line . . . that this is not all me. It's the situation in which life has placed me.

C.: Yeah. And still . . . a rather *private* conviction that . . . there isn't anything I can do except with the *me*.

Many of the significant experiences of therapy occurred outside of the interviews themselves. Here is a description of one of these.

(*Twenty-fifth interview.*) *C.*: (Long pause: 2 minutes, 30 seconds.) I'm quite ashamed of myself in the night. I just was. . . I wasn't feeling well, and I began to go over this whole thing . . . and . . . it was just this . . . well, feeling of . . . frustration, weepiness . . . and . . . I don't know, just involving all kinds of things about myself. . . . . And then . . . being confronted with, well, why don't you do something? And not *knowing* why. (Pause: 19 seconds.) Fighting . . . fighting all kinds of . . . possible reasons, some of them flattering, some of them very . . . uncomplimentary. And yet actually the part that really gets me is not being able to . . . say, well *this* is the reason. Or it's . . . it may be a combination of this and that. . . Actually not knowing why. And just sort of filing it, just giving the whole thing up in a sort of complete frustration. Sort of thinking, oh, to hell with it. And . . . sort of dozing off to sleep. And . . . of waking with sort of a jolt. With a . . . wishful thinking, shall we say? I don't know, but it was a something . . . a feeling, "Well, you *can* do something about it. You *can*, and you will." And then, well, I mean, sort of . . . well, shall we say, maybe hopeful.

Twenty-sixth through Fortieth Interviews

There was another experience, coming between the twenty-ninth and thirtieth sessions, which Mrs. Oak later referred to as the most meaningful point in therapy for her. She opens the thirtieth interview with an account of it.

C.: Well, I made a very remarkable discovery. I know it's . . . (*Laughs.*) I found out that you actually *care* how this thing goes. (*Both laugh.*) It gave me the feeling, it's sort of well . . . maybe-I'll-let-you-get-in-the-act sort of thing. It's . . . again you see, on an examination sheet, I would have had the correct answer, I mean . . . but it suddenly dawned on me that in the . . . client-counselor kind of thing, you *actually care* what happens to this thing. And it was a . . . revelation, a . . . not that. That doesn't describe it. It was a . . . well . . . the closest I can come to it is a kind of relaxation, a . . . not letting down, but a . . . (pause) more of a kind of straightening out without tension if that means anything. I don't know.

T.: Sounds as though it isn't as though this was a new idea, but it was a new *experience* of really *feeling* that I did care and if I get the rest of that, sort of a willingness on your part to let me care.

A moment later she relates this experience to her own feeling toward people.

C.: The next thing that occurred to me, that I found myself thinking and still thinking, is somehow . . . and I'm not clear why . . . the same kind of a caring that I get when I say, "I don't love humanity." Which has always sort of . . . I mean I was always convinced of it. So I mean, it doesn't . . . I knew that it was a good thing, see. And I think I clarified it within myself . . . what it has to do with this situation, I don't know. But I found out, no, I don't love, but I do *care terribly*.

A little later she amplifies somewhat the way in which the relationship has changed now that she can permit the therapist's feeling for her to enter her experience.

C.: I mean, the same thing to a certain extent . . . has happened in here. I mean there's been this tearing-through the thing myself. Almost to . . . I mean, I felt it . . . I mean, I tried to . . . verbalize it on occasion . . . a kind of . . . at times almost, not wanting you to restate, not wanting you to reflect, the thing is *mine*. Course, all right, I can say it's resistance. But that doesn't mean a damn thing to me now. But I mean, which . . . you see, makes me feel that it's a more subtle thing than just not wanting to . . . appear strong. Because . . . well, consciously anyway, I certainly don't care here. The . . . I think in . . . relationship to this particular thing, I mean, the . . . probably at times, the strongest feeling was, it's mine, it's *mine*. I've got to cut it down myself. See?

T.: It's an experience it's awfully hard to put down accurately into words, and yet I get a sense of difference here in this relationship, that from the feeling that, this is mine. I've got to do it, I am doing it, and so on, to a somewhat different feeling that . . . "I could let you in."

C.: Yeah. Now. I mean, that's . . . that it's . . . well, it's sort of, shall we say, volume two. It's . . . it's a . . . well, sort of, well, I'm still in the thing alone, but I'm *not* . . . see . . . I'm. . .

T.: M-hm. Yes, that paradox sort of sums it up, doesn't it?

C.: Yeah.

It seems that this very meaningful interview is followed by one in which doubt and vacillation and resentment toward the therapist are evident. Two excerpts will indicate something of this phase of the process.

(*Thirty-first interview.*) *C.*: You know, I sort of have a feeling that . . . (pause) I'm sort of in the middle of . . . an experience, of a growth process. Well, not of conflict. There's a feeling that . . . I've got to go forward simply because I can't go back. But if I . . . were given a choice. . . I mean, if it were something of more or less . . . well, something I were buying, I might very much be tempted to go back.

T.: You feel very betwixt and between them. It somehow seems almost impossible to go back. Yet, if that were really a free choice between going backward and forward, there's lots to be said for going back. (Pause.)

C.: M-hm. (Long pause: 2 minutes, 15 seconds.) I don't know. I'm awf-quite upset. I just can't look at it yet. (Pause.)

A minute later.

C.: I don't know just why this comes out, but maybe if it's out, maybe it'll help. Maybe it'll be just curtains. Mean, I am sure I never did . . . t-tell you my past . . . I mean, I just realized it myself . . . weapon that I had. I mean my sure-fire resistance that always worked for me. And it's, course, it's the fact that I can say this, this proves what a . . . the kind of a climate this is. But I always get the feeling, and it's . . . always directed to you. You don't add a damn thing to my status. And it's . . . it's always helped me to . . . now that I've said it, maybe it just won't work any more, you see.

T.: At this point there's always very strongly the feeling, "You don't add a *damn thing!*"

C.: That's right. Not a damn thing to my status somehow to. . . (Pause.)

T.: Sounds like a feeling of annoyance and pulling away.

C.: M-hm.

T.: A little bit of resentment.

C.: Course, now that I've caught on to it, it's not going to work too well.

T.: Kinda spoils it as a weapon.

Having expressed this doubt and resentment, the client is also able to experience, in this same interview, two very deep aspects of her feeling.

C.: And I have the feeling that it isn't guilt. (Pause.) (*Weeps.*) So . . . course I mean, I can't verbalize it yet. It's just being *terribly hurt!*

T.: M-hm. It isn't guilt except in the sense of being very much wounded somehow.

C.: (*Weeping.*) It's . . . you know, often I've been guilty of it myself, but in later years, when I've heard parents . . . say to their children, "Stop crying," I've had a feeling, instead I've thought it through, so that . . . I mean . . . a hurt as though, well, why should they tell them to stop crying? They feel sorry for themselves, and who can feel more adequate-a-a-adequately sorry for himself than a child. Well, that is sort of what . . . I mean, as-as though I mean, I-I thought that they should let him cry. And . . . feel sorry for him too, maybe. In a . . . rather objective kind of way. Well, that's . . . that's something of the kind of thing I've been experiencing. I mean, now . . . just right now. And in-in . . .

T.: That catches a little more the flavor of the feeling, that it's almost as if you're really weeping for yourself. . . . .

C.: And then of course, I've come to . . . to see and to feel that over this . . . see, I've covered it up. (*Weeps.*) But . . . and . . . I've covered it up with so much *bitterness*, which in turn I had to cover up. (*Weeps.*) *That's* what I want to get rid of! I almost don't *care* if I hurt.

T.: (*Gently.*) You feel that here at the basis of it, as you experienced it, is a feeling of real tears for yourself. But that you *can't* show, mustn't show, so that's been covered by bitterness that you don't like, that you'd like to be rid of. You almost feel you'd rather absorb the hurt than to . . . than to feel the bitterness. (*Pause.*) And what you seem to be saying quite strongly is, "I do *hurt*, and I've tried to cover it up."

C.: I didn't *know* it.

T.: M-hm. Like a new discovery really.

C.: (*Speaking at the same time.*) I never really did know. But it's . . . you know, it's almost a physical thing. It's . . . it's sort of as though I-I-I were looking within myself at all kinds of . . . nerve endings and-and bits of-of . . . things that have been sort of mashed. (*weeping.*)

T.: As though some of the most delicate aspects of you—physically almost—have been crushed or hurt.

C.: Yes. And you know, I do get the feeling, oh, you poor thing. (Pause.)

T.: Just can't help but feel very deeply sorry for the person that is you.

Two interviews later she is able to experience quite the opposite side of herself. The excerpt below comes from the final moments of the interview and contains one of the few references in the interview to her research tasks.

(*Thirty-third interview*.) *C*.: One thing worries me . . . and I'll hurry because I can always go back to it—a feeling that occasionally I can't turn out. A feeling of being quite pleased with myself. Again the Q-technique. I walked out of here one time, and impulsively I threw my first card, "I am an attractive personality"; looked at it sort of aghast but left it there, I mean, because honestly, I mean, that is exactly how it felt . . . a. . . Well, that bothered me, and I catch that now. Every once in a while a sort of pleased feeling, nothing superior, but just . . . I don't know, sort of pleased. A neatly turned way. And it bothered me. And yet . . . I wonder . . . I rarely remember things I say here, I mean I wondered why it was that I was convinced, and . . . something about what I've felt about being hurt that I suspected in . . . my feeling when I would hear someone say to a child, "Don't cry." I mean, I always felt, but it isn't right; I mean, if he's hurt, let him cry. Well, then, now this pleased feeling that I have. I've recently come to feel, it's . . . there's something almost the same thing. It's . . . we don't object when *children* feel pleased with themselves. It's . . . I mean, there really isn't anything vain. It's . . . maybe that's how people *should* feel.

T.: You've been inclined almost to look askance at yourself for this feeling, and yet, as you think about it more, maybe it comes close to the two sides of the picture, that if a child wants to cry, why shouldn't he cry? And if he wants to feel pleased with himself, doesn't he have a perfect right to feel pleased with himself? And that sort of ties in with this, what I would see as an appreciation of yourself that you've experienced every now and again.

C.: Yes. Yes.

T.: "I'm really a pretty rich and interesting person."

C.: Something like that. And then I say to myself, "Our society pushes us around, and we've lost it." And I keep going back to my feelings about children. Well, maybe they're richer than we are. Maybe we . . . it's something we've lost in the process of growing up.

T.: Could be that they have a wisdom about that that we've lost.

C.: That's right.

Another section which Mrs. Oak also referred to later as being a very meaningful part of therapy can only be presented in a rather lengthy and incoherent quotation which is, however, full of psychological meaning. She is exploring the quality of her own basic nature and comes to a deeply significant though tentative conclusion.

(*Thirty-fourth interview.*) *C.*: I'd like to be able to utilize it, to . . . as a kind of descending into this thing . . . of . . . you know it's . . . it's as though . . . I . . . I don't know, damn, I'd sort of . . . sort of acquired some place, and picked up . . . all along the way, and some beyond my way, a . . . a certain instinct, and I don't mean instinct when I say that, a . . . for all that has happened, a . . . the . . . things that have happened to you and why they've happened, and . . . and the result. The . . . a kind of acquaintance with the structure. An . . . almost as though I knew it brick for brick kind of . . . thing. Ah, it's a something that . . . an awareness . . . I mean, that . . . of . . . a feeling of not being fooled, of not being drawn into the thing. And a . . . critical sense, a . . . of knowingness. But in a way . . . the reason it's hidden and . . . I mean, it almost is a part of . . . it's a part of me, but it somehow can't be a part of everyday life. And there's something of . . . at times I feel almost a little bit terrible in the thing, but again terrible not as terrible. And why? I think I know. And it's . . . it's an exciting thing too. Because it's hidden, and . . . it's hidden, well, then . . . I mean, it's . . . just somehow, I mean it just isn't something that . . . can intrude into any place but with me. And . . . it can't . . . it isn't something that I've learned to use. It's something that can occasionally excite me. And . . . I want to put it out. It's like . . . well, because I guess maybe I am the kind of . . . person that likes to, I mean, probably even torment myself, or . . . to chase things down, to try to find the whole. And I've told myself, "Now look, this is a . . . pretty strong kind of feeling which you have. It isn't constant. But you feel it sometimes, and, as you let yourself feel it, you feel it yourself" . . . you know, there are words for that kind of thing that one could find in abnormal psychology. Might almost be like the . . . feeling that is occasionally is . . . attributed to things you read about. I mean, there are some elements there . . . I mean, this pulsation, this excitement, this knowing. And . . . I've said . . . I tracked down one thing, I mean, I was very, very . . . very brave, what shall we say . . . say . . . a sublimated sex drive. And I thought, well, *there* I've got it. I've really solved the thing. And that there's nothing more to it than that. And . . . for a while I mean I . . . I was quite pleased with myself. That was it. And then I had to admit, no, that wasn't it. 'Cause that . . . that's something that had been with me . . . long before . . . I became so terribly frustrated sexually. I mean, that wasn't . . . and, but in the thing, then I began to see . . . a little, within this very core is . . . an acceptance of sexual relationship, I mean, the only kind that *I* would think would be possible . . . it was in this thing. It's not something that's been . . . I mean, sex hasn't been sublimated or substituted there. No. Within this, within what I know there . . . I mean, it's a different kind of . . . sexual feeling to be sure. I mean, it's one that is stripped of all the . . . the things that have happened to sex, if you know what I mean. There's no . . . no chase, no pursuit, no . . . battle, no . . . well, no kind of hate, which I think, seems to me, has crept into such things. And yet, I mean, this . . . feeling has been . . . oh, a little bit disturbing.

T.: I'd like to see if I can capture a little of what that means to you. It is as you've gotten very deeply acquainted with yourself on kind of a brick-by-brick experiencing basis, and in that sense you have become more *self*-ish, and the notions of really . . . a in the discovering of what is the core of you as separate from all the other aspects, you come across the realization, which is a very deep and pretty thrilling realization, that the core of this self is not only without hate but is really something more resembling a saint, something really very pure, is the word I would use. And that-that. . . You can try to depreciate that. You can say., maybe it's a sublimation, maybe it's an abnormal manifestation, screwball, and so on. But inside of yourself you know that it isn't. This contains the feelings which could contain rich sexual expression, but it sounds bigger than, and really deeper than, that. And yet fully able to include all that could be a part of sex expression.

C.: It's probably something like that. . . . . I mean, it's kind of a descent. It's a going down where you might almost think it should be going up, but no, it's . . . I'm sure of it; it's a kind of going down.

T.: This is a going down and immersing yourself in your self almost.

C.: Yeah. And I . . . I can't just throw it aside. I mean, it . . . it just . . . just seems, oh, it just *is*. I mean, it seems an awfully important thing that I just . . . had to say.

T.: I'd like to pick up one of those things too, to see if I understand it. That sounds as though this sort of idea you're expressing is something you must be going up to capture, something that *isn't* quite. Actually though, the feeling is, "This is a going-down to capture something that's more deeply there."

C.: It is. It really. . . There's something to that which is . . . I mean, this . . . I have a way, and of course sometimes we're going to have to go into that . . . of . . . rejecting . . . almost violently, that which is righteous, that which is good. I would suppose though that there's a kind of rejection of . . . the ideal, the . . . as . . . and that expressed it; I mean, that's sort of what I mean. One is a going up . . . into I don't know, I mean, I just have a feeling, I can't follow. I mean, it's . . . it's pretty thin stuff if you ever start knocking it down. This one went . . . I wondered why . . . I mean, has this awfully definite feeling of descending.

T.: That this isn't going up into the thin ideal. This is a going-down into the astonishingly solid reality.

In the next interview she puts more coherently one portion of what she has discovered.

(*Thirty-fifth interview.*) *C.*: Then there's something else . . . a feeling that's starting . . . to grow; well, to be almost formed, as I say. A . . . this kind of conclusion that I'm going to stop looking for something *terribly* wrong. Now I don't know why. But I mean, just . . . it's this kind of thing. I-I'm sort of pretty *sure* . . . I've ruled out fear, and I'm positive I'm not afraid of shock . . . I mean, I sort of would have welcomed it. But . . . in view of the places I've been, what I learned there, then also kind of, well, taking into consideration what I don't know, sort of, maybe this is one of the things that I'll have to date, and say, "Well, now, I've just . . . I just can't find it." See? And now without any . . . without, I should say, any sense of . . . apology or covering up, just sort of a simple statement of what, at *this* time, appears to be fact.

T.: Does this catch it? That . . . as you've gone more and more deeply into yourself, and as you think about the kind of things that you've discovered and learned and so on, the conviction grows very, very strong that, no matter how far you go, the things that you're going to find are not dire and awful. They have a very different character.

C.: Yes, something like that. Something like that.

It is at this point that she first discusses the feeling that the end of therapy may be in sight.

(*Thirty-sixth interview.*) *C.*: Well, I think one of the things I wanted to see if I can do . . . is to put some of the things I'm feeling into a . . . street clothes. I don't know. I mean, I don't feel myself getting into it, but (pause) seems to me that's what I'd like to do if I could. (Pause.) Maybe I can get into it from a different way. Let's just say . . . well, think I'll just drop it. (Pause.) I might . . . sort of let . . . some thoughts catch up with me. A . . . one of the things that's been formulating, a kind of growing in . . . in a . . . shape, into some kind of shape, is this . . . first recognizing it, yes, I felt dependent on *this* thing. I think a change coming there, a . . . growing into something else. It a . . . it, it has its meaning on the outside in that . . . well, the recordings don't bother me, I mean, not in the *least*. I mean it's . . . at one time there was this feeling of, just that. . . . Oooh. Now, I mean, just, this seems to me the only ego involvement I-I would feel would be. Oooh, what deplorable grammar, what . . . what terrible mispronunciation, what . . . possible contradictions. But I mean, aside from that, it just sort of has no meaning at all, just . . . a . . . a, well, just that's that, kind of . . . a thing, and you're welcome. I mean, that's the kind of outside feeling. Then there's another kind of feeling that I feel is something that, well, grew from this, "Yes, I feel the dependency," the, a, knowledge it's a . . . (*sighs*). I feel as being comparable to the feeling that (pause) that you sometimes get, I'm sure that . . . everyone gets, feels . . . when you're just about finishing up a . . . very meaningful kind of a (pause) book. A . . . a certain feeling of almost being a little sorry to know there's a few pages left, and a little regret . . . a-a, sort of wishing that, well . . . a, sort of, it just seems so darn meaningful . . . a-a, that you wish you could prolong it. And then a-a sort of feeling I had, well, really, I mean, you do close the book, you finally do close the book. And, a, yes, there's regret, still . . . well, it's been awfully good; it's sort of with you, and you can still have the book and feel the book, you can touch the book, or . . . kind of occurs to you that you can give the book *away*, and yet if need be . . . go back to it . . . somehow go back to it. I mean, I feel this kind of thing . . . a (pause).

In this interview and the following one she discusses quite freely the fact that she has not fully resolved the area of sexual conflict. The factual picture she gives seems to match that given by the TAT. The contrast is in the tone. The TAT analysis of the post-therapy test pictures "the sexual area as a very sensitive one indeed. The panic reaction is not so strong, but she is evasive and defensive here." Here are Mrs. Oak's comments on the sexual area.

(*Thirty-sixth interview.*) *C.*: Because I mean, a kind of feeling that, well, one just doesn't battle there. If it's a battle, it's . . . I don't know *what*, but it's accomplishing nothing. (Pause: 9 seconds.) I don't know what, now, I mean, I'm confronted with a . . . the thing and it's kind of a high step . . . the . . . feeling of, well, I mean, almost quoting . . . paragraph such and such . . . "as to a sex outlet, the patient remains *neurotic*." You know (*fondly*), I'm beginning to have a kind of easiness about *that;* a kind of, well . . . (*smilingly*) at least . . . maybe so, but no . . . well . . . but maybe that's just one of those . . . I mean, comes to me again it's strange though that kind of gets me off. . . I said once, certain passageways are . . . probably blocked . . . are blocked up. I feel maybe I should explore them. Well, maybe . . . maybe this . . . maybe it will . . . *have* to stay blocked, and it's just a question of . . . where I drop matches. I don't know. A . . . I can't see myself pursuing a . . . a kind of . . . back-street affair. I mean it just isn't very . . . well, it just wouldn't be me. It's just kind of . . . nothing shocking, but . . . just doesn't . . . isn't my language.

T.: And it may say in the books that, with no sex outlet, you would have to be neurotic, but you can sort of look at that with a different attitude . . . just, well, maybe. But maybe there are some areas that, that you can't quite clear up.

C.: Yeah.

T.: At least that the alternative answers such as going out to *seek* a sex life, as it were, just aren't *you.*

C.: Just. Unh-unh. No. . .

(*Thirty-seventh interview.*) *C.*: There's still . . . I mean, there's . . . a few little fronts. There's a . . . I mean, there's the area of sexual relationship, but . . . I won't . . . I mean, I realize now that I-I-I could probably rationalize the thing outside; I couldn't here. I went as far as I did. And I knew it. And it's sort . . . I mean, that it's alright with me. I mean that's the way it *should* be. That's sort of . . . that . . . in that particular area, that's my salvation . . . that I stop now; I mean, that's as far as . . . so, I mean, that to, that wasn't what we wanted, but there isn't very much to say.

T.: You went as far as you were ready to go or felt it helpful to go and stopped at that point in that area.

C.: That's right. That's right.

There is much in the closing interviews which is quotable, but a great deal of it would be repetition of themes already illustrated. Perhaps three additional excerpts, all from the thirty-ninth interview, can close our account of the process as it occurred in this series. In the first she expresses the realization of the scope of the implications of her therapeutic experience.

C.: Well of course I think I mentioned the . . . I mean, how far I feel this thing really carries over in just amazing kind of areas. It's . . . oh, it's just sort of unbelievable. Things of importance, and things not so important. . . . . Oh, I mean I could tie it up with my war e-e-experience when we found ourselves in the midst of a national scandal kind of thing. The . . . well, I was sent down there and rea-realized, "My God, what terrible things are happening to people down here." Mean, knowing what had to be done and working to get this democratic . . . process rolling. And . . . knowing, you see, and yet the terrible frustration of knowing that the educational process would take hundreds of years. And I mean, now knowing that my own frustration was just because I couldn't bring into this thing a kind of climate. A . . . I mean, I know what was lacking, see. I mean, it's that it just branches out, I mean, where I find myself saying to myself, "Well, this is the most, it's the damnedest, most revolutionary thing I've ever encountered."

There are also two rather vivid reactions to the relationship and what it has meant to her.

C.: That's right. It's terrific. (Pause.) And then, of course, I mean there is a certain pulling from behind what in my thinking is probably the most dramatic episode. The realization at a certain point, a kind of diathermy had actually been set up, a . . . something that could be measured, if it could be. I mean, just that, a kind of . . . kind of radiant warmth which completely restores. . . .

C.: (Later.) I mean, I still don't believe it that I'm going to just casually walk out. Well, of course I'm going to do it. But I'm never going to believe it, never. I . . . I mean it's just one of those things in talking about therapy and all these things . . . I can see, I mean how this is different. I mean I've heard all kinds of jokes, I mean because I have friends in deep analysis, I mean who are talking about transference to me and what I'm missing, and I mean answering, "Well, you can't fall in love with a microphone, you know . . . really, you just can't do it." (*Laughs.*) But, on the other hand, I'm never going to be casual about you. I mean, a contact has been established that's going to carry on, and I want it that way. So. . .

T.: Something that has a very real meaning. . .

C.: That's right. But I think I've gone as far as I can go.

T.: Okay.

C.: And I think it's been pretty thorough. I hope. And . . . well, I mean, there are a lot of little ends. . .

In the two weeks following the "end" of therapy (which concluded with the fortieth interview) Mrs. Oak came in for two additional sessions, simply talking into the recording machine, the therapist being out of town. These were vivid and meaningful sessions. In the first such session she talked at some length about the meaning which the therapist had begun to have for her, during the last interview and since that time—that suddenly she was much more aware of him as a person, more aware of his clothes, his movements, his personality.

(*First self-recorded session.*) *C.*: The thread to the thing was a-a . . . being aware I mean . . . that . . . at that session, I had . . . had sort of run the a-a, the whole gamut of-of very complex and very evolv-involved emotional feelings about my therapist. I . . . a sense of-of . . . a kind of pride in . . . something that I-I interpreted as a kind of courage, a . . . a kind of . . . of tenderness which was . . . that developed, of a sense of understanding, a kind—a very personal kind of understanding which-which actually, I mean . . . which actually couldn't be personal. It's just because I-I know nothing about my therapist. A kind of brilliance, and this over-all feeling of-of . . . of really, I mean, of a . . . I mean, quite a guy, leaving with that feeling, leaving very satisfied; satisfied with-with-with the sessions and the relationship.

With this acceptance of the close personal relationship on her part came "a very special bonus."

C.: The telling myself . . . that when I had walked out of the counseling room on that day, I had walked out knowing . . . actually knowing, and later of course, confirming, that I would never again in my life need a father. . . Just that. It's *just* that. (Pause.) And . . . a . . . here-here again, I-I sense what seems to me to be so *awfully* important, a realization that . . . that actually I didn't have to *know* that; that actually I-I . . . it would have been the same whether I knew it or not, that it isn't necessary to verbalize those things.

From the second of these sessions we shall take only one excerpt—an expression of deep feeling which was first worked through very incoherently with much weeping and then restated somewhat more clearly.

C.: It seems to me that what I'm saying is that somewhere, (pause) very deep in self, is a kind of force, which-which apparently seems clearer to me in terms of a flame, a (pause) a flame which is, is cold, ah, so very, very, ah (pause), crystal, and that isn't the word, but so much generated, so much heat generated, ah, that it's cold, and-and, so bright that ah, it's almost, you can't, you can't look through it, it's a kind of blinding, then it seems to me that I said, that it is the individual, ah, who has somehow gotten there, has somehow made the journey. It begins to-to (pause) it somehow may be a terrible journey, I mean, there *is* something of that in it, and it seems to me that-that if I can just not be afraid of the word. Well anyway, ah, if once they've gotten there, a sort of having dared, and then begin to walk away, to walk back up the road, backward, facing this thing, and just-just, a very little way, they begin to feel the warmth, and see the color. I guess what I'm saying, I know I'm saying, is that it's kind of big. . . And of course this ties up so completely with my conflict. . . . . the apparent rejection of a love philosophy. (Pause.) I *know* what it is, it's a feeling that so much in this love philosophy. . . . . is too far off the road, a kind of thing that has turned its back on this flame of self.

We may close our account of the first forty interviews with this characteristically allegorical or poetic expression of Mrs. Oak in which she reaffirms her deep conviction that constructive social relationships grow out of a full appreciation of the force and power of self, not a turning of one's back on self.

Forty-first through Forty-eighth Interviews

It will be recalled that Mrs. Oak returned, at the time of the first follow-up, for additional interviews, saying that there were a few more things she wanted to clear up and that she did not think it would take long. Some have expressed surprise that a client who was "through with therapy" should return. Actually this has been a very common experience with therapists of a client-centered orientation. If therapy is thought of as a "cure" for an "illness," then a return to therapy would seem as though the cure had been unsuccessful. But where therapy is conceived as learning to experience and be one's self, then it is a process which can go on through a lifetime, and returning to the atmosphere of therapy for a temporary acceleration of this process is not a matter for surprise. It has been our experience that clients use such returns to push ahead from where they are rather than to rework old material. The reader will perhaps be able to judge from the excerpts which follow whether this statement applies to Mrs. Oak.

The sociologist would be especially interested in Mrs. Oak's description of the risk of defining one's self, as compared with the security of accepting a definition of self from others.

(*Forty-first interview, speaking of the "challenge of responsibility" which therapy had meant for her.*) *C.*: I really wondered, when did this happen; did . . . when did I first start dodging this responsibility? And of course, I don't know; I really don't know. Probably, probably sometime oh, when . . . when I was very, very young. But I-I-I have sometimes realized (*whispering*), "By golly, you *are* different; you aren't really this-this thing that people think you are". . . . . And then all along the line the-the . . . the acceptance of-of others' definitions, really. The-the-the thought that—I don't know this, I think it, I don't know, but I was going to say that thinking perhaps that there is—there is more security in-in the definitions of o-o-other people for your "I." I don't know, I'm sure I was never . . . I certainly was never very clear on the subject.

An important theme of this second series of interviews had to do with relationships—the relationship to the therapist, especially, and also relationships with others. Two excerpts will illustrate some of her thinking about this theme.

(*Forty-second interview.*) *C.*: You see as the thing went on—I wasn't actually . . . too aware of you, I mean I was aware of certain . . . certain forces . . . shall we say. As a person I don't think aware of you other than putting my coat on your chair. So I was through with therapy. Well, that of course was a very delightful kind of thing, but then later, you see, *much* later, the impact of-of-of this human contact hit me, along with so many other things, so many other significant things. See . . . well, at that time it disturbed me very much; it disturbed me psychologically, shall we say, as a psychological approach to this thing . . . as being a transference . . . I rather gag on the term, really I do. . . . .

C.: (Later.) Actually what I'm saying is . . . it's aw- it's impossible to-to . . . in the accepted terms, to *love* someone else. The moment you do . . . and it seems, it seems to me that's probably the secret of therapy, is this, is this (*sighs*). I can't say *not* loving, until I go on . . . and . . . say what-what . . . what loving in its . . . accepted concept seems to me to be. But the moment you-you accept that concept and the moment you say, "I love," then there's somehow . . . the other person becomes a justification to your own . . . well, for your life. So you see, I mean I capture that point. If what I have discovered before, if all of these things I felt about myself are true, then that has to be true for me too. (Pause.) I don't know. . . It's frightening. . . It's frightening. Because I don't (*sighs*) . . . it isn't the kind of thing that's easily understood.

T.: What it really means is that . . . that love as it is culturally defined and understood is for you really fallacious because it means finding the-the reason or the justification for *yourself* in this other person.

C.: And that isn't really possible, I don't think . . . it isn't possible. Now isn't that true of therapy, am I wrong? See I found that here, somehow. Now isn't that true? . . . . . There might, there might be something I don't know what it is. I mean there might . . . there might be a communication . . . rather than "I love you" . . . now I'm thinking, I'm talking about a therapeutic situation, I don't know. . . There might be a recognition . . . a projection . . . of this, of this, of this bit of self-love that one has, . . . this secretness . . . so that rather not "I love" but that "You are my love." I think that there might be something to that. I don't quite know.

Another theme which recurs from time to time in these interviews is her changing attitude toward being a woman. In the forty-fifth interview she speaks of various things she has learned since the end of therapy and includes this:

C.: I began learning, oh, a lot of other things . . . (pause) one for-for-for instance, rather shocking thing to me. . . I just-just stopped rejecting the feminine role, just . . . well, I mean, quite by magic. Which of course, really I wasn't aware of; I just . . . how can one do it and be so completely . . . I might have recognized why yes, there was something wrong, but always got powerful guilt feelings in the end. (Words lost.) But I hadn't realized the extent of. . .

T.: But in some way that you don't understand, and don't understand how you could have been blind to it before, . . .

C.: No. No. It's *just* amazing. And, of course, I couldn't bring it out any place but here, I'm sure.

T.: . . . you find that it isn't so necessary to protest against being a woman.

C.: Yeah. It's kind of amaz-kind of an amazing thing. And there's-there's a difference, believe me, in-in . . . there's a difference in the way a man lights my cigarette. Now, that doesn't seem believable. And of course, I'm-I'm still just-just a little bit amazed by the whole thing; sort of a, oh my, a little bit shocked by it, I think.

Often in these interviews she includes a theme with a minor key —that to live in the way which therapy has opened up for her involves a type of loneliness, a differing with the culture, a pain-in-pleasure experience which has much meaning for her. A lengthy excerpt from the forty-fifth interview conveys this theme and some of her other feelings toward therapy.

C.: However, I mean, again, realistically, you see, and of course that's going to be a conflict in life, you see, realistically. I mean, very soon, *you* are going to be simply a book. Now that's pretty damn insulting, really. Sort of on a par of . . . how we used to feel when we were very young and were kinda shocked to learn that all great men weren't dead; I mean, you-you felt that. It is interesting. But I don't think I'm to blame for that. It-it-it's . . . it's (*whispering*) pretty—. You see, it-it . . . it's a cultural thing, it-it's the . . . the realism that . . . well, that . . . will let you have-have a report of the atomic-bomb testing with your coffee. It-it's the . . . (pause) realism of-of . . . it seems to me, very peculiar kinds of values, primarily based on . . . "it-it's forbidden." That-that's the world, you see, all of these things, I mean, the world outside, of realism . . . I-I'm beginning to think I'm more than a little bit contemptuous of it. Not just conflict, not just resistance to, but just the kind of contempt for . . . (pause). . .

T.: Is this it? That you're saying that our relationship has been very meaningful, that, in the future, it looks as though that would . . . be ended, and I would just be a book . . . and that, you feel, is fairly necessary in terms of the culture. Yet, you can't help but look with a certain amount of contempt upon the artificial realities that the culture imposes.

C.: M-hm. Precisely. Yeah. Hits it *very* well. Oh, and then of course, too, (pause) I . . . I have a hunch I'm not coming back; I'm coming back once more, or twice more, but I've a hunch I'm through with therapy.

T.: This time you would be . . .

C.: Yeah.

T.: . . . really finished.

C.: M-hm. I may be wrong.

T.: You're not trying to be dogmatic about this, but it's just the feeling . . .

C.: Yeah. Yeah.

T.: . . . about it.

C.: And it's based on-on . . . on something pretty doggoned deep, a-a . . . a feeling that (pause) sort of, that from here on in, I'm sort of going to have to play this thing on my own, with my own ship. And . . . I'm scared. (Pause.)

T.: It seems like a slightly . . . lonesome and risky affair.

C.: Yeah. Well, I mean it's a little bit more than that, or not quite that. 'Cause actually, really on one side and what I consider it, actually I wouldn't . . . I wouldn't trade my loneliness for-for anything in the world; it's too, it's too much, it's too much me. I couldn't, or I wouldn't be me.

T.: So that the loneliness that comes from being you, you'll take and . . .

C.: Yeah.

T.: . . . you wouldn't trade it for anything.

C.: I'll take . . . I mean, knowing . . . somehow knowing, and I may . . . I mean, that may be something that works out, although I don't think so. Knowing that . . . that I'm not going to win, see. Of course, that scares me.

T.: Feeling that . . . it is certain to be a losing battle in some way, and yet . . .

C.: M-hm.

T.: . . . yet, you wouldn't back out of it.

C.: I-it seems to me the only thing I can think of is-is . . . Saint Matthew said it, I think: "rejoice and be exceedingly glad" that . . . (Pause.)

T.: A—that kind of . . . paradoxical . . .

C.: That's it.

T.: . . . rejoicing in, I don't know what terms, something negative that . . .

C.: No, it isn't negative. . . . . I don't know, I mean, it-th-the only kind of imagery that I can bring into the thing is-is a feeling sometimes of-of . . . walking through life, with the whole goddamn world just kind of-of . . . going to . . . to pieces, and-and kind of picking my way, and still this sense of-of "rejoice and be exceedingly glad." . . . So, I suppose there is, there is the-the . . . element of-of the thing being negative.

T.: I guess you're saying that that description sounds paradoxical, and to you, it really isn't; it's all one piece.

C.: That's right. That's right.

At times Mrs. Oak shows profound insight as to the dynamics which have operated in her. In the forty-sixth interview, speaking of her past struggles to express anxiety, she says:

C.: Maybe we are settling what is neurosis. I don't know. Yes, I really think that is precisely what I mean, is that because you can't . . . I don't know why, but you somehow aren't permitted to recognize the . . . aren't permitted . . . I don't know if I mean that, I think I do, because you can't recognize and sort of simply embrace your fear that this kind of thing results.

T.: Because you can't recognize your fear as it is right in you, then it can become that unhealthy, vague fear that seems outside of you.

C.: Yeah. That's it. That's the difference.

From time to time during this series she gives indications that there have been significant changes in her inner adjustment to sex. Again the excerpt is from the forty-sixth interview.

C.: (Long pause.) I think perhaps I'm going to tell you something else I found out about myself, and I'm not too eager and it's not too pleasant. No, that isn't quite so, but anyway, we will find out whether it's pleasant or unpleasant; whether that's the right word to use. Going back, it was so *very* difficult for me to get to *any* part of the sexual problem at all, very difficult. And, do you know, I haven't the slightest idea of what I said, not the slightest. And yet, which of course, I mean, wouldn't the critics make something of that! I should *know*, you see, but I don't know and I really think, I really think, it's because I don't *want* to know; I have no need to know, I just don't want to know. And yet, *miracle*, I mean the areas that have been walled up are no longer walled up. It's unbelievable, again it's an unbelievable thing.

Another statement from the forty-sixth interview will indicate something of the depth of the understanding of the process and its implications which Mrs. Oak achieves. It also illustrates the gradually changing nature of the relationship toward the conclusion of this series—a give and take between therapist and client which had not been present before, as they discuss issues which are general rather than personal.

C.: Has it ever . . . I don't know, I don't quite know what I am doing now. Has it occurred to you that doing this kind of therapy is a little dangerous? Again, because you see, it isn't important that the client really know what happens, what happens to himself, what I mean is, maybe it's a little dangerous to participate in a situation whereby the individual becomes aware of . . . he needn't become consciously aware, even . . . of the fact that *he can make choices?*

T.: That it really is taking a very genuine gamble to venture with people into the realization that choices are possible.

C.: Yes. Yes. It's frightening. I wonder how long it's going to take people to catch on. I just wonder. They probably won't, or a good many won't. I sometimes think that what might happen is that, bit by bit, that which is "useful" would be taken over and the *real* significance lost. Dammit I mean . . . I *do care* about that.

T.: Well, all those thoughts have occurred to me, all right. I think I understand them.

C.: And, of course, you know, it isn't accidental but could you really tell people how it is done? I don't think so.

T.: Tell? No.

C.: I don't think so.

T.: My own feeling is that, if a person has ever had anything in his experience of this sort, so that he knows *inside*, some inkling of what this is about, then you can tell him; it makes sense, you can talk about it together and so on. Otherwise telling doesn't help.

C.: I can almost just imagine (word lost) it's really (word lost) I'm convinced of that. Just as I'm convinced, and again I may sound textbookish, that therapy is only as deep as this combination, this relationship, as the *need* in the client is as deep as the need, and as deep as the *willingness* for the relationship to grow *on* the part of the therapist. And I don't think he has to know that, do you? I mean he. . .

T.: I think he *doesn't* know half the time.

C.: Yeah, M-hm. And then it's . . . and then of course it's . . . did I know, did I know that I had this need? No. I mean for a type of love, for which there is no personal gratification? . . . . . Now it seems to me that because this whole thing *is* a way of life, that there are many other factors, many levels of . . . I don't know what . . . devotion, warmth. But it seems to me that *that*, by golly, is what does it, and of course, of course it seems to me that personally it means something to me because it was something I was struggling with and struggling for.

In talking about the relationship with the therapist, she mentions several times that it was her conversations with friends, some of them in therapy, which raised a doubt in her mind. This doubt seems to have been primarily: "Did he really value me? Was it a real relationship? Or was it something that was pseudo—that was 'professional'?" It was questions of this sort which brought her back for further interviews. But by the forty-seventh interview she seems to have resolved this issue.

C.: This whole relationship was a-a-a kind of-of picture on sunbeam material, was caught in the breeze, and was *there*, you see, I knew that, but there was too much motion to it and too much of a, well, I'll say out of focus, but it had to be br-brought to a standstill. Well, that happened last week. (*She continues with some of the details of this.*) Now I don't know if that—if it does make sense, except that it does to me (*as she slaps her hand on the desk*), by golly, the lines are straight!

T.: Somehow those feelings that you caught clarified things for you till it brought this into a clear and real focus, is that . . . ?

C.: That's right, that's right, that's right, completely right.

She mentions, in this same interview, a way of seeing her experience which has occasionally troubled her.

C.: Oh, another thing, I recognized that the-the therapeutic experience for me, in comparing others that I've known—and this'll be difficult, I think it will, oh, no I don't—has . . . has been somewhat akin to the . . . religious kind of experience, which last summer rather bothered me. And yet. . .

T.: That is, sort of mystical.

C.: Yes.

The forty-seventh interview was the final recorded interview. The forty-eighth was, at the client's request, not recorded. It was largely a recapitulation of the themes which have already been illustrated, together with more of a give-and-take discussion of therapy in general. It closed with expressions of warm mutual regard on the part of the client and therapist. Consequently, we shall close these excerpts with two portions from the forty-seventh interview. The first expresses the belief that the primary problem for therapy is that the person has deserted his own experience, his own *self*.

C.: I think there's one other thing that . . . that followed me (words lost), the question of what really happened . . . someplace along the way, or *all* along the way. And . . . of course, I don't think it's important to really know. But it-it seems to me, I'm certainly not alone in-in this thinking—that the whole problem —not only for myself but for so many others—is really this-this idea of-of getting away *from* self and . . . where it starts, I don't know. I'm convinced that with me, it started as a very young child, a-a-a . . . this . . . it comes, I'm *sure*, in the . . . the awful, the awful, devastation that there is in-in . . . recognizing that there *is* self. That . . . I mean, probably you can't cope with. . .

T.: Just kind of a frightening realization.

C.: Yes. One suddenly . . . I mean . . . you suddenly just are *you*, and nothing else . . . and everything else seems to fall away; there just aren't any props, you see. And what happens, I don't know, except I'm sure . . . that . . . that you . . . begin building according to others' concepts, which is of course culturally impos- almost impossible *not* to be, but . . . well, it just seems to me that-that . . . that's the whole thing.

The final excerpt gives something of her tentative assurance about ending the interviews and her feeling about the therapist.

C.: Of course I'll never cease to be amazed the way one works through all these things without conscious effort. (Pause.) Oh, and I think too, I think too, I've-I've-I've kind of reached the point, or very near the point where . . . I'd sort of like to be processed out (*laughingly*). You know . . . I'd sort of like to be through. . . . . Oh, and I might tell you, I might tell you that . . . this time in I've been, I mean . . . *very* much aware of your skill, I mean really . . . and it hasn't detracted one bit from the. . . In fact, I've appreciated it. Of course I wasn't before. . . And I don't quite know what that means. . . But . . . (words lost) I mean, I have, I've-I've been aware of your skill.

T.: It seems as though this time you've let part of yourself watch me in operation while you were working with yourself.

It is to be hoped that this lengthy series of excerpts from the recorded interviews will have given the reader something of a feeling for the complex process, the subtle relationship between persons, which underlies the personality changes reported in the research section of this report.

XI. A SUMMARY OF THE THERAPEUTIC PROCESS

If we try to avoid high-flown abstractions and inferences and keep our description of the process close to the client's perception of it, we come out with statements such as the following. The only liberty that has been taken is to arrange some of the elements in groups and to change their order to make a somewhat more logical presentation. We may then say that the process of therapy for this client is crudely described in the following statements, each of which may be, without too much difficulty, turned into an operational statement and thus become a testable hypothesis.

The therapist provides an atmosphere of warm caring which gradually becomes experienced as a real diathermy—a safe warmth.

The client finds that she changes the emphasis from dealing with reality problems to experiencing self.

Experiencing self comes to mean feeling one's feelings to the full, in the immediate present, without inhibition—whether feelings of anger, hurt, bitterness, childishness, adolescent disillusionment, or pleasure and appreciation of self.

Experiencing of self means letting feelings bubble through into awareness which formerly have been denied to awareness.

This is a process which seems to open up new channels of thought—experienced as a physiological alteration.

It is a process which has its own organismic time table and cannot be forced by self or others.

As previously denied feelings (feelings not recognized as part of self) are admitted to awareness, the self as perceived tends to break down, become more disorganized. In spite of this, there is the feeling that this is the right path, that "I can rebuild."

The essence of this process is not that certain *content* material is admitted to awareness but that the client discovers that recognizing an experience for what it *is* constitutes a more effective method of meeting life than does the denial or distortion of experience.

What one *is*—a woman, a person with a wide range of feelings, a person who is "seventy-five per cent poet"—comes to be experienced as acceptable and enjoyable and as having rich potentialities.

A part of the process is being this more complete self—even a self with hostile feelings—and discovering that such a being is healthy, constructive for self and others—and satisfying.

Therapy is experienced as being a defining of one's self and a being of one's self instead of accepting other's definitions of self.

One of the most important elements which is fully experienced is the relationship with the therapist—the full awareness and acceptance of the therapist's warmth and caring.

The client discovers in experience that what has been needed is a love which is not possessive, which demands no personal gratification.

A further part of the process is that the therapeutic experience generalizes—that the client can create a genuine relationship with others in which they can be self-experiencing and self-directing.

There is the discovery that there is, at the core of one's being, nothing dire or destructive of self and nothing damaging or possessive or warping of others.

Instead, the attitude toward self becomes one of confidence in one's own experience, and toward others a caring which is free of persistent antagonism, hate, or possessive love.

There is an increasing feeling of self-responsibility, even responsibility for refusing, at this time, to explore certain denied areas.

The client comes to feel that it is rewarding though not pleasant to bear the aloneness of making one's own choices.

The client comes to feel that it is possible to walk with serenity through a world that seems falling to pieces.

The process ends with the client able to feel a tentative but basic confidence in herself and her capacity for functioning in impersonal reality and in interpersonal relationships.

XII. FINAL SUMMARY

In this extended (perhaps overlong) report we have presented the wealth of objective data which has been derived from the intensive research study of one client, Mrs. Oak, before, during, and after forty-eight interviews with a client-centered therapist. The data illustrate the type of information which has been obtained on all the clients in the current research program at the Counseling Center of the University of Chicago.

The findings for this one client have been reported for each of six research projects. The first had to do with the degree of over-all personality change exhibited in four TAT's, administered during an eighteen-month period. The second dealt with the data concerning the perceived self and self-ideal, as obtained through Q-sorts. Some qualitative analysis was given, a correlational analysis was made, and the outcome of a factor analysis of this material was also presented. The third project had to do with the relationships between the TAT diagnosis and the self-picture, utilizing Q-technique as the method of the study. The fourth examined the objective Q-sort data regarding the therapist-client relationship. The fifth project investigated the degree of change in the maturity of the client's behavior, using the E-M Scale as the instrument. The sixth project measured the degree of change in attitudes toward others, particularly the acceptance of others, using as instrument the S-O Scale, drawn from several sources.

In addition to these research studies, the effort was made to present a body of data on the process of therapy by quoting from the verbatim interviews all the portions which seemed to be most relevant to an understanding of process.

XIII. CONCLUSIONS

Since many of the data have been discussed in connection with their presentation, only the summarized conclusions will be stated here.

Cautions and Limitations

It should be quite clear that the present study does not justify any statement that psychotherapy in general, or client-centered therapy, produces on the average such changes as have been measured in this case. Nor can we say that such changes are typical of "successful" cases in client-centered therapy. The limited type of statement which can be made is that these changes did occur in one client and, consequently, that such changes *may* occur in other individuals undergoing client-centered therapy and that the effective agent of change appears to be the therapeutic interviews. Before proceeding to summarize these changes, certain more general conclusions should be noted.

Conclusions as to Methodology

This study indicates that hypotheses drawn from a theory of therapy or from a theory of personality can be given a meaningful and objective test in the single case. Stephenson has maintained this on a theoretical basis. It is believed that this study is one of the first to demonstrate the fact.

The researches which utilized the Q-technique indicate that complex data drawn from the internal frame of reference of the client may be treated objectively and that meaningful findings can emerge. Since there has been much misunderstanding of this problem, it may simply be said that these researches show that subtle and fluctuating aspects of the client's phenomenological field can be operationally defined and dealt with on a rigorous scientific basis. It is hoped that this sort of research will lead to a merging of two points of view which have regarded themselves as mutually exclusive.

A correlated conclusion is that data drawn from the internal frame of reference by instruments designed to capture aspects of the phenomenal field appear to be fully as useful scientifically as material drawn in the more conventional fashion from the external frame of reference.

It is especially noteworthy that the study of *relationships* between data gathered from the internal and external frames of reference is very fruitful indeed (V, VI).[6]

Some Tentative Conclusions regarding the Process of Therapy

Though the researches presented focus more upon the outcomes than the process of therapy, certain tentative conclusions may be drawn from the research findings and the verbatim material.

A change in self-perception appears to be central to the process of therapy in this case (IV, V).

6. The Roman numerals in parentheses following each of the more specific conclusions indicate the section or sections of this report in which data are found to support the conclusions.

The conclusion is suggested that "experiencing"—the complete *awareness* of the *total* organismic response to a situation—is concomitant with, or basic to, the process of therapy (X).

The warmth of the therapist's relationship to the client—a *caring* which is not possessive or demanding—is also suggested by the verbatim material as being an important (essential?) aspect of the process of therapy (X).

The evidence shows that in this case the therapist's perception of the client's phenomenal field included material which was not consciously admitted to the client's awareness at that time. Whether this is significant for therapy is unknown (VI).

Some Conclusions Related to Personality Theory

Most of the researches described were based on hypotheses drawn from the personality theory which has been developing out of client-centered therapy. A number of the propositions of self-theory have found support in our findings, and some provocative new propositions added.

Change in the perception of self, or concept of self, appears to be basic to personality change in this case (IV, V, VI). It is this concept of self which is reorganized during the therapy period (IV, V).

Change in self-organization is accompanied by disturbing feelings of disorganization (X).

The self, at the beginning of therapy, is defensively organized in such a way that it denies to awareness certain aspects of experience, as can be seen by comparing the self and the diagnostic picture (V).

The self as reorganized a year after the conclusion of therapy includes a much larger proportion of experience, with less of experience denied to awareness (III, V).

The self appears to be, in an important sense, the "architect of self," in that the client tends to become, both phenomenologically and diagnostically, the self she desired to be (V, VI).

A change in behavior is concomitant with, or follows, a change in the perceived self (VII).

A somewhat surprising new proposition which is suggested is that, when the individual is able to admit much of his experience to awareness, the total personality organization which will exist in the near future is best predicted, not by a diagnosis of the total personality organization at the present, but by the self as experientially perceived at present (V, VI).

Another new proposition which is suggested is that changes in total personality organization may be of a drastic order, such that within an eighteen-month period the final personality may be negatively correlated with the initial personality (V).

Conclusions as to Outcomes

The most firmly based conclusions which we can draw from the total study all have to do with the outcomes of client-centered psychotherapy in this case. In general, the major finding of this research analysis is that we have solid, objective evidence that client-centered psychotherapy *may* bring about in a client: changes in the structure of the perceived self; change in both surface and deeper levels of personality as measured by the TAT; change in attitudes of acceptance of others; change in behavior as observed by self and friends. In every one of these respects the change is in the direction which would be predicted by client-centered theory.

While this supplies the general picture, a more detailed statement of the outcomes appears to be warranted in order to pull together the findings from all the studies. The data which have been given would lend support to the following statements, each of which is given as descriptive of some aspect of the outcome of therapy in the case of Mrs. Oak.

The client becomes less panicky, less anxious (III).

She becomes less driven, less compulsive (III, IV).

She becomes less guilty, less hostile (IV).

She becomes more secure (III, IV, VII).

She develops much more confidence in self (IV).

She becomes more expressive, less guarded and inhibited (III, IV).

She becomes aware of experiences and conflicts which previously were denied to awareness (III, V).

She perceives herself as being more nearly what she wants to be (IV).

She becomes, according to a diagnostician, much more nearly what she wants to be (V).

She becomes less dependent and passive, more self-directing, more able to make her own contribution (III, IV).

She finds social situations less threatening (III).

Her interpersonal relationships become more pleasant and satisfying (III, IV).

She is more able to give and receive affection (III).

She is less fearful of any elements in her self (III).

She is able to formulate her own values, even when these run counter to socially accepted values (III, IV).

She understands herself better (III, IV, V, VII).

She becomes less defensive of her self (III, IV, V, VII).

She becomes better organized in her reactions to distracting and disorganizing situations (VII).

She is more acceptant of her own capacities and limitations (III, VII).

She perceives herself as being more mature in her behavior (IV, VII).

She becomes, in the judgment of her friends, more mature in her behavior (VII).

She becomes more accepting of others as separate individuals, with a right to be separate (VIII).

She places more value upon the individual, herself included (IV, VIII).

She is less inclined to reform or change others (VIII).

She tends to place more value upon the contributions of others to group thinking and action (VIII).

She exhibits a stronger tendency to use and favor democratic means in the achievement of goals (VIII).

She is less frightened by sex and more accepting of her sexual role (III, IV, VII).

She still exhibits unresolved conflicts in the area of sexual attitudes and behavior in spite of progress in this respect (III).

She is more unified, better integrated, less ambivalent and conflicted in her personality and behavior (III, IV, V, VII).

The changes which took place in her during the period of therapy continued for the most part in the same direction during the follow-up periods (III, IV, V, VI, VII, VIII).

In the few exceptions to the preceding statement, there was slight regression toward the pre-therapy status during the follow-up period (VIII).

In no instance does a post-therapy or follow-up measurement indicate poorer adjustment than at the pre-therapy point (III, IV, V, VII, VIII).

In every type of measurement obtained there is change from the pre-therapy status in the direction of a more realistic, more comfortable, more confident, more unified, less defensive adjustment (III, IV, V, VI, VII, VIII).

Perhaps we may conclude this review of all the evidence with a statement written many months before this research was undertaken. It was an attempt to summarize, from the theory of client-centered therapy, the types of outcomes which might be expected. It finds strong support in this research.

Thus therapy produces a change in personality organization and structure, and a change in behavior, both of which are relatively permanent. It is not necessarily a reorganization which will serve for a lifetime. It may still deny to awareness certain aspects of experience, may still exhibit certain patterns of defensive behavior. There is little likelihood that any therapy is in this sense complete. Under new stresses of a certain sort, the client may find it necessary to seek further therapy, to achieve further reorganization of self. But whether there be one or more series of therapeutic interviews, the essential outcome is a more broadly based structure of self, an inclusion of a greater proportion of experience as a part of self, and a more comfortable and realistic adjustment to life [3, p. 195].

REFERENCES

1. Boyer, Jacques K. "A Study of the Relationship between, and the Changes in, a Client's Concept of Her Self, the Ordinary Person, and Her Self-ideal during Client-centered Psychotherapy." A.M. thesis, University of Chicago, 1951.
2. Hartley, Margaret W. "A Q-Technique Study of Changes in the Self-concept during Psychotherapy." Ph.D. dissertation, University of Chicago, 1951.
3. Rogers, Carl R. *Client-centered Therapy*. Boston: Houghton Mifflin Co., 1951

CHAPTER 16

The Case of Mr. Bebb: The Analysis of a Failure Case

CARL R. ROGERS

I. INTRODUCTION

The purpose of this chapter is to present a body of research and clinical data bearing on an individual who must, by several criteria, be regarded as a "failure" in psychotherapy. There are a number of reasons for regarding this as worth while. Very few unsuccessful cases have been presented, and the portrayal of such a case is thus a step in the consideration of the whole range of therapeutic effort. Further, the fact that a wealth of objective information is available on this client makes the value of the presentation greater to the profession. Finally, there is the long-standing and distressing fact that, though each therapeutic orientation has fairly clear-cut hypotheses to explain those instances in which constructive change occurs, the hypotheses offered to explain failures are vague, confusing, and often contradictory. We stand in need of more significant hypotheses to account for lack of change, and it is hoped that analysis of such a case may provide some leads for better hypotheses.

The reader who wishes a more complete picture of the several research projects by means of which the data were collected on this case should consult chapter 3, which describes the complex program out of which the data grew. Those who wish to compare the findings from this case with the findings in a case in which significant change occurred should read the case of Mrs. Oak, described in the preceding chapter. In order to facilitate such a comparison, the material from this case will be presented in much the same fashion as in the presentation of the case of Mrs. Oak.

II. THE CLIENT AND HIS THERAPIST

The Gathering of Data from the Client

"Mr. Bebb," as we shall call this client, was a young man of foreign birth, a student, who came to the Counseling Center at the suggestion of a friend. He agreed to participate in the research, with the understanding that his therapy would in no direct way be influenced by the research. In terms of our experimental design he was assigned to the own-control group and was immediately given the battery of tests utilized in the first block (Block I) of our research: the Thematic Apperception Test (TAT); a set of one hundred Q-sort cards with self-referent items which he sorted to portray himself, the self he would like to be, and the ordinary person; the Willoughby Emotional-Maturity Scale (E-M Scale); and the Self-Other Attitude Scale (S-O Scale). He was then asked to wait for sixty days before the first appointment with his therapist. At the end of the sixty-day period all the tests were repeated before his first interview, giving a control period of sixty days without therapy. The first through seventh interviews were held in the next thirty-one days, all interviews being recorded. At the conclusion of the seventh interview he was requested by the psychometrist to again carry out the threefold Q-sort. At this time the counselor also sorted the Q-cards as he thought the client would sort them. There were two more interviews in the next twelve days, and he then concluded therapy after the ninth interview, therapy having extended over a six-week period. After he had concluded therapy, the whole battery of tests was repeated. After a follow-up period of six months the battery of tests was readministered, and he was interviewed by both the psychometrist and the therapist in regard to his experience during and since therapy. This concludes the contacts through which the objective data were collected.

Each of the instruments used was selected to test one or more specific hypothesis concerning the process or the outcome of therapy. The hypotheses for each portion of the study will be stated in the appropriate section in which the data are given (Secs. IV through IX of this chapter).

The Client as Seen by the Therapist

The therapist supplied the following qualitative description of Mr. Bebb very shortly after the conclusion of therapy.

When I first saw Mr. Bebb, he seemed to me to be an extremely shy, deferential, rigid, frightened person. He was concerned about himself because of physical symptoms (heart palpitations) which he had been told by a physician were psychological in origin. These seemed to be part of a general anxiety.

In his interviews he revealed himself as having extremely high expectations for himself. In comparison with these standards, he thought of himself as completely worthless. He tentatively revealed some auditory hallucinations, which he never thoroughly explored. He felt that he must have guidance in his thinking and that he could not possibly make any choices on his own initiative. He wanted very much to have some external and objective decision as to his normality.

His progress in therapy was evident but centered around a very limited issue. As he discussed the necessity of being guided by external standards, he explored the different answers he might receive and recognized that some of these answers he would accept and others he would reject. Evidently the impact of these discoveries struck him between interviews, and he came in, in the ninth interview, with a decidedly changed view. He had concluded that he *was* capable of making evaluations himself and that he could accept himself as having this capacity. With this interview, he concluded therapy.

The therapeutic process was clear cut in that he achieved the courage to place the locus of evaluation within himself. It was also clear however that he was a long way from having achieved integration. I cannot predict whether therapeutic change will continue beyond the end of the interviews. If not, he will at some point need further help, because he did not fully admit all significant experiences to awareness. I regard the case as successful in a limited way.

The Relationship

Because of the probable importance of the relationship to the process of therapy, the counselor was asked to give his impression of the relationship between himself and Mr. Bebb. These are his comments.

Mr. Bebb was such a frightened and self-depreciating person that a real relationship was very difficult to establish. I felt warmly toward him, partly I am sure, because he was so obviously in need of help. It seemed to me that he was never able to accept my feeling for him, because he could not believe it.

In the relationship he frequently wanted and asked for guidance and for answers. I did not feel in any sense pushed by these requests, because the desperate need for inner assurance showed through these so clearly. I usually handled such requests by trying to understand the feeling behind them. When he wanted very much to have an objective evaluation of his normality, I dealt with this in somewhat the following fashion: "It seems to you that, if I would tell you that in my judgment you are normal, this would settle the issue for you, and that, on the other hand, if I said you were definitely abnormal, then you could accept that and be guided by it." This helped him to explore his own feelings much further and to discover resources of self-confidence of which he had been unaware.

His confidence in himself took a sharp upward turn which was fairly dramatic. I was surprised to have him conclude his interviews at this point, however, and thought it likely that he would return. In our parting I expressed my sincere attitude of willingness to see him again if at any point, then or later, he felt a need of further help. To date he has not returned.

Counselor Ratings

The ratings of the case, made by the therapist at the conclusion of the interviews, give in summary form his judgments of the somewhat contradictory elements in the situation. The judgment was made that therapy for this client had been largely an intellectual-cognitive process and only to small degree an emotional-experiential one. It was felt that Mr. Bebb had made very little use of the relationship itself for therapy. As for over-all ratings regarding outcome, it was judged that at the beginning of therapy the client was near the extreme of highly defensive psychological organization and that in therapy he made only slight progress toward real integration. (On the "degree of personal integration" he was rated on the nine-point scale as being at 2 at the beginning of therapy and at 4 at its conclusion.) As to his life-adjustment, it was felt that this was poor and that little progress had been made. (Rating of 3 at beginning, 4 at conclusion.) As to "outcome of therapy," the counselor first gave him a rating of 5 but then changed it to 6 on the nine-point scale, feeling that the therapeutic process had been clear cut and positive, even though the gains were relatively small.

III. THE DYNAMICS OF THE THERAPEUTIC INTERVIEWS

Undoubtedly the reader will wish to form his own clinical judgment as to the basis of the failure of personality or behavior change to occur in this case. For this reason, numerous and somewhat lengthy excerpts have been taken from the nine interviews, and they are presented in this section. Since it was obviously impossible to present the whole case, selections had to be made. The effort was made to include all the segments which appeared to have the most meaning to the client, those excerpts which seemed to have any bearing on the therapeutic process, and those portions where questions might be raised as to the adequacy of the therapist's handling. It is believed that this basis of selection has provided, in a relatively small number of pages, an accurate picture of the client, the process, and the relationship. The material will be presented with a minimum of interpretation to facilitate the forming of independent judgments.[1]

In presenting the material, it may be helpful to state that the client's voice was very low and hesitant and that sometimes it would trail off into such self-directed mumblings that it was inaudible to the therapist. The client was quite inarticulate, and speech was slow, with many pauses. This seemed to be a matter of temperament rather than a matter of speaking in other than his childhood tongue.

First Interview

In the first moments of the first interview Mr. Bebb states his problem as he sees it.

C.:[2] I just . . . had a general feeling of being depressed. . . . . And, well, it's the way it . . . it . . . manifested itself that sort of . . . worried me. . . . . The way I became aware of it was more or less in the physical manifestations, I mean, palpitations of the heart . . . . . and, I seen the doctor over at the hospital, and, well, he tried to say that . . . its a functional disease . . . some sort of a psychiatric . . . that's what's wrong.

He tells how he saw a psychiatrist for two interviews and was told that his difficulty was an Oedipus complex and that he should think about it and come back in three months. He has tried to think about it but to no avail.

C.: (Pause.) I mean, I've been thinking about this stuff, but . . . I've tried to get at it and really . . . I mean seek it out, seek out the problem and . . . try to recognize it. But . . . I mean, all I'm confronted with, ever, I think, is just the effects. . . The cause is completely . . . unidentified, completely concealed. And . . . it's just like . . . diving, I mean, with a hood over your head or something. You don't know just where to look for it.

1. Some readers may prefer to study the objective research evidence before forming a clinical impression. With this in mind, the present section has been prepared as a unit and can be read either before or after the sections which present the data (Secs. IV through IX, pp. 372–400) without any loss of meaning.

2. We shall attempt to indicate short pauses or hesitations by three-dot ellipses (. . .), while longer pauses are indicated in parentheses "(pause)." Where irrelevant material as been omitted in editing, the omission is indicated by five-dot ellipses (. . . . .). "*C.*" refers to the client; "T.," to the therapist.

T.: M-hm. You tried very hard to look within yourself . . .

C.: Yeah. M-hm.

T.: . . . and see what the cause could be but it's just . . . the causes just remain completely unknown to you, and you're scrabbling around in the dark. (Pause.)

C.: And the . . . I mean, the physical effects are still there and . . . that gives me reason to believe that whatever is the catalyzer, initiator of the whole thing, is still there.

He tells something of his childhood and talks of his feelings both of inferiority and of superiority.

C.: People generally thought I was . . . a kind of idler or idle person . . . . . and . . . had no ambition or no backbone. And . . . also in the school I went . . . which was . . . well, it's sort of an orphanage and sort of an . . . institution . . . which I was put into after my father and my mother was divorced. And there the . . . well, the kids always made fun of me because I was sort of dull, inactive . . . in their activities, and . . . which I'm quite sure gave me a sort of inferiority complex. . . . . Then I have the opposite feeling, namely that . . . . . I'm really much better than some people. . . . . Sometimes, I mean, I just feel depressed, morbid, and I just feel that I'm no good; and other times I feel . . . very elated. That is I . . . I . . . just feel that . . . well, practically ready to take on anybody because I feel that, sometimes, I'm so much better than they are. But there's never really any . . . any . . . golden medium.

Second Interview

In the second interview he compares this country and his own and his feelings about going back. In this segment he also presents again the two views of himself.

C.: I'm actually . . . sometimes I'm fearful of the fact of . . . going back and . . . well, then, I think, I believe I've changed a great deal since . . . since I lived in my own country, you see. My . . . people in my country, they know me. . . . . Mean, I have this notion of feeling compelled to do something which is really good and worth while before I can go back. . . . . And I still feel that there's a certain amount of prejudice involved in . . . people I know in my country . . . in respect to my individuality, my personality, which . . . is not the case here because . . . I don't, well, I don't know what you would call it, maybe a bad impression, but . . . well, I guess you could say that. I don't think that that has been the case over here. And (pause) it's (pause) mean, my (pause) well, my achievements . . . regardless of how small they may be, have been . . . been greater in this country than they have in my own. And . . . but the people in my country don't . . . don't seem to be aware of it, perhaps because of . . . I told you when I went to this orphanage when I was . . . ten till I was fifteen, well, they considered me sort of dull. But I don't know . . . I mean, somehow the—I mean a great many times I knew that . . . for instance in studying, I mean, I was among the lowest in the class and . . . but still 'way in myself I felt . . . . . that I knew more, I mean about the courses that we focused on, our studies, than, the . . . persons who were considered to be the best in the class. I just felt that I . . . I wasn't recognized. I don't know why that is. Seems I was, well, rather sort of emotional because sometimes, somehow I mean, I'd just start crying. I don't know, that . . . meant nothing and . . . so I mean they'd make fun of it, I mean, the kids. . .

T.: So that one of the reasons why you feel quite sure that you couldn't really be accepted back there unless you do something quite important and quite significant over here is that . . . there is quite a discrepancy between the way you felt inside yourself where you felt even in those younger days that you *did* know something, you really knew more than some of the others and so on; but because of your feelings and emotions, somehow that didn't get expressed, and so others had a poor opinion of you. Is that something like it?

C.: Yeah. It's also this . . . well, now, when I look upon those years, I also thought that I sort of . . . withdrew myself, and probably it easily could have been . . . probably justified, and . . . considered sort of dull or . . . inactive. . .

He is annoyed that he cannot believe in himself, and two statements from the remainder of the interview will indicate his attitudes on this point.

C.: Now I'm working on a novel in my own language, and I just thought maybe if I could finish that and have it published in my country that maybe. . . Somehow I just get, I mean get sort of angry with myself because I feel that I have to do something before I dare show up, mean I just get angry with myself because I don't have, seem to have, enough faith in my, in own capabilities.

T.: (*Later, responding to a statement client has just made.*) You want so much to prove to them, "I am worth while; I am somebody."

C.: Yeah. But of course I mean, it would also prove to myself something.

T.: Feel it isn't only to them that you have to prove this; it's to yourself too.

C.: Yeah. But, sorta feel, I mean, I'm more convinced essentially . . . than . . . I feel they are. (Long pause: 2 minutes.)

Third Interview

The third interview was spent mostly in expressing his comparative attitudes about this country and his home country. Much of the material was not very deeply related to himself. At one point he expresses his need of belonging.

C.: Well, I mean, somehow . . . I still feel a need of belonging by common . . . consent . . . I mean, to (pause) living or (pause) more or less be part of some (pause) collective mentality which is in . . . is in concord with one's own, I mean, my own . . . way of looking at things.

T.: You want to be identified with some group or with its way of living and its culture. With a group that sees life somewhat in the same terms that you do. Is that . . . ?

C.: M-hm. (Pause.)

Fourth Interview

The fourth interview is very full of quotable material, as he plunges more and more deeply into his own attitudes. First is his desire to be told and then his fear about his sanity.

C.: (Long pause.) (*Sighs.*) I feel like (*deep sigh*) I wish you could tell me what you wanted me to say. And I don't know . . . talk about something (pause).

T.: You mean you'd be quite willing to talk about something if I would indicate what . . . what it might be useful or helpful to talk about, hm?

C.: Yeah. (Long pause.) I don't know why, I mean (*sighs*) always seem to . . . want to have . . . I mean, be told things like. . .

T.: M-hm. (Pause.) As though there's a certain amount of . . . *satisfaction* in being . . . guided, is that . . . ?

C.: Well not (pause), not necessarily being guided, but (pause) just (pause) at least just have suggestions . . . be given suggestions . . . having suggestions made about . . . things which . . . I'm not sure about. Like about myself somehow. And (Pause.)

T.: That is, in areas where you're not *sure*, like about yourself (pause) you prefer it if somebody *else* gives you a lead a little bit . . . or makes a little suggestion.

C.: Yeah. (Pause.) Sometimes I just feel that (pause) I'm not . . . fully sane and I just . . . want somebody to have some sort of . . . test made, you know, or just be . . . I mean, I want somebody to ascertain whether it's true or not. I mean I just sort of (pause) feel in doubt, or dubious. And . . . I mean I can't . . . ascertain that for myself because I don't feel, I mean I don't feel I have capacity for—either the capacity or the competence for it in that sense. (*Sigh of relief.*)

T.: M-hm. When you . . . when you wonder if you really are normal or if you're abnormal, or insane, then it seems as though—if someone who was more competent than *you* would test you, would judge you . . . and say, either "Yes, you are," or "No, you aren't" . . . that . . . there would be something about this that you'd like . . . very much.

C.: Yeah. M-hm. That's it. (Pause.) There occurs . . . (*clears throat violently*) within myself I find, I mean, such . . . a sort of . . . dichotomy between . . . well, not . . . maybe it's two selves or . . . maybe there's just . . . two halves of the one . . . I mean, it's just two extremes, and (*sighs*) sometimes I just feel the one is normal, and the other one is abnormal, by others' preconceived standards, judgments. And . . . then . . . I just wanta . . . *know* whether it would (pause).

T.: Is this it, that when you feel such a deep *discrepancy* within your*self* . . . as you say, maybe between two selves (pause), and then it's . . . well, I'm not quite sure there. Then it seems to you as though perhaps one self is abnormal and the other one . . . is *not*. . .

C.: Is not, yeah. This . . . is the way it seems to me, but then . . . I mean in cases like that I'd just like to have some competent person, I mean, who knows about it . . . tell me just . . . which is which and . . . then I feel that maybe I could look at it differently rather than . . . being aware of the . . . of the . . . symptoms or whatever it is. . . Not know . . . just . . . how they are to be interpreted or . . . what they mean.

In discussing this, he tells of trends in himself toward turning within and turning out.

C.: (Long pause.) And then sometimes I (pause), I don't know if this makes sense, but . . . sometimes I just feel that . . . I want to exist, so to speak, completely . . . within myself, I mean, within . . . without any . . . normal social intercourse, and then . . . but when I feel like that I (*sighs*), I sort of feel sorry for myself. And then I become sorta depressed. And then (*sighs*) at other times I feel that I don't want to exist within myself at all because it . . . brings sort of agony or torment or sort of mental . . . hardships. And then I just want to . . . indulge in complete . . . normal . . . social . . . relationships, and I don't want at all to exist within myself, but (*sighs*), well, then I become . . . then I feel it's that somewhat . . . I mean I feel that's good. And then I become . . . rather elated. And I (*sighs*), I feel that . . . I've taken the right course . . . but I mean I don't know . . . again I mean, there's nothing, there's nothing in between. (*Sighs.*)

T.: Sort of swings back and forth, but there are the two . . . two pulls, as I get it. That sometimes you feel pulled in the direction of just living completely within yourself and never mind relationships with anyone else; only then you . . . feel dissatisfied and depressed somewhat by that feeling. Then again the pull is in the other direction, to . . . live in your relationships with others; and that feels very good, but it . . . doesn't necessarily last that way. Is that what . . . ?

His desire for social relationships makes him realize his need for affection, and this in turn makes him angry.

C.: But then when I . . . when I get this feeling that . . . I need affection, then . . . I become angry . . . at myself because I . . . or become angry at other people because they . . . bring about my realization that I do need it. . .

T.: M-hm. You feel . . . angry at others because they kind of awaken in you that . . . that sense of *need* for affection, and then you feel angry at yourself because . . . why are you so weak or something as to . . . need any affection from others? Is that something like it?

C.: Yeah. M-hm. (Long pause.)

Later in the interview his desire for outside evaluation is explored much more deeply, and he comes to realize the positive opinion he has of himself.

C.: I feel that (pause) if you, if you should tell me something now . . . something which you . . . thought would-would sum me up . . . I mean, sum my personality up pretty well and pretty accurately . . . now, if . . . it didn't click, or if you say something which . . . wasn't very flattering, I . . . well, I'd just feel that . . . I'd probably say that . . . you just couldn't say that after . . . such a short time like . . . I'd feel that you wasn't competent to say it . . . after such a short time, whereas, on the other hand, if it's something that (pause) I thought I could accept, I . . . I wouldn't question it at all. (Pause.)

T.: The way you use the phrase "not flattering" there made me wonder . . . if I said something about you . . . and it was somehow . . . rather deeply *disapproving* of you, then you could find a lot of reasons why . . . it shouldn't be *accepted;* where if . . . does the opposite hold true? Where if it was something that . . . rather deeply *approved* of you . . . then perhaps that would click with your own feelings. Is that . . . ?

C.: M-hm. Yeah. (Pause.)

T.: Is this going too far, then, to say that . . . it looks as though your own feelings . . . were looking for some basis on which they could really . . . approve of you?

C.: Yes. That is . . . I just want some sort (*sighs*) of . . . verification. . . And . . . if it didn't coincide . . . I'd just . . . not accept it . . . I mean, just reject it.

T.: M-hm. If you could find some *confirmation* . . . something that would *support* you in feeling positively about yourself . . . then you could accept that . . . and if it was anything else you'd just . . . toss it out.

C.: M-hm. (Pause.) Seems just that I feel uncertain . . . of myself. But yet-yet I hope and I want (*sighs*) confirmation for. . .

T.: M-hm. You have real hope in regard to yourself but you . . . you doubt that hope, you wish that something could confirm it, could support it. Is that . . . ?

C.: Yeah. (Pause.) Since . . . I mean, I want to . . . I mean, rationally I feel that I have to . . . accept myself . . . for what . . . competent people, who know me, evaluate me to be. (Pause.) But sometimes if it . . . doesn't . . . coincide with . . . what I hope . . . (*sighs*), I just feel that I wouldn't accept it. (Pause.)

T.: In other words, you know within yourself (pause) that your acceptance of yourself . . . would have to be in the terms that you . . . that you hope for yourself. Does that make sense?

C.: Yeah. I mean, I know . . . I mean, rationally, I know that . . . as I may say . . . I mean, I'm only what I am . . . I mean, I'm nothing more or nothing less than that. But I hope that what I am is . . . is something *good* rather than something *bad* . . . but if someone should come along and say that . . . tell me that it's something bad . . . I just wouldn't accept it, but then I feel . . . I'd just go elsewhere to seek some confirmation.

T.: Almost as though your feelings were pretty well convinced that what you are is basically good . . . and if someone says, "No, you're not; you're basically bad" . . . you just know that you couldn't and wouldn't accept *that.*

Fifth Interview

In this interview he strikes a new note in this thinking about the evaluation of himself.

C.: Somehow I feel that . . . I never get . . . I mean, any real external proof of . . . of one's own . . . abilities or capacities for doing something well. Somehow it (*sighs*) . . . don't you think it all depends upon . . . an inner awareness or an inner . . . conscious feeling of one's own . . . abilities? Somehow I feel that even if I should get a degree, it would really mean nothing to me unless I felt convinced myself that I really had accomplished something and produced something . . . something good. And, well, in that case, a degree is never really any proof. I feel that there's inner awareness of, a feeling of . . . that what one does is *good*, and . . . is appreciated, I mean, has to be . . . judged just mostly by one's self.

It is in this interview, too, that he becomes more specific as to the reason why he feels insane.

C.: And I . . . sometimes I (*sighs*) sort of hear noises which I know they're not . . . I mean, I know they're not there. That, of course may just be. . . I don't know, it may just be different levels of consciousness, I don't know enough about it. But at that time . . . I mean at the times like . . . these, I just feel that, well, it's. . . I mean, it's just something which . . . which is there. Maybe I'm just (pause), just abnormal, I . . . mean. . . (*Sighs*.)

T.: M-hm. It's when you hear sounds that intellectually you know aren't there, then there's the feeling, "Oh, my gosh, I'm really abnormal." (Pause.)

C.: Well, I mean, at times like that I just feel like (*sighs*) I mean, just more or less like . . . just resigning to my fate or whatever you want to call it. Just accept whatever consequences are involved.

At the close of the interview he is discussing his feelings about abnormality, when there comes a segment which is of considerable interest from the point of view of therapist handling.

C.: Yeah, and then I feel that, well, I've tried, and I've, so to speak, just failed. Then . . . instances like that I'd just like for someone to sit before me just to give me the answers. And tell me just . . . what is up.

T.: And so you feel that the answers can't be . . . haven't been able to come from within you, and you'd like very much to . . . have someone else . . . put the answer before you.

C.: Yeah. That's right.

T.: Guess we'll have to call it quits for today. (Arrangements for next appointment.)

C.: Say . . . I'd like to . . . have some kind of an answer. Is there any reason to worry about it if you hear noises or could it just be levels of consciousness?

(*Laughs.*) I know it's an unfair question. I know that . . . and you don't have to answer it.

T.: But that doesn't mean that you wouldn't like an answer, I mean, you wish that you. . . .

C.: Yes. But I mean, it's an unfair question, because it's against your. . . You don't have to. . .

T.: Well, you feel it's an unfair question because it's against my method. I would just feel that . . . I don't know of any answer I can quite give, because the fact is, you *are* worried about it.

C.: Yeah.

T.: I mean, that's why you talked it over.

C.: Yeah.

T.: And I guess my feeling is that, as we explore your concern about it, then maybe we can find out whether there is anything there to be concerned about. I mean, as I look at it, take some of these other things. You felt first: "Here are a lot of *problems* that I want to get the answers to." Now today, you're saying: "No . . . that isn't quite it. I want to see what I can do about *myself*." Well, the thing looks differently to you perhaps than it did at first. Now . . . that may be the kind of thing that would happen if we get down and talk of these other things.

C.: Yeah. M-hm.

Sixth Interview

In this interview most of the time is spent in discussing the standards by which one should live with some reference to the question of how "abnormalities" are to be judged. Toward the end of the interview he explores his fear of insanity a bit more directly, though still cautiously and in the third person.

C.: And I feel that the thing which really brings about the conflict in a person is . . . when he finds similarities between phenomena described and labeled in a . . . in a scientific book perhaps and phenomena observed in himself. I mean it might not have seemed very significant to him. But then when he reads a book or maybe is lectured, given certain labeled phenomena, he . . . I mean, he begins to . . . think about it, and . . . this . . . well really like this, I think the conflict might arise. (*This last in almost a trembling voice.*)

T.: So it can really set up conflicts in a person to find that things that he has observed within himself . . . are categorized and labeled . . . by the . . . experts . . . as being this or that . . . and then he may become concerned about it. Is that . . . ? (Pause.)

C.: That is why . . . I mean, if you become completely yourself, I mean, or just accept yourself for what you are, I mean. . . In that case, you just exclude any labeling or any . . . any way of handling(?) things by words. But that I feel is impossible because of your . . . of the way we live . . . I mean, in reality (*tone more confident*).

T.: From your tone of voice it almost sounds as if you felt it might be desirable to simply be yourself and not be . . . labeling all aspects of experience. But you feel that's just impossible in the present-day world.

C.: (*A few moments later in the interview.*) But maybe . . . I mean, even if you did label certain phenomena in your own personality, (pause) it might not make much difference . . . until you observed the same phenomena in other people just carried to a . . . more extreme, I mean to a larger degree like . . . you might find within yourself . . . sometimes that you might be somewhat neurotic or even somewhat psychotic which might not worry you, but then when you see . . . an extremely psychotic person, you know that they are insane and, I mean . . . by and large are beyond any help or any . . . repair, I mean, I feel that you become worried . . . maybe this will happen to me, and. . .

T.: Quite a frightening thing if some of the things that you observe within yourself . . . you see carried to a much greater extreme in others . . . and those others are psychotic.

C.: M-hm.

T.: Because then it seems to you they're hopeless and therefore . . . does it mean that . . . a—I harbor within me the beginnings of this hopeless . . . a. . .

C.: It might evolve to the same. (Pause.)

T.: That can really worry you.

C.: Yeah. I mean, if you just . . . so to speak . . . existed within yourself . . . and didn't have any contact with other people . . . that would be . . . I mean, would be fine . . . and might even be (*sighs*) an ideal, because you . . . I mean, you wouldn't be put in contrast with—to other people . . . but I mean your daily contact with other people . . . reveals these contrasts . . . makes them more apparent.

Seventh Interview

Mr. Bebb opens the seventh interview with the feeling that his need for counseling is a sign of weakness.

C.: I've been thinking about this counseling service. And I've somewhat questioned my necessity for . . . for seeking . . . counseling help. Because it seems . . . well, maybe not quite apparent but it . . . just . . . seems to be a reasonable inference that (pause) the solution to any problem that you might find . . . more or less it lies . . . within the individual, I mean it . . . seems that . . . to me that he should be capable of reasoning and . . . reflecting about them himself. Thus . . . he might, arrive at some solution . . . since we'll agree that . . . I mean it's not the problems but . . . it's to look within the person. And . . . well . . . it's just . . . a little . . . sort of . . . well, ridiculous. I mean, seeking out . . . seems to me it's sort of a . . . manifestation of my own . . . inferiority in trying to solve my own problems. Well, I'm not. . .

T.: Seems like kind of a . . . weak and . . . ridiculous thing that . . .

C.: Yes, I feel. . .

T.: . . . that you feel that you have such a need. (Pause.)

C.: And . . . well, I'm not saying that I don't think it will help. But . . . well, I just feel that it's sorta just . . . declaring my own . . . incapability to solve my own problems. Well, I just don't know how to. . .

A bit later he goes further, saying that counseling thus far has been both discouraging and disturbing. He mentions the possibility of stopping.

C.: I also feel that this . . . introspection is . . . not necessary because it doesn't . . . seem to have taken anywhere, or lead anywhere. And I feel that . . . what I see within myself I should just . . . accept rather than asking how and why. But somehow that doesn't satisfy. (Pause.)

T.: But you feel as though looking within . . . hasn't led to any progress and . . . you think you have to just stop that and accept whatever is . . . within; then you can't quite let yourself do that either.

C.: No. (Pause.) But as I said, I mean . . . it seems that the more I try to look at myself, the more pecu-confused I become. . .

T.: And is what . . . is this part of what you're saying today, that as you look at yourself . . . it does seem more confusing . . . and that that confusion seems a little frightening? (Pause.)

C.: Well, it seems discouraging. . . . . And I feel that, rather than . . . *help* me, it disturbs me.

T.: M-hm. That by and large to discover . . . confusion within yourself . . . has been disturbing . . . rather than helping.

C.: Then I also think that . . . could be that I just want to . . . to know too much about myself, or maybe that I just indulged in too much introspection. . . Mean, it appears to me that . . . sometimes, that I should just stop where I am . . . and just, just stop there and don't . . . not speculate any more about it. But . . . well, I, again I don't.

T.: It looks kind of attractive to say. . . "Okay, I'll just shut the doors here. I won't look at myself any further and go on from here." . . . But somehow you don't find yourself . . . doing that.

C.: I don't . . . no.

Later in the interview he explores the possibility that his discouragement may be due to the fact that what he is finding within himself is not in accord with his hope and intuition. He tells how much he wishes to discover that he is a positive and worth-while person.

C.: Maybe the fact that it appears to me that I'm not getting anywhere . . . might be or might . . . yeah, might be indicative of (pause) the fact that what I find within myself is not in concord with my . . . intuitive or my . . . intuitive . . . knowledge of what I hope to find. . . But yet . . . seems that I don't want to abandon my intuition.

T.: M-hm. M-hm. M-hm.

C.: I mean, if there were any definite traces within myself . . . which might bear out the . . . intuition, then, I mean, I would know that I was getting somewhere, because I would know that I was getting closer to . . . my original . . . or . . . the things which I see verification for. But the fact that I don't seem to get anywhere might be . . . indication that it doesn't exist. . . I don't know if it's clear.

T.: I think it is. That perhaps the reason you feel . . . no progress and so on is that . . . perhaps in this exploration of yourself . . . you haven't yet, at least . . . well, I'll put it the other way around . . . that you have discovered things that aren't entirely in accordance with what . . . somehow basically . . . you feel you are. . . And perhaps that's a disturbing . . . thing. Is that . . . something of what you're saying?

C.: Yes. (Pause.) And I suppose it's because of this fact that the things which I find are not in accordance with my intuitive knowledge of myself, that I feel the need of some person whom I suppose . . . or hope, would feel the same way about it might guide me to what . . . I mean, I hope that his evaluation of me might coincide with my intuition about . . . what I . . . basically am.

T.: That almost sounds, and I'm not quite sure that I understand it, but that almost sounds as though (pause) as though you feel concerned that what you're discovering within yourself . . . may make you a less worth-while person than you had intuitively felt . . . you were, and if you could find somebody who says, "But you are a worth-while person," and who would confirm that side of your self . . . that that would have a good deal of meaning. Is that . . . ?

C.: Yes. I was just going to say that. That what I've been saying here, I mean, would . . . give the implication that (pause) what I . . . intuitively feel that I am is something good . . . and . . . from what I've been saying it rather appears that . . . what I *do* find is . . . I mean, is not good. (Pause.) But, other times, I feel that I find something within myself which is good, but then that . . . it doesn't develop far enough to . . . I mean for me to be completely convinced of its validity. I mean, it just seems . . . to stop, and you have . . . sort of . . . opposites . . . just . . . entering in, disturbing the . . . distorting the picture, so to speak.

T.: M-hm. In other words . . . in this exploration, it isn't just that you find bad things about yourself, but when you find things you *value* about yourself, they don't seem too *certain* or too sure, and there are often contradictions involved . . . ?

C.: Yeah. . . They just don't seem to be . . . strongly enough set off . . . to be convincing.

T.: M-hm. Sorta gives you kind of an . . . *uncertain* feeling about that aspect of it. Is that . . . ?

C.: Yes. In fact (pause) I mean, I feel that basically what it is, I mean what is troubling me about myself is that uncertainty as to, as to just what I am. And (pause) I feel that what I'm seeking *for* . . . within myself is just . . . a convincing . . . verification of (pause) good qualities which I might discover. (Pause.)

At the close of this period he recognizes that perhaps he is trying to escape the effort which would be involved in becoming the person he wants to be. At this point he also reduces the number of interviews from two per week to one.

C.: I mean if that is the case, and I have to conclude that I consist . . . of both good and evil, the only thing I can do is just . . . work toward elimination of the . . . I mean elimination of the evil (pause) by working for something good. (Pause.) That is to say, I mean to be truly good, just seems to be . . . a process of just hard . . . plain hard work rather than something which you . . . you *are* . . . inherently . . . I mean that you are innately.

T.: That is, *possibly* it isn't the (pause) possibly being really good isn't a type of *description*, but a type of *effort*. Is that . . . ?

C.: Yeah. (Pause.) Then maybe if that is the case the problems which I seem to encounter might just be (*sighs*) obstacles in my . . . conscious effort to . . . becoming good. (Pause.) Well, I might . . . I mean, rather than trying to fight them (pause) just try to (pause) resign and try to rationalize, attempt to find some . . . logical (pause) necessity for the existence. (Pause.)

T.: M-hm. That is, a part of what's going on in *you* may be a (pause) a need to kind of . . . escape seeing them as obstacles which might yield to effort, and maybe it's just an attempt to see them in some more absolute light. Is that . . . ?

C.: Yeah. Just try to become convinced of the . . . necessary reason for their existence rather than try to eliminate them. (Pause.)

T.: Guess our time's about up.

C.: Yeah. (Arrangements for next appointment.) Really, only one meeting a week would be all right.

T.: All right. Want to make it a week from today?

Eighth Interview

Our client opens the interview by considering further the process of effort which is necessary to become "good." He feels that one has to have incentive to work toward the goal of realizing one's potentialities. Very tentatively he concludes that even if one's potentialities are not great, but "sort of limited," it might still be some reason to work toward their realization.

He wishes very much that he knew whether he had potentialities. He explores this uncertainty further in the passage that follows:

C.: Sometimes I just feel that . . . personally I'm (pause) well, I'm working or sort of . . . directing my life or my existence . . . on the basis of some sort of hypothesis which is really . . . there's no rational . . . a, basis for, for accepting it in the first place. I mean, sometimes I feel that I am worth while and other times . . . I feel that I'm not. Again . . . it's just this uncertainty.

T.: M-hm. (Pause.) Does that . . . does that feeling almost amount to being . . . a very deep wish that . . . someone did regard you as worth while? . . . Or isn't it? I don't know.

C.: Yes. In a sense. But then (pause) if it does happen that . . . people should compliment me on something I've done . . . it just doesn't seem to be enough . . . and I just seem to want more . . . and that's. . .

T.: M-hm. You know very well . . . that praise for achievement . . . that isn't the thing that satisfies this need.

C.: No, it's . . . mean, it's . . . more or less boils down to what I said before. I mean, it has to be some sort of . . . an inner realization of your . . . I mean, of your own worth-whileness. (Pause.) But then again . . . I mean, it's a contradiction . . . because that may not at all be attained by (*sighs*) . . . even if someone . . . or if I should . . . should agree for someone to tell me what he . . . what he, what he thought. I mean, someone whom I considered . . . well, competent. That's why. (Pause.)

T.: That there is the feeling that you would so much like to regard yourself as a worth-while person . . . and it seems to you as though perhaps . . . someone else by some kind of evidence . . . could convince you that that's true. (Pause.)

C.: Ah, yes. (Pause.) I mean (*sighs*) there exist such . . . conflicting and contradictory . . . notions within myself that I just don't. (Pause.)

T.: You don't see *how* you can find the . . . sure sense of your own worth within yourself because there are such . . . contradictory feelings *in you*.

Later he discusses an intelligence test as a way of proving his worth to himself.

C.: (Long pause.) So I mean, the problem is really how to (pause) how to, to achieve some sort of stability within . . . I mean, some stable . . . belief . . . about myself . . . I'm just . . . not sure. (Long pause.)

T.: I can't help but wonder there . . . if what you are asking basically in your feelings . . . may not be this . . . ah, "Is there *anyone* . . . who really . . . deeply believes that . . . I'm worth while?"

C.: Yeah. I'm . . . I've been thinking about that. (Pause.) If that is so, I mean then it is . . . a more or less universal . . . problem for . . . the human. (Pause.) Like, I mean at times I've just felt . . . oh, it sounds silly, I mean. . .

T.: You were saying it seems kind of silly but. . .

C.: Yes. I mean . . . at least it does . . . to me . . . that it is silly because sometimes I do want it that way. Like . . . I mean, great many times I'm just sort of . . . obsessed with the idea . . . of having an intelligence. . . I mean, having an intelligence test made . . . on me. (Pause.) In a way that seems sort of artificial, but, on the other hand, sometimes I feel it would serve a purpose. But here again I feel that . . . if it didn't sort of mark up to the I.Q. of my friends, I just feel that I wouldn't accept it because . . . I have this . . . innate . . . desire . . . to try to be like my friends, at least . . . meet their standards.

A long quotation from the end of this interview indicates something of the depth of his despair about himself and his doubt about continuing in the interviews.

C.: (Long pause.) Now, here again I just feel the need of some sort . . . well, sort of universal standard by which to . . . to measure myself, I mean (pause) attempt to get some sort of definite (pause) certain way . . . or notion about myself.

T.: M-hm. (Pause.) This seems like such a strong desire to have someone say, or give you evidence that . . . this is the way you should look at yourself, or this is why you do the things you do or. . .

C.: Yes. I mean, sorta the key to myself. Key to my personality.

T.: M-hm. You'd like so much to get the key to yourself that would enable you to measure yourself and understand yourself. (Pause.)

C.: Just at least get . . . get something which would explain . . . my certain basic . . . recurrent traits . . . behavioristic traits. (Pause.)

T.: You'd like to know, "Why do I behave recurrently in this way?" (Long pause.)

C.: Mean, it's also a confusion, I mean, sometimes I just feel that I should have this, and other times I feel that I shouldn't. Mean, feel that I shouldn't because it's artificial. I should be able to discover those truths or these truths about myself, and by my own efforts. And then when I feel that that's impossible, then I . . . would like for someone else to do it.

T.: M-hm. When you feel a little bit hopeless about finding the answers to some of those things within yourself, then it just seems as though you've got to have someone else to provide that assurance. (Long pause.)

C.: But as I said . . . I mean, deep within myself, I feel that it has to be. I mean, no external assurance would really alter anything or . . . would make any modification or . . . well, I mean, it has to be some sort of . . . some inner realization or inner awareness or inner realization of just what I am. (Pause.)

T.: You're very sure that in the long run it's got to be that inner realization of what you are, or a realization that comes from within you. But still, that doesn't. . . . And you realize that the other would be somewhat artificial, but still that doesn't stop you from feeling . . . at times that, "By gosh, that's what I want." (Pause.)

C.: Yes. You're right. And also I feel that, at times, that this outside assurance or information about myself . . . might work as a clue toward this ultimate self-realization.

T.: M-hm. You might sort of get some leads from an outside evaluation. (Long pause.)

C.: But here . . . I mean, this desire, those doubts about myself (*sighs*) I mean, I've had them for years, and I sort of think about them perpetually, constantly, but (pause) I never reach any solution though. I feel that now, while I'm in here, I should attempt to talk more about them, sort of feel that maybe I'm just trying to shun away from them because they appear so futile.

T.: M-hm. Feel that you've struggled for so long with those feelings of worthlessness that . . . well, that you just don't know what . . . what you can hope for there. And I gather that you even . . . even criticize yourself in the interview for not . . . why don't you get at them more and so on. You're feeling somewhat critical toward yourself in that.

C.: Yeah. (Pause.)

T.: As though you (pause) can't quite accept yourself in the interview either. I mean, you should be doing something different and better. (Pause.)

C.: Yes. I mean, I feel that (pause) I don't think that I make enough of any personal effort. . . I mean, somehow I just feel that I don't decide to tell about it or . . . try to sort of shut it out.

T.: Seems to you that you can't . . . or that you don't think well of yourself in the interview any more than you do outside. That you're just not making an adequate effort.

C.: M-hm. (Pause.) Mean, I sometimes feel that . . . I really shouldn't be . . . taking or undergoing these interviews, that I feel it's . . . what I see within myself is just . . . I mean, is just *me*, and it's . . . it's unchangeable. And I feel that that is manifested in my desire sometimes . . . my speaking language about it, and just trying to remain quiet.

T.: M-hm. Just sort of feel, "Look, all I get at in the interview is *me* . . . and that's a pretty hopeless futile kind of . . . thing. I can't change that worthless me. What right have I to take up anybody's time?" Is that putting it too strongly or is that . . . ?

C.: No, that's . . . I mean, that's pretty. . .

T.: (*Very sympathetically.*) Maybe it doesn't quite seem to you that (pause) that anybody *could* feel it was worth while to spend time with you when you are only *you*. (Pause.)

Ninth Interview

He opens this contact with the possibility of working things out entirely within himself.

C.: Well . . . (*sighs*) I've been thinking about what I told you. And . . . a . . . I've concluded that (pause) that since (pause) if I (pause) achieve some inner realization . . . that what I'm doing . . . is right . . . well, then everything, it appears, would . . . would be all right . . . and . . . but then if that is the case . . . I mean, there's no . . . use . . . I mean, for me . . . to . . . talk it over with other . . . other people any more when, when I've . . . if I've come to this realization.

T.: M-hm. That is, seems to you as though if the thing seems inwardly right to you . . . then you really believe perhaps you can *trust* that . . . that inner feeling. But if you have really and fully come to that conclusion . . . then . . . counseling wouldn't particularly be needed.

C.: No. Because (pause) I mean, since it all depends upon how I feel about myself, and . . . because of the fact that . . . now . . . I've come to the belief that it all . . . depends on my own attitude toward it . . . then . . . a . . . I don't think . . . I should take (*sighs*) any more of your time. I mean . . . I feel that, I mean, that as of now it's more or less up to me. . . That is, I . . . I'll have to act in accordance with . . . what I think is right, and then the rest will be trying to (*very softly*) eliminate whatever is troubling me. (Pause.) I may not always know when (*sighs*) I mean, I might set up problems but . . . least I'll know what they are and then abandon whatever I'm doing and then go back and try to do it over. See if I'll be satisfied with that. (Pause.) Mean more or less the sensible . . . thing . . . I'll have to follow is just that (pause) if I feel bad about something, it is because it's not . . . what I . . . I mean, deep within me, I really want to do, but what I think that I *should* do. So . . . the thing to do would just be to . . . go back and then try to do it over. And it seems to me I have to . . . work . . . on the basis of that-that principle.

A little later he explores much more fully his growing confidence in his own capacity for self-evaluation. A lengthy quotation seems justified here to give the full flavor of his feeling.

C.: But I've come to believe that . . . whatever I do . . . I just will have to be the judge of it myself. I mean, at least . . . in important questions or personal questions maybe.

T.: You're the only one who can really . . . put the value . . . on what you do.

C.: Yeah. M-hm. (Pause.) And what I've wanted . . . I mean, having the . . . trying to get assurance or . . . sanction or confirmation or verification or whatever you want to call it, from other people . . . I mean, it's really no good unless . . . it agrees with what I . . . I myself want to do, or what I myself think of it. (Pause.)

T.: Are you sort of saying there that. . . since the opinion of others and the judgment of others about *you* . . . is only really of value to you when it . . . confirms your own . . . judgments, then it isn't really quite as important as . . . as . . . you had previously thought. Is that . . . ?

C.: Yes. M-hm. (Pause.) I mean it's part of what I feel that . . . if I think what I'm doing is good . . . and other people don't think it's good, I still give my . . . own judgment preference. . . And if other people think it is good . . . and I also think it is good, well, then I don't really care about . . . a . . . the other people's judgment because it just—fits in—it's according to my own, coincides with my own. (Pause.) But still it just (pause) just occurred to me that . . . I mean, I might have found a principle (pause) to, so to speak, work under . . . follow, but still if I have to . . . mean if I have to apply this principle very much, it would imply that there's still something, I mean . . . which must be bothering me, whatever it may be. Because of the fact that I have to apply the principle. I mean . . . the fact that I have found something . . . to . . . to work by, or to . . . yes, to work by . . . it doesn't mean that . . . whatever problems I think I have, or I thought I had, I mean, it doesn't mean they're eliminated. Just that I've found maybe some sort of a cure for them, or . . . I mean, it may eliminate them. But then again . . . it may not.

T.: Are you saying there that . . . as you think it over, you really feel . . . somewhat *uncertain* as to just . . . how much the . . . recognition of this principle or any use of this principle will do for you in terms of the problems that you feel. Is that . . . ?

C.: Yes. I mean, I feel that it may be . . . a good . . . therapy, I mean, for the elimination of them or. . . What I mean to say is that with this principle, or this . . . yeah, principle . . . I haven't found the, so to speak, the cause of the problem. . . But . . . what I mean is that I've found some sort of . . . medicine, or some sort of . . . thing which might help solve them or be superior to them . . . might even eliminate them.

T.: M-hm. You might have found a way . . . of dealing with your problems, but without ever being completely aware of what the causes of these problems were. Is that . . . ?

C.: M-hm. Yeah. (Pause.) Well, I also feel that . . . mean, I'll probably (*sighs*) continue having problems as long as I live, and . . . could be that . . . maybe I'm only overemphasizing them. . . And . . . if I just look at them possibly a little differently, I may get more confidence, might not think as much about them.

T.: These *problems* may be something that you'll always have with you, but if . . . if you found a *constructive* way of looking at them . . . that might be a very important . . . step . . . or very important thing. (Pause.)

C.: But I think that the most important thing . . . is the fact . . . I feel that . . . well, that I realize that . . . in reality that . . . the people of . . . I mean, the judgment of other people . . . outside yourself is not really . . . important. And you can only realize your own value . . . I mean through some inner awareness of what you feel that you are. And no matter what other people think of it, it makes really no difference unless you . . . you yourself feel that way about it . . . if you don't agree with them, then you . . . it just won't (*sighs*) just won't help any.

T.: Feel that for you that's a pretty important . . . discovery that . . . the only values you can ever be sure of are the ones you actually *experience* within yourself.

C.: And the ones you really accept or believe in. (Pause.) I mean, someone might come along and pat you on the shoulder and say that . . . you're an excellent fellow, you're good, but . . . if you don't believe it in yourself I mean, it's just . . . doesn't help any. You might just think the person is insincere. (Pause.) So I'm just . . . convinced it all depends on me . . . or, least, depends on myself.

T.: And you feel, I gather, much more . . . *willing*, and perhaps much more able, to rely on yourself in that kind of thing. Is that right? Or am I. . .

C.: Yes. M-hm. I do, because . . . as I've said, I don't know . . . I just. (Pause.) My own . . . judgment is not absolute. At least it's . . . but . . . or my own judgment about myself anyway . . . may not be absolute, but . . . it's relatively higher than the . . . judgment which other people might pass upon me. (Pause.) I feel that if I ultimately should become (pause) convinced of the fact that . . . what I do or what I have done . . . is good, well, there's just . . . nothing that anyone ever could say about it that I think would change my mind.

T.: M-hm. (Pause.) If you have the *inner* conviction that what you've done is worth-while . . . then you doubt if a thousand people telling you the opposite could . . . change your mind.

C.: Yeah. M-hm. I feel that . . . I mean, previously, a great deal of my trouble has . . . stemmed from the fact that I've . . . I've sought too much the opinion of other people without relying too much on myself; and that . . . though I did rely a little on myself, I also relied on . . . other people; and that . . . brings up the uncertainty. But that was really what caused difficulties.

T.: M-hm. That actually you weren't quite relying on one or the other.

C.: M-hm.

T.: And . . . so never had a firm . . . basis.

C.: M-hm. That's right. And I feel now that . . . I'm much more certain about. . .

T.: You just feel more assurance about yourself, hm?

C.: Yeah. I think. (Long pause.) I mean, I feel that the thing to do is just to be . . . be honest with yourself and be sincere.

Toward the end of this interview comes a portion in which the therapist's handling is likely to be much questioned.

C. (Long pause.) Well, I may be (*sighs*) repeating myself again. But (pause) I think it's a major . . . achievement or . . . a major step . . . in individual progress to come to realize . . . well, that you should . . . depend on your own judgment rather than the judgment of other people. I know I've said this before, but . . . the more I think about it, the more I realize how important it is. I just want to stress that . . . most important . . . I mean, I think. . .

T.: That's something that has a lot of meaning . . . for you.

C.: M-hm. I feel it has eliminated the uncertainty. (Pause.) I feel that participation and things like that would only be meant toward this end that . . . coming to depend more upon yourself. (Pause.) Well, I mean, not depend on yourself to the extent that you exclude, I mean, human relations or anything like that. (Pause.) Just depend on yourself so that (pause) you realize that you (pause) do have the . . . potentialities, I mean, of doing something, instead of having to ask people all the time whether they think it's right or not.

T.: M-hm. This isn't an independence that shuts other people out or anything like that. It sounds more as though . . . it was an experience of trusting yourself more in . . . in the directions that you're going.

C.: M-hm. (Long pause: 2 minutes.) Well, I don't know if I can say more without just repeating myself.

T.: You really feel you've . . . said almost what you have to say.

C.: Well, yeah, I feel that . . . I just found the essentials, and (pause) I could . . . probably talk more about it. I'd just . . . be elaborating on details rather than . . . I don't know just. . .

T.: It just sorta seems to me that . . . what you're saying in your feeling is, "I think I'm through" . . .

C.: M-hm. Yeah.

T.: . . . but that you're having kind of a hard time putting that in words. Is that right?

C.: Yeah. (*With relief.*) (Pause.) I mean, I don't want to imply that I have no use for you any more. (*Sighs.*) I mean. . .

T.: Sort of fearful that if you said you think you're through, that would seem as though you were somehow. . . ?

C.: It would be just sort of selfish, I mean. (Pause.) Just . . . talk to clarify my own thoughts maybe. (Long pause.)

T.: Okay?

C.: Yes. I think I'm through. (*Sighs.*)

T.: Okay. And I'd just say that . . . I think so too. But that if . . . if, on the other hand, next week or next month or some time, you feel, well, "By gosh, I see more things that I want to work out or something," all right, I'll be very glad to see you.

A comment probably needs to be made here which would be unnecessary if we were presenting a recording rather than a transcript. When the counselor attempts to respond to the client's unspoken feeling, "I think I'm through," the relief in Mr. Bebb's voice is very obvious. It seems clear that this *is* his feeling and that he is greatly relieved to have it recognized. This comment is only a description of a fact which would be evident to anyone who listened to the recording. Whether the therapist was wise to respond in this way is an entirely separate question upon which the reader can form his own judgment.

A few minutes after this excerpt the client concluded his interviews, with thanks to the therapist and with the therapist's repetition that he should come back in if he wished to.

Follow-up Interview

Six months later Mr. Bebb was asked to return to the Counseling Center for follow-up interviews. He was interviewed both by the psychologist who had administered the tests and by the therapist. The content of both interviews was very similar. An excerpt from the interview with the psychologist will illustrate the flavor of both interviews.

Test Administrator: Jim, I'm interested in . . . right now in your reaction to your counseling experience and whether it meant anything to you, then or during the last months. How do you feel about . . . ?

C.: Well. (Pause.) It . . . seems to me that, right after I completed it and even during the latter part of the counseling service . . . it meant a great deal more to me than . . . it does now.

T.A.: Some diminution in benefits, sort of . . . as time has lapsed, it's become less beneficial or meaningful?

C.: Yeah. I wouldn't say *beneficial*. I mean, rather the, apparent value, uh, at least . . . for me, it's seemed to decrease. (Pause.) Let me explain it this way: I don't know if everyone who undergoes counseling feels this way or not, but I felt that . . . when I . . . went to counseling, went to my therapist about myself, I felt that the . . . the ultimate thing that I had to . . . do, I mean, effect by myself was . . . I mean, by my own efforts, was a change in *myself*, I mean a change in my way of doing things or in looking at myself or in looking at other people. Now . . . while undergoing counseling with the help of the therapist I . . . apparently . . . or I thought . . . seemed to me that I (pause) realized the value of a great many things and that's not. . . I mean, I was very sincere about certain resolutions that . . . was implicitly inferred by the . . . by. . . I mean, some of the answers I gave in the . . . in the counseling, and the answers I gave to myself. And . . . so, I mean, I was very sincere in my . . . in my hope of fulfilling these . . . resolutions and doing everything that I myself wanted to do about myself. However, as it is now, it seems that (pause) at that time, of course it only remains in theory, I mean, I don't think I ever sincerely tried to . . . *do* what I've talked about. I mean, I rather just talked about it, instead of doing it, although I did have the very sincere intention of . . . starting doing . . . starting to . . . I mean, starting to do what I . . . sincerely believed I should try to, about changing myself.

In these interviews Mr. Bebb also stated that he felt he gained more respect for his own individuality and that he came to recognize that it is a lifelong job to mold one's self. He wished the therapist had given his opinion, a "temporary answer," which might have helped to provide a tentative goal.

His major feeling, however, was that he had not put into action some of the things he had seen. In response to direct questions he said that his physical symptoms were pretty much unchanged, though he did not feel they were quite as alarming. He was also asked by the therapist, "You once mentioned that you were kinda concerned about some experiences that you'd had, sort of hallucinations. . . . . Anything to say about that?" His response was: "I haven't had any for a long time. When I have them, I become concerned, but I haven't really any cause for concern."

IV. GLOBAL PERSONALITY CHANGE

In the total research program one of the projects was concerned with measuring, on a continuum of adjustment and integration, the degree of general personality change. The TAT was the instrument used for this purpose (see chap. 8). In this section the findings of this portion of the research in the case of Mr. Bebb will be presented.

The hypothesis for this project was that if a competent psychologist placed the TAT's in an order from most poorly integrated to best integrated, the pre- and post-therapy and follow-up tests would show increasing integration. This hypothesis was made, of course, in regard to all the cases in the study as one of the outcomes which could be expected from client-centered therapy. A special investigation was made of the TAT's available in the case of Mr. Bebb which was parallel to, but goes further than, the study thus far made of the whole group.

TABLE 1

Ranking	TAT	Time of Administration
4. Least integrated and adjusted...	Z	Pre-wait (1st TAT)
3.	W	Follow-up (4th TAT)
2.	Y	Pre-therapy (2d TAT)
1. Best integrated and adjusted...	X	Post-therapy (3d TAT)

There were four TAT's available for analysis: from the pre-wait battery, the pre-therapy battery, the post-therapy test, and the follow-up. The respective intervals between tests were as follows: 60 days, 49 days, and 180 days. The stories as given by Mr. Bebb were electrically recorded and transcribed. A set of these four transcriptions, with the dates removed, and identified only by letter, were then given to a psychologist who was experienced in the interpretation of the TAT[3] but who had no knowledge of the case or its outcome and no knowledge of the order in which the TAT's had been given. She was asked to study each TAT and to summarize her impression of the individual and his psychological state. She was also asked to order the TAT's from least well adjusted and integrated to best adjusted and integrated.

The psychologist carried out this assignment but stated that the ordering of the tests was difficult in this case, since the differences in degree of integration seemed small, and hence the placements were made with considerable uncertainty. The order is, however, of considerable interest. They were rated as shown in Table 1. It

3. Thanks are due to Dr. Carol Bowie, at that time psychologist of the Municipal Court of Chicago, for her assistance in this task.

is evident that the first, second, and third TAT's showed improvement in adjustment as predicted but that the fourth TAT, the follow-up, showed a regression toward the initial status.

In order to give the reader somewhat more of an opportunity to make these judgments for himself, the summarized personality pictures, as written by the psychologist without knowledge of the case, are presented in the order in which the tests were administered.

First TAT: Code Letter Z[4]

This is a passive, dependent individual whose characteristic response to frustration is to withdraw, to retreat either by removing himself bodily or by becoming as inconspicuous as possible physically while withdrawing mentally and emotionally into a kind of passionless nirvana. He is strongly ambivalent but as strongly represses his own aggressiveness. A favorite retreat from too deeply experienced emotion is intellectualizing, a philosophical approach which makes discussion possible by making it impersonal. This is a highly complex and very intelligent individual who is very anxious, very insecure, and rather guilt-ridden. There are masochistic trends in his passivity, and, although he wishes to give the impression of being impervious to persuasion, to continue on his own chosen path "in spite of..... pleading," he is very unsure of his own strength and ability to choose and hold to any goal requiring real effort for attainment. There is ambivalence expressed in both father-son and mother-son relationships, with a heightening of guilt feelings in these areas. The Freudian "death wish" is strongly expressed. A depression, a desire to quit the uneven struggle, a despair of ever being accepted as the noble creature he is in his secret heart—are all lying as an undercurrent in everything he thinks and says. The fairy-tale changeling prince, of finer clay than those about him but unacknowledged and unrecognized, he is desperately unhappy. His refusal to accept challenge and to be the aggressor is based upon a real fear of discovery that these delightful fantasies are far from reality—and because the lone dissenter *always* fails if he becomes aggressive. The only thing to do is to withdraw, in lofty superiority, to his ivory tower. Since warm human relationships can undermine even this security, they, too, are thrown aside with finality—"there can be no means of altering" the "facing in an opposite direction" from love and affection. Freedom is seen as the ability to do nothing. This individual may be rather too close to a real break with reality for comfort, having shut off all feeling, all desiring, all hoping, all struggle as too painful and too hopeless. It might be that he is a victim of an actual catastrophe which has actually overwhelmed and rather benumbed him; it might be a very deep feeling of inadequacy and impotence for physical reasons—or perhaps the whole depression is basically self-induced. *Something* is sensed as catastrophic, inescapable, and

4. Given prior to waiting period; ranked No. 4, least well adjusted.

bearable only by complete passivity with an almost panic reaction when the possibility of being overcome by this "it" is faced. The individual holds himself in with a very tight rein indeed.

Second TAT: Code Letter Y[5]

This individual is torn by ambivalence but not to the extent of panic or complete dissolution. He feels impotent to utilize his own gifts, either because the world won't listen or outside forces prevent it or "things" are just too much for him. The ivory tower is still seen as desirable—contemplation of the conflict between good and evil, of strife versus inertia is still the safest way to handle himself. "Someone" will come along and fix everything—it will not need effort on his part. However, the eventuality of having to take an active part in effecting harmony is beginning to dawn upon him. There is a tentative facing of the problems which produce panic with almost immediate flight into "nirvana"—but with more and more cautious but continuing, positive steps toward action. There is realization of the need for love and support in a faint realization that rejection results in utter misery. He is afraid to allow himself to hope for happiness, and he refuses to admit to himself how strong his feelings of hostility and aggression are—especially toward men. He turns his back upon emotional involvement, refusing to admit how necessary love is to him and affirming stoutly that the conflict of intellect versus emotion must be won on the intellectual level.

Life and struggle seem empty, futile, and nonrewarding. He despairs of being recognized as the superior person he feels he is and is desperately lonely while at the same time denying the need for deference. There is a guilt about failing to come up to the expectations of the mother (or other women) in affectional responsiveness.

Outstanding in this record is the feeling of futility—struggles against terrific odds only to find the object, once gained, turning into dust. The individual is gravely ambivalent; he wants to be "above" or aloof from all feeling tone, but can't. Being aloof, refraining from aggressiveness is seen as "good"; displays of strength are "evil." The individual is so insecure, so unsure of his invulnerability, that he still runs—escapes into depersonalization. The unconscious desire to show great hostility in aggressive, almost antisocial, ways is very close to the surface but not quite—there is always the hasty interpolation of "This is only make-believe." Instead of overt aggressiveness, the individual prefers manipulation of others (power over others without resistance or competition) with a corresponding fear of being manipulated by others. His determination to ignore or minimize familial ties is a denial of deep dependency needs and may point toward a strong oedipal complex deeply buried. He is afraid and knows he is afraid—of people and contacts with people. Life is futile; therefore, one must acknowledge no needs, feel no emotion. He is afraid of the challenge of living, but cessation from struggle is not now seen as an end in itself; it is just a resting place. Inertia—

5. Given prior to therapy; ranked No. 2 in adjustment.

nirvana—is a temporary withdrawal into a "secure" place, where strength may be gathered to go on from there. This is not the feeling of utter chaos and black despair; although the individual has a long way to go, he has seen that there is a way out and feels that it is available to him if and when he is ready for it.

Progress may be illusory—and the feeling of superiority may be hollow—but the converse *may* also be true.

There is a constant swing from feelings of desperate inadequacy to an almost equally desperate demand that everyone recognize his superior qualities; but gradually the value of some kind of compromise is making itself felt. Since this way of life has resulted in nothing but futility and loneliness, there is a need, not to negate life, but to seek a substitute for the present or established ways of meeting its challenge. The safety of the known—safe although unrewarding—is being sensed as an insufficient reason for clinging to it. The individual wants to protect himself from others—is highly suspicious of others—and his impulse to stand aside and observe life flow by is beginning to seem both impossible and undesirable in the long run. Dimly he senses that if enough of the facets of personality are integrated, the "strays" or "mavericks" may be ignored or may even be swept along with the rest—they are not necessarily potential shatter points.

Third TAT: Code Letter X[6]

The individual admits his own ineptitude in handling life. Passivity and dependency have not "worked"—rather sluggishly, some degree of activity is stirring. Action is seen as preferable to inaction, but the individual still cannot trust others or himself in relationship to others. There must be manipulation, and therefore there must be eternal vigilance. Emotions and frustrations are acknowledged—grudgingly—and the familiar cover-up ("This isn't real; this hasn't actually happened; it's a horrible nightmare, and I'll soon wake up") is readily assumed. The individual is now aware that his panicky flights into a nirvana state solve nothing; attempts to withdraw from reality have failed. The outlook is weakly positive, weakly optimistic, but dissolution of personality is no longer so frankly feared. Love, as a real, warm, living thing between two peers, is still a threat, and there are strong indications of almost overt homosexual activities (as the passive partner), which have caused grave concern. Love and affection are almost deliberately placed "in the background" for later fulfilment but are no longer ignored or blacked out completely. The alternative to giving up is to try again in a different direction. The patient feels lost; he doesn't know the terrain—but no longer utterly helpless. There is great guilt feeling with respect to the mother figure, with pronounced dependency needs almost desperately denied and defied. He is both drawn to and repelled by men—and has no real convictions as to which will predominate. There is an increased compulsivity, increased ambivalence, but *some* decrease in anxiety and insecurity. The preferred aloof, onlooker role is reluctantly given up; it is so safe, so Jovian! But man's attempts to alter the unalterable are futile; struggle is of no avail. The struggle between good

6. Given after therapy; ranked No. 1, best adjusted.

and evil within himself is never going to be resolved "for keeps," and reinforcement of "good" relationships or a "split" may ensue. Aggressiveness is seen as "lurking in wait." Life is a monster, lying in wait to trap the unwary—which it always does. It is futile to try to escape. Hence nirvana is no answer. The individual still feels helpless in the influence of stronger forces than himself; he is weak and cannot overcome evil by himself. Masochistic trends are apparent, but there is the "maybe"—rather stronger than in any other record—that to struggle is really preferable. The possibility of finding a way out is seen as, *perhaps*, even pleasant. *Maybe* he will "enjoy the light"—*maybe* he will "return to the dark." The present sense of confusion and loss is here seen as, possibly, of his own doing; and therefore it can, maybe, be undone. This is tentative, but sensed for the first time. All is still "vanity," and the irrevocability of the way he has handled life can be borne only if it can be depersonalized. This takes real strength. Dependency is still highly necessary, but there is still, also, distrust of the stronger person and a need to find some *impersonal* support for the dependency. Some people, he feels, *like* dependent individuals and can help develop them into potential leaders. There is still much self-doubt—"Am I going anywhere or not?" Competition can still exist only where there is no question of his superiority—he is still sure that weakness is equivalent to death—but there is now the possibility of facing some of his fears; and the reassurance of being able to "see for a little way" helps.

Fourth TAT: Code Letter W[7]

This record seems to split into two distinct parts, as if given on separate occasions. The first ten responses delineate a very disturbed person indeed, so close to a schizoid break that one cannot be quite certain he has not slipped over the brink. The complete disorganization is focused around Cards I and II, which may indicate a despair so profound he cannot bear to remember it—a guilt so deep it throws him completely. He does not recover for the first ten cards. The sense of loss begun in Card I ("Outside forces have destroyed . . . . . the thing they like"—note he does not say "love") reaches its culmination at Card III and results in utter chaos. The possibility of some crime of violence contemplated or actually performed should be considered, although the probability of actual performance by this patient is not too great. He is struggling very hard to fight through the chaotic currents, and throughout there is a general feeling of slight optimism—that having reached the "depths of dark despair" there's a possibility of ascent, that any descent implies an eventual ascent. The individual "prefers" the "dark," "fears" the "light"—yet struggles toward it. Withdrawal is futile even though comparatively safe, and, while the individual is passive, the flight into complete inactivity is less headlong—the tendency to overintellectualize is strong, and there is a determined effort to depersonalize all situations. This effort is not always successful; then the individual shows deep dependency needs and a sense of complete inadequacy. He is constantly asking, "Who am I? Where am I? Where do I go from here?" Almost in spite of himself a feeling of the necessity for com-

7. Given at follow-up point; ranked No. 3 in adjustment.

promise, for acceptance "both/and" rather than his desire for "either/or" grows upon him. There is considerable guilt feeling centered around the mother figure. He fears aggressiveness and offers only passive resistance to frustration, at best; this easily breaks down into an almost overtly desired dependency. Panicky when activity seems to be forced upon him, he is equally panicky at the idea of uncertainty in the natural forces around him, and the real sense of his inadequacy to deal with reality. Escape would be a "miracle," yet he begins to hope for such a miracle, *very* tentatively. His attempts to face real emotional depths are extremely inadequate; he quietly retreats into an immature, unreal "Bang, bang, you're dead—now get up and shoot me" kind of wishful thinking. Yet he gropes toward a realization of the necessity for facing painful facts. He can't actually *do* so; but he sees, dimly, that some people can; maybe, someday, he can learn to do so. There is revealed for the first time a feeling of having been rejected, of being alone *not* of his own volition. The changeling prince may be a mortal among men—but still of somewhat finer clay . . . people should value him, and be willing to "carry" him even though he is dead weight. Passivity, dependency, competition only against nonexistent competitors—it is still the picture of inadequacy, although some beginnings of insight may be inferred, and fear of personal involvement is slowly losing its deep emotional loading enough to be faced—or at least talked about, in the latter half of the record. The complete breakdown in the first half and the consequent feeling of terrific and almost hopeless struggle smooth out to less desperation and to a clinging to abstraction as to a life-raft.

Comments

These TAT's indicate that this client was a rather deeply disturbed person, and it is quite clear that at no point does he approach a real resolution of his conflicts or a genuinely good adjustment. The range of change is narrow.

One point of interest is that some change is seen by the TAT analyst between the first and second TAT's. This would seem to indicate that in a person motivated for therapy, and looking forward to the beginning of therapy, some change may take place even in the absence of any interviews or other contacts (see chap. 14 for a more complete discussion).

It seems clear that some change occurred during the period of therapy. The post-therapy record seems well described as "weakly positive" and showing constructive indications not present in the other TAT's. It is also evident that in the ensuing six months Mr. Bebb dropped back to a state in which inner catastrophe or breakdown again seems very close.

V. CHANGES IN SELF-PERCEPTION

The General Findings

We may turn now to the process of change as reflected in the Q-sorts of self-referent items. The hypotheses of this portion of our study were these: (*a*) that the perceived self as measured by the Q-sort would become increasingly congruent with the self-ideal as therapy progressed; (*b*) that the perceived self would change more than the perceived self-ideal; (*c*) that the self as perceived at the end of therapy would be more confident, more self-directing, less divided, less inhibited than the self prior to therapy; and (*d*) that the changes in the perceived self would be greater during a period of therapy than during a period of no therapy. We will now have an opportunity to examine the data relevant to these hypotheses from the case of Mr. Bebb.

TABLE 2*

CORRELATION MATRIX OF Q-SORTINGS
CASE OF MR. BEBB

	SBW	SB	S7	SA	SF	IBW	IB	I7	IA	IF	OBW	OB	O7	OA	OF	CS7	CI7	CO7
SBW																		
SB	63																	
S7	55	62																
SA	22	41	45															
SF	54	45	39	54														
IBW	−18	01	−06	35	10													
IB	−16	06	00	37	14	77												
I7	−25	−16	−29	02	−03	51	47											
IA	−13	−09	−13	26	13	70	67	49										
IF	−01	03	03	35	21	67	68	43	73									
OBW	−42	−38	−31	−28	−17	06	06	35	15	01								
OB	−38	−51	−42	−49	−47	−03	−12	20	04	13	65							
O7	−50	−48	−45	−44	−49	01	−08	16	−05	−14	43	10						
OA	−31	−29	−26	−20	−30	−07	−14	11	01	−06	28	52	39					
OF	−11	−25	−24	−16	02	−10	−10	15	05	04	31	37	25	24				
CS7	55	30	30	09	30	−38	−35	−28	−35	−22	−18	−19	−31	−11	11			
CI7	−23	−16	−29	17	01	68	71	54	69	64	29	19	13	11	05	−38		
CO7	−24	−25	−27	−25	−14	−03	−01	23	07	01	50	53	34	30	42	−03	20	

CODE

S = Self
I = Self-ideal or wanted self
O = Ordinary person
BW = Before waiting period
B = Before therapy
7 = Following the seventh interview
A = After the conclusion of therapy
F = Follow-up, six months after end of therapy
C = Counselor's prediction of client's sorting

* Decimal points omitted.

From the design of the research (chap. 3) it will be shown that Mr. Bebb, on five different occasions, sorted the cards to represent his perception of himself, his perception of the self he desired to be, and his perception of others as he thinks they generally are. These fifteen sortings, together with the three made by the therapist at the end of the seventh interview, were correlated with each other, and all the intercorrelations are given in Table 2, although only a portion of these can be specifically commented on.

We shall first be concerned with the correlations related to self and self-ideal, since we know from previous experience that these often change markedly during and after therapy. Some of the most pertinent relationships are indicated in Figure 1. Let us summarize some of the general findings which may be drawn from this figure and from a study of the correlation matrix.

A certain amount of change takes place in self-perception and in the perception of self-ideal during the sixty-day waiting period, and the characteristics of this change are those that we have found to be associated with therapy. Thus the correlation between SBW and SB is .63, and between IBW and IB is .77, both figures being lower than the ordinary self-sort reliability. Also the direction of the change is toward greater congruence of self and ideal, indicating somewhat less tension at the pre-therapy point than at the initial examination (*r* SBW · IBW = −.18; *r* SB · IB = .06).

In the whole period under scrutiny there is change both in self and in ideal, with the more marked change occurring in the perceived self (*r* SBW · SF = .54; *r* IBW · IF = .67).

For both self and ideal, particularly the former, the change during the six-week therapy period is greater (correlations lower) than the change during the sixty-day waiting period or the six-month follow-up period, suggesting that the therapeutic interviews are influential in the change (*r* SB · SA = .41, while *r* SBW · SB = .63, and *r* SA · SF = .54. Also *r* IB · IA = .67, while *r* IBW · IB = .77, and IA · IF = .73).

The over-all change which occurs in the perception of self and ideal is such as to increase to some degree the congruence between the two (*r* SBW · IBW= −.18; *r* SF · IF = .21). Evidently some progress was made toward greater internal comfort, as represented by this measure, but the discrepancy is still great.

Two Significant Sortings

These are some of the very general results of the Q-sort study, and they add up to the statement that, in terms of the client's perceptions as revealed by his sortings, some change occurred, and to some degree tension was reduced. The more significant findings come, however, from a much more detailed scrutiny. A careful study of Table 2 will reveal that the self-ideal as perceived after the seventh interview is definitely distinct from the other ideal sortings. Likewise the self as perceived at the conclusion of therapy is much the most distinctive of the self-sorts. The following paragraphs will attempt to depict the facts in this connection, from which certain inferences will be drawn.

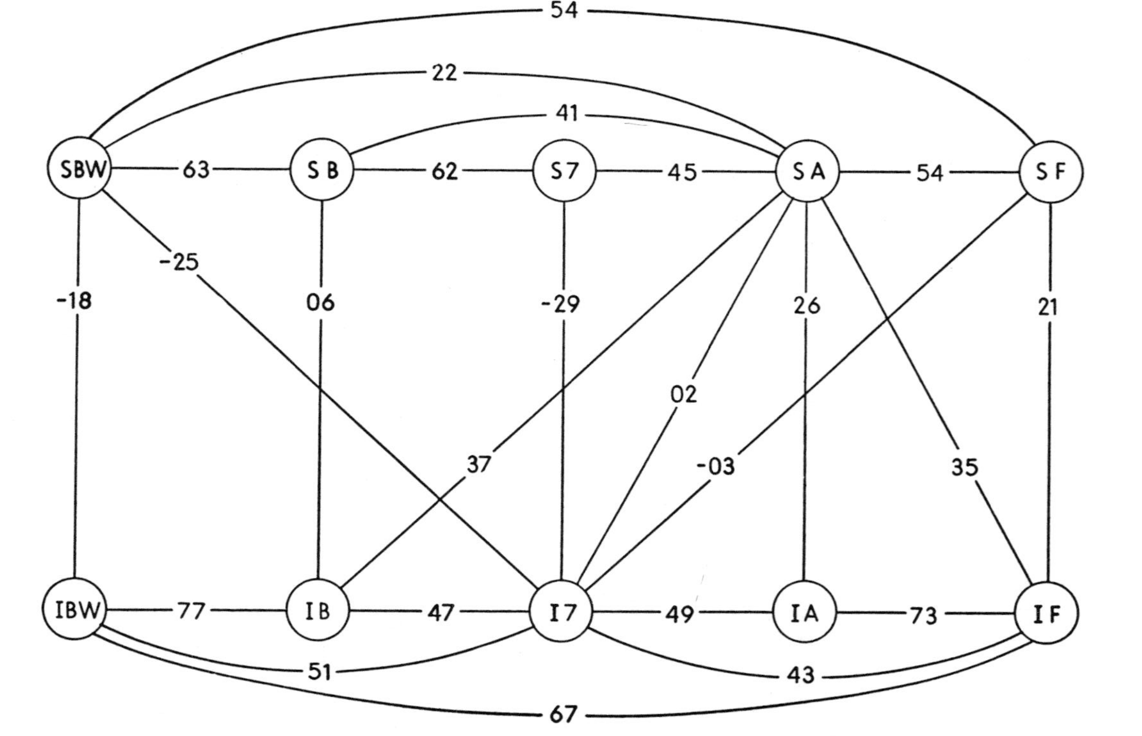

Fig. 1.—Relationship between self and self-ideal. (Figures are correlations, with decimal points omitted.)

The perceived self changes markedly by the end of therapy (*r* SBW · SA = .22).

The sharpest change in the self occurs during a period of two interviews, the eighth and ninth (*r* S7 · SA = .45; also *r* SBW · S7 = .55, *r* SBW · SA = .22).

During the follow-up period the perceived self regresses to a picture which bears more similarity to the initial perception (*r* SA · SBW = .22, but *r* SF · SBW = .54).

It may illuminate this statement of the statistical relationships to give something of the qualitative picture. An examination of the items as they were sorted at the pre-wait point, the end of therapy, and the follow-up point justifies the following description. The self at the end of therapy was seen as being much less dependent on the opinions of others, and as being much more self-reliant and acceptable, than at the pre-wait point. In comparing the self as first perceived by Mr. Bebb with the self at the end of therapy, there are some sharp changes. The two items which show the most radical shift illustrate the above. "I am afraid of what other people think about me" shifts from 7 ("very characteristic of me") to 1 ("very unlike me"). (The maximum possible change is from 8 to 0.) The item "I take a positive attitude toward myself" shifts from 2 ("unlike me") to 8 ("most characteristic of me"). These are the most extreme changes in item placements, but others are in the same direction. The client pictures himself as less afraid of others' opinions; he feels himself to be more social in his behavior. He is less afraid of sex and more expressive of his emotions. He can admit that he is often lonely and often disliked by others and that he feels insecure and confused. He feels, however, that he understands himself much better, this item having changed from 2 to 7 in his placements. This sorting for the self at the end of therapy thus shows a very considerable amount of change in a constructive direction. It appears to be realistic rather than defensive. The direction of change appears very similar to the alterations which have occurred in cases where significant permanent change has taken place.

Let us leave this picture of the self at the end of therapy and turn to the self-ideal at the seventh interview, which also stands out as distinctive.

The self-ideal at the seventh interview is definitely unlike all the other four ideals, which are quite similar to each other (mean *r*, I7 with other self-ideals = .48;[8] mean intercorrelation, all other ideals = .70).

The ideal shows its maximum change at the seventh interview and then quickly regresses, so that the ideal two interviews later, and the ideal at follow-up, are both similar to earlier ideals (*r* I7 · IBW = .51; *r* I7 · IF = .43; but *r* IA · IBW = .70, and *r* IA · IF = .73, and *r* IF · IBW = .67).

The qualitative picture is also of help in understanding these facts. Examining the item placements, and comparing the pre-wait self-ideal with this ideal at the seventh interview, gives us this description.

The changes in item placement are frequent but not extreme. The ideal at the seventh interview seems definitely more personalized, less stereotyped, than the first ideal. He places less stress on achieving social conformity, on being a good mixer, etc. There is less stress on being ambitious. There is more stress on understanding himself, being satisfied and content with himself, more value placed on being unafraid of sex and sexuality. His ideal now places more weight on being a person of worth, not helpless or hopeless. Greater value is given to tolerance, and one gains the impression that this is tolerance of himself. He is less inclined to wish for compulsive perfection, and his ideal seems somewhat closer to the person he may internally be. He wants very much to achieve a state where his hardest battles are not with himself.

The Dynamics of Failure as Seen in the Q-Sorts

Let us now try to draw the natural inferences and to interpret the dynamics of this failure in therapy as they are revealed by the Q-sorts. It would seem that by the time of the seventh interview Mr. Bebb had come to re-perceive the self he wished to be, achieving a more uniquely personal goal. But this achievement increased the discrepancy between self and ideal (*r* S7 · I7 = −.29) and probably the internal tension.

In two more interviews he comes to perceive himself quite differently, in a way which marks the high point of self-reorganiza-

8. In calculating this and other means of correlations, the correlations were first changed to Z' scores, the average computed, and the result translated into its corresponding *r*.

tion. He is now closer than at any other time to his usual self-ideal and is making definite progress in the direction of his unique ideal as held at the seventh interview.

But already a regression process is at work, owing perhaps to fright or concern at the tension which existed at the seventh interview. The self-ideal has been sharply modified in a regressive direction. At this point he leaves therapy. During the follow-up period the self joins the self-ideal in regression, and, though not all the change is negated, he never comes near achieving the self-ideal which he glimpsed at the seventh interview.

TABLE 3*

RELATION OF SUCCESSIVE SELVES TO SUCCESSIVE SELF-IDEALS

SELVES	IDEALS				
	IBW	IB	I7	IA	IF
SBW.....	−18	−16	−25	−13	−01
SB.......	01	06	−16	−09	03
S7........	−06	00	−29	02	−03
SA.......	35	37	02	26	35
SF.......	10	14	−03	13	21

* Decimal points omitted.

Table 3 lifts from the matrix a few of the correlations most pertinent to the dynamics we have been discussing. Note that the initial self was in the greatest state of tension, as compared with all the ideals, while the self after therapy is much the closest to the general run of self-ideals. Looking down the columns, it is clear that the self-ideal at the seventh interview is much the most uncomfortable to live with, the mean correlation being −.14, while the ideal at follow-up time is the most "comfortable" in relation to his various selves, having a mean correlation of .11.

It would appear to be true that in the waiting period both self and ideal changed in such a way as to reduce the extreme tension to some degree. The exploration of the therapeutic interviews increases this tension to its maximum by the seventh interview. This is unbearable, and, though a sharp and constructive change takes place immediately thereafter in self-perception, the self-ideal retreats to a more and more comfortable form, and the self later regresses too.

The Counselor's Perceptions

The only other portion of the matrix upon which specific comment will be made is the counselor's sortings at the seventh interview, which attempted to predict the sortings the client was doing at this same time. Unfortunately, these are the only counselor sortings we have, because, when therapy concluded two interviews later, and a post-therapy counselor sorting was called for, the therapist felt that it would be so similar to his previous sortings as to be of no value. In view of the changes occurring in the client sorts, it is quite unfortunate that we do not have this comparative picture.

TABLE 4*

COUNSELOR'S SORTINGS IN RELATION TO SUCCESSIVE SELVES AND IDEALS

Counselor Sortings	Selves				
	SBW	SB	S7	SA	SF
CS7......	55	30	30	09	30
CI7......	−23	−16	−29	17	06
	Ideals				
	IBW	IB	I7	IA	IF
CS7......	−38	−35	−28	−35	−22
CI7......	68	71	54	69	64

* Decimal points omitted.

Table 4 selects what appears to be the most interesting and significant correlations in connection with the counselor's sortings. It will be observed that the counselor's sorting for the client's self was much more predictive of an earlier sorting (SBW) than of the self at the seventh interview. It was not at all predictive of the self two interviews later. Likewise the counselor's sorting for the client's ideal was very much in line with any of the other ideals but is not so close to the more differentiated ideal at seven, which it was intended to predict. However, the counselor's ideal sort bears the expected relationship to the client's selves, being most discrepant from the self at seventh interview and most like the self two interviews later.

Evidently the therapist perceived the client more as he had been than as he was and perceived his self-ideal as it generally was rather than as it existed at the time of the interview.

Factor Analysis of the Matrix

Thus far all our analysis of the correlation matrix has been made by a logical and inspectional type of analysis. To check this and to see what additional information might be gained, the matrix was also subjected to factor analysis.[9] Tables 5, 6, and 7 present the pertinent data from this analysis, Table 6 being a duplication of a portion of Table 5, to bring out more strongly those sortings which showed a significant weighting on each factor.

Factor A is clearly a self-factor. It is most strongly exemplified by the sorting for self at the seventh interview. It is to be noted that all self-sortings, those made by the client and the counselor's sort for the client's self, have significant loadings on this factor. Of the client's self-sorts, the one at the conclusion of therapy (SA) has the lowest loading.

It is possible, by a somewhat elaborate analysis, to obtain a qualitative picture of this (and the other) factors. If we examine the rating of every item on the Q-list on each of these six sortings which have a significant loading, it is possible to determine those which are characteristic of the factor. Thus Item 37 had ratings of 2, 2, 2, 3, 2, and 3 on these six sortings. Because the range is only 2, it is regarded as characteristic of this factor, with an average rating of 2. Item 20 has ratings of 6, 6, 7, 6, 5, and 5, respectively, on the different "selves," and with its range of 3 is also selected as characteristic, with an average rating of 6. In this fashion the characteristic items, in which the range was narrow and the rating

9. Full credit for the factor analysis is due Miss Sarah Counts, who was responsible for this portion of the study.

TABLE 5

Factor Loadings of All Q-Sorts

	A	B	C	D		A	B	C	D
SBW......	48	−15	−14	26	IF........	18	78	09	04
SB........	54	10	−11	−03	OBW......	−03	01	51	27
S7........	62	07	00	−19	OB........	−01	00	70	00
SA........	40	43	−13	−07	O7........	−17	−02	50	−19
SF........	45	11	−10	36	OA........	07	−02	51	−09
IBW......	02	86	−01	−11	OF........	08	−15	40	38
IB........	03	83	−06	−04	CS7.......	38	−41	04	32
I7........	−11	46	14	23	CI7.......	−06	70	13	12
IA........	−04	73	00	14	CO7.......	09	−07	54	34

TABLE 6

The Four Factors

	A (Self)	B (Ideal)	C (Ordinary)	D (Conventional)		A (Self)	B (Ideal)	C (Ordinary)	D (Conventional)
SBW......	48	......	......	26	IF........	......	78	......	......
SB........	54	......	......	......	OBW......	......	......	51	27
S7........	62	......	......	−19	OB........	......	......	70	......
SA........	40	43	......	......	O7........	......	......	50	−19
SF........	45	......	......	36	OA........	......	......	51	......
IBW......	......	86	......	......	OF........	......	......	40	38
IB........	......	83	......	......	CS7.......	38	−41	......	32
I7........	......	46	......	23	CI7.......	......	70	......	......
IA........	......	73	......	......	CO7.......	......	......	54	34

TABLE 7

Correlation between the Four Primary Factors

	A	B	C	D
A.......	1.00	....	....	....
B.......	− .17	1.00	....	....
C.......	− .60	.03	1.00	....
D.......	− .03	.28	.02	1.00

similar on all six sortings, were selected out. This list is given in Table 8. It will be seen that the cluster represents a person who is critical, depressed, confused, and insecure. He is indecisive and uncomfortable in social situations. He does not regard himself as a complete failure and does not live entirely by others' standards, but he is tense and dissatisfied.

Factor B is almost equally clearly interpretable as an "ideal" factor. All the client's sortings for the self he would like to be have heavy loadings on this factor, except the self-ideal following the seventh interview, which has a more modest loading. The coun-

TABLE 8

ITEM DESCRIPTION OF FACTOR A ("SELF")

Average Rating	Item No. and Item
7*	(31) I am critical of people.
6	(20) I am often down in the dumps.
	(47) I am impulsive.
	(70) I can't seem to make up my mind one way or another.
	(71) I am confused.
	(85) I feel insecure within myself.
	(88) I am intelligent.
5	(1) I feel uncomfortable while talking with someone.
	(4) I make strong demands on myself.
	(10) I am an aloof, reserved person.
	(21) I am really self-centered.
	(24) Usually in a mob of people I feel a little bit alone.
	(27) My hardest battles are with myself.
4	(7) I doubt my sexual powers.
	(26) I can live comfortably with the people around me.
	(33) I am liked by most people who know me.
4—*Continued*	(35) I am sexually attractive.
	(44) I am poised.
	(50) It is pretty tough to be me.
	(59) I am no one. Nothing really seems to be me.
	(74) I am likable.
	(75) My personality is attractive to the opposite sex.
	(95) I am unreliable.
3	(16) I have few values and standards of my own.
	(19) Self-control is no problem with me.
	(25) I want to give up trying to cope with the world.
	(73) I am a failure.
	(100) I dislike my own sexuality.
2	(14) I live largely by other people's values and standards.
	(37) I can usually make up my mind and stick to it.
	(72) I am satisfied with myself.
	(78) I feel relaxed and nothing really bothers me.

* An average rating of 7 indicates that this is most characteristic of the "self"-factor, with ratings of 6 and 5 being decreasingly characteristic. The rating of 4 is neutral, neither like nor unlike, while 3 and 2 are increasingly unlike the self.

selor's sort for the client's ideal also has a heavy loading on this factor. The client's self, as the counselor sees it, has a significant negative loading.

Much the most interesting element in this second factor is the presence of the self at the conclusion of therapy. It would appear that the client came so much closer to being the self he wished to be that his picture of his self at the conclusion of therapy has approximately equal loadings on the self and wanted-self factors. However, by the follow-up period this is no longer true, and at follow-up time his self has a negligible weighting on the ideal factor.

TABLE 9

ITEM DESCRIPTION OF FACTOR B ("IDEAL")

Average Rating	Item No. and Item	Average Rating	Item No. and Item
7*	(96) I understand myself.	4—*Continued*	(35) I am sexually attractive. (46) I often feel resentful. (49) I don't trust my emotions. (50) It is pretty tough to be me.
6	(31) I am critical of people. (41) I am contented. (47) I am impulsive. (51) I am a rational person. (53) I am tolerant. (67) I take a positive attitude toward myself. (80) I feel emotionally mature. (88) I am intelligent. (91) I am self-reliant.	3	(39) I often feel guilty.
		2	(14) I live largely by other people's values and standards. (16) I have few values and standards of my own. (58) I feel inferior. (60) I am afraid of what other people think about me.
5	(33) I am liked by most people who know me.	1	(71) I am confused.
4	(7) I doubt my sexual powers. (17) I have a hard time controlling my sexual desires.		

* Again the listing is from 7 (most characteristic of this factor) to 1 (least characteristic).

The qualitative picture of this second factor is contained in Table 9. It seems to contain some contradictory elements, the desired self being both impulsive and rational, critical and tolerant. In general, this desired self is a person who has insight, is emotionally mature, likes himself, and has his own standards and values. It is a self which is assured and not confused.

Factor C is his concept of the ordinary person, and there is little that is remarkable about it except that it indicates a more stable picture of the ordinary person than is indicated by the correlation matrix itself. The correlation between the picture of the ordinary person before therapy and after the seventh interview is only .10—one of the sharpest changes in the matrix. The factor analysis indicates, however, that underlying such changes is a more stable element which runs through all the sortings for the ordinary person. The qualitative picture of this factor indicates that the ordinary person is regarded as one who lives by herd standards, is a good mixer, and is definitely not different from others.

The fourth factor is a more complex one, which, after examining all the data, it seems reasonable to label as the "conventional self" or the "social stereotype." It has modest loadings contributed by the self before therapy and at follow-up time, but a rather strong (though insignificant) negative loading from the self at the seventh interview. The ideal at the seventh interview contained something of this conventional person. It is natural that two of the sortings for the ordinary person also contribute. The counselor saw something of this in the client in his sort at the seventh interview.

The items which are characteristic of this factor show that this self is primarily formed to suit other people. It is intelligent, competitive, well liked, and not emotionally upset. Feelings of resentment are not too prominent.

The factor analysis confirms what we have seen previously from other sources in regard to Mr. Bebb. His self-picture changes quite markedly by the end of therapy, becoming more like his ideal, but drops back in the post-therapy period to something not unlike the self with which he started. The desired self changes considerably by the seventh interview but then changes back gradually to something much closer to his initial ideal. Running through all these facets of self is the fact that a conventional self, concerned primarily about what others think, is evident when he first comes in and at the follow-up time but not in between. His picture of the ordinary person is also weighted with this stereotype at the same points.

VI. THE RELATION OF THE PERCEIVED SELF TO DIAGNOSIS

It has been evident that the preceding section deals with the objective analysis of the client's self-perceptions, as made operationally available through the Q-sorts. But the psychologist who is accustomed to think of clients solely from an external or diagnostic frame of reference may continually be asking himself the question as to what is "really" happening, judged from the outside. Though the material from the TAT has been given, it is not directly relatable to the Q-sorts in the form in which it was given.

The present section deals with the relationship between these two ways of viewing an individual. The hypothesis was that in effective therapy the self as perceived by the client would become more similar to the client as perceived by the diagnostician. As denied material enters awareness, the client should view himself more realistically and hence in a manner more similar to that of the diagnostician.

The tool for this investigation was again the Q-sort. The four TAT's which had been given to Mr. Bebb—both the protocols and the summarized diagnosis—were given to a psychologist[10] who had no contact with any of the case material, knew nothing of the client, and did not know how the case was regarded or, indeed, whether the individual had been in therapy. Neither did he know the order in which the TAT's were administered. He was asked to take each TAT protocol and its summary, study it carefully, and then sort the Q-cards to represent this individual as he actually was, diagnostically, at that time. It was of course recognized that the cards were not ideal for this purpose, since they are self-referent rather than diagnostic statements. It was also learned that different diagnosticians do not sort the cards in any very similar fashion for the same TAT (two judges, sorting for two of these TAT's independently, had a mean correlation of .45), so that the results must be interpreted cautiously. Nevertheless, this method gives both the external and the internal frame of reference operationally expressed in a fashion which permits direct comparison.

The findings in this case are somewhat puzzling and not too easy

10. Thanks are due to Mr. Richard Farson for his help on this portion of the study.

to interpret. Table 10 contains the correlations between each of the four diagnostic sortings and all the sortings for self and ideal. It will permit the reader to formulate theories and explanations of his own, since those to be given by no means exhaust the data. Some of the more pertinent relationships are diagrammed in Figure 2. Some of the findings may be summarized as follows.

TABLE 10*

CORRELATION MATRIX FOR SELF, IDEAL, AND DIAGNOSIS

	SBW	SB	S7	SA	SF	IBW	IB	I7	IA	IF	DBW	DB	DA
SBW													
SB	63												
S7	55	62											
SA	22	41	45										
SF	54	45	39	54									
IBW	−18	01	−06	35	10								
IB	−16	06	00	37	14	77							
I7	−25	−16	−29	02	−03	51	47						
IA	−13	−09	−13	26	13	70	67	49					
IF	−01	03	03	35	21	67	68	43	73				
DBW	38	38	32	01	00	−41	−41	−27	−49	−41			
DB	40	14	25	23	22	−13	−15	−09	−15	−02	39		
DA	20	06	02	11	23	03	02	10	01	10	15	49	
DF	29	28	16	−11	02	−44	−48	−29	−44	−36	54	35	30

CODE

S = Self
I = Self-ideal
D = Diagnostic picture
BW = Before waiting period
B = Before therapy
7 = Following the seventh interview
A = After therapy
F = Follow-up, six months later

* Decimal points omitted.

It will be noted that significant change occurs in the diagnostic picture by the end of therapy (*r* DBW · DA = .15) but that at the follow-up point the picture is more similar to the initial status (*r* DBW · DF = .54).

The degree of change during the whole period happens to be identical whether measured in terms of the diagnosis or in terms of the perceived self (*r* DBW · DF = .54; *r* SBW · SF = .54).

The diagnostic picture becomes increasingly *unlike* the self as time goes on (successive *r*'s of .38, .14, .11, .02), thus going entirely counter to the hypotheses set up regarding effective therapy. The self as perceived by the client has become *less* like the client as perceived by a diagnostician.

The above statement might make it appear that the client had grown steadily worse during the whole period, denying more and more of the reality of his personality in the picture he maintains of self, but such an inference is contradicted by the statements which follow.

The diagnostic picture at the end of therapy clearly shows constructive change. It is the diagnosis which is least like the initial one, and it is the diagnosis which is most like the client's self-ideals. (It has a low positive relationship to all the

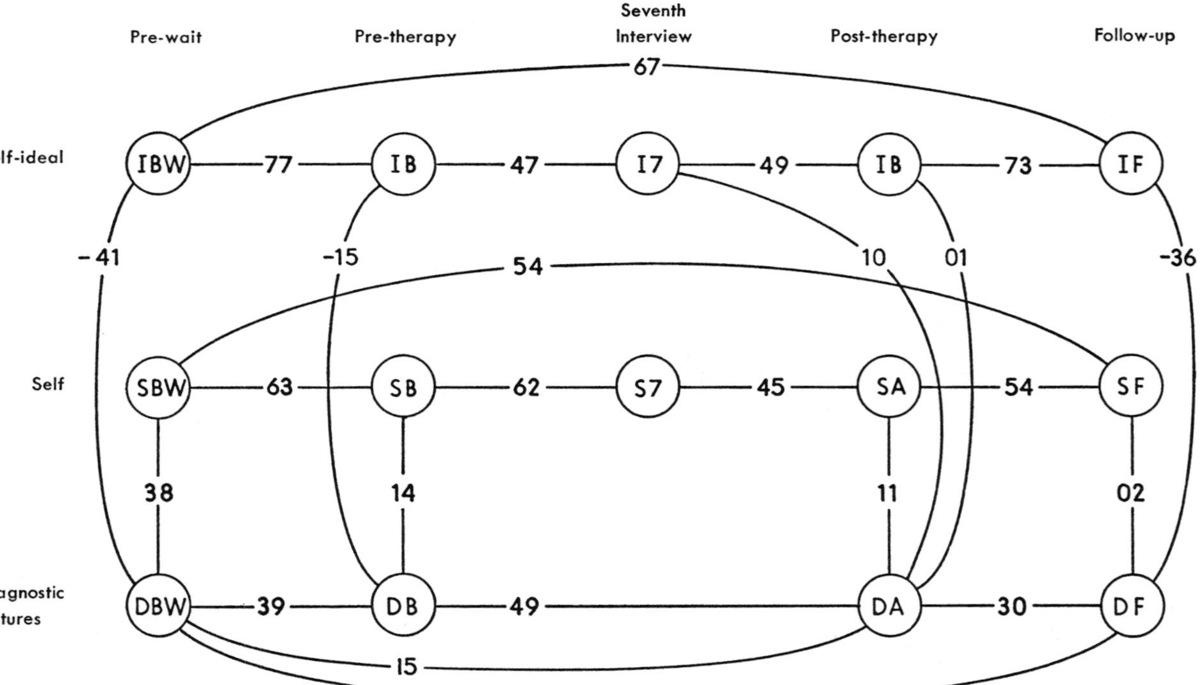

Fig. 2.—Some relationships of self and ideal to the diagnosis. (Figures are correlations, with decimal points omitted.)

ideals, where the other diagnoses have mostly strong negative correlations.) This diagnostic picture at the end of therapy even has a very modest positive correlation with the unique and personal ideal achieved at the seventh interview (r DA · I7 = .10).

In view of our previous comments about the self-ideal at the seventh interview as being an ideal which seemed more acceptant of himself, it is interesting to see the facts turned up by this different type of analysis. This self-ideal seems to be slightly the most achievable of any held by the client having a mean correlation of −.14 with all the diagnoses, where the other four self-ideals have mean correlations with the diagnoses of −.25, −.27, −.28, and −.18, respectively.[11]

It will be noted that the diagnosis shows, in every instance but one, more discrepancy from the ideal than does the self. In other words, the individual, judged externally, is further from his desired ideal than he judges himself to be.

It is of interest that the one exception is in connection with the ideal at the seventh interview (r DA · I7 = .10, while r SA · I7 = .02, and r S7 · I7 = −.29). Here it appears once more that this ideal was achievable and that the client was closer to it than he recognized.

Another finding of significance is the instability of the diagnostic picture. Even in this case where relativity little change seems to have occurred, the mean intercorrelation between diagnoses, all of them made during a period of less than ten months, is .38, with a range of .15 to .54. There is less consistency in the diagnostic picture than in the client's self-perceptions. Yet frequently, in clinical practice, the diagnostic label or description is considered to be a fixed or semipermanent classification. Our finding raises grave question as to such a practice.

It is a matter of interest that some diagnostic change occurs during the sixty-day waiting period, and this change is constructive, bringing the diagnosis somewhat closer to the client's self-ideals (mean r of DBW with five self-ideals = −.40; mean r of DB with these same ideals, −.11). It appears evident that a person motivated for therapy and expecting therapy may change constructively without therapeutic interviews.

Comment

It is obvious that the findings are not clear cut and unambiguous in the foregoing section. Yet the basic finding of constructive change in this client, followed by regression, is confirmed, and also the crucial importance of the self-ideal at the seventh interview. The other findings are sufficiently suggestive to warrant further use of the method in other "failure" cases, as well as those showing permanent change, in order to isolate out the necessary elements in effective therapy. Furthermore, if diagnosis proves, upon further study, to be as unstable as it is in this case and in the previously

11. The means are calculated as indicated in n. 8 above.

reported case of Mrs. Oak,[12] some drastic rethinking as to the place and function of diagnosis in clinical psychology will become necessary.

VII. CHANGES IN ADJUSTMENT SCORE

Following the collection of the foregoing Q-sort data, a new method of looking at this material was devised by one of our staff (see chap. 5 for a full account). All the items of the Q-sort were submitted to a number of clinical psychologists with the instructions: "Place in one pile those items which a well-adjusted person would regard as characteristic of himself, and in another pile those which he would regard as not characteristic of himself." A very high degree of agreement was found on the placement of seventy-four of the one hundred items. These seventy-four were then used as a basis for a very crude score of adjustment. When the subject had sorted one of these items in that half of his sorting which would be predicted by this concept of "good adjustment," he was given a score of 1. Obviously the total possible score is 74.

TABLE 11

"ADJUSTMENT" SCORE

	Self	Ideal	Diagnostic Sorting
Before wait	24	52	6
Pre-therapy	25	54	18
Seventh interview	25	38	....
Post-therapy	33	54	27
Follow-up	27	51	10

Using this method gives us another way of examining the Q-sort data, this time in a normative way. The data are shown in Table 11. It is of interest that the data provided by this approach confirm several of the findings already given. Again we find that it is the self after therapy which is best adjusted. Again we find evidence of the regression after therapy toward the initial status.

By calculating the degree of adjustment indicated by the sorting

12. Chap. 15, pp. 287–95.

for the wanted self, we find confirmation of another finding already stated. All the ideals except the seventh are very similar. The ideal at the seventh interview is the least "adjusted" or stereotyped; it has the greatest negative correlation with the self-picture. It thus appears to be distinctive but less idealized and more achievable.

The "adjustment" score was also calculated for the diagnostic sortings described in the preceding section, based upon the four available TAT's. Several elements stand out if we examine the scores given in Table 11. The first is that, as would be predicted, the total personality as seen by the diagnostician is scored as much more poorly adjusted than the self as seen by the client. This would be a crude measure of the degree of defensiveness. The improvement during the waiting period is given some additional (though not entirely independent) confirmation by the increase in "adjustment" score of the second diagnosis. The improvement during therapy likewise receives further confirmation. It is of some interest that the degree of adjustment as perceived by the client and as perceived by the diagnostician approach each other at the close of therapy and at this point only. Finally, of course, the evidence of regression in the follow-up period is very marked.

While providing us with little new information, this method of analyzing the Q-sort data tends to corroborate the findings previously described.

VIII. CHANGE IN MATURITY OF BEHAVIOR

As part of the general research design, the Willoughby Emotional-Maturity Scale was used to measure any alteration in the behavior of the individual as seen by himself and by his friends (see chap. 13 for the complete account). Not only was the client to be rated by himself and two friends at four points during the entire period but, as a check on their reliability as raters, the two friends were each to rate some other individual well known to them, presumably not in therapy.

The hypothesis in this project, as applied to all the cases in the study, was that the client's behavior, as perceived by himself and by his friends, would change during therapy in a direction defined by experts as constituting greater emotional maturity. The behavior of control persons, rated by the same friends, would, it was hypothesized, show less change in the direction of maturity.

The data from this segment of the project, as related to Mr. Bebb, are given in Table 12. The findings which may be drawn from this table are relatively few.

TABLE 12

E-M SCALE SCORES: CASE OF MR. BEBB
(Higher Scores Indicate Greater Maturity)

	Pre-wait	Pre-therapy	Post-therapy	Follow-up
Rating of Mr. Bebb by:				
Self	33.2	38.5	34.2	35.9
Friend No. 1*	47.8	48.0	38.4	53.1
Friend No. 2	38.1	27.2	†	†
Mean of Self and Friend No. 1	40.5	43.3	36.3	44.5
Percentile (Willoughby's norms for students)	7	17	2	23
Rating of controls:				
Control A by Friend No. 1	56.4	53.6	55.3	57.9
Control B by Friend No. 2	62.3	59.0	†	†

* A misprint form, omitting some items, was given to Friend No. 1 at the pre-therapy point. To make his ratings strictly comparable, all four of his ratings were treated in the same way, omitting these same items. Hence his scores are comparable among themselves but are not directly comparable to the scores obtained by other raters.

† Forms not returned.

The ratings on Mr. Bebb show more variation than do the ratings on the controls. Either he is a more changeable individual than the controls or else therapy has been a factor in this variation.

The two series of complete ratings suggest a decrease in maturity of behavior at the end of therapy, though most of this variation is contributed by the rating of Friend No. 1.

During the total period there is a suggestion of a slight increase in maturity of behavior, though it is unlikely that this increase is statistically significant.

Willoughby's finding is borne out that a self-rating on this scale is as satisfactory as a rating by others.

This client is decidedly immature in his behavior throughout, his scores ranging from the 2d to 23d percentile, according to Willoughby's norms for a student population.

The net result of this portion of the study is that there is little striking change in the quality of Mr. Bebb's behavior, except possibly a slight deterioration during therapy and a slight improvement during the follow-up period.

IX. CHANGE IN THE ACCEPTANCE OF OTHERS

Still another project in the experimental design had to do with the changes in attitudes toward others (chap. 11 gives the full description). It was hypothesized that, when therapy was effective, a change would occur in the direction of greater acceptance of others, increased respect for the individual, the placing of greater values upon other individuals and their contribution, and a decrease in political and economic conservatism and in authoritarian beliefs. The instrument for the investigation of this hypothesis was the Self-Other Attitude Scale, a compilation of items largely from scales developed elsewhere.

Table 13 gives the scores for each subscale and for the total scale,

TABLE 13

S-O SCALE SCORES: CASE OF MR. BEBB

(Decrease in Score Indicates Increase in Acceptance of Others)

	Pre-wait	Pre-therapy	Post-therapy	Follow-up	Change First to Last
F-scale (30 items): Basic anti-democratic, authoritarian, fascistic tendencies	94	95	103	112	+18
L-scale (10 items): Ideology regarding leadership; acceptance of leadership role as function of the group; acceptance of group decision rather than leader decision or control	45	44	40	45	0
A-scale (10 items): Acceptance of the worth of members' contributions to the group	21	24	40	38	+17
D-scale (10 items): Acceptance of differences of opinion and ideas in group discussion; willingness for the group to review its decisions and consider new evidence	22	42	36	35	+13
M-scale (10 items): Tendency to believe in and use democratic means of achieving goals; acceptance of individual responsibility	30	49	44	49	+19
C-scale (10 items): Desire to change others versus willingness for others to be themselves	34	37	36	41	+ 7
E-scale (20 items): Ethnocentrism; tendency to exalt own group above all others; antagonism to minority groups	51	52	58	58	+ 7
PEC-scale (10 items): Political and economic conservatism	25	15	18	21	− 4
Totals	322	358	375	399	......
Change	36	17	24		......
Mean change, total scale	......	......	......	......	77

at each of the four points at which it was administered to Mr. Bebb. The findings are striking.

Mr. Bebb becomes increasingly *less* acceptant of others, precisely the opposite of the results hypothesized for effective therapy.

This direction is consistent, being evident on six of the eight subscales. No subscale changes significantly in a democratic or acceptant direction.

The four scales showing the greatest change indicate a move toward authoritarian, antidemocratic beliefs, toward placing less value on the worth of an individual's contributions or opinions, and an increasing willingness to use other than democratic means to achieve an end.

The sharpest shift in these directions occurred during the waiting period, before therapy began; but the trend continued during therapy and during the six-month follow-up.

Illustrations

The quality of change which has occurred may be illustrated by the following items. The letter in parentheses indicates the scale from which it is taken, and the four numbers indicate his four successive scores, the higher the score the less acceptant the answer.

(F) If people would talk less and work more, everybody would be better off (1, 1, 4, 5).

(F) It is essential for learning or effective work that our teachers or bosses outline in detail what is to be done and exactly how to go about it (1, 7, 5, 5).

(A) It is more efficient in a group if experts tell the group what it should do (1, 3, 5, 5).

(A) No matter how many authorities one has consulted, no question should be considered finally closed (1, 1, 5, 7).

(D) There are always some people in a large group who should not be accepted on the same level of equality as others (1, 5, 5, 4).

(M) Because of the nature of the world in which he lives, an individual should look out for his own interests first (1, 7, 3, 3).

(M) It may be necessary to make use of autocratic methods in order to attain difficult democratic objectives (1, 7, 5, 5).

Comment

Here is a clear-cut reversal of one of the outcomes which has been hypothesized for client-centered therapy. It would appear that Mr. Bebb has moved away from, not toward, acceptance of others. It is barely possible that his increased scores are caused by an increased willingness to state his own authoritarian beliefs. Thus, a greater frankness in avowing beliefs unpopular in a democratic country would increase the score. The only evidence for this speculation is that he seems most consistent in his views on the first taking of this test. Later his views show definite internal contradiction at times, which might represent a more accurate portrayal of his real sentiments rather than an "official" ideology. While this possibility cannot be entirely discarded, there is little evidence to support it.

In general, then, it would seem that in the successive periods before, during, and after therapy Mr. Bebb became more authoritarian in his views, less acceptant of others, and more willing to use any means to reach a goal. The fact that this direction is most sharply seen during the waiting period before therapy indicates that it was not caused by therapy, but neither did therapy alter or stop this trend.

X. DISCUSSION OF RESULTS

Extent to Which Hypotheses Were Upheld

Though Mr. Bebb has been referred to throughout as a "failure" case, the objective reasons for this have not been summarized. It may be well to take the hypotheses from each of the separate projects and draw them together, indicating the extent to which they were upheld or negated in this case. These hypotheses were initially drawn from the theory of client-centered therapy and were hypotheses as to the types of change predicted in client-centered therapy (see Rogers [4] for a statement of this theory, and chaps. 2 and 3 of the present volume for the way in which the hypotheses were drawn from theory).

It was hypothesized that if a competent psychologist placed the TAT's in an order from most poorly integrated to best integrated, the pre- and post-therapy and the follow-up TAT's would show an increasing degree of integration. This hypothesis was not confirmed in the case of Mr. Bebb. The post-test showed more integration than the pretest, but the follow-up test showed regression.

It was hypothesized that the perceived self as measured by the Q-sort would become increasingly congruent with the perceived self-ideal during and after therapy. This hypothesis was upheld, although the process was irregular and the increase in congruence was slight.

Another hypothesis was that the perceived self would change more than the perceived self-ideal. This hypothesis was upheld.

It was predicted that the self as perceived at the end of therapy would be more confident, more self-directing, less divided, and less inhibited than the self prior to therapy. This hypothesis receives some qualitative confirmation at the end of therapy, but most of this confirmation had disappeared at the follow-up point.

Another hypothesis was that the changes in the perceived self would be greater during a period of therapy than during a period of no therapy. This hypothesis was upheld, whether the change in the therapy period was compared with the control period (the wait period) or with the follow-up period.

It was hypothesized that the self as perceived by the client would become more similar to the client as perceived by a diagnostician. The evidence proved the reverse of this hypothesis.

It was hypothesized that the client's behavior, as perceived by himself and by his friends, would change in the direction of emotional maturity. The evidence provided no confirmation of this.

It was hypothesized that the client's score on the S-O Scale would change in a direction indicating more acceptant and democratic attitudes toward others. The data show a steady decrease in democratic attitudes and acceptance of others from the first to the follow-up test.

With only three of these hypotheses clearly upheld, it seems fair to conclude that this is a failure in client-centered therapy, in which the predictions made by the theory of client-centered therapy are not confirmed.

Since the hypotheses of these studies had to do with the prediction of changes which were likely to occur in successful therapy, there are no specific hypotheses formulated in advance which were concerned with possible concomitants of failure. Hence we cannot prove or disprove hypotheses regarding the failure to change significantly. All we can do is to examine first the clinical data of the recorded interviews and then the objective data, to see if we can formulate objectively supported explanations of this failure and get leads which will provide hypotheses for future studies.

Inferences Drawn from the Clinical Data

If we examine the material from the interviews in the endeavor to understand why lasting personality changes did not occur in this case, two conclusions seem to this writer justified. In the first place, it is the client's fear of what he is finding within himself which tends to drive him from therapy in spite of the progress he is making. In the second place, the therapist makes at least two serious mistakes in handling the client's desire to leave therapy. Let us state the bases for these conclusions.

From the sixth interview onward Mr. Bebb is pulling away from therapy. In the sixth contact he voices his real fear of the psychotic phenomena within himself, which he regards as essentially beyond help. In the seventh interview he talks of his need for therapy as an evidence of weakness. He also feels that therapy has been confusing, discouraging, and disturbing, because what he is thus far finding within himself is not "in accordance with my intuitive knowledge of myself." It is at this point that he partly leaves therapy by reducing the number of interviews from two per week to one. In the eighth interview he feels that he is trying to "shun away" from dealing with his doubts about himself. He also expresses the feeling that he should not be undergoing these interviews because what he is discovering is just himself and hence unchangeable. In the ninth interview he begins by stating that he does not think he should take any more of the counselor's time. It seems clear that the underlying reason for pulling away from therapy is his fear of the unacceptable or abnormal aspects of himself which he is in the process of discovering.

This brings us to the therapist's handling of this material. Was the therapist partly responsible for the premature closure which occurred? Undoubtedly there will be as many opinions about the therapist's procedures as there are orientations, or possibly as many opinions as there are readers. In regard to the therapist's general handling of the material, some will feel that he should have given the client more reassurance. Others will feel that he should have interpreted to the client his fear and his desire to leave the relationship. Others will feel that he did not provide enough support for a dependent client. Others—and this opinion is shared by the writer—will feel that his two most serious mistakes occurred within one moment of time during the ninth interview. In this moment he voiced *for* the client the client's feeling that he was through and then added his own support to this, "I think so too." If one listens to the recording, there can be no doubt that Mr. Bebb was endeavoring to leave therapy. His voice shows great relief when the therapist recognizes this feeling and voices it. The therapist was not, it is clear, injecting this feeling into the situation. But by voicing it before the client could bring himself to voice it and then by supporting it, he helped to truncate therapy. Had he refrained from this response, Mr. Bebb might or might not have left therapy at this time. But if Mr. Bebb had voiced this feeling or this decision, and the therapist had accepted it, the client would still have been left with his own deep ambivalence about continuing and would have had to live with that ambivalence. As it was actually handled, it would seem that the therapist sided with one side of the ambivalence and thus helped to give the client a premature and defensive closure.

Another possible mistake of the therapist is that both in respect to leaving therapy and in respect to the client's desire for liking from another person, the therapist accepts feelings which have not yet been expressed. There is not much doubt as to the accuracy of the therapist's responses. The client did, at some level, wish love and approval from someone; he did wish to leave therapy. But to respond to these feelings prematurely may well have been frightening to an already frightened individual.

The Objective Findings

Let us now draw together the various findings of the objective studies so that we may see what they contribute to the understanding of a failure in therapy.

Mr. Bebb shows some personality change, in a favorable direction, during the sixty-day wait period (IV, V, VI, VII).[13]

He makes progress toward integration during the therapy period (IV, V, VI, VII).

Greater congruence of self and ideal is achieved, both during the waiting period and during therapy (V).

From the point before the wait period to the conclusion of therapy there is a decided and favorable change (IV, V, VI, VII).

During the follow-up period the client regresses toward his original status, whether the measure is the TAT, the Q-sort for self, or the "adjustment" score (IV, V, VI, VII).

Changes in both the perceived self and the self-ideal are sharper in the therapy period than in the waiting period or the follow-up period (V).

Changes in both the self and the ideal are at one point very

13. Following each conclusion Roman numerals in parentheses indicate the section or sections of this chapter in which data are found to support the conclusions.

sharp, as indicated by a correlation of only .45 between the self of the seventh interview and the self of the ninth interview, and a correlation of only .49 for the ideal during the same period (V).

The self-ideal moves from a rather stereotyped ideal before therapy to a more unique and more achievable ideal at the seventh interview and then regresses (V, VII).

The self at the conclusion of the interviews shows many characteristics of better adjustment but regresses (V, VII).

The self after therapy had a significant loading on the client's generalized ideal, but the self at follow-up time had no such loading (V).

The change in the diagnostic picture was as great as the change in the self-picture and showed a similar fluctuation (VI).

There is no significant trend in the maturity of behavior, as observed by self or others (VIII).

There is a trend toward a lessened acceptance of others throughout and after therapy (IX).

This change is sharpest in the waiting period prior to therapy (IX).

Inferences Drawn from the Objective Data

It may be helpful to sketch the dynamics of therapeutic failure in this case from the information provided by the objective data.

In the first place, a degree of therapeutic change appears to take place in this seriously disturbed person motivated for therapy, even in a period of no therapy. This change in the sixty-day period is supported by evidence from the TAT analysis, the diagnostic sorting based on the TAT, the Q-sort for self and ideal, and the behavior rating. The only contrary evidence is in the sharply lessened acceptance of others, which is difficult to explain.

In the second place, if this study had been concluded at the time of the ninth interview, the evidence indicates a definite amount of therapeutic progress in a person who was close to a psychological breakdown. The counselor rating, the TAT analysis, the diagnostic sorting based on the TAT, the Q-sort for self and ideal—all support this. The behavior ratings show some contrary trend, and there is a somewhat lessened acceptance of others. If the ninth interview had been merely a point *in* therapy, rather than the *end* of therapy, all the evidence would have fallen into line. It would have been interpretable as genuine progress in therapy, with a decreasing defensiveness helping to account for the lessened acceptance of others and the temporary deterioration of behavioral maturity.

From the objective point of view, the most likely influence in the client's leaving therapy is the increased tension indicated by the sharp and increased discrepancy between self and ideal as he moves forward in therapy. This point is also supported by the low loading of the seventh interview ideal on the ideal factor and the ninth interview self on the self factor, indicating that these particular perceptions are very different from those which precede or follow. They are thus likely to be tension-creating.

Finally, the objective evidence of regression is strong. It begins with a regression in the self-ideal between the seventh and ninth interviews and is evidenced by the TAT analysis, the diagnostic Q-sort, the "adjustment" score, and the self and ideal Q-sorts. The S-O Scale shows still further decrease of acceptance of others. Only the behavior rating shows an increase in maturity, back to approximately the pre-therapy state.

The over-all picture from the objective point of view is that the client was making progress—progress in which greater tension was being experienced—with some painful fluctuations in perception of self and ideal and perhaps some deterioration of behavior. These kinds of "constructive disorganization" are known to be often evident in successful cases. But at this point therapy was truncated, and thereafter regression toward the original status set in.

A Meaningful Parallelism

It will have been noted that all our data, clinical and objective, show in most respects a surprising degree of parallelism. An improvement during the therapy period is indicated whether we rely on the client's statements during the therapeutic and follow-up interviews, the objective analysis of the client's frame of reference through his Q-sorts, an adjustment score based on the Q-sorts, the counselor rating, the TAT analyzed in conventional fashion, or by means of an objective method. The later regression is equally well indicated by any of the above except the counselor rating, which was made only at the conclusion of therapy and hence offers no evidence on this issue.

This point is worth making, since some psychologists have been concerned about the objective analysis of material from within the client's phenomenological field. They are fearful that the client's desire "to impress the therapist" or the "hello-goodbye" effect will vitiate such material. Where a case is generally successful, it is difficult to refute such a view. In this case, however, the improvement and the later regression show up just as strikingly, and sometimes more meaningfully, from analysis of the internal frame of reference as from analysis of external observations such as the TAT.

Both this case and the previously reported case of Mrs. Oak (chap. 15) show that diagnostic representations of the client reveal even greater variability than do self-representations. If then one is looking for some stable objective fashion of representing the individual through time, the suggestion is that such stability does not truly exist, either in the internally perceived picture of self or in the externally perceived picture of the personality.

"A Flight into Health?"

This phrase has not been used because its meaning is so ambiguous, but, since it is a term very commonly used by clinicians and therapists, it deserves comment. Is this case "a flight into health"? If the phrase is understood to mean a defensive pretense of therapeutic progress, when none in fact exists, then Mr. Bebb did not exhibit a flight into health. The picture of definite improvement seems real, whether judged by conscious or by projective material. But if "flight into health" is interpreted as leaving therapy because further progress appears very frightening, then Mr. Bebb would fall into that category.

Hypotheses for Future Study

Have we been able to achieve our goal of discovering fruitful hypotheses regarding failures in the therapeutic process? It would seem that from this exhaustive study of one unique failure have come four hypotheses worthy of inclusion in future research. Each of them could, with our present knowledge of research method, be given operational meaning.

The first and simplest is as follows: The concomitants of client-centered psychotherapy are less likely to occur if the client is in therapy for a "short" time than if he is in therapy for a "long" time. Studies by Seeman, reported in chapter 7, by Porter (3), and by Bartlett (1) give some beginning support to this hypothesis. Porter's follow-up study shows that clients are much more likely to regard therapy as helpful when the number of contacts is greater. Seeman, on another group, shows that counselor ratings of success show a positive correlation with length of therapy. Bartlett's study shows that supervisors and employers of clients are more likely to have noticed positive change when the number of interviews is greater. Thus a beginning has been made in investigating this hypothesis.

A second hypothesis may first be stated informally and then more formally. It appears clear that it is the very depth of the disturbance in Mr. Bebb which makes therapy seem so frightening. Put in a somewhat oversimplified form, we may say that, the more deeply the person needs therapy, the more difficult it is for him to overcome his fear of the therapeutic relationship and what it holds for him. Let us try to state this second hypothesis in a more general and formal way. It is hypothesized that the greater the experienced inner tension—measured by the discrepancy between perceived self and perceived ideal—the greater must be the perceived safety of the relationship if therapy is to continue. This hypothesis could be made completely operational if a Q-sort were developed to represent the quality of the relationship, somewhat in the fashion already done by Fiedler (2).

A third type of hypothesis is suggested by the therapist's part in defeating therapeutic progress in the case of Mr. Bebb. It would seem that his overstrong acceptance of the client's desire to *leave* therapy and his failure adequately to accept the client's desire to continue and fear of continuing helped to bring the unsatisfactory closure. It also appears that his acceptance of some unexpressed feelings was premature and frightening to the client. Perhaps two generalized hypotheses could be stated in these terms. Third hypothesis: Failure by the therapist to accept all aspects of a client's expressed feelings is associated with a lessened degree of change in the client or with a greater likelihood of premature closure. Fourth hypothesis: The therapist's expressed acceptance of feelings and meanings not expressed by the client is associated with a lessened degree of change in the client or with a greater likelihood of premature closure. There is little doubt but that reliable categorizations of client and counselor statements could be set up to test these hypotheses. It is less clear whether Hypotheses 3 and 4 are the most significant hypotheses to test.

To the writer, these are the only significant general questions which grow out of this analysis of Mr. Bebb's experience, but it is hoped that an examination of the data may provide others with additional issues for investigation.

XI. SUMMARY

In this chapter an analysis has been presented of the data from the case of a seriously maladjusted young man undergoing client-centered therapy in which the hypothesized concomitants of such therapy did not occur. In addition to the counselor's ratings, extensive excerpts from the recorded interviews have been given to supply the clinical evidence for this failure. Data from the repeated administrations of the TAT, analyzed both by conventional and by objective methods, have been given. The data from repeated self-referent Q-sorts and their factor analysis have been presented. Information is also given from repeated ratings of the client's behavior by self and friends on the Willoughby Emotional-Maturity Scale and from repeated administrations of a test of attitudes toward others.

The findings from these data have been summarized, and the attempt has been made to formulate both a clinical and an objective picture of the reasons for the progress exhibited and the regression which followed. Some hypotheses have been developed from this analysis for testing in future studies.

REFERENCES

1. Bartlett, Marion R. "A Six Month Follow-up of the Effects of Personal Adjustment Counseling of Veterans," *Journal of Consulting Psychology*, XIV (1950), 393–94.
2. Fiedler, Fred E. "A Comparison of Therapeutic Relationships in Psychoanalytic, Nondirective and Adlerian Therapy," *Journal of Consulting Psychology*, XIV (1950), 436–45.
3. Porter, E. H., Jr. "Clients' Evaluations of Services at the University of Chicago Counseling Center." Unpublished manuscript.
4. Rogers, Carl R. *Client-centered Therapy*. Boston: Houghton Mifflin Co., 1951.

PART IV

Conclusion

CHAPTER 17

An Overview of the Research and Some Questions for the Future

CARL R. ROGERS

It is the purpose of this chapter to present, in brief compass and in nontechnical terms, the plan of this research, its major findings, and some of the issues which it raises.

I. THE RESEARCH DESIGN

The general aim of the total program was to gain objective knowledge in regard to the end results and the process of one form of psychotherapy—the client-centered approach. Without trying to use such unsatisfactory global concepts as "success" or "failure," it was desired to learn more precisely what the measurable concomitants of a period of client-centered therapy are.

To this end, it was planned to use a series of objective research instruments to measure various characteristics of a group of clients before therapy, after the completion of therapy, and at a follow-up point six months to one year later. The clients were to be roughly typical of those coming to the Counseling Center of the University of Chicago, and the aim was to collect these data, including the recording of all interviews, for at least twenty-five clients. The choice was made to make an intensive study of a group of moderate size rather than a more superficial analysis of a larger number.

A part of the therapy group was set aside as an own-control group. This group was given the battery of research instruments, asked to wait during a sixty-day control period, and then given the battery a second time before beginning counseling. Thus if change occurs in individuals simply because they are motivated for therapy, or because they have a certain type of personality structure, then such change should occur during this control period.

Another group of individuals not in therapy was selected as an equivalent-control group. This group was equivalent in age and age distribution to the therapy group and roughly equivalent in socioeconomic status, in the proportion of men and women, and of students and nonstudents. This group was given, at matched time intervals, the same tests as the therapy group. Thus if change occurs in individuals as the result of passage of time only, or as the result of repeated contact with the tests, it should be evident in the findings from this group. Obviously if the therapy group shows changes during and after the therapy period which are greater than those which occur in the own-control period or in the equivalent-control group, then it will be reasonable to attribute these changes to the influence of the therapy.

It was recognized from the first that, in obtaining the material desired from the "therapy group" of clients, some of them might fail to begin therapy, drop out of therapy for various reasons, or end their contacts in such a short time that personality change could not be presumed to have occurred. It was planned to study and investigate these individuals as a separate group.

II. THE THERAPY GROUP

There were nearly thirty clients in the therapy group. They came to the Counseling Center voluntarily for personal help. In age they ranged from twenty-one to forty. There were more men than women, as is characteristic of the clientele of the Center, and more students than nonstudents. In socioeconomic status they ranged from "lower-lower" class to "upper-middle," but they tended to cluster at the lower-middle class level. They presented a wide range of initial problems, from concern over near-psychotic behavior to concern over a lack of positive goals; from homosexuality, unhappy marital life, or failure on the job or at school to more general problems, such as difficulty in making decisions or feelings of social inadequacy (*3*).[1] In their adjustment, in their degree of inner tension, and in their degree of personality disturbance they were significantly worse off than the control group (*4*, *8*). They were like the control group, however, in being, on the average, somewhat accepting and democratic in their attitudes (*11*).

1. Throughout this chapter each significant factual statement—sentence or paragraph—is followed by the number (in italics) of the chapter giving the data upon which the statement is based. Thus the basis for these condensed statements about our therapy group is found in chapter 3.

III. THE COUNSELORS

It was the goal of the program to discover the results of therapy as carried on by a group of average counselors, not by some select group of experts. The sixteen therapists who carried on the therapy for this program were individuals who had had at least one year of experience in counseling, and most had had from one to six years of experience. The writer was an exception, with more than twenty years of experience. Six of the group had Doctor's degrees in psychology; the others were close to the doctorate level (*3*).

The counseling of the experimental clients by these counselors was judged by the counselors to be, on the average, modestly successful. The counselor ratings of the therapeutic experience of these clients at the close of therapy ran the whole gamut from completely unsuccessful to highly successful (*7*).

IV. THE HYPOTHESES AND INSTRUMENTS

The many hypotheses out of which the separate projects grew were derived from the theory of client-centered therapy or out of other bodies of recognized psychological theory. In general, a variety of changes were hypothesized in the self of the therapy client, in his personality characteristics and structure, in his personal integration and adjustments, in his attitudes toward others, and in the maturity of his behavior. In regard to each of these it was hypothesized that there would be significantly more change in the clients in therapy than in the control group or in the control period (*3*). In some of the special studies there were hypotheses having to do with the nature of the process of therapy and with the limitations of its application.

The instruments used to test these hypotheses included a variety of psychological tests previously developed by others, some developed for the purpose, and other special instruments such as the Q-technique. Some use was made of rating scales, but, except in the case of the counselor's rating, all ratings were made "blind" so as to eliminate any subjective bias—that is, the rater did not know whether the material he was rating was produced before therapy began or after it was completed or whether it came from a client or a control individual.

V. THE TASK

With this general plan of operation we then launched on a program which involved complex and frequent contacts with nearly eighty individuals—clients, "drop-outs," and controls—over periods ranging from a few months to four years. Involved was the administration of a six-hour battery of tests on more than two hundred occasions to these individuals, the recording of well over a thousand therapeutic interviews, and the transcription of many of these interviews for further research analysis. It has been estimated that over five hundred man-hours of effort were necessary to collect and transcribe the data from one typical client (thirty interviews) and the matched control individual; this does not include any of the time given to *analysis* of the data. The general design of the research, in other words, is relatively simple and clear cut; its application to a group of human beings has proved to be a task of massive complexity.

VI. THE FINDINGS

The previous chapters have given, in considerable detail, the various findings, with the methods leading to them, and the qualifications which should be made in regard to each one. Here the attempt will be made to weave all these into a meaningful pattern which the reader can trace back to its multiple origins by means of the parenthetical chapter references. There is no doubt that deeper meanings, more significant interrelationships, will be discovered in these data as we continue to study the different investigations; but it is hoped that the following summary will at least accurately reflect our results as they have emerged in the various studies and as we at present understand their interrelated meaning.

Changes in the Self and the Self-in-Relationship

Let us first approach the outcomes of therapy from the vantage point of the client himself and take note of the measurements made at various points (by means of Q-technique) of the client's perception of himself, of the person he would like to be, and of the ordinary "other" person.

The characteristic person who enters therapy has a picture of himself which is far removed from—or even negatively correlated with—the concept of the person he would like to be. This seems to indicate a considerable degree of inner distress or tension (*4*, *6*). During the process of therapy sufficient change occurs so that at the conclusion of therapy, and at the follow-up point, there is a significantly greater congruence of self and ideal (*4*, *6*, *15*). In other words, the client has come to be—in his own eyes—a person who is much more similar to the person he would like to be. This change is especially marked in those clients rated as showing considerable therapeutic movement (*4*). During the follow-up period there may be some falling-away from this achievement, some small degree of regression in the direction of the previous state (*4*, *6*). In some individuals this regression has been sharp, and little of the gain of therapy has been retained (*16*); in others there has been no regression at all, but a continuance of the trend noted in therapy, so that the individual has become increasingly a person such as he would like to be, a person whom he values more highly (*6*, *15*).

That this whole process of change is due to therapy seems abundantly clear. The control group shows little tension to begin with and no significant change in this respect (*4*). In our therapy clients the change during therapy is significantly greater than during the control period (*4*, *6*) and significantly greater than the change occurring in the control group (*4*). The fact that this change in self-perception is quite central to therapy is perhaps indicated by the fact that the self changes much more than the concept of the ideal self or of the ordinary person (*6*).

Thus far we have mentioned only that the self has changed but nothing of the generalized direction of the change. In terms of adjustment, as defined by psychologists, our clients see themselves when entering therapy in ways that clinicians would term "poorly adjusted." This is not true of the control group (*5*). Over a sixty-day waiting period our clients show no change in their adjustment picture. It appears that a desire for help and personal reorganization is not by itself sufficient to bring change. During the process of therapy the clients change markedly to self-descriptions indicative of much better adjustment. At the conclusion of therapy they are still somewhat less well adjusted, in their self-descriptions, than are the controls, but this is no longer a significant difference (*5*). In general, these changes in the self are in the direction of greater self-understanding, increased inner comfort, greater confidence and optimism, increased self-direction and self-responsibility, more comfortable relationships with others, and less need for self-concealment (*6, 15*). During the follow-up period there is somewhat less feeling of ability to cope with the problems of life (*6*).

Not only has the self changed in these ways, but some of its relationships are also perceived as changing. The goal of what the client would like to be has become less perfect, less "adjusted," more realistic, thus becoming a more achievable goal (*6*). Likewise the perception of others has altered. The ordinary person is seen as more like the client's self and as being somewhat better adjusted. At the conclusion of therapy the gap between the self and others is perceived as significantly less (*6*).

One of the major theoretical hypotheses of client-centered therapy is that during therapy the concept of the self is revised to assimilate basic experiences which have previously been denied to awareness as threatening. The tools of the current research are not adequate to test this hypothesis, but there is some pertinent and suggestive data. In a detailed study of a case in which therapy brought about constructive change, the client's perception of self came to have a substantial similarity to a diagnostician's perception of the client. Since the diagnostician was attempting to assess the total personality, including the denied or repressed elements, it seems accurate to draw this conclusion; at follow-up time the self of the client had assimilated into itself a greater proportion of the individual's total experience, including those sorts of experiences previously denied to awareness (*15*). In a case in which therapy was a failure, studied in equal detail, the reverse was found to be true. The client's self-perception came to be increasingly *unlike* the diagnostician's perception of the client (*16*).

In general, then, the individual sees himself as entering therapy in distress, decidedly maladjusted, very unlike the person he wants to be. During therapy he moves significantly in the direction of adjustment and integration, becomes inwardly more comfortable and less tense, sees others as more like himself, and relates more comfortably to them. He understands himself better and is more confident and self-directing. He alters his personal goal in a realistic and more achievable direction. There is some data suggesting that the new self-concept includes more of his inner experience than the old and is thus less easily threatened. During the period following therapy he may retreat in some degree from these gains he has made, or he may continue in the directions he has begun during his interviews.

Neither the control group nor the clients during the control period show significant changes in self-perception or in the perception of the self-ideal or other people. Unlike the group in therapy, their perceptions remain relatively constant. The significant differences between the therapy and no-therapy groups seem to be attributable to the influence of the counseling hours.

Changes in Personality and Integration

We now shift from this internal frame of reference of the client to an external view, in order to see what changes in personality characteristics and in degree of integration may be observed from a diagnostic point of view.

A trained psychologist took the projective personality tests (Thematic Apperception Test) which had been administered to clients and controls and rated them on a scale which ranged from psychotic, or severe disturbance bordering on psychotic, to "well-integrated, happy person, socially effective." In making these ratings, the psychologist had no knowledge about the specific test—whether it came from a client or a control or from a pre-therapy, post-therapy, or follow-up point.

When the results were analyzed, it was found that the therapy group was significantly more disturbed than the controls at the pre-therapy point, ranging from maximum disturbance to "problems of some difficulty." During therapy there was significant change in a positive direction, and this gain was maintained through the follow-up period. The improvement was not due to the phenomenon of regression toward the mean. The control group showed no change during the period studied (*8*).

Of the therapy group, twenty of the twenty-five showed personality change in a positive direction. In most instances, however, this change was not extreme, and even at the follow-up point the test protocols of over half the group were rated as showing the existence of serious problems. The alteration in personality structure and in personal integration was, in other words, moderate and did not constitute a change to complete integration or a problem-free personality (*8*).

The changes found through this "blind" analysis of the personality measure correlated positively and significantly with the changes in adjustment score based on the client's own perceptions of himself. They also were positively and significantly related to the counselor's rating of "success" or movement in therapy (*8*).

In another study a "blind" analysis of the same TAT material was made, using scales based on classical psychoanalytic theory, the ratings being made by a research worker with a strongly diagnostic orientation. The central findings were the same. On one of the major scales which rated the diagnostic status of the individual from psychotic to healthy adult, significant positive change was found in the clients during the therapy period. No marked change was found in the control group, and the difference between the two groups was significant. For the clients who underwent a sixty-day control period before therapy, it was found that they evidenced more personality change during therapy than during the control period. The findings from this study, however, showed no significant correlation with any other measure used, except for a rather low correlation with the preceding TAT study (*9*). It appears that a different type of change was being measured by this method, and, while this change was positive, it was not significantly related to the kinds of change hypothesized by the theory of client-centered therapy.

In general, then, the personality characteristics of clients in therapy tended to show significant change away from those labeled as border-line psychotic, severely neurotic, and severe discomfort, in the direction of those labeled as milder problems or as being the characteristics of an essentially well-functioning person. This change, while on the average not great, tends to be maintained through the period following therapy. No such change is discovered in the control individuals or in therapy clients during a control period.

Changes in Attitudes toward Others

To what extent do our clients, as a concomitant of psychotherapy, change in their general attitudes toward others? When this problem was examined in a small group of cases studied intensively, it was found that certain changes occurred in the perception of others. The ordinary person came to be seen as better adjusted, more of a separate individual, with his own standards and values, more responsible, and less guilty. These trends were not all statistically significant, but they tended to confirm previous studies of this question. Perhaps the most significant finding was that others came to be perceived as being much more like the client (*6*).

When the question is asked regarding the whole group, as to whether the clients become more acceptant and democratic in their attitudes toward others, or more nonacceptant and authoritarian, then the answer is inconclusive. In terms of the test used, both clients and controls are rather accepting in their attitudes, and neither shows any significant over-all change during the periods studied. There is a tendency for the clients who show the greatest therapeutic change (as judged by a number of criteria) to become more acceptant of others, while those showing the least change move in the reverse direction. This tendency is not significant, however. It also appears that the clients who show the greatest movement in therapy tend to de-emphasize their attitudes toward others, becoming less insistently acceptant or less strongly rejectant (*11*).

The methods used in these studies reveal no clear-cut change in the attitudes toward others during or following the period of therapy. The findings are complex, and, though suggestive trends emerge, the major hypothesis is not upheld. Since some of the findings are at variance with earlier studies, further investigation is needed.

Changes in Behavior

Thus far our concern has been entirely with psychological change within the individual client. In what way, if any, does his everyday behavior change? In order to measure his behavior, both the client himself and two of his friends were asked to indicate, from a list of specific behaviors, those which were characteristic of the client. By comparing the ratings made at different times, any change could be detected. The behaviors on the list had been evaluated by a group of a hundred clinical experts as to the degree of maturity of behavior each represented.

It was found that there was no significant difference between the pre-therapy and post-therapy behavior of our clients, on the average, according to the friends' observations. However, this lack of change in the average was found to be due to two divergent underlying trends. The friends (who were not in contact with the Center and knew nothing of the therapy) observed a definite increase in the maturity of behavior of those clients judged to be showing movement in therapy and a definite decrease in the maturity of behavior in those clients judged to be failing to progress in therapy. This relationship was significant and was even more marked when the whole period from pre-therapy to follow-up was considered (*13*).

The clients themselves observed a significant change in their behavior over the therapy period, a gain which was held, but did not significantly increase, over the follow-up period (*13*).

When the clients' ratings of their own behavior were compared with the ratings by their friends, it was discovered that our clients consistently rated themselves less favorably than did their friends; but this discrepancy steadily diminished, so that by the follow-up point their perception agreed much more closely with that of their friends (*13*).

It was also found that the clients' estimates of amount and direction of behavior change tended to agree with the friends' ratings and with the counselor's judgment of therapeutic movement, except in those cases which the counselor deemed unsuccessful. In such cases, the counselor saw little or no movement in therapy, and the friends saw marked deterioration in behavior; but these "failure" clients perceived themselves as having made marked gains in their behavior. This appears to be a pure and measured instance of defensiveness in self-appraisal (*13*).

No significant change was found in the maturity of behavior of control individuals rated by friends or in the behavior of the clients during a no-therapy period (*13*).

Thus we may conclude that the quality of the therapeutic experience is responsible for the fact that, where therapy "takes," the client becomes more mature in his behavior—becoming less dependent, less boastful, less compulsive, less easily upset, better organized, more tolerant, more open to the evidence, behaving in ways that show more concern for the discovery of the facts in the case, more concern for the welfare of all. On the other hand, where therapy is judged by the counselor to be a failure, there is a marked deterioration in these same qualities of behavior (*13*).

Factors Which Favor or Limit Change

What factors make it likely that a client will make progress in therapy? Or fail to make progress? Our studies throw a certain amount of light on these questions.

Age, for example, which is often thought to be an important consideration, shows no relationship to movement in our clients (*7*). However, it must be remembered that the age range is from twenty-one to forty only. The initial adjustment or integration of the client likewise shows no relationship to the gains made in therapy, the deeply disturbed and the mildly disturbed progressing about equally well (*7, 8*).

It is a clear-cut fact that in our group the women clients made significantly more progress than did the men (*5, 7, 8*). Since our counselors were, with one exception, men, it cannot be said whether this means that clients make more gain when working with a counselor of the opposite sex or whether women are more able to effect a personality reorganization than men.

Another factor associated with therapeutic movement is the length of the series of interviews. Where there were more than twenty interviews, there is considerable assurance of therapeutic gain, while in shorter cases the results are more variable (*7*). It is also perhaps important that a seriously disturbed client can show evidence, on almost every measure, of having made progress and yet regress to his former disturbed state primarily because therapy was too brief (*16*).

An unexpected finding was that those clients who were asked to wait for sixty days before beginning therapy were less likely to become involved in therapy, became more extreme in their social attitudes, liked the counselor less when they began their interviews, and showed less benefit from therapy (*11*). From this evidence in a small number of cases, it appears that having to wait for therapy (or at least where this wait is in part necessitated by a research design) makes therapeutic gain less likely.

It has sometimes been suggested that the most important factor in change is the client's decision *to* change—that the motivation for therapy is itself perhaps a sufficient cause of change. Our findings show that, for the group which waited sixty days before beginning therapy, no significant degree of constructive change occurred during that period, although there was some trend in that direction on several of the measures (*14*).

In this connection it is of interest that, of this "wait" group, those who dropped out of therapy after a few interviews were those who were somewhat better adjusted to begin with (*7, 14*) and who had made positive gains on most of our measures during the sixty-day waiting period (*14*). It seems to be at least suggested that there is an element of "spontaneous recovery" in some of the less disturbed individuals and that these clients then fail to become really involved in therapy.

In certain ways our findings are related to recent studies of the authoritarian personality. There is a suggestion in our material that clients with moderately democratic and acceptant attitudes toward others benefit the most from therapy (*11*). Conversely, clients with a high degree of ethnocentrism, who make sharp and rigid distinctions between their own and other groups (*12*), and those who are generally anti-democratic (*11*) tend to be failures in therapy (*11, 12*).

While further study is clearly needed on a number of these points, it appears that empirical studies can help to discover the factors which make it likely that client-centered therapy, as it exists at the present time, will be effective or ineffective in helping the client to change.

The Therapeutic Process

Though most of the studies reported in this volume deal primarily with the outcomes of psychotherapy, the findings in a number of ways help us to give a more complete and objective account of the process of client-centered therapy.

A relationship in which the client comes to feel a strong liking and respect for the counselor is the type of relationship most associated with progress in therapy (7). When the counselor develops similar feelings for the client (7) or an attitude of caring which is not possessive or demanding (*15*), then success is likely.

Although the therapist endeavors to relate to the client as the client sees himself, he may actually be relating to the client as the latter will come to see himself when he is more aware of all his feelings (*15*).

During the interviews the most distinctive characteristic is for the client to move, in his discussion, away from specific and situational problems to an exploration of himself. His interviews also become less an intellectual or cognitive or thinking process and more and more an emotional or experiencing process, in which he is feeling and being rather than dealing with problems on an intellectual basis (7). It appears that perhaps "experiencing"—the complete awareness of his total organismic response to a situation—is an important concomitant of the process of therapy (*15*). These directions in the interviews are associated with constructive change in therapy (7). Interestingly enough, though the quality of the relationship is important, as indicated in the preceding paragraph, the extent to which the client focuses on the relationship itself in his interviews has little correlation with the degree of personality reorganization which will be effected (7).

The change in self-perception appears to be a central element in the process of client-centered therapy. The emergence into awareness of new perceptions of self is characteristic of our cases, particularly of those rated as successful (*10*, *15*). There is some evidence that these emerging self-perceptions are based on material previously denied to awareness (*15*).

The degree of emergence of new self-perceptions correlates positively with three other criteria of progress in therapy but correlates negatively with a measure developed out of a diagnostic and psychoanalytic orientation. There is a suggestion that client-centered therapy produces the changes hypothesized by client-centered theory but may not necessarily produce those changes hypothesized by other theories of personality or therapy. The evidence is insufficient to make a definite statement (*10*).

In summary, then, the process of client-centered therapy, as caught in the factual evidence of these various studies, appears to be based on a warm relationship of mutual liking and respect. The client begins with a somewhat intellectual discussion of his "problems" but moves toward a personal exploration of himself and an experiencing of his actual organismic reactions to situations. As he permits more of these actual experiences to enter his awareness, his picture of himself keeps changing and enlarging to include these newly discovered facets of self. When the process is of the sort we have just described, the degree of reorganization of personality and behavior is likely to be considerable.

VII. SOME PERPLEXING ISSUES

For those of us who have carried on the research each aspect of it contains a multitude of tantalizing unanswered questions, tempting us forward into further investigations which may discover further aspects of lawfulness in this most subjective of relationships. It would be impossible to list all the questions which have been raised for us by these studies, but we trust that the reader will already have experienced many of these questions in himself. It may be profitable, however, to describe and discuss briefly a very few of the more important issues which remain unanswered by the studies completed to date.

The Question of Selective Regression

Several of our studies have shown in our total client group, or in certain subgroups, a slight average regression from the end of therapy to the follow-up point (*4*, *5*, *6*, *13*). This falling-away from the peak point of therapy is not significant and from a statistician's point of view could be ignored. However, a close examination of the data in chapter 6, for example, shows that the slight average regression in the correlation of self and ideal is actually based, in these eight intensively studied cases, on a somewhat dichotomous picture. Two clients regressed very sharply, and two clients made sharp gains during the follow-up period, only four remaining relatively constant (two gaining slightly, two regressing slightly) (*6*). This sort of contrast is made even sharper in the complete analysis of two cases, one showing constructive change during follow-up (*15*), and one showing significant regression (*16*).

What underlies this difference? Why is it that, following the conclusion of therapy, some clients continue to show marked personality and behavioral change of a constructive sort, and others equally sharply regress? Is it due to the initial personality characteristics of the client, to factors in the relationship, to the attitudes or feelings in the counselor, to the length of therapy, to the presence or absence of certain elements in the process of therapy? At the present time we do not know. It is possible that further analysis of the available data may assist us in finding partial answers. It may be that new studies will be necessary. It is obvious that, if the answers were available, we might be able to be more effective in providing the conditions for permanent positive personality change.

Factors Favoring or Limiting Therapeutic Change

A somewhat similar but broader question is: What are the factors which facilitate or block therapeutic change? If we consider our twenty-five "attrition" cases—those who never became deeply involved in therapy—we find that two were dropped because of circumstances, and six gained real help in a few interviews in mastering a situational problem. This leaves seventeen who "dipped their toes" into therapy and retreated, compared with twenty-nine who entered fully (*3*). This is, we believe, characteristic of the experience of most organizations offering psychotherapy. Then, of the twenty-nine entering therapy, there were varying degrees of personality reorganization and "success."

What personality factors are associated with this facilitation or lack of movement in therapy? One bit of objective evidence had been provided by Haimowitz,[2] before the present program commenced. The studies reported here add some additional evidence. We may now say that the data suggest that those who are poorly

2. See Natalie R. and Morris L. Haimowitz, "Personality Changes in Client-centered Therapy," in Werner Wolff (ed.), *Success in Psychotherapy* (New York: Grune & Stratton, 1952).

adjusted (*5*), conscious of a high degree of internal tension (*4*, *14*), intra-punitive in their personality characteristics (Haimowitz), and moderately acceptant of others in their attitudes (*11*) are likely to make constructive change in therapy. Conversely there is some evidence that those who are better adjusted (*14*), who are aware of less internal tension (*14*), who are ethnocentric in their attitudes (*12*), and extra-punitive in their personality characteristics (Haimowitz) are more likely to drop out of therapy or, if they remain, are less likely to profit from it. Also, in the judgments of counselors, whose ratings have proved to have validity in other respects, a relationship of mutual liking and respect is associated with favorable outcomes (*7*). On the negative side, we find nothing in our data to indicate that the initial diagnostic status of the individual has any marked relationship to therapeutic outcome (*7*, *8*).

This is a beginning—but only a beginning. These findings are suggestive, not conclusive. They need much more thorough investigation. And there are many other aspects of this question which have not even been touched. Does the personality of the therapist make a difference? (Probably not, judging by one unpublished pilot study.) Do the attitudes of the therapist make a difference, as seems clinically to be true? Is the number of years of experience of the therapist related to favorable outcome? The content of his professional preparation? Is the preconceived picture of the therapeutic relationship, on the part of both client and therapist, related to the likelihood of therapeutic movement? These and many other questions remain as no more than interrogation points at the present time.

It should be emphasized that such a search as has here been suggested would not have as its goal the discovery of those individuals who are "untreatable," who cannot profit by psychotherapy. Rather its goal would be to find those individuals or groups who have not found client-centered therapy, as it exists today, a fruitful approach to the personality and behavioral changes which they desire. Such findings would constitute a challenge to therapists to discover new or revised ways of dealing with their clients to the end that the desired personality reorganization can be more widely achieved.

How Make the Best Use of Phenomenological Data?

This is possibly the first major psychological research to build heavily on the objective analysis of phenomenological data. In our use of the Q-sort to obtain the client's picture of self, self-ideal, and other (*4*, *6*, *15*, *16*), in our study of the counselor's frame of reference as a worth-while datum (*7*), in the use of the client's awareness of self as revealed in the interviews (*10*), we have frequently used material which is gained by sampling the individual's awareness, his phenomenological field, as a basis for our study. In one sense there is nothing new in this. Psychologists have in many ways drawn upon such samplings of consciousness—in questionnaires, in survey interviews, in responses to inkblots and pictures, in responses to intelligence tests. But the usual use of such material has been to make inferences from it regarding some concept *not* in the subject's frame of reference—his "intelligence," "schizophrenia," "social maladjustment," "psychopathy," and the like. We too have used such material in this fashion in our analysis of the TAT (*8*) in determining the degree of ethnocentrism (*12*) and in other ways. But we have also made our heaviest use of this material to infer from it the client's internal frame of reference—to infer his own picture of some aspect of his world. In this respect our work has been similar in intent to that of Piaget, for example, rather than to that of most American psychologists. Piaget's study of the stages in the development of intelligence and reasoning in the child, based on the analysis of the way these processes *seem to the child*, is a significant instance of this sort of approach.

With a similar type of intent, we too have aimed at discovering the order which exists in the phenomenal world of the individual. We may thus investigate the relationship between perception of self and perception of the ordinary person and determine whether this relationship alters during therapy. In so doing, we regard it as quite irrelevant for the moment whether the self is "really" as it is perceived, or whether the ordinary person "really" has the characteristics perceived by the client. It is the possibility of lawful relationships within the phenomenal field which interests us.

Now we have found this approach most fruitful and rewarding.

In fact, it appears to the writer that, in those portions of our research where we have endeavored to discover the underlying order or lawfulness in such phenomenological data, the findings contain much more stimulation in the direction of forming new hypotheses, and in raising new and profound issues, than in those portions where our approach has been more conventional. In those instances where we have tried to relate the order discovered in the phenomenal field to some of the external observations—perception of self compared with diagnosis, for example (*15*, *16*)—we seemed to have uncovered some unexpected and important relationships. Thus we have little question as to the profitable nature of this whole quest for the natural order inherent in the internal frame of reference, the private perceptual world, of the individual.

But being pioneers in this field, we are also very much aware of the puzzles which attend the use of such data. Let me try to state very briefly the most serious practical problem. A negatively described aspect of the individual's private world—a depreciative self-sort, a high discrepancy between self and ideal, or a perception of one's behavior as immature—has, we have found, only one sort of meaning. It indicates stress, tension, maladjustment, etc., within the individual, and this meaning tends to be definitely corroborated by evidence external to the person's frame of reference. A positively described aspect of the individual's private world—a confident self-picture, a small discrepancy between self and ideal, a positive picture of one's behavior—may, on the other hand, have either one of two meanings. It may mean, as in the case of Mrs. Oak (*15*), a reasonable degree of adjustment, inner comfort, and maturity, a meaning which is verified by external evidence. Or it may mean, as mentioned by Butler (*4*), a highly defensive paranoid individual. It may be the defensively "good" picture of behavior put forth by individuals who are threatened by their failure to experience progress in therapy (*13*). Each picture is a "real" picture of the phenomenal field of the individual, but this picture may have one of two quite discrepant generalized meanings.

In other words, we have not learned how to adapt most effectively to what the writer has come to think of as "the Y-shaped meaning" of most measures of the phenomenal field. If one thinks of the base of the Y as representing negative aspects of the phenomenal field, direct inferences may be made from these as to internal states of tension, which will be corroborated by other evidence. But those aspects of the phenomenal field which are positive may have one or the other of two widely divergent meanings: (*a*) a general validity borne out by other evidence in those individuals for whom the pertinent experiences are accessible to awareness or (*b*) a defensive or "façade" meaning in those individuals in whom the relevant experiences are denied to awareness.

For the present, this constitutes a dilemma. Some would have us resolve it by throwing overboard any attempt to make objective measurements of the phenomenal field. This seems most unwise in view of the tremendous fruitfulness of this approach (*4*, *6*, *10*, *14*, *15*, *16*) and in the richly stimulating findings which emerge when efforts are made to relate these measurements of the internal frame of reference to measurements of a more external order (*5*, *6*, *10*, *14*, *15*, *16*). Consequently, we prefer to live with this dilemma until we understand it more deeply and perhaps can develop more sensitive theories as well as better instruments to deal with it.

The Problem of Perceptual Vantage Points

There is a closely related problem which perplexes us. The observant reader may have noted, as he went along, this odd assortment of facts which seem to be variations on one theme. When the client describes himself, and is in turn described on the same instrument by a diagnostician, the correlation is generally low (*15*, *16*). When the clients describe their behavior, and their friends describe their behavior on the same instrument, the correlation is low (*13*). Such facts are easily brushed aside by most psychologists, because it is easy to mistrust the client. But the other facts are not so easily evaded. When two diagnosticians report objectively their diagnostic picture of a client, the correlations between the two are in the thirties and forties (*15*, *16*). When two friends observe the behavior of each client, the correlation between the observations by the "first" friend and the observations by the "second" friend is in the twenties (*13*). When one psychologist analyzes the TAT from one orientation, and another psychologist from another, the correlation is low, or in some aspects even negative (*9, 10*). Yet in every one of these instances the individual observer or perceiver—whether the client, the diagnostician, the TAT analyst, or the client's friend—exhibits a high degree of consistency with himself in his repeated observations and judgments. As one examines this complex material, which has been considerably oversimplified in this description, one gets the picture of each observer (including the client as an observer of himself) consistently and reliably reporting, in objective fashion, a given aspect of the client's personality or behavior. Yet, when another individual is asked to make the same type of objective report of the same aspect of personality or behavior, this report may differ considerably.

It would be quite easy to attribute all this to the crudity of our measures and the newness of the field and to say that as yet we have no adequate way of measuring what the person "really" is or what his behavior "really" is. This kind of explanation, however, does not account for the significant relationships found, and the high degree of order discovered, when our methods of analysis are such as to stay within one given perceptual vantage point at a time. Nor would it account for such findings as the significant relationship between the counselor's judgment of movement in therapy and the friend's observations of change in behavior (*13*).

There is at least another possibility which may be approached by way of analogy. The physicist has become accustomed to the fact that he cannot know "reality." Even time and space and motion have no absolute meaning but exist only as the ordering of events in the mind of an observer and are relative to the vantage point of the observer. There is not even any such thing as "now"—the present instant—which applies to the universe as a whole, but only a "now" for a given vantage point.[3] Is it possible that in dealing with problems of personality the quest for "reality" may be equally unsound? Is it possible that in place of this hypothetical single reality we shall have to substitute a recognition that there are various perceptual vantage points from which to view the person, one of these being from within the consciousness of the person

3. See Lincoln Barnett, *The Universe and Dr. Einstein* (New York: William Sloane Associates, Inc., 1948), for an interpretation of the findings of modern physics.

himself? Certainly our evidence would suggest the lawfulness and internal order within each of these perceptual views. There is also the suggestion of significant and perhaps predictable relationships between these perceptual systems. But whether there is *a* reality with which the science of personality may deal remains a question.

Issues as a Result of Research

The four perplexing questions which have been singled out are not necessarily the most important issues to emerge from our research program. It is not at all certain that there would be any agreement among our staff as to what constitutes the most important unresolved questions. They are presented merely as a sampling of the many perplexities which have grown out of our investigations. It is to be hoped that both our own efforts and those of the readers of this volume will move such issues in the direction of solution. And if in the process of resolving these questions even more perplexities are discovered, then we will know that the pursuit of a scientific search is having its usual result.

VIII. CONCLUSION

This chapter has endeavored to give a condensed and simplified account of the research program described in this volume. It has indicated that various changes in the self-perception of the client, in his personality organization, and in his daily behavior occur as a concomitant of a period of client-centered therapy. It appears reasonable to conclude that the psychotherapy is the effective agent of change, since changes of comparable magnitude do not occur in a control group or in our clients during a control period. In our judgment the research sets forth for the first time objective evidence that one defined approach to psychotherapy produces certain measurable and significant changes in the individual coming for help and that certain other changes which have also been hypothesized failed to occur in significant degree.

In addition, the findings from our studies have been analyzed for the light they throw on the process of therapy. In general, these findings tend to support the description of the process as set forth by the theory of client-centered therapy.

Finally, a presentation has been made of a few of the many unanswered questions and unresolved issues posed by the research. Though to the community at large the most significant outcome of our studies lies in their positive factual findings, to us as therapists and research psychologists it is the unanswered questions which are most important. These will, we trust, lead us further into unexplored areas as we attempt to comprehend and identify the orderly processes by which the human personality is altered through the influence of experience in an interpersonal relationship.

Index

Index

A-scale; see Authorities, dependence on
Adler, Alfred, 12
Adjustment; *see* Personal adjustment
Adjustment score; *see* Q-sort adjustment score
Adorno, T. W., 171, 172, 196, 208, 209, 211
Anderson, Robert P., 23
"Atomistic hypotheses," 6–7
Attitudes toward others, 4, 10, 14, 25, 37, 82, 123, 132, 134, 148, 154–56, 196, 242
  and attitude toward self, 4, 146, 167–69, 170, 212, 214, 216
  changes in, 175–88, 421
  as criteria of success, 238
  de-emphasis of, 184, 185–86, 194–95
  effect of wait period on, 188–91, 248
  and extent of personal contact with other, 195
  in Mrs. Oak, 273, 285, 287, 305–7
  and personality theory, 167–69, 216
  relation of changes in, to initial score, 183–84, 186–88
  significant others, 124–25, 195
  in "successful" clients, 181–84
  see also Ethnocentrism
Attitudes toward self, 81, 82, 123, 132, 148, 154, 156
  and attitudes toward others, 4, 146, 167–69, 170, 212, 214, 216
  changes in, over wait period, 188–89
  in Mrs. Oak, 262, 266, 272, 287
  and personality change, 188–91
Attrition group, 6, 52, 241
  description of, 43–44
  effects of wait period on, 188–91, 192, 253
  and Emotional-Maturity Scale score, 246–47
  initial status of, 106, 107, 245–46
  and Mental Health Scale scores, 249–51
  and Q-adjustment score, 245–46
  and self-ideal correlations, 243–45
  and Self-Other Attitude Scale, 247–49
Authorities, dependence on, 37, 170, 173, 178, 180, 197, 247
  and democratic attitudes, 173
  in Mr. Bebb, 398–99
  in Mrs. Oak, 305, 306, 307
  and submissiveness, 170
Autism, 124, 128, 161, 210–11, 249

Ballard, R. G., 197
Barnett, Lincoln, 432
Barron, F. X., 183, 197, 199, 200
Bartlett, Marion R., 407
Bebb, Mr., case of, 10
  counselor's Q-sorts for, 385–86
  Counselor's Rating Scale for, 352
  defensiveness in, 352, 396, 403, 406
  Emotional-Maturity Scale scores of, 396–97, 404
  factor analyses of Q-sorts, 386–90
  and ideal-self concept, 379–81, 382–85, 389–90, 391–95, 403–4
  locus of evaluation, 351, 357–58
  ordinary person, concept of, 379, 390, 395
  personal integration in, 352, 403
  process of therapy in, 158, 351, 352–72
  Q-adjustment scores of, 395–96
  regression in, 404–5, 406
  as seen by client, 379–90, 391–95, 396, 397
  as seen by diagnostician, 372–78, 391–95, 395–96
  as seen by friends, 396–97
  as seen by therapist, 350, 385–86
  self-concept, 379–82, 383–85, 386–95, 396, 403–4
  self-ideal correlations for, 379, 380–81, 383–85, 386, 387–90, 403–4
  Self-Other Attitude Scale scores of, 398–400, 404
  TAT analyses of, 372–78
  and therapeutic relationship, 351–52, 352–72, 401–3
Berger, E. M., 168, 170
Bergman, Daniel, 167

Bico, Mrs., case of
  and self-awareness, 158–60
  "success" rating for, 158
  therapeutic process in, 158–60, 163
"Blind" ratings, 6, 415
  in Mr. Bebb, 372–8
  in Mrs. Oak, 267–73
  of TAT material, 9, 111, 115, 119, 120, 121–22, 142
Block, Jack, 197, 210
Block, Jeanne, 197, 210
Block IV, 26, 119
Bowie, Carol, 267, 271, 373
Bowman, Paul, 23
Bown, Oliver, 24
Boyer, Jacques K., 283, 285
Bronfenbrenner, Urie, 198
Butler, John M., 36, 76, 86, 243, 244, 273, 430

C-scale; *see* Desire to change others
California Scale of Ethnocentrism, 196; *see also* Ethnocentrism (E) Scale
Carr, Arthur C., 100
Cartwright, Desmond, 189, 196, 204, 247
Client-centered Therapy, 5
Client-centered therapy, 13, 31
  hypotheses of, 3–5
  limitations of, 10, 183, 202, 206–7, 213
  and other orientations, 8, 121, 141–42, 161–64
  personality theory of, 4–5, 6–7, 25, 30, 56–58, 85–86, 94, 167–69, 215–16
  research in, 6–7, 12–34
Client group; *see* Experimental (E) group
Client-therapist interaction, 14; *see also* Therapeutic relationship
Client wait group; *see* Own-control (O-C) group
Clients
  attitudes of, toward counselor, 102, 103, 104, 188–91, 264, 266
  capacities of, 3, 4–5
  and research program, 7, 42, 49, 51, 52
  selection of, for research, 45–46
Concomitants of psychotherapy, 3, 6, 30; *see also* Outcomes of psychotherapy
Conservatism, 194–95
Control features, 6, 9, 10, 20, 21, 44–47, 64–65, 97; *see also* Controls
Control groups; *see* Equivalent-control (E-C) group; Own-control (O-C) group
Control phenomena, principle of, 21–22
Controls, 6, 9, 10, 21, 44–47, 64–65
  for age, 44, 45, 65, 239
  for biosocial characteristics, 44
  difficulties of, 6, 7, 19, 20–21, 44, 46–47, 97, 188–91, 239–40
  on Emotional-Maturity Scale, 37, 218–19, 223–24
  for environmental influences, 44–45
  for expectations of therapy, 44
  experimental, 21
  for motivation, 21, 38, 44, 45, 65, 239
  for passage of time, 38, 44, 45, 65, 82
  for personality characteristics, 21, 38, 44, 65
  for repeated testing, 39, 65, 82
  for sex, 44, 45, 65, 239
  for socioeconomic status, 44, 45, 65
  statistical, 21
  for student-nonstudent status, 45
Correlates of psychotherapy, 22–23, 25, 26; *see also* Outcomes of psychotherapy
Counseling Center, 3, 16, 17, 35, 41, 42, 48, 49, 122, 134, 148, 172, 189, 196, 199, 200, 202, 218, 219, 221, 240, 260, 301, 343, 349, 371, 413, 414, 422
Counseling Center Staff, 3, 4, 5, 16, 17, 35, 42, 48, 100, 196, 433
Counseling relationship, 5; *see also* Therapeutic relationship
Counselor judgments, 9, 50, 81; *see also* Counselor's Rating Scale
Counselor's Rating Scale, 9, 81, 180, 261, 415
  description of, 100–103
  and Emotional-Maturity Scale, 220, 222–23, 227–30, 231–32, 236
  and Ethnocentrism (E) Scale, 201, 205–7, 210, 213, 214
  and Mental Health Scale, 141–42, 155–57, 160–64
  on personal integration, 99–100, 106–7, 295–300
  on process of therapy, 50, 100, 101, 102, 103, 104, 188–91
  and Q-adjustment score, 81, 83, 84, 87, 105, 109, 155–57, 181, 205
  reliability of, 103, 106–7
  on therapeutic relationship, 50, 100, 101, 102, 103, 104, 105
  and Self-awareness Measure, 148, 150, 151–52, 153–55, 157–58, 161–64, 165
  and self-ideal correlations, 69–70, 72
  and Self-Other Attitude Scale, 181–91, 192

Counselor's Rating Scale—*Continued*
and TAT Rating Scale, 69–70, 105, 117–18, 119, 120, 155–57, 181
Cowen, E. L., 198
Curran, Charles A., 146

D-scale; *see* Differences of opinion, acceptance of
Data collection, problems of, 7, 8, 26–27, 221
Defensiveness, 4, 14, 23, 30, 82, 146, 167–69, 216, 235, 430–31
and adjustment ratings, 160–64
and attitudes toward others, 167–69, 211, 248–49
in attrition group, 248–49
and denial of material to awareness, 57–59, 167–69, 345
and emotional maturity, 231–32, 235
in Mr. Bebb, 352, 396, 403, 406
in Mrs. Oak, 281, 290–95, 296, 298, 304
and Q-sorts, 59, 72–73, 75
and self-awareness, 146, 147
Democratic attitudes, 37, 170, 171, 172, 178, 180, 247
and attitude toward leadership, 174
and dependence on authority, 173
in Mr. Bebb, 398–99
in Mrs. Oak, 305, 306, 307
and personal adjustment, 170–71
Democratic means, belief in, 37, 174, 178, 180, 247
in Mr. Bebb, 398–99
in Mrs. Oak, 306, 307
Denker, P. G., 238, 239, 240, 252–53
Department of Psychology (University of Chicago), 17
Desire to change others, 37, 168, 174, 178, 180, 247
and attitudes toward others, 174
in Mr. Bebb, 398
in Mrs. Oak, 305, 306, 307
Desired self; *see* Ideal-self concept
Differences of opinion, acceptance of, 37, 174, 178, 180, 247
and democratic attitudes, 174
in Mr. Bebb, 398–99
in Mrs. Oak, 305, 306, 307
Dorfman, Elaine, 5
Drop-out group, 6
Dymond, Rosalind F., 81, 91, 96, 105, 142, 148, 149, 155, 156, 157, 161, 165, 205, 245, 282, 295

Edwards, A. L., 137, 242
Einstein, Albert, 235
Emotional-Maturity Scale (E-M Scale), 49, 50, 141, 142, 215–37, 242, 246, 247, 249, 250, 260, 261, 301–5, 396, 397
controls for, 218–19, 220
and Counselor's Rating Scale, 227–30, 231–32, 236
description of, 37, 216–17, 234
and difficulties of data collection, 221
findings on, 221–33, 246–47
and Mental Health Scale, 141–42
reliability of, 223–25
scores for Mr. Bebb, 396–97, 404
scores for Mrs. Oak, 301–5
Empathic understanding, 4, 24; *see also* Therapeutic relationship
Equivalent-control (E-C) group, 38, 39, 52, 64, 97, 241, 250
description of, 45–46, 413–15
and Emotional-Maturity Scale, 246–47, 218–19, 223–25
and Ethnocentrism (E) Scale, 202–3
and Mental Health Scale, 122, 123, 131–37, 138–39, 143, 249–51
and Q-adjustment score, 78, 80-81, 82, 84, 109, 115–16, 119, 120, 245–47
selection of, 45, 47
and self-ideal correlations, 64–67, 68, 70–71, 73, 74, 77, 116–17, 119, 120, 243–45
and TAT Rating Scale, 110, 111, 114–18, 119, 120
wait group of, 38, 78, 80, 242, 244–46, 247–48, 251
Ethnocentrism, 10, 37
changes in, 172, 178, 180, 196
changes in, and initial score, 183
definition of, 172–73, 196–97
effects of group therapy on, 197, 203
in interpersonal relations, 196–97, 210–12
in Mr. Bebb, 398
and perceptual functioning, 196, 197–98, 209–10
and personality organization, 198–99, 209–10
pervasiveness of, 198
and range of effectiveness of therapy, 10, 202, 205–7, 213
in self-referred clients, 208–9
and success in therapy, 183, 201–7, 212
tenacity of, 197

Ethnocentrism (E) Scale, 10, 37, 167, 178, 180, 183, 200
  and Counselor's Rating Scale, 201, 205–7, 210, 213, 214
  findings, 201–7, 212, 213
  and PEC-scale, 173
  and Self-awareness Measure, 168–69
  and Self-Other Attitude Scale, 206–7, 213
Experimental controls; *see* Controls
Experimental (E) group, 8, 9, 10, 38, 52, 65, 97
  changes in, over wait period, 238–58
  and Counselor's Rating Scale, 102–6, 117–18, 119, 120, 158
  description of, 39–41, 414
  and Emotional-Maturity Scale, 218, 219, 221–23, 226–34, 236, 246–47
  and Ethnocentrism (E) Scale, 201–8
  and Mental Health Scale, 122, 131–37, 138–39, 143, 153–55, 249–51
  and Q-adjustment scores, 78, 80–81, 82, 84, 91–94, 109, 115–16, 119, 120, 245–47
  selection of, 41–44
  and Self-awareness Measure, 152–65
  and self-ideal correlations, 60–64, 67–68, 70–71, 73, 74, 77, 116–17, 119, 120, 243–45
  and self-ideal-ordinary interrelationship, 89–91, 94–96
  and Self-Other Attitude Scale, 175–80, 181–83, 184–88, 188–93, 247–49
  and TAT Rating Scale, 110, 111, 114–18, 119, 120
  typical client in, 39, 41
  wait group of; *see* Own-control (O-C) group
Experimental wait group; *see* Own-control (O-C) group
Eysenck, Hans, 238, 239, 253

Factor analysis of Q-sorts, 36, 62, 98
  for Mr. Bebb, 386–90
  for Mrs. Oak, 283–86
Failure, 6, 10, 24, 28, 29, 43, 109
  case study of, 349–409
  on Emotional-Maturity Scale, 231–32
  and ethnocentrism, 208–14
  factors contributing to, 104–5, 188–91, 208–14, 407, 423–24, 427–28
  nature of, 24–27
  and Q-sort changes, 97–98
  and self-ideal correlations, 71–72, 73–74, 407
  and Self-Other Attitude Scale, 184–88
  and therapeutic relationship, 50, 100–105, 345, 407–8
  as therapeutic risk, 199, 201, 202, 208, 212, 213, 423–24
Fascist scale (F-scale), 37, 178, 180, 247
  changes in Mr. Bebb, 398–99
  changes in Mrs. Oak, 305–6, 307
  and outcome of therapy, 170–71
  and Self-Other Attitude Scale, 171–74
Fiedler, Fred E., 407
Fisher, J., 197
Fisher, R. A., 60, 103
Follow-up interview, 50–51, 371
Follow-up period, 38, 82, 221
  changes over, 85, 134, 304–5, 307–8, 310
    on Emotional-Maturity Scale, 222–23, 226, 227–28, 230
    on Mental Health Scale, 134–35, 138, 143, 153–55, 156
    on Q-adjustment score, 80, 153–55, 156, 282, 293
    on Self-awareness Measure, 153–55, 156
    on self-ideal correlations, 63–64, 68, 70, 71–72, 73, 74, 282, 293–94, 384, 389, 403
    on self-ideal-ordinary interrelationships, 90–98, 281
    on Self-Other Attitude Scale, 179–80, 181–83, 184, 305–6, 309, 398, 404
    in TAT analysis, 308, 378
    on TAT Rating Scale, 114, 117–18, 153–55, 156
Follow-up questionnaire, 51, 371
Fox, Margaret, 23
Frenkel-Brunswik, Else, 171, 172, 196, 208, 209, 211
Freud, Sigmund, 12, 249
Fromm, Erich, 12, 167
Fromm-Reichmann, Frieda, 167
Functional leadership, 18

Gestalt, 62, 159
Gordon, Thomas, 5, 25, 37, 41, 196, 247
Group-centered functioning, 17–18
Group-centered values, 173
Group leadership, 5, 174, 178, 180, 247
Group therapy, 5
  and attitudes toward others, 195
  and ethnocentrism, 197, 203
Grummon, Donald L., 41, 68, 249

Index

Haigh, Gerard V., 36, 57, 86, 146, 243, 273
Haimowitz, Morris L., 427, 428
Haimowitz, Natalie Reader, 100, 427, 428
Hartley, Margaret W., 23, 46, 57, 86, 298
Hathaway, S. R., 29, 64
Hebb, D. O., 238, 239, 240
"Hello-goodbye" effect, 28–29, 64, 406
  and Q-adjustment rating, 82
  and self-ideal correlations, 74
Hobbs, Nicholas, 5
Hogan, Richard A. 30, 146
Horney, Karen, 12, 96–97, 167
Hutchins, Robert, 5

Ideal-self concept, 23, 59, 85, 260, 261
  adjustment rating of, 62, 73, 76, 85–86, 91–94, 98
  changes in, 59–75, 85, 95–97, 416–19
  definition of, 56, 85
  of Mr. Bebb, 379–81, 383–85, 389–90, 391–95, 403–4
  of Mrs. Oak, 276–78, 279, 280, 282, 283–86, 290–95, 295–300
  and ordinary concept, 85–86, 89–91, 283–86
  reorganization of, 58–59
  and self-concept, 23, 58–59, 60–74, 85–86, 89–91, 96–97, 345
  stability of, 87–88, 285
Ideal-sort (Q-sort), 9, 36, 50, 57, 85, 260, 261
  changes in, 59–75, 85, 95–97
  description of, 36, 57–58, 77, 85
  for Mr. Bebb, 379–81, 383–85, 389–90, 391–95, 403–4
  for Mrs. Oak, 276–78, 279, 280, 282, 283–86
  and ordinary sort, 85–86, 89–91
  and self-sort, 23, 58–59, 60–74, 85–86, 89–91, 96–97

Jeffrey, Thomas E., 57
Jenkins, David H., 172, 173, 174
Jenkins' inventory; *see* "Sentiments Inventory" (Jenkins)
John, Eve S., 148, 155, 156, 157, 160, 161, 162, 163, 165, 249
John's (TAT) ratings; *see* Mental Health Scale
Jonietz, Alice K., 100
Jung, Carl, 12

Katz, Edward, 121
Kell, Bill L., 24
Kendall, M. G., 129
Korchin, S. J., 197

Langley Porter Clinic, 200, 208
Leadership scale (L-scale), 174, 178, 180, 247
  measure for Mr. Bebb, 398
  measure for Mrs. Oak, 306, 307
Learning theory, 20
Levinson, D. J., 171, 172, 196, 208, 209, 211
Liberalism, 194–95

M-scale; *see* Democratic means, belief in
Mann, H., 67, 71, 72, 137
Mann-Whitney test, 67, 71, 72, 137
Marquis, Donald G., 16
Maturity of behavior, 4, 10, 14, 37
  changes in, 218–37, 421–23
  definition of, 216–17, 234
  in Mr. Bebb, 396–97, 404
  in Mrs. Oak, 287, 301–5
  and personality theory, 215–16
  as seen by client, 217, 218, 219–21, 222–23, 225, 230–33, 236
  as seen by friends, 217, 218, 219–21, 222–23, 225, 226–30, 233, 236
Mental Health Scale (TAT), 10
  and Counselor's Rating Scale, 141–42, 155–57, 160–64
  description of scales, 122, 123–28
  findings, 131–42, 144
  and Emotional-Maturity Scale, 141–42
  psychoanalytic basis for, 123–24, 127
  and Q-adjustment score, 141–42, 155–57
  reliability of, 128–30
  and Self-awareness Measure, 148–49, 150, 151–52, 153–55, 157, 158, 161–64, 165
  and Self-Other Attitude Scale, 141–42
  and TAT Rating Scale, 142, 143, 155–57
  validity of, 130–31
Minnesota Multiphasic Inventory, 100
Mosak, Harold, 100
Motivation for therapy, 10, 240, 424
  controls for, 21, 38, 44, 45, 65, 188–90
  and Emotional-Maturity Scale changes, 246–47
  and length of therapy, 106
  and Mental Health Scale changes, 249–51

Motivation for therapy—*Continued*
  and personality change, 10, 238–58
  and personality organization, 24
  and Q-adjustment changes, 78, 80–81, 245–47
  and Self-Other Attitude Scale, 247–49
Muench, George A., 100
Murray, Henry A., 28

No-therapy control group; *see* Equivalent-control (E-C) group
No-therapy group; *see* Equivalent-control (E-C) group
No-therapy period; *see* Wait period
Nondirective psychotherapy, 3; *see also* Client-centered psychotherapy
Null hypothesis, 251

Oak, Mrs., case of, 10, 406
  attitude toward others, 273, 305–7
  attitude toward self, 262, 266, 272, 287
  Emotional-Maturity Scale scores of, 301–5
  outcomes of, 346–47
  and personal integration, 266, 273
  Q-adjustment scores of, 282, 295
  and Q-sort changes 273–86, 295–300
  and remembered-self sort, 261, 279, 280, 281, 290–300
  as seen by client, 288, 291–300, 302–5
  as seen by counselor, 261–63, 264–65, 290–300
  as seen by diagnostician, 267–73, 288, 290–95, 298–300
  as seen by friends, 302–5
  and self-awareness, 158, 159, 160, 262–63, 317–19
  self-ideal correlations for, 282, 285, 286
  Self-Other Attitude Scale scores of, 305–7
  sequence of testing in, 260–61
  TAT analyses of, 267–73
  therapeutic process in, 263, 264–65, 310–42
  and therapeutic relationship, 263, 264–65, 266, 295–300, 315–16
Oedipus complex, 124, 353
"Openness to experience," 23, 55, 168, 235
Ordinary person, concept of, 85, 260, 261
  adjustment rating of, 85–86, 91–94, 98
  changes in, 85, 87–88, 89–91, 94, 95, 418–19
  definition of, 85
  and ideal-self concept, 85–86, 89–91
  in Mr. Bebb, 379, 390, 395
  in Mrs. Oak, 279, 282–86, 290–95
  stability of, 87–88
Ordinary sort (Q-sort), 9, 36, 50, 85, 260, 261
  adjustment rating of, 85–86, 91–94, 98
  changes in, 87–88, 89–91, 94, 95
  description of, 36, 77, 85
  forced normal sorting of, 57–58, 77
  and ideal-sort, 85–86, 89–91
  in Mr. Bebb, 379, 390, 395
  in Mrs. Oak, 279, 282–86, 290–95
  and self-sort, 85–86, 89–91
Outcomes of psychotherapy, 3, 4, 23, 30, 413–34
  criteria for, 25–26, 27–31, 109, 238–39
  measurement of, 288–300, 344–46, 347–48, 391–95, 405–6, 431–33
  studies on, 6, 14, 16, 21, 22, 25–26, 27, 35–37, 109
  see also Personality change
Own-control (O-C) group, 38, 39, 50, 52, 65, 78, 86, 238–58
  and changes over wait period, 238–58
  description of, 45, 413
  and Emotional-Maturity Scale, 218, 220, 222–23, 226, 236, 246–47
  and Mental Health Scale, 122, 139–41, 143, 249–51
  and Q-adjustment rating, 77, 78, 80, 81, 84, 92–94, 245–72
  and Q-sort interrelationships, 87–88, 92–94, 94–96
  selection of, 45–46
  and self-ideal correlations, 68, 69, 74, 243–45
  and Self-Other Attitude Scale, 175–78, 182–83, 184, 185, 186, 188–91, 192, 193, 247–49
  see also Experimental (E) group
Own-control method, 21, 45–46, 65, 240, 413
  effects on
    attitudes toward self and others, 188–91, 192, 193
    client, 188–91
    length of therapy, 188–91, 192
    outcome of therapy, 188–91, 192, 193
    therapeutic relationship, 188–91, 192

Pearl, David, 168, 195, 197, 203, 208
Perception, theory of, 7, 20

Index

Personal adjustment, 9, 36, 38
  conflicting concepts of, 121, 123, 141–42, 143, 161–64
  criteria for, 27–31
  as measured by counselor, 9, 50, 81, 83, 84, 99–107
  as measured on mental health scales, 131–42, 144, 420
  as measured by Q-sortings, 76–84, 85–86, 91–94, 109, 417–18, 420
  as measured on TAT Rating Scale, 36, 114–19, 419–20
  see also Personality change
Personal counseling, 3; *see also* Client-centered psychotherapy; Psychotherapy
Personality change, 4, 6, 20, 25, 26, 28, 31, 35, 74, 235
  in attitude toward others, 36, 51, 175–78, 424
  in behavior, 51, 218–37
  and changes in self, ideal, and ordinary person, concepts of, 85–98
  and degree of ethnocentrism, 183–84
  dynamics of, 6, 12, 26, 31, 58, 145–66
  in ethnocentric attitudes, 198–99, 424
  evaluation of, 161–64, 235
  factors limiting, 10, 43, 81, 97, 104, 105–6, 107, 143, 188–91, 423–24
  as judged by counselor, 99–108
  as measured by Q-adjustment score, 76–84, 91–94
  and self-ideal discrepancies, 60–75
  in self-perception, 36, 51, 58
  after therapy, 117–18, 404–5, 406, 426–27
Personality dynamics; *see* Personality change, dynamics of
Personality organization, 20, 23, 58, 102, 406
  and adjustment, 161–64
  controls for, 21, 38, 44
  and ethnocentric attitudes, 196–99
  and length of therapy, 105
  and motivation for therapy, 24
Personality reorganization; *see* Personality change
Personality theory, 3, 4, 16, 20, 31
  development of, 3, 5, 31
  and hypotheses for research, 6–7, 20–21, 35, 347–48
  and research, 3, 4, 5
  see also Client-centered therapy, personality theory of

Phillips, E L., 168, 170
Piaget, Jean, 429
Play therapy, 5, 22
Political-economic conservatism (PEC-scale), 37, 178, 180, 247
  and ethnocentrism, 173
  for Mr. Bebb, 398
  for Mrs. Oak, 305, 306, 307
Porter, E. H., Jr., 407
"*Pragnanz*," 197
Prejudice, 171–73, 195
Preliminary interview, 260
Problem-solving, 30–31, 198
"Program design," 16
"Proper" self, 23; *see also* Self-concept
Psychoanalytic theory, 123–24, 127, 142
  and client-centered theory, 121, 123, 143, 161–64
Psychological climate, 4–5, 24
  in other interpersonal relationships, 5
Psychosexual development, stages of, 124, 128, 148, 161, 249
Psychotherapy, 3, 6, 8, 12, 31
  and behavioral sciences, 12
  contributions of, to other fields, 12–13
  research in, 3, 5, 8, 13–14, 27, 31, 109
  study of, 12, 55
  see also Client-centered psychotherapy

Q-sort adjustment score, 9, 76, 180, 242
  and Counselor's Rating Scale, 83, 84, 87, 105, 109, 155–57, 181, 205
  description of, 77–78, 79
  findings, 78–82, 83, 417–18
  and Mental Health Scale, 141–42, 155–57
  for Mr. Bebb, 395–96
  for Mrs. Oak, 282, 295
  reliability of, 82–83
  and Self-awareness Measure, 148, 150, 151–52, 153–55, 163, 164, 165
  and self-ideal correlations, 83
  and self-ideal-ordinary Q-sort changes, 91–94, 98
  and Self-Other Attitude Scale, 181–91, 192
  and TAT Rating Scale, 115–16, 119, 120, 155–57, 181
Q-sorts, 9, 49, 77, 109, 148, 151, 260, 261, 350
  by counselor, 50, 260, 261, 295–300
  description of, 36, 57–58, 77
  as a description of the therapeutic process, 277

Q-sorts—*Continued*
forced normal sorting of, 57–58, 77
instructions for, 57, 86, 96
as measure of change, 286–87
origin of Q-sort items, 57
see also Ideal sort; Ordinary sort; Self-sort
Q-technique, 6, 9, 23, 57, 58, 242, 287, 343, 344, 415, 416

Raimy, Victor C., 99, 145–46
Rank, O., 12
Raskin, Nathaniel J., 99–100, 146, 148
Recording equipment, Gray Audograph, 50
Recording of interviews, 8, 35, 37, 49, 50, 52, 261, 267, 401, 402
problems of, 27, 42
Remembered self (Q-sort), 261, 279, 280, 281, 290–95, 296
"Repression," 55
Research Group (of Counseling Center Staff), 3, 8, 22, 25, 27, 38, 169, 240
and consultants to, 17, 19–20
description of, 16–17
functioning of, 17–20
Research methodology, 12–34, 36–40
of "blind" ratings, 6, 9, 415
and controls, 20–21, 44–47, 64–65, 97
and criteria problem, 19, 27–31, 238–39
and measurement problem, 288, 289, 290, 295–300
new issues for, 429–33
of single-case analysis, 6, 10, 259–60, 308–10, 344
and theory-hypothesis relationship, 6–7, 16, 20–21, 239, 347–48, 400
Research program, 3–4, 5, 29, 35
aims and objectives of, 14–16
consultants for, 8, 17, 19–20
contributions of, 7–8
controls for, 7–8
and data collection, 7, 8, 26–27
deficiencies of, 7–8
design of, 9, 19, 36–40, 42, 49–51, 413–14
and hypotheses-theory relationship, 4, 6–7, 16, 20–21, 347–48, 415
instrumentation for, 21, 26, 51, 415–16
planning of, 9, 16–21, 35
problem of criteria for, 19, 27–31
projects in, 9, 20–26
and selection of counselors, 47–49, 415
and selection of subjects, 41–47
Rogers, Carl R., 5, 12, 20, 23, 55, 94, 167, 168, 199, 201, 202, 212, 213, 215, 246, 265, 400
Rokeach, Milton, 198
Role-playing test, 25, 37, 49, 51, 260
Role-taking test; *see* Role-playing test
Rorschach, 25, 100, 198
Rudikoff, Esselyn, 24, 46, 244

Sanford, R. N., 171, 172, 196, 208, 209, 211
Seeman, Julius, 24, 26, 81, 146, 148, 407
"Selective regression," 117–18, 404–5, 406, 426–27
Self-awareness, 10, 55
admission of material to, 23, 30, 55, 145, 161–62
and changes in self-concept, 147
and defensiveness, 161–64, 235, 345
definition of, 147, 149–50
and ethnocentrism, 168–69
as measured by self-descriptive statements, 147, 149–51, 153–55
in Mrs. Oak, 262–63, 281, 317–19
of new aspects of self, 147, 150–51, 153–55, 157–64
of old-self patterns, 147, 150, 153–55
and process of personality change, 345
Self-awareness measure
and Counselor's Rating Scale, 148, 150, 151–52, 153–55, 157, 158, 161–64, 165
description of, 147, 149–50
and Mental Health Scale, 148–49, 150, 151–52, 153–55, 157, 158, 161–64, 165
and Q-adjustment score, 148, 150, 151–52, 153–55, 163, 164, 165
reliability of, 152–53
and TAT Rating Scale, 149, 150, 151–52, 153–55, 164, 165
Self-concept, 14, 22, 85, 145, 260, 261
adjustment rating of, 76–84, 85–86, 91–94, 98, 188–91
changes in, 60–73, 85, 87–95, 145, 416–19
definition of, 55–56, 85, 145–46
and ideal-self concept, 23, 58–59, 60–74, 85–86, 89–91, 96–97, 283–86, 345
in Mr. Bebb, 379–85, 386–96, 403–4
in Mrs. Oak, 273–75, 278–81, 283–86, 295–300
and ordinary person, concept of, 85–86, 89–91, 283–86

Self-concept—*Continued*
and personality change, 345
stability of, 87–88
values attached to, 56–57, 58
Self-evaluation, 56–57, 74, 75, 76, 84, 116, 146
and adjustment, 188–91
changes over the wait period, 188–89
as criteria for therapy, 238
and ethnocentrism, 168–69
as motivation for therapy, 58
Self-ideal (Q-sort) correlations, 23, 60–74, 75, 89–91, 95–97, 242, 243–45
changes in, 60–75, 416–17
and Counselor's Rating Scale, 69–70, 72
and length of therapy, 244
as measure of self-esteem, 56–57, 74, 75, 84
and motivation for therapy, 243–45
in Mr. Bebb, 379, 380–81, 383–90, 403–4
in Mrs. Oak, 282, 285, 287, 293–94
and Q-adjustment scores, 83
and TAT Rating Scale, 116–17, 119, 120
Self-Ideal-Ordinary Q-Sort (SIO Q-Sort), 35, 76, 86; *see also* Q-sort
Self-Other Attitude Scale (S-O Scale), 37, 49, 196, 242, 260, 350
and Counselor's Rating Scale, 181–91, 192
description of, 171–75
and ethnocentrism, 206–7, 213
findings, 175–88
and Mental Health Scale, 141–42
for Mr. Bebb, 398–400, 404
for Mrs. Oak, 305–7
and Q-adjustment scores, 181–91, 192
and TAT Rating Scale, 181–91, 192
Self-perception, 4, 35
and adjustment, 9, 37, 344
changes in, 9, 145–46
definition of, 145–46, 149–50
and perception of ideal self, 9, 58–59
and personality organization, 286
see also Self-concept
Self-sort (Q-sort), 9, 14, 36, 50, 57, 85, 145, 260, 261
adjustment rating of, 76–84, 85–86, 91–94, 98, 188–91
changes in, 60–73, 85, 87–95, 145
description of, 36, 57–58, 77, 85
as description of therapeutic process, 277
forced normal sorting of, 57–58, 77
and ideal sort, 23, 58–59, 60–74, 85–86, 89–91, 96–97, 283–86, 345
instructions for, 57, 86, 96
as measure of personality change, 286–87
for Mr. Bebb, 379–85, 386–96, 403–4
for Mrs. Oak, 273–75, 278–81, 283–86, 290–94, 295–300
and ordinary sort, 85–86, 89–91, 283–86
Self-structure
as affected by counseling, 58–59
definition of, 55–56
see also Self-concept
Self-understanding, 4, 14, 146
Self-value; *see* Self-ideal (Q-sort) correlations, as measure of self-esteem
"Sentiments Inventory" (Jenkins), 172, 173, 174
Sheerer, Elizabeth T., 146, 168, 170, 195
Singer, J. L., 197
Single-case analysis, 6, 10
methodology of, 308–10, 344
of Mr. Bebb, 349–409
of Mrs. Oak, 259–348
Snyder, William U., 146
Spontaneous recovery, 77, 251–53, 254, 424
controls for, 239–40
Spontaneous remission; *see* Spontaneous recovery
Statistical controls; *see* Controls
Steele, Betty L., 146
Stein, Morris I., 25
Stein Sentence Completion Test, 25
Stephenson, William, 36, 57, 288, 344
Stock, Dorothy, 146, 168, 170, 195
Success, 6, 10, 43
case study of, 259–348
criteria of, 28, 69–70, 238
as a criterion, 27–31, 109, 239–40
and degree of self-awareness, 147–65
and degree of selfhood, 212, 214
effect of wait period on, 188–91, 423–24
and Emotional-Maturity Scale scores, 227–31, 232, 236
and ethnocentrism, 196, 198–99, 201–7, 183, 424
factors limiting, 104, 105–6, 135–37, 143, 183, 188–91, 196, 198–99, 201–7, 210, 212, 423, 424, 427–28

Success—*Continued*
and initial Self-Other Attitude Scale scores, 186–88
as judged by counselor, 9, 29, 99–108, 160–64, 201, 205–7, 210, 213, 229
psychoanalytic theory of, 121, 160–64
and self-ideal correlations, 59, 69–72, 73, 74
and self-ideal-ordinary interrelationships, 97–98
and Self-Other Attitude Scale score, 183, 238
and therapeutic relationship, 50, 100–105, 345
Sullivan, H. S., 12, 199, 201, 202, 212, 213

Thematic Apperception Test (TAT), 9, 10, 25, 36, 37, 49, 51, 69, 70, 72, 81, 84, 105, 109–44, 148, 149, 150, 151, 153, 154–57, 180, 181, 241–42, 249–51, 260, 267–73, 287, 288, 350, 372–78, 404, 419–20; *see also* Mental Health Scale (TAT); TAT Rating Scale
TAT mental health rating; *see* Mental Health Scale (TAT)
TAT Rating Scale, 36, 72, 81, 84, 109–10, 180, 205, 242
and counselor's rating, 69–70, 105, 117–18, 119, 120, 155–57, 181
description of, 110–14,
findings, 114–19
and Mental Health Scale, 142, 143, 155–57
Q-adjustment score, 115–16, 119, 120, 155–57, 181
and Self-awareness Measure, 149, 150, 151–52, 153–55, 164, 165
and self-ideal correlations, 116–17, 119, 120
and Self-Other Attitude Scale, 181–91, 192
Therapeutic outcomes; *see* Outcomes of psychotherapy
Therapeutic process, 4–5, 10, 58–59, 235, 424–26
and awareness of self, 10, 145–66, 425–26
counselor's description of, 100, 101, 102–4
in Mr. Bebb, 351, 352–72
in Mrs. Oak, 263, 264–65, 310–42, 345
and psychological climate, 4–5, 24
studies of, 3, 14, 16, 22, 23–25, 27, 35, 37–38
"Therapeutic readiness," 21, 105; *see also* Motivation for therapy
Therapeutic relationship, 4–5, 13, 22, 24, 198–99
and client's attitudes toward counselor, 102, 103, 104, 264, 266, 407, 425
and counselor's attitudes toward client, 4, 102, 104, 265, 266, 407, 425
and effects of wait period, 188–91
and ethnocentrism, 198–99, 204–5
as focus of therapy, 102, 103, 104, 266, 345
and interaction in, 145
and length of therapy, 105
in Mr. Bebb, 351–52, 352–72, 401–3
in Mrs. Oak, 263, 264–65, 266, 295–300, 310–42
as seen by client, 24, 102, 104, 261–63
as seen by counselor, 24, 100, 101, 102, 103, 104, 105, 264–65
and self-ideal correlations, 407
and success in therapy, 50, 100–105, 345
"Therapeutic risk," 199, 201, 202, 208, 213, 423–24
Therapists, 3, 7
attitude of, toward clients, 4, 102, 104, 188–91, 265, 266
functions of, 3, 4–5
psychological orientation of, 47–48
selection of, for research program, 47–49
training of, 3
Therapy group; *see* Experimental (E) group
Therapy period, 38, 82, 221
changes over, 85, 86, 307–8, 310, 403, 405
on Counselor's Rating Scale, 102–4, 107, 117, 153–55, 156
on diagnostic Q-sorts, 290–91
on Emotional-Maturity Scale, 222–23, 225, 226, 227–30, 236, 301–2, 398, 404
on Mental Health Scale, 134–35, 136–37, 138, 139–41, 143, 153–55, 156
on Q-adjustment rating, 80, 81, 82, 153–55, 156, 282, 295, 381–82, 395–96
on Self-awareness Measure, 153–55, 156

Therapy period—*Continued*
changes over—*Continued*
on self-ideal correlations, 63–64, 68, 69, 71–72, 74, 282, 285–86, 293–94, 389, 403
on self-ideal-ordinary interrelationships, 89, 90–98, 281, 286
on Self-Other Attitude Scale, 177–79, 181–83, 184, 305–6, 309, 398, 404
on TAT Rating Scale, 84, 109, 114–16, 117, 119–20, 153–55, 156, 378
Therapy wait group; *see* Own-control (O-C) group
Thorndike, Edward L., 13
Thorndike's dictum, 13
Tippett, L. H. C., 61, 62
Tougas, Rolland R., 183, 186, 188
"Transference cure," 105

University of California, 200, 202, 203
University of Chicago, 3, 39, 122, 200, 343, 413

Valued self; *see* Ideal-self concept
Vargas, Manuel J., 142

Wait group; *see* Equivalent-control (E-C) group, wait group of; Own-control (O-C) group
Wait period, 38, 45, 65, 77, 81, 221, 252
changes over, 85, 86, 251–52, 254
on diagnostic Q-sort, 391, 404
on Emotional-Maturity Scale, 222–23, 225, 226, 236, 246–47, 397, 404
on Mental Health Scale, 139–41, 143, 249–51
on Q-adjustment rating, 80, 81, 245–46, 382, 395–96
and Q-sort changes, 89, 90–98
and self-ideal correlation, 68, 69, 74, 243–45, 380, 384, 403, 404
on Self-Other Attitude Scale, 176–78, 182–83, 184, 247–49, 398, 404
on TAT analysis, 378, 404
effect of, 188–91
as a selective factor, 42, 46
Wechsler, I. S., 128
Wechsler-Bellevue Scale, 128
Whitney, D., 17, 71, 72, 137
Wilcoxon, Frank, 67
Willoughby, R. R., 216, 217, 218, 231, 301, 302, 397
Willoughby Emotional-Maturity Scale (E-M Scale); *see* Emotional-Maturity Scale (E-M Scale)
Wished-for self, 23; *see also* Ideal-self concept
Wolfson, Kate S., 146

Yates, F., 83, 117, 202

Zubin, J. A., 238